THE STORY OF

ROCK 'n' ROLL

THE STORY OF
ROCK 'n' ROLL

The Year-by-Year Illustrated Chronicle

CONSULTANT EDITOR

PAUL DU NOYER

A MUSIC BOOK SERVICES PAPERBACK

This is a Carlton Book
Exclusively distributed in paperback in the U.S.A by MBS Corporation,
P.O. Box 16295 N.W. 13th Ave., Suite B, Miami, Florida 33169

Text and Design copyright © 1995 Carlton Books Limited

ISBN 1-886894-22-1

Printed in Spain

Contents

1950s — Ed Ward

1960s — Johnny Black

1970s — Lloyd Bradley

1980s — Sylvie Simmons

1990s — Andy Gill

Introduction

One night in the late Eighties, Paul McCartney was at home watching the TV news. On screen he could see unfolding the most dramatic event of that era – the fall of the Berlin Wall. Something about those young East Berliners, tearing with bare hands at the concrete, scrambling in hope and jubilation over the rubble, fascinated the former Beatle.

Suddenly it hit him. "That's our lot," he said to himself. "They're our people."

Paul McCartney realized that these escapees from the Communist bloc with their blue jeans and Pink Floyd T-shirts and punk rock hairstyles, were the children of rock 'n 'roll, of Elvis and the Beatles. They were the inheritors of something that their Soviet superiors could never allow, yet could never suppress. Whatever the forces that brought down Communism, the gloriously corrupting influence of Western pop culture was, in the end, as deadly to that system as anything else.

It was an ironic achievement. Rock 'n' roll was the juvenile art form that back in the Fifties got denounced as a communist plot itself. In the decades since then, rock music came to embody a dream of freedom. Since the early Sixties it has been unrivalled as an expression of youthful creativity. Its influence on the post-war generations has been profound. No account of the late 20th century would be complete without an awareness of the way that rock culture has impacted on young people's hearts and minds in every part of the world.

So it is an important story. But also it is an astonishing one, rich in every element of human drama. In this book you will meet the stars, the bit-part players, the heroes and the villains. In some of their careers they encounter fortune and fame beyond compare, but sometimes terrible tragedy too. We find individuals who are conceivably possessed of true genius and many more who clearly are not – yet are hugely entertaining all the same.

More than anything *The Story of Rock 'n' Roll* is about a thrilling, liberating noise, full of excitement and sex and escapism. It can often be the vehicle of great emotional expression, or of valuable social insight. Over the years rock music has adapted to each innovation in technology; it has likewise found a voice to express maturity as much as youth. Its range today is unlimited.

Rock music began in many different places, has followed many different paths, and has arrived at many different destinations . . . simultaneously! It is not a simple business. But you will not find that a problem here. With its logically-ordered approach *The Story of Rock 'n' Roll* needs no 'How To Use' section. The whole picture is spread out before you, unrolling decade by decade. A team of experienced writers, British and American, leads you through the maze of music from old-time jive, rockabilly and doo-wop, right up to ragga, rap and grunge. Nothing happens in isolation. Everything overlaps and few things ever came out nowhere. This book makes all the connections. So whether you're looking for soul, psychedelia or new wave, for the Doors, Led Zeppelin or Prince . . . enquire within. They'll not be far away.

At the heart of rock 'n' roll is absurdity – and only some of it is intentional. In this spirit our history finds ample room for the fads, fashions and follies that have distracted us at every step of the way. When UK teenagers first heard rock music – the most bizarre import from the United States ever! – thousands of boys were moved to cavort before their bedroom mirrors strumming their cricket bats. In their mind's eye they looked the very image of Chuck Berry or Eddie Cochran. From a US perspective, perhaps the British Isles have been producing outlandish sights ever since: the Beatles and the Stones looked other-worldly at first; David Bowie, the Sex Pistols and Boy George were no easier to assimilate. On the other hand, we in England could never fully understand that all-American Fifties phenomenon the Davy Crockett hat, and we await an explanation at your earliest convenience.

Pop crazes and 'trash' history are duly noted, then – and who can deny the central role of scandal in rock 'n' roll's continuing fascination? That's all in here, too. Outside the main text of our book are biographies of key artists and story-boxes on some extra-special aspects.

Underground musical movements are always influential, and they're looked at closely. Our 'Rock 'n' Roll Record' runs throughout to give you a quick checklist of musical events in chronological order. For background reference, we've added a running tab of World Events – use it if you ever wish to place all this sound, fury and nonsense into some kind of wider context.

Nearly anyone who picks up this book has already had their lives enriched in some measure by rock 'n' roll music. I hope it will increase your understanding of that music and, in so doing, deepen your enjoyment and appreciation. If it makes you want to explore music you haven't heard before, then I hope you'll go right ahead. The catalogue of recorded music is fabulously rich. In this, the digital age, it is more accessible than ever before. And The Story of Rock 'n' Roll is not over yet.

Paul Du Noyer

'Awop bop a loo bop a lop bam boom'

The Fifties

1950s

Ed Ward

was when rock'n'roll began and 1954 is often chosen as the year of rock'n'roll's birth. But really it was thanks to a lot of trends that had been coming together since the end of World War II. Minority populations in the US now had more money, so it made economic sense to sell them records. The major record labels weren't about to do it, so a lot of small labels, particularly in the black music (Rhythm & Blues, or R&B) field, sprang into existence. Teenagers, too, had more money than ever before, and began to define themselves as a distinct class of people with their own wants, tastes and spending power.

In country music, electric instruments and the popularity of boogie meant that music was developing a harder beat and more black influence than ever before. War jobs had brought a lot of country people to the city, with the result that black people were exposed to more jazz and big-band 'jump' blues, resulting in hits like **Roy Brown**'s 'Good Rockin' Tonight'. Younger urban black people liked the stripped-down mellow harmonizing of groups like the **Orioles** and the **Ravens**, who sang in front of minimal instrumental accompaniment.

Around 1952, things started to get mixed-up. White urban teenagers began buying R&B records in sufficient quantity that a record-store owner in Cleveland, Ohio approached his friend Alan Freed, a DJ on a local station, and told him he should put together a programme playing black music for white kids. He did and it paid off in a big way. In New York, two jazz fans started a label, Atlantic, and found they were recording more and more black pop music by singers like **Ruth Brown** and **LaVerne Baker**. When they got a mediocre blues-singer, **Ray Charles**, and encouraged him to sing more like he did in church, they found themselves with a new kind of music that would one day be called "soul". In Chicago, two brothers who owned a nightclub started Chess Records to record a down-home kind of blues that they could sell to the nostalgic Southern blacks who came to their club and soon **Muddy Waters** and **Howlin' Wolf** found themselves stars. Down in Memphis, Sam Phillips was recording blues and dreaming of a white kid who could sing black, while across town a poor white teenager named **Elvis Presley** was buying every black record he could lay his hands on. The powder was packed, the fuse was lit and the explosion was not far off.

◄ Little Richard: 'Tutti Frutti'

Rock'n'roll wasn't born in 1954. To be honest, it wasn't born at all – well not in any one place, at any one time: it just sort of coalesced and, as the new year dawned, that process was already well underway. You can see the development on the R&B charts, at least: the top record there in the first week of January 1954 is 'Money, Honey' by the **Drifters**, a number most people would consider rock'n'roll.

More significantly perhaps, on January 4, a Memphis truckdriver makes a second visit to the Memphis Recording Service to pay for another recording of himself playing guitar and singing. **Elvis Presley** who is about to turn 19 had been there before, in September 1953, to cut two tunes for his mother when the secretary-cum-office-manager, Marion Keisker, had noticed his unusual voice. Something clicked in her mind. Her boss, Sam Phillips, had once said, "If I could find a white man with the Negro sound and the Negro feel, I could make a billion dollars," and Keisker had a feeling she'd found that white man. Phillips, who also has a record label called Sun operating out of the same studio, had missed Presley's first visit, but he is around this time and, although he doesn't think much of

the two recordings, country songs entitled 'Casual Love Affair' and 'I'll Never Stand In Your Way', he takes down the kid's phone number (which actually belongs to the rabbi who lives downstairs) for future reference.

For some time now, being a Negro artist with the Negro sound and the Negro feel had been none too good for your career: the watchdogs of public morals in the US had been vigilant against 'lewd and lascivious' lyrics and it seemed the first place to look for them was on R&B records. On February 26, a bill is introduced in the US House of Representatives to make mailing or transporting dirty records a crime punishable by a $50,000 fine (it doesn't get through) and, in April, **Johnnie Ray**'s version of the Drifters' 'Such a Night' is banned as too suggestive for the American air-

waves. On May 8, the BBC follows suit.

In this climate, it's much wiser to play it safe as **Bill Haley**, a Western Swing bandleader from Pennsylvania, knows. On April 12, he and his band the **Comets** record two songs for their new Decca contract, '(We're Gonna) Rock Around The Clock' and 'Thirteen Women'. The songs flop – 'Rock Around The Clock' will later hit the top of the charts in the summer of 1955 – and, on April 28, while recording a version of **Big Joe Turner**'s 'Shake, Rattle And Roll' with rewritten lyrics, Haley tells a reporter, "We steer clear of anything suggestive."

Not so **Hank Ballard & The Midnighters**, though. On April 14, their first hit since changing their name from the **Royals** (after getting stuck with a lawsuit from the much

Hank Ballard (left) and the Midnighters workin' hard, although Annie is nowhere to be seen. Maybe she's home with the baby.

more successful **'5' Royales**) enters the R&B charts. 'Work With Me Annie' is about as suggestive as rock'n'roll music gets until the Seventies – when **Marvin Gaye** and **Donna Summer** will help push the boundaries even further – and the song becomes a touchstone for the growing numbers of hip white youngsters around the country who are seeking out R&B records for their passion and thumping beat.

These same kids have been the backbone of success for a disc jockey in

Lowman Pauling, inventor of the crotch-level guitar stance, main song-writer for the "5" Royales, preparing to launch into one of the group's patented outrageous on-stage routines.

Cleveland, Ohio, over the last couple of years. Alan Freed, a classically-trained trombonist and Wagner fan, had been floundering with his late-night show until a friend with a record store alerted him to the number of white teenagers buying records by black artists and persuaded him to give these songs a try on his show. The *Moondog Show* quickly became the hottest

thing on radio and Freed took advantage by staging live performances featuring the artists whose records he was playing. On May 1, he takes a daring leap by presenting the *Moondog Coronation Show* in Newark, New Jersey, drawing in excess of 10,000 fans, and turning away nearly that number again. There's no doubt about it: pop music is undergoing a revolution and, on June 17 in Britain, the first issue of the pop weekly *Record Mirror* rolls off the presses.

Sam Phillips roadtests **Elvis Presley**'s 'That's All Right'/ 'Blue Moon of Kentucky' by pressing up an acetate and taking Elvis himself down to Dewey Phillips' show on radio station WHBQ. Elvis knows Dewey as the white DJ who plays black music in Memphis and he is terrified. But Dewey has promised he'll play the record then interview Elvis, and he's as good as his word making sure Elvis mentions he'd gone to school at Humes High so people know he is white. The phone lines go nuts, and Phillips has to order a second pressing before he's even gotten the first: he already has in excess of 7000 orders for the record.

Nonetheless, the glory of being the first white guy with the R&B hit falls not to Elvis but to **Bill Haley**, whose version of 'Shake, Rattle And Roll' winds up in the pop Top 10, at this time an unusual feat for a record with mostly teen appeal. And it seems the teens are heating up to

APR 28 : Harold Wilson replaces Aneurin Bevan in the labour shadow cabinet

Elvis Begins

And so it came to pass that Sun Records boss Sam Phillips heard something that knocked him out. It was a song called 'Without You' submitted to him on a tape by a black songwriter from Nashville which Sam knew would be a hit in the right hands. But whose? Marion Keisker reminded him of the 19-year-old kid who'd been in earlier in the year and Sam started to hunt for his phone number. Before he had even hung up the phone from Phillips, **Elvis Presley** had streaked down to the studio to get to work.

There was, however, one problem. Try as he might, Elvis couldn't get the song right. Neither he nor Phillips could figure out what was wrong. If the songwriter hadn't disappeared after recording the demo, Sam would have shown Elvis the door and pressed up the demo, but instead they hammered away, getting nowhere.

They took a break. "What can you do?" Sam asked the kid. "I can do anything," he answered. Phillips, perhaps sensing a last chance, said "Do it."

And Elvis did. Literally just about everything: pop standards, gospel songs, country music, "real heavy on the Dean Martin stuff", Keisker remembered years later. Elvis probably realized it was his last chance: he'd been turned away by the Memphis office of Modern Records, one of the country's top R&B labels, before coming to the Memphis Recording Service anyway. If Sam — and, through him, Sun Records — didn't take him, nobody would.

In the end, they didn't get anything on tape, but Sam agreed to help Elvis get together with a band and called his friend Scotty Moore, a country guitarist who ran a local club band, to ask him to meet Elvis and see if they couldn't work some stuff up. Although Scotty thought the name Elvis sounded like something "out of science-fiction," he invited him over to the house where they spent an afternoon jamming on country and blues tunes.

In the midst of all of this Scotty's bass-playing neighbour, Bill Black, showed up and played a little, too.

Scotty and Bill were almost as anxious to record as Elvis was, so they were happy to hear that Sam wanted them to come down to the studio to see if they could get something on tape. Instead of a recording-session, this turned into months of gruelling rehearsals, but they were gradually turning into a band.

On July 5, 1954, Sam decided to tape it. "Okay, this is the session," he said (since much of this tape still exists, we can hear his words today), and they began to play. First up was 'I Love You Because', a crooning ballad of the sort Elvis loved. Then there was some sort of delay and, while everybody was hanging around, Elvis started a hyped-up version of **Arthur Crudup**'s blues 'That's All Right', laughing and jumping around, with Scotty and Bill joining in the fun. Suddenly Sam burst into the room. "What in the devil are you doing?" he demanded. "We don't know," Scotty answered, honestly. "Well, find out real quick and don't lose it," Sam commanded. "Run through it again and let's put it on tape." And they did.

Then they went cold again. Eventually, they went home, but they came back the next day to try for something to put on the other side of the record. Again, the results were desultory until they started fooling around in a dull moment. This time, the song being messed with was **Bill Monroe**'s 'Blue Moon Of Kentucky' with Elvis mocking the bluegrass pioneer by giving the song a jumped-up, bluesy reading. It was just fun, but Sam was taping it, and after they stopped, he came into the studio (he'd left the tape running again) and said "Fine, fine, man. Hell, that's different. That's a pop song now, little 'Vi. That's good." And, just to be safe, they cut it again.

Now all that remained was to see what the public thought.

▲ Elvis Presley (note leather-coated guitar) in full jiggle.

APRIL 10: Blues giant Big Joe Turner puts out the lyrically-uncensored version of 'Shake Rattle And Roll'.

MAY 10: Release of Bill Haley's 'Rock Around The Clock': the disc that will, for a wider public, mark the beginning of rock-'n'roll.

MAY 15: Clyde McPhatter of the Drifters gets called up for the US army.

JUNE 5: Early rock classic 'Riot In Cell Block No. 9' is released by the Robins.

JULY 12: Sam Phillips signs Elvis Presley to a contract at Sun Records.

OCTOBER 5: Boomtown Rat and Live Aid's prime mover Bob Geldof is born in Dublin, Ireland.

DECEMBER 1: Death of country music publisher Fred Rose, whose legendary protegé Hank Williams had passed on nearly two years earlier.

DECEMBER 7: Annie Lennox of Eurythmics is born in Aberdeen, Scotland.

R&B in great numbers: Alan Freed's popularity is such that he is wooed away from Cleveland by New York's WINS, where he reports for work on September 9. Meanwhile, his Los Angeles counterpart, Hunter Hancock, is doing well syndicating his own radio show and promoting concerts on the West Coast.

Elvis' career starts to inch forward: in the August 7 issue of *Billboard*, the country & western reviewer calls him a "strong new talent" and, three days later, he makes a hometown appearance at a show in the Overton Park Bandshell. On September 9, he plays the opening of Katz' Drugstore in downtown Memphis, before going into the studio to record 'Good Rockin' Tonight', a hit for blues shouters **Wynonie Harris** and **Roy Brown**, with 'I Don't Care If The Sun Don't Shine' on the flip-side. The record's release coin-

cides with a big break: Elvis, Scotty and Bill play Nashville's hallowed venue *Grand Ole Opry*. At the end of their slot, the talent director tells Elvis he should stick to truck-driving and Elvis never again plays the Opry. Instead, he goes over to the competition, playing his first appearance on the *Louisiana Hayride* on October 16. He quickly becomes a regular on the popular radio show.

The year winds down with a flurry of controversy over obscene lyrics. **Hank Ballard & The Midnighters** have continued their 'Annie' saga with a natural sequel, 'Annie Had A Baby' ("Can't work no more," is the next line) and, while it sails to the top of the R&B charts, in October, following an editorial decrying filthy lyrics, *Billboard* reports that the 'Annie' songs have even been banned by WDIA, Memphis' 'Mother Station of the Negroes'. People are

so nervous about obscenity that even **Rosemary Clooney**'s 'Mambo Italiano' gets banned, because radio programmers are afraid of what the Italian lyrics might be saying. As if in conciliation, the **Drifters** release their soon-to-be-classic version of 'White Christmas', which becomes a year-end chart perennial.

As the old year merges into the new, a tragedy hits the world of R&B as **Johnny Ace**, a 25-year-old singer named the Most Programmed Artist of 1954 in a national poll of DJs and one of the most popular new performers, dies of a gun wound at Houston Civic Auditorium, where he is playing a New Year's show. Strange stories circulate about the exact nature of what happened - the official line is that he was playing Russian roulette – but the result is a death cult round Ace similar to that which will later emerge around actor James Dean.

State of the Art

At the start of 1954, the pop music landscape in America was much as it had been ever since the end of World War II. The pop charts were dominated by sweet pop music, white singers fronting lush, string-laden orchestras, with the occasional rhythm novelty, usually of a pseudo-Latin nature, thrown in for variety. This music was overwhelmingly pressed on ten-inch 78 rpm shellac records, although RCA Victor had done a good job of hustling their seven-inch 45 rpm singles. This new industry standard ("the little record with the big hole") had smaller grooves resulting in better sound and, in fact, 1954 would also be the year the term "high fidelity" caught on to describe the enhanced sound possibilities inherent in microgroove 33 1/3 rpm twelve-inch long-playing records (LPs), which were collected by a small but influential bunch of audiophiles who bought

expensive equipment on which to play them. Needless to say, the music on the majority of the LPs was classical: popular music wasn't worth the expense, let alone such minority-interest stuff as R&B and hillbilly music.

It would be a long while before the LP became the standard for popular music, but the 45 was another matter: comprising only 28% of the record market in 1953 (78s were 52% of the sales, LPs 20%), by the end of 1954 they had grown so popular that pundits were predicting the death of the 78 at the hands of the 45. All new singles were being sent to disc jockeys on 45 starting in June and, although the 78 would hang on in some parts of the world until as late as 1966 (when Parlophone in India pressed the **Beatles**' 'Paperback Writer' on 78), the 45, which became synonymous with rock'n'roll, was on its way.

NOV 28 : The US National Cancer Institute claims a definite link between cancer and cigarette smoking

1954 - HEADLINE NEWS

1950s Trash

From the moment it began, rock-'n'roll was trash in the eyes of the public, no matter how much its performers, from **Elvis Presley** to **Bill Haley**, or its promoters, most notably Alan Freed, protested to the contrary. Still, it must be admitted, from the garishness of Elvis' clothes (bought at Lansky's) to **Little Richard**'s eye make-up, the early days saw their share of bad taste and misbehaviour.

Sometimes rockers just wouldn't play by the rules: Ed Sullivan's first foray into rock'n'roll in 1955 saw him booking **Bo Diddley** on his Sunday evening show. Sullivan wanted Diddley to perform 'Sixteen Tons', but the singer had other ideas. During rehearsals, they patiently went

▼ Besides hit songs, one thing Elvis generated his whole life through — and even afterwards — was merchandise.

over the song, and had the lyrics printed up on big cue cards for the near-sighted, bespectacled singer. Come the live broadcast, Bo hoisted his guitar, strummed a few chords ... and played his personal anthem, 'Bo Diddley'. "Man, maybe that was 'Sixteen Tons' on those cards," he said afterwards, "But all *I* saw was 'Bo Diddley'."

Then there was the question of taste in these repressed times: **Gene Vincent**'s smouldering 'Be Bop A-Lula', he said, was named after the *Little Lulu* comic book, but it's unlikely the girl with the pear-shaped head was the one who, in the words of his song, kept giving him "more, more, more".

This may have been scandalous, but it caused less of a stir than some of the records that followed in the summer of 1956, when rock-'n'roll 'novelty' records began to appear. First off came 'Transfusion', by **Nervous Norvus**, a 40-something truck driver, who sang about serious automobile accidents that required hospitalization, concluding each verse with a line like "Pass the claret to me, Barrett." Next came the notorious 'Flying Saucer', which incorporated snippets of currently-popular songs in a scenario in which a radio news reporter breathlessly described the landing of aliens in a downtown area. It sold like crazy despite a flurry of lawsuits from various copyright-holders and gave parents and DJs alike migraines. There were more on the way, though.

Not all of the trash was on vinyl, either. 'Colonel' Tom Parker, Elvis' manager, was an old carnival hand,

so the idea of selling cheap exploitation products came naturally. In 1956, Parker jumped in with both feet, licensing everything from cologne to stuffed hound dogs to lipstick (available in shades such as Heartbreak Pink, Hound Dog Orange and Tutti Frutti Red) to glow-in-the-dark pictures, all stamped with Elvis' name and likeness.

Another stunt in August 1956, involved a little known songwriter climbing a tree in Penn Township, Pennsylvania, swearing not to come down until a song he'd written had sold a million copies. Equipped with a mattress and phone, with food handed up to him by friends, he's probably still up there, since the record sank without a trace. Getting a song played could really be hard work, so when Okeh Records released **Screamin' Jay Hawkins**' 'I Put A Spell On You', they took out an ad in the trade papers urging DJs to play it. "If you get fired," it said, "we'll get you a job." So Bob Friesen, in Chilliwack, British Columbia

▲ "Won'tcha wear my ring around your neck" the King sang, but this Fan would rather have him around his neck.

played it – and got fired. Doing the natural thing, he appealed to Okeh. They ignored him.

Sometimes just cutting a song could be a thorny matter. Eager to follow up on **Jerry Lee Lewis'** first big hit, 'Whole Lotta Shakin' Goin' On', Sam Phillips got him back into the studio in 1957 with a number, 'Great Balls Of Fire', that Sam was sure was a winner. What he didn't count on was Jerry Lee's sudden flip-out into religious fervour. In an argument that was partially taped by the engineer, Sam and Jerry Lee argued about the Bible and rock'n'roll, with the tape ending on Jerry Lee's insistence that "... I have the Devil in me. If I didn't, I'd be a Christian." Fortunately, the Devil won out, and the song became a smash.

Naturally, there were plenty of unsavoury goings-on: in early 1958, Chicago police raided Lormar Distributors, a record-distribution firm that was under investigation for using rather physical means to convince jukebox owners to buy from them and found a slew of counterfeit records. Lormar, the police told the press, seemed to be owned by Joey Glimco, head of Chicago's taxi-drivers' union and owner of a jukebox-distributing company and, in Washington, rumours abounded of a Federal crackdown on the jukebox industry.

1958's crop of novelty records was worse than ever before. Someone discovered the sound of a speeded-up tape, allowing for the birth of such atrocities as 'Witch Doctor' and 'Flying Purple People Eater'. Teens' insatiable fascination with horror movies resulted in John Zacherle, a horror-movie TV host from Philadelphia, recording 'Dinner With Drac' which, in its original version, really overstepped the bounds of good taste – so much so that a watered-down version had to be recorded.

Satan, however, would not be so easily thwarted: the man with the Devil in him managed to undo a lot of careful image-making with one move. **Jerry Lee Lewis** landed at Heathrow Airport in London on May 22 with two women, his sister, Frankie Jean, and his third cousin, Myra Gale. Although his manager tried to get the women out of the way for the press conference Jerry Lee stood firm. A reporter asked who the young woman was. "This is my wife, Myra," Jerry Lee says. Wife? Sure enough, they'd been married since December 11. Asked if she wasn't a bit young – Jerry had told the reporter she was 15 – Myra blithely replied that "back home" you can get married at 10. Naturally, the story got splashed all over the British press and made it by wire back to the US, where a Memphis reporter found

that not only was Myra just shy of her 14th birthday, but she was Jerry Lee's third wife and there was more than a hint that his second marriage hadn't been legally dissolved. Undaunted, Jerry Lee went on to do three tour dates playing just 10-minute sets before the Rank Organization and Jerry Lee's manager agreed that he'd blown it and decided to call it a day. On his way out of the country, Lewis called the British press "jealous" and then, his way to the plane blocked by photographers, he lashed out with his foot. The shock waves from this incident eventually ended his rock'n'roll career.

The Fifties, in fact, seem to have ended with a rock'n'roll crime-wave. The payola scandal was heating up in Washington. The three male members of the **Platters** were arrested in a hotel room in Cincinnati with three white 19-year-old women – all concerned were in various states of undress. And that icon of rock'n'roll himself, **Chuck Berry**, was arrested for transporting a 14-year-old prostitute across state lines. Although not much came of the payola scandal, the Platters were exonerated and Berry's first trial was thrown out of court on appeal, the die had been cast. If you thought that rock'n'rollers would have gotten the message and learned to behave, you couldn't have been more wrong.

Elvis Presley celebrates his twentieth birthday on January 8 with the release of his third single, 'Milk Cow Blues Boogie'. Like his previous two releases, this goes nowhere on a national level but, like the previous two, does get some recognition on the about-to-be-discontinued regional country charts that *Billboard* publishes.

The practice of white performers 'covering' R&B songs, however, is growing. Although few get as close to the spirit of the originals as Elvis, such established artists as **Georgia Gibbs**, **Rosemary Clooney** and **Perry Como** are now jumping on the bandwagon, while newcomers the **Crew Cuts** have all but obliterated the **Chords**' original version of 'Sh-Boom'. By the end of February, this trend has started to annoy R&B performers, and **LaVern Baker**, an Atlantic Records artist (whose hit 'Tweedle Dee' has been effectively kept off the pop charts by near-identical copies from Georgia Gibbs and **Vicki Young**) writes a letter to her Congressman asking him to revise the copyright law so that arrangers and performers will at least be compensated when this happens. The net result of this is that Baker is out three cents for a stamp, although by the end of the year powerful radio

station WINS in New York will ask that its disc jockeys play only original versions whenever possible. Meanwhile, the **McGuire Sisters**' version of the **Moonglows**' 'Sincerely' floats happily atop the pop charts. Like the original this, curiously enough, lists Alan Freed as co-composer. This problem is even about to hit Britain. Although the UK charts are dominated by American crooners like **Eddie Fisher** and homegrown talent like **Alma Cogan** and **Petula Clark** (whose first record, 'Majorca', is released on February 2), the Crew Cuts have a smash hit in mid-April with their smoothed-out version of the **Penguins**' doo-wop hit 'Earth Angel'.

The trick now is to make records that no one else can copy. For that you need unique songs sung by truly original talents. The first of these in 1955 is by a 27-year-old R&B veteran from New Orleans, **Antoine 'Fats' Domino**. The gentle-looking, portly pianist had a R&B smash in 1950 with 'The Fat Man' and, despite a dozen subsequent releases, hasn't enjoyed much success since. Suddenly, his infectious 'Ain't That A Shame' becomes the hottest-selling R&B record of spring 1955, even winding up in the pop Top 10 despite stiff competition from **Pat Boone**'s cover version. Another 27-year-old, Elias McDaniel, has nothing to fear from Pat Boone, though. The thick-spectacled ex-boxer, recording under the name **Bo Diddley**, is most famous for his patented 'Bo Diddley beat' which he crunches out on his guitar beginning with his debut record, 'Bo Diddley'. (The flip-side is 'I'm A

Man', which will become a standard with British blues bands in the mid-Sixties.) Although 'Bo Diddley' won't bother the pop charts this year, the record becomes a two-sided R&B hit denied the glory of the top slot only by Fats Domino. But the real revolution will come in July, when **Chuck Berry**'s 'Maybelline' will smash into the pop Top 10 with no serious cover problems to challenge it.

Meanwhile, Elvis Presley is still slogging along: beginning in March with an appearance on a TV version of *Louisiana Hayride,* he is trying to expand his audience. On April 1 he puts out record number four and

Sartorially impeccable Bo Diddley (aka Elias McDaniel) with his trademark square guitar. He later acquired one ▽ covered in mink.

FEB 10 : MPs in Britain vote by a majority of 31 to keep the death penalty • MAR 12 : US jazz musician Charlie Parker dies

Rudy Pomili's bass-riding antics were a notable feature of Bill Haley and the Comet's shows. Haley (centre) looks appropriately amused.

again only regional sales result, albeit in more widespread regions than before. On May 13, he plays a show in Jacksonville, Florida, and a riot breaks out. The tour will inch its way through the South, with weekly returns to Baton Rouge, Louisiana, to allow Elvis to perform on the radio show *Louisiana Hayride* before moving into Texas, where he is doing comparatively well by the autumn.

However, at this time, the rock-'n'roll crown still perches on the head of **Bill Haley**. 'Rock Around The Clock' is America's Number 1 record nearly all summer long and it is proving to be quite controversial. In May, at Princeton University, one of the more prestigious schools in the US, a student plays 'Rock Around The Clock' on his phonograph one night: another joins in and, within minutes, a full-scale riot with burning rubbish and chanting students erupts outside

the dormitory. Proof that the Sixties have not yet arrived comes when a dean succeeds in talking the students down not long afterwards and they all file meekly back into their dorm-rooms. Meanwhile, in Britain, despite the success of smooth yodelling **Slim Whitman**, an American country star who will continue to sell better in Britain than at home, Haley's fans are determined to be heard. At the end of August, a

London man is fined £3 10/- for "making an abominable noise," the said noise being 'Rock Around The Clock' played straight for two and a half hours with the intention, it is alleged, of driving his neighbours crazy. Haley must have been anxious that nobody find out about the really wild stuff he recorded earlier, because on August 5, he files suit against Essex, the small Pennsylvania label he had been with before his success with Decca, to keep them from releasing his previous work, saying it is "of inferior quality." Haley's doing so well that at the start of September he turns down $2000 a week for an Australian tour, claiming that he and the band are afraid to fly.

1955 is a watershed year for black music, as the R&B charts show more groups and fewer old-fashioned blues singers gaining popularity. The vocal-harmony groups, who sing a kind of music that will latterly be dubbed 'doo-wop' after the nonsense syllables the back-up singers frequently use, are forging a romantic style that appeals to teenagers black

The Platters' suave look was mirrored by their silky sound, which was propelled by the gorgeous tenor of Tony Williams (top left) and the airy harmonies of Zola Taylor (front).

and white (and brown: doo-wop, as **Johnny Otis** and **Hunter Hancock** find out putting on shows at the Barrelhouse Club in Los Angeles' Watts district, is a big hit with the Chicanos in Los Angeles). This is the year that sees such fully-developed examples of the style as the **Nutmegs**' 'Story Untold', the **El Dorados**' 'At My Front Door', the **Cadillacs**' 'Speedo' and the

Coasters' 'Smokey Joe's Cafe' and 'Riot In Cell Block No. 9'. The real group success-story of the year, however, is the **Platters**, whose smooth rendering of classics like 'Only You' and 'The Great Pretender' manages to build a bridge between the older, mellow stylings of the **Mills Brothers** and the younger sound of the doo-woppers, thereby selling to both generations.

Fads: Davy Crockett

Probably 1955's most unlikely pop icon is a hard-drinking, crude Tennessean who has been dead for over a hundred years. Davy Crockett was a frontiersman who left his native state under something of a cloud, despite having been elected to national office from there and, like so many others from Tennessee, drifted down to Texas, where he joined the independence movement. He was one of the many killed at the Battle of the Alamo in San Antonio, and languished in obscurity until somebody working for Walt Disney thought he'd make a good subject for a multi-part saga on their *Disneyland* television show in 1955. For reasons that are hard to explain, Davy

Crockett mania is suddenly sweeping the US and the previously-unknown actor, Fess Parker, who'd played the role, is catapulted to stardom. 'The Ballad of Davy Crockett', available in a plethora of versions, can be heard everywhere, and American kids go crazy for Davy Crockett products. Besides the obligatory coonskin cap with the tail hanging down the back, there are toy rifles, clothing of all kinds including the buckskin fringe jacket, books, comics, lunch pails… And then, almost as fast as it had appeared, it vanishes. Subsequent attempts to elevate Jim Bowie and Daniel Boone to the same stardom fail, and the raccoon population of America breathes much easier.

JANUARY 8: Elvis begins his breakthrough year with a new single 'Milk Cow Blues Boogie' b/w 'You're A Heartbreaker'.

MARCH 12: His body battered by substance abuse, jazz genius Charlie Parker dies aged 35.

JUNE 17: Eddie Fisher marries Debbie Reynolds.

JUNE 26: Mick Jones of The Clash and Big Audio Dynamite is born in London.

JULY 23: Chuck Berry re-writes country song 'Ida Red' and, as 'Maybelline', it becomes his first single release.

AUGUST 25: The other Elvis, Elvis Costello, is born Declan McManus in London.

SEPTEMBER 14: Little Richard completes his first recording session for Specialty Records in New Orleans.

OCTOBER 10: David Lee Roth is born.

DECEMBER 3: 'Great Pretender' by the Platters is released.

By the end of the summer, **Elvis** is beginning to show signs of catching up: two of his records make the national country charts and he winds up in West Texas playing the Cotton Club in Lubbock. The next day, performing at the opening of a car dealership, he narrowly escapes violence at the hands of some of the local lads upset by his effect on their girlfriends. It's not only the women who are stirred up: his opening act at the Cotton Club is Buddy and Bob, two locals who play 'Western and Bop', according to their business card. **Charles Hardin "Buddy" Holley** is a tall, lanky kid with glasses who has been paying attention to Elvis all along – he regards opening for Elvis as much more prestigious than opening for **Bill Haley**, which he did the night before. It's at the Haley show, however, that Holley is noticed by a talent scout for Haley's label, Decca, who reports back to New York that he's found something interesting. Fortunately, Elvis' tour of tiny clubs turns out to be his last. He soon finds himself on a country package show headlined by **Hank Snow**, whose manager, 'Colonel' Tom Parker, can't help noticing how the young Memphian is getting to the teenagers in the audience.

It seems as if everybody's getting stirred up: down in New Orleans, Richard 'Bumps' Blackwell is presented with the unenviable task of coming up with a record by a talent he's finally convinced his boss, Art Rupe of Specialty Records, to sign. Blackwell had been impressed with a tape submitted to Specialty in LA but, in the flesh, **'Little' Richard Penniman** is something else entirely: flamboyantly dressed, obviously gay and, although they have engaged Fats Domino's band as his back-up, incredibly nervous. Nothing happens at the recording session all morning but at lunch they go into a bar where Richard gets onto the piano and screams out a filthy song he'd picked up playing the blues circuit. Hearing the energy he'd picked up on the original tape, Blackwell rushes Richard back to the studio, where a young songwriter named Dorothy LaBostrie has been hanging around trying to pitch songs. With almost no time left to record, Richard whispers the lyrics of the song to her and she rewrites them into something more innocent. Richard then flies to the piano, hits a chord and hollers: "A wop bop a loo bop a lop bam boom! Tutti frutti, aw rootie!" About two minutes later, another of rock'n'roll's classic records has been created.

By the end of the year, rock'n'roll is a landslide that can't be stopped. 'Rock Around The Clock' tops the charts in Britain, Little Richard is climbing both the pop and R&B charts and, in Memphis, an incredible announcement is made: RCA Victor has paid $45,000 for Elvis in a deal that gives Sam Phillips $25,000 for the rights to all of Elvis' Sun recordings (which he will use to invest in the fledgling Holiday Inn hotel chain) and Elvis himself $5000 cash. In addition, Tom Parker has taken over as the boy's manager and negotiated a separate deal for music publishing with the prestigious Hill & Range firm. RCA announces that, despite Elvis' success in the country field, they are going to promote him to the pop and R&B markets as well. Clearly, 1956 will tell the tale of whether rock'n'roll is here to stay.

▲ Little Richard gets sent by a female fan. Or is she whispering makeup secrets?

1950s Underground

If rock'n'roll could have been talked out of existence, it would never have had a chance. Pundits and sages came out of the woodwork all during its childhood to prophesy its disappearance, warn about its pernicious effect on modern youth, and to explain why, even though it was becoming the most popular music in America, they wouldn't play it. The reasons went beyond mere distaste for the music: the entire entertainment industry was used to teenagers being passive consumers of what it decided to make available to them, and suddenly they were spurning this "good" music, much of which was on major labels that picked up on rock'n'roll only belatedly, if at all. Furthermore, the teen culture that emerged simultaneously with rock'n'roll was making its own rules. Teens were no longer just the older children in the family: they seemed to be a new species, another hideous development in a post-war era already haunted by the spectres of Communism and the Bomb. Reactions were strong, sometimes violent, and occasionally tinged with racism. Herewith some choice examples.

"We have decided that we can combat the teenage swing to R&B by playing more and better Dixieland and jazz. It seems to be going fine. They go for it." Bernard Zuward, WIBC, Baton Rouge, Louisiana, November 1954.

NBC radio's censor passes 'Long Tall Sally' by **Little Richard** for play, saying "How can I restrict it when I can't even understand it?" March 1956.

"Rock'n'roll is mainly performed by coloured artists for coloured people, and is therefore unlikely to ever prove popular in Britain." British bandleader **Ted Heath**, May 1956.

The Birmingham (Alabama) White Citizens' Council asks jukebox operators to ban all rock'n'roll records, saying that the rock'n'roll craze has been instigated by the NAACP and other integration forces, April 1956.

Dave Pringle at WPAG, Ann Arbor, Michigan, hands out membership cards for the "I Hate **Elvis Presley**!" club. The cards say "He makes me feel surgical – like cutting my throat," and come with a razor blade. August 1956.

"As a Christian, I could not morally justify playing the music of Mr. P[resley]. I would like to begin an organization (of DJs) to help eliminate certain wreck and ruin artists." Terry McGuire, WCMC, Wildwood, New Jersey, September 1956.

"A top rock'n'roll label executive told me that each of his recording sessions is geared more and more to appeal to the pop field because he realizes that the long-term trend of rock'n'roll is levelling off and the rock'n'roll is levelling off and the teenagers themselves are tiring of the monotony and sameness of beat and performance which have marked so many rock'n'roll records." Jerry Marshall, WNEW, New York's highest-rated DJ, October 1956.

"I banned Little Richard's 'Lucille' because I feel the lyrics advocate immoral practices. I'm happy to say that the general consensus of my listeners – teenagers and adults – is that I did a most praiseworthy thing." Noble Gravelin, WAMM, Flint,

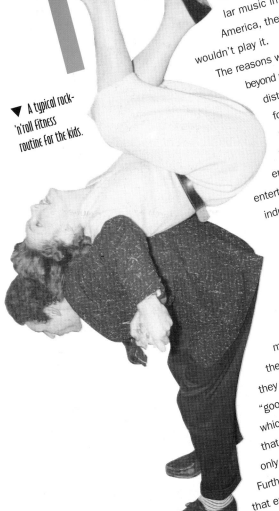

▼ A typical rock-'n'roll fitness routine for the kids.

▼ Poor Ted Heath! He didn't know any 'coloured people', so he never got hep to the jive!

Michigan, May 1957.

Veteran journalist Donal Henahan publishes an exposé of "vulgar cheap junk" on the radio in the Chicago *Daily News*. Henahan says pop hits are a product of "the manipulation by money-hungry adults of the half-felt cravings of teenagers." June 1957.

"Calypso is on the wane, and Hawaiian music will make the complete circle and come to the forefront in a resurgence bigger than the late Twenties within a year, because America's musical ear has been too long tortured by non-melodic forms,

▲ Conway Twitty continued to smoulder as a country & western singer.

rock, R&B, and calypso, too." Dolph Martin, Boston songwriter, June 1957.

"Clean up the show or else." Los Angeles Police Department to **Elvis Presley**, November 1957.

Al Priddy, at KEX, Portland, Oregon, is fired for playing Elvis' 'White Christmas'. Management says "The treatment is in poor taste." December 1957.

KWK, St. Louis, Missouri, bans all rock'n'roll and smashes every rock-'n'roll record in its library after playing it a last time. Says president Robert T. Convey, "It's simply a weeding out of undesirable music." January 1958.

Rock'n'roll is banned in Iran and Egypt on the advice of Iranian doctors who say that many young rock'n'roll dancers have injured their hips with the extreme gyrations. February 1958.

WCFR, Springfield, Virginia, auctions off the "worst" rock'n'roll records to benefit the March of Dimes charity. 'Hound Dog' is bought by a local merchant who mails it to the Kremlin. February, 1958.

Best-selling sociologist Vance Packard tells a Senate Subcommittee on Commerce that rock'n'roll has been foisted on "passive" teenagers by conniving DJs and is not the teens' own taste. He says broadcasters have been "manipulated" to keep "cheap music" – hillbilly, Latin American, R&B and rock'n'roll – on the air because they're cheaply obtained and easy to record. March 1958.

"A girl can't sing rock'n'roll too well. It's basically too savage for a girl to handle." **Connie Francis**, June 1958.

Contacts, the Catholic Youth Council newspaper, publishes an article on lyrics. Among the suspicious songs named are 'Wear My Ring Around Your Neck' and 'Secretly', because they sanction or promote going steady; 'All The Way' and 'Witchcraft' because of the suggestion in the lyrics; and 'Why Don't They

◀ Connie Francis thought she wasn't savage enough to sing rock and roll. She was right.

Understand' because it challenges youngsters' attitudes towards their parents. The editorial page urges readers to "smash the records you possess which present a pagan culture and a pagan way of life. Resist the pressures created by the money-mad record hucksters and popularity-hungry disc jockeys..." July 1958.

The Esso Research Center reports that rock'n'roll on a car radio can cause the driver to jiggle the accelerator pedal in time to the music, causing a decrease in miles per gallon. July 1958.

Representative Torget McDonald of Boston argues against educational matter postal rates for records because it subsidizes "musical illiterates" like Elvis, **Little Richard**, **Conway Twitty** and the **Royal Teens**. March 1959.

KAVI, in Rockyford, Colorado, breaks one rock'n'roll record over the air every 10 minutes until the whole 500-disc library is destroyed. Station manager Ken O'Donnell says "any announcer on my staff who plays a rock'n'roll record in the future will be fined on the spot. There comes a time when human endurance reaches a limit. This is it on KAVI for rock'n'roll." July 1959.

Rock'n'roll in 1956 can be summed up in a word: **Elvis**. With the power of a major record label behind him and with that label motivated by its huge investment, Elvis Presley is going to be out there on display for all to see. It's not as if nothing else is happening in 1956, it's just that Elvis is way ahead of the pack as rock'n'roll's figurehead, its ambassador and its scapegoat.

His first move is television: he makes his national television debut on CBS' the *Dorsey Brothers Stage Show* with whom he's signed a three-week contract. The show's talent booker, Jackie Gleason, sees him as a guitar-wielding Marlon Brando but, by the end of the first broadcast, he must be wondering if he's done the right thing. The theatre is half-full with a scattering of teenagers, the applause perfunctory. The band is nervous and sounds it. But the boys also use their time in New York to record a raft of new songs in RCA's studios. Elvis has already recorded 'Heartbreak Hotel' in Nashville over the Christmas holidays, but here he is concentrating on rock'n'roll, recording 'Tutti Frutti', 'Lawdy Miss Clawdy' and 'Shake, Rattle And Roll'.

Elvis also records 'Blue Suede Shoes', a song by one of his former label-mates at Sun. **Carl Perkins**

had grown up in the only white family sharecropping on a west Tennessee farm and he and his brothers Clayton and Jay B had their own band as soon as they could afford instruments. Once again, Marion Keisker's keen ears had heard something they liked and the band signed a deal with Sun in January 1955 – although Sam Phillips insisted on recording only their country stuff. Finally, perhaps in desperation, Carl recorded 'Blue Suede Shoes', a thinly-masked anthem of teenage defiance. Released early in 1956, it shoots up the charts, going as high as Number 2 on the R&B charts, which must have pleased Carl. Sensing a new Elvis, the *Perry Como Show* invites Carl and the boys to play in New York, so they set out from Tennessee, and in Wilmington, Delaware, they collide with a pick-up truck, which puts everybody into the hospital and severely injures Jay B. Although his career isn't over, the momentum is lost, and he will never be a serious threat to Elvis. Elvis, for his part, refuses to allow RCA to release his version of 'Blue Suede Shoes' as a single. It remains a track on his first LP, 'Elvis Presley', which sells 155,000 copies in its first two months.

Everybody is looking for the next Elvis, on the supposition that the current one won't last much longer than the Davy Crockett fad did. **Buddy Holley** heads for Nashville in January to record some numbers for the Decca subsidiary Brunswick, which include his own tribute to the **Midnighters**' 'Annie' records, 'Annie's Been Workin' On The

Midnight Shift'. (He does so without the services of his partner **Bob Montgomery** who is of a more traditionally country bent and who graciously bows out to allow Buddy his chance. Montgomery will later become an important country songwriter in Nashville). Buddy's first single, 'Love Me', sinks without a trace, which is bad enough, but his name is mis-spelled as 'Buddy Holly' on the record's label, a change Buddy decides to stick with.

Capitol Records, home of **Frank Sinatra**, finds their Elvis in Eugene Vincent Craddock who, as **Gene Vincent**, leads a band called the Blue Caps in Virginia. Vincent is, not to mince words, something of a thug: he drinks heavily, and his first record, 'Be Bop A Lula' is as suggestive as anything the Midnighters ever released. On stage, he cuts an odd figure: a motorcycle accident has left him with a bad leg, on which he pivots as he sings. The band is hot though and the record shoots into the Top 10. Perhaps the most musi-

Gene Vincent (second from right) in a pensive moment with the Blue Caps, one of the era's greatest unsung bands.

22

ROCK'N'ROLL record

JANUARY 21: Carl Perkins releases 'Blue Suede Shoes' b/w 'Honey Don't', songs famously covered by Elvis and the Beatles respectively.

JANUARY 25: 'Heartbreak Hotel' is Elvis' first single for RCA.

JANUARY 31: John Lydon, the future Johnny Rotten of the Sex Pistols, is born in London.

MARCH 3: James Brown's debut is 'Please Please Please'.

MARCH 15: Elvis signs a management contract with "Colonel" Tom Parker, who will oversee the rest of his career, and control his affairs long after his death.

AUGUST 14: A young guitarist, Eddie Cochran, gets to play his song 'Twenty Flight Rock' in a Jayne Mansfield movie The Girl Can't Help It.

DECEMBER 8: The movie Rock Rock Rock, starring Chuck Berry, Frankie Lymon, LaVerne Baker and Johnny Burnette opens in US cinemas.

cally exciting of the newcomers is the **Johnny Burnette Rock & Roll Trio**, featuring one of the era's best guitarists, **Paul Burleson**. Burnette's music is a bit too hard-core to be popular on a mass level and it will be up to a later generation to rediscover him, when the **Yardbirds**' version of 'The Train Kept A-Rollin'' makes him posthumously famous.

Sun, too, with its infusion of cash from RCA, is on the lookout for more Elvises. **Billy Lee Riley**, from Pocahontas, Arkansas, is one: his 'Flying Saucers Rock And Roll' and 'Red Hot' still fail to make waves. **Johnny Cash**, another Arkansasan, is too country, although he sells well, and **Carl Smith** ('Rock And Roll Ruby') and **Roy Orbison** ('Ooby Dooby'), are other contenders – although only Orbison, from Wink, a small Texas town near to where **Buddy Holly** grew up, manages to get onto the charts. Sam Phillips needn't worry, though: playing piano on some of these sessions is a young dynamo from Ferriday, Louisiana, namely **Jerry Lee Lewis**, who is biding his time waiting for a chance to record on his own.

One place they're not looking for a new Elvis is in the world of R&B. Fired by the acceptance the music has had from teenagers and conscious that things are changing, black musicians are experimenting. The **Robins**, who had had some success with 'Smokey Joe's Café' late in 1955, have regrouped and renamed themselves the **Coasters**, since they are the only West Coast (LA) group signed to Atlantic Records. They have formed a solid partnership with two

young Jewish guys, Jerry Leiber and Mike Stoller, who have been writing R&B songs since the early Fifties, when they were still in high school. Leiber and Stoller have a gift for wacky stories, amusing wordplay and coming up with exactly what teenagers want to hear, so no wonder the first Coasters record, 'Down In Mexico', is a hit.

Another school of thought holds that what teenagers most want to see up on stage is other teenagers and George Goldner, who has mostly been recording salsa bands in New York, is presented with **Frankie Lymon & The Teenagers**, an all-teen group of black and Puerto Rican kids from Harlem, by one of his talent scouts. Frankie is only 13 and adorable, a born performer, and although Goldner has his doubts (he'd only taken the group on because he thought they played salsa) he releases 'Why Do Fools Fall In Love?' which climbs to Number 6 on the pop charts and the top of the R&B charts.

Others are convinced that it is easier for solo performers like Elvis to be the focus of teens' attention, which is how **James Brown**, a 28-year-old ex-convict and gospel singer, winds up recording 'Please Please Please' for the same label as the

A young, tuxedo-clad James Brown, around the time of "Please Please Please."

Midnighters, Federal. This sounds like nothing else in the world, consisting of mostly one word, 'please', repeated over a sinuous 6/8 groove while Brown's backup singers, the **Famous Flames**, sing 'Please Don't Go'. Released in April, the record takes a long time to gather momentum and although it never enters the pop charts, it is the start of one of the longest-lived careers in popular music.

Elvis himself is certainly keeping busy — and making mountains of money for RCA, for whom he represents a neat 50% of their popular music sales. In Hollywood, Paramount Pictures announce he's been signed to a three-picture contract and that production on the first of them, *The Reno Brothers*, will begin presently. His only stumble on the way up occurs when he opens at Las Vegas' New Frontier Hotel as the warm-up act for the **Freddie Martin Orchestra** and comedian Shecky Greene. After a week, the hotel and

Colonel Parker mutually agree to terminate the booking due to mass audience apathy. No big deal: with his records topping the charts nearly as quickly as they're released, Vegas isn't to be an important part of the equation just yet.

The May 2 issue of *Billboard* carries some very interesting news for those who like to crunch the numbers. Five records appear simultaneously on the Pop and R&B Top 10: 'Heartbreak Hotel' by **Elvis Presley** (Number 1 pop, Number 6 R&B), 'Blue Suede Shoes' by **Carl Perkins** (Number 4 pop, Number 3 R&B), 'Long Tall Sally' by **Little Richard** (Number 9 pop, Number 1 R&B), 'Magic Touch' by the **Platters** (Number 10 pop, Number 7 R&B) and 'Why Do Fools Fall In Love?' by

Frankie Lymon & The Teenagers (Number 7 pop, Number 4 R&B). Presley and Perkins also claim the top two positions on the country charts that week.

This will be the first rock'n'roll summer: the music is all over the radio, on television and in the cinema. Proof that people are beginning to speak the rock'n'roll language comes from one of the weirdest records yet to be a hit. **Bill Buchanan and Dickie Goodman**'s 'The Flying Saucer' is a fake radio programme interrupted by news reports of a flying saucer landing. Interviewed by a newsman, the aliens reply with short snippets of recent rock'n'roll hits by Little Richard, **Chuck Berry**, **Fats Domino** and Carl Perkins. You can't dance to it and

it's blatant copyright infringement but Alan Freed loves it and, after he plays it all the time, it winds up on the charts for three months.

Among the summer's hits are slow-dance classics like the **Five Satins**' 'In The Still Of The Nite', 'Oh What A Night' by the **Dells**, the Platters' 'Great Pretender', 'A Thousand Miles Away' by the **Heartbeats**, 'Devil Or Angel' by the **Clovers**, faster numbers like 'This Little Girl Of Mine' by the **Cleftones**, 'Let The Good Times Roll' by **Shirley & Lee** and a double-sided smash from Fats Domino, 'My Blue Heaven' and 'I'm In Love Again'. But the clarion call of the revolution is sounded by Chuck Berry with 'Roll Over Beethoven' gleefully declaring all other types of music irrelevant in the

▶ Britain's first teen idol, Tommy Steele, fresh from a career as a pantry boy for the Cunard Line, tries out the Elvis look as he performs "Rock With The Caveman."

Elvis on TV

Although television in 1956 is not quite the ubiquitous medium it later becomes in the US, it has caught on in a big way in the larger cities, where all three major networks (ABC, CBS, and NBC) usually have outlets competing with a couple of smaller local stations. In these pre-MTV days, the idea of promoting a popular music artist on this medium is, if not unheard of (**Perry Como**, among others, had his own show), at least quite novel.

After his *Dorsey Brothers* debacle, **Elvis** has learnt a lesson in the ways of TV: on April 3, two days after his screen-test, he appears on the *Milton Berle Show*, a venerable institution that sees Elvis play live from the aircraft carrier USS Hancock, watched by an estimated 40 million people (a quarter of the population of the United States). On June 5, he appears again on the weekly show and, by now, the anti-Elvis forces are ready with their brickbats: the *New York Times* calls it "a rock and roll variation on…the hootchy kootchy" and their competition at the *Journal-American* moralistically opines that stripper Georgia Southern ought to get equal time. Even more damning is the statement by *New York Daily News* columnist and variety TV show host, Ed Sullivan, that he would never allow anything so suggestive on his stage. This only prompts his rival, Steve Allen, to sign

Elvis onto *his* show, which airs at the same time as Sullivan's. Just to make sure nothing untoward happens, though, Allen dresses Elvis in a tuxedo, makes him promise not to dance, and has him sing his new single, 'Hound Dog' to a mournful-looking basset hound. Seeing the ratings, Sullivan caves in and offers Elvis $50,000 for three appearances beginning in September.

Sullivan himself doesn't even bother to host the September 9 show, on which Elvis first appears, leaving the duties up to actor Charles Laughton, of all people. Elvis performs in front of a live audience of teenagers and the ensuing pandemonium — including the spectacle of him in full jiggle — makes American broadcast history. Despite overwhelmingly negative press response and even a warning from the *Catholic Sun*, Sullivan has him back for a second appearance and is there to greet him in person. Finally bowing to the onslaught of criticism, for a third show (and, despite what's been written subsequently, *only* for the third show), Sullivan instructs the cameramen to show Elvis from the waist up, but the audience can't forget what's going on down there and the screaming continues.

And is any of this helping RCA sell Elvis records? More than ever before, thank you very much.

face of rock'n'roll.

Film, too, will be immortalizing rock 'n' roll, first with a quickie featuring Alan Freed and Bill Haley, unsurprisingly entitled *Rock Around The Clock*, with few other memorable stars. The real winner is *The Girl Can't Help It*, with Tom Ewell, Edmund O'Brien and Jayne Mansfield and musical appearances by **Little Richard**, **Gene Vincent and the Blue Caps**, **Fats Domino**, the **Platters** and **Eddie Cochran**. Unlike most of the early rock'n'roll movies, this one has a plot that ingeniously manages to weave in the musical numbers fairly seamlessly. And great numbers they are, too: Gene Vincent's 'Be Bop A Lula' is his transcendent moment, and Little Richard performs with an energy that makes one suspect he's waited all his life for the opportunity. Of course, the film everyone's waiting for is *The Reno Brothers*, **Elvis**' debut. The title has been changed to *Love Me Tender*, to help promote the theme song (adapted from 'Aura Lee', a Civil War hit), and plot-wise it's a complete disaster, but it's nearly 90

minutes of Elvis, even if he does get killed in the end (which gives him the perfect opportunity to reprise 'Love Me Tender' from a cloud as his family walks away from his grave). Predictably, cinemas are packed.

Towards the end of 1956, rock'n'roll finally jumps the Atlantic. *Blackboard Jungle*, a film about juvenile delinquency, has caused trouble in Britain already, with teens wrecking cinemas as soon as 'Rock Around The Clock' comes on the soundtrack and with the single (along with 'Why Do Fools Fall In Love?') having hit the charts. However the ball really starts rolling when Radio Luxembourg starts beaming Alan Freed's syndicated radio show across Europe and into England. On September 21, *New Musical Express* devotes a four-page supplement to the new music and soon not only has the Queen invited **Bill Haley** to do a command performance (which occurs on the same day the Syria Mosque in his home town of Pittsburgh bans him) but British performers start recording rock'n'roll records. First comes **Johnny Brandon**, The King of Zing, with 'Do You Love Love Love Me', followed quickly by **Tommy Steele**, whose 'Rock With The Caveman' charts in early November. (The same chart

sees Gene Vincent's 'Blue Jean Bop' entering at Number 19 a good 30 places higher than it ever gets in the US: Vincent will always be more popular in Britain than at home.)

It's been a great year for rock-'n'roll, and particularly for Elvis, who has managed to put a whopping 16 records on the charts, five of which were double-sided hits and one, 'Don't Be Cruel'/'Hound Dog', a double-sided Number 1 record. Weary of touring and film-making, he goes home to Memphis for Christmas (he gives his parents a Cadillac each), and he heads over to Sun Studios to see his friends. **Johnny Cash**, **Carl Perkins**, and **Jerry Lee Lewis** are all there and the engineer slips a tape on as Jerry fires up the piano. For over an hour there is spontaneous music-making and conversation, as they sing hymns, blues tunes and whatever comes into their heads. The so-called '**Million Dollar Quartet**' is no great shakes here at making music, as people will hear in 1981 when the tape finally surfaces, but it's a heartwarming affirmation of some sort of community, a community built on rock'n'roll.

A carefully-staged shot of the Million Dollar Quartet, left to right, Jerry Lee Lewis, Carl Perkins, Elvis Presley, and Johnny Cash, who left almost immediately afterwards.

Rock'n'roll has been blessed with several perfect years, when the shops are filled with great records, the airwaves are playing your favourite song all the time and musicians are coming up with ideas that just catch the mood of the times. The first of these golden years is 1957, a stunning twelve months when more good records come out than the charts can accommodate, established artists produce some of their most classic work and a host of major new stars are born.

Britain observes New Year's Day with the initial broadcast of its first rock'n'roll show, *Cool for Cats*, and a week later **Bill Haley** takes off for an Australian tour (with a new set of **Comets** who aren't afraid to fly) that will also bring him to Europe and the British Isles. One week later, the Cavern Club opens in Liverpool, featuring jazz and skiffle bands in the venue that the **Beatles** will make their own in a few years' time.

Elvis celebrates his 22nd birthday in ominous fashion on January 16 by taking the physical examination that will determine his suitability for Army service and, unfortunately, passes it.

Whispers abound that the passing fad that was rock'n'roll is over: the country charts are once again loaded with traditional sounds, old-

fashioned blues seem to be making a comeback on the R&B charts and America's best-selling album for most of the first half of the year is 'Calypso' by **Harry Belafonte**, whose 'Banana Boat (Day-O)' is selling like hot cakes. Record companies immediately rush to release their own calypso records, all of which stiff, even when they're by American performers like **Richard Berry**, a Los Angeles R&B studio piano player, whose fake Trinidadian dialect just renders the lyrics of his calypso attempt, 'Louie Louie', meaningless.

Others, however, keep the faith: back home in West Texas, **Buddy Holly**, stung by his treatment in Nashville and his inability to sell records, has been rehearsing a new band called the **Crickets**, after the insects that chirruped along in their

Skiffle

Although American folk music will become one of the elements of the rock music of the Sixties (see 1959), it is overseas that its first revival takes place in the form of the skiffle movement in Britain. The key to the music's popularity is its simplicity: using acoustic guitars, washboard percussion and a bass that is often home-made out of a tea chest or washtub, the musicians play good-timey blues and play party music taken from the repertoires of **Leadbelly**, **Big Bill Broonzy** and other American blues musicians that they've encountered during the course of the British trad jazz craze.

Americans, of course, perceive this new music as silly and foreign, although a few British musicians, like a former member of Chris Barber's jazz band, **Lonnie Donegan**, who does manage to chart a novelty hit: his 'Rock Island Line', a Leadbelly tune, makes the Top 10 in 1956. In fact, skiffle is more important for its influence on other forms of music than for what it actually comes up with itself. One effect it has is to open up British ears to blues, as performers like **Alexis Korner** and **Cyril Davies** pursue the subject further and

discover **Muddy Waters** and the whole Chicago blues scene, a taste they will help future members of the **Rolling Stones** to acquire. Skiffle also popularizes acoustic instruments among the younger generation, leading to protest songs being an important part of the Campaign for Nuclear Disarmament in the late Fifties and, on a parallel track, the rediscovery by a new generation of Britain's own folk heritage. (It is worth noting that both of these movements happen in Britain before they do in the US.) But probably most importantly, in a country with no rock'n'roll tradition, it brings people together to play: the **Vipers**, one of skiffle's bigger groups, metamorphose into one of Britain's most influential groups, **Cliff Richard**'s backing band the **Shadows**. And, perhaps most importantly, in 1956-7 a skiffle band appears in Liverpool, the **Quarrymen**, founded by John Lennon and later to include Paul McCartney, George Harrison and Stuart Sutcliffe. They may be no great shakes as a skiffle band, but once they figure out that it's really rock'n'roll music that they love, they'll do okay as the **Beatles**.

FEBRUARY 5: Via the liner Queen Elizabeth from New York to Southampton, Bill Haley arrives amid scenes of mob hysteria to begin his first UK tour.

25: In Clovis, New Mexico, Buddy Holly and band record 'That'll Be The Day', its title taken from a John Wayne catch-phrase in the movie The Searchers.

JULY 6: John Lennon and Paul McCartney meet at a church fete in Woolton, Liverpool, after a set by Lennon's skiffle band the Quarrymen.

OCTOBER 24: The Elvis movie Jailhouse Rock debuts at Loew's State cinema in Memphis.

NOVEMBER 11: As Jerry Lee Lewis unleashes his masterpiece 'Great Balls Of Fire', the hell-raising singer secretly marries his 13-year-old cousin Myra Gale Brown.

NOVEMBER 25: A New York duo called Tom & Jerry release 'Hey Schoolgirl'; they'll later become Simon & Garfunkel.

rehearsal room the previous year. Fed up with recording in Nashville, Holly finds a small recording studio just across the border in Clovis, New Mexico, run by Norman Petty, who seems to be more understanding than the Nashville people and who is willing to advise him on his songs. But Norman still thinks the reworking of 'That'll Be The Day' isn't going to do any better than the slower version he'd cut in Nashville. Holly disagrees and mails a tape of it off to New York.

Holly's problem in Nashville had been that he'd been dealing with the Music Establishment in the shape of Bradley Owen, who was so successful with his mainstream country artists that he had no time for 'Texan hicks'. But others in Nashville are hungrier, like Archie Bleyer, whose Cadence label is on the verge of folding. Desperate to survive, he's signed, among others, the **Everly Brothers**, Phil and Don, country singers in the **Louvin Brothers** tradition who have had one flop record on Columbia. Then, to supply his new artists with material, Bleyer has a husband-and-wife team from Acuff-Rose Music come in and pitch them songs. By the time Felice and Boudleaux Bryant get round to the Everlys, most of their country material is gone, and all that remains is one song, 'Bye Bye Love', which has been turned down by 30 previous artists. Surprisingly, the boys love it, and it takes them straight to the Number 2 position on the pop and country charts. It's also the beginning of a close working relationship between the Everlys and the Bryants

(who, despite being among the first professional songwriters to work in Nashville, remain best known for their work with the duo) and, needless to say, the salvation of Cadence Records.

Hungrier still is **Jerry Lee Lewis**, toiling away as a sideman playing piano on sessions at Sun. The kid's been chafing to record on his own, but his sole attempt so far has been a strange version of **Ray Price**'s 1956 hit 'Crazy Arms', which has gone nowhere. On live dates, he's been doing a song recorded by **Roy Hall** in 1955 called 'Whole Lotta Shakin' Goin' On', which he's remodelled considerably mainly thanks to the fact that he's forgotten the original lyrics. Finally, Sam Phillips agrees to record it with him and, after a long theological discussion (Jerry Lee is torn between religion and rock'n'roll, a problem usually faced by black singers such as the **Soul Stirrers' Sam Cooke**), they cut it and Lewis' career starts its meteoric ascent.

As the weather warms up, rock-'n'roll starts creeping back on the charts, its presence heralded by a song that perfectly captures whatever it is that's been driving so many kids wild: 'School Day (Ring Ring Goes The Bell)' by **Chuck Berry** begins by listing the things that makes school a drag before, musically and lyrically, giving the release. Ring, ring goes the bell and you're free to go down to the malt-shop, drop a nickel in the jukebox, and have fun at last. "Hail

The Everly Brothers, Don (left) and Phil, regularly appeared on their parents' radio shows throughout the Forties.

hail rock & roll", Berry sings, "Deliver me from the days of old." He's referring specifically to history homework, but everybody who hears the song knows that it goes a lot deeper than that.

Songwriters are learning how to talk to teenagers, as Leiber and Stoller conclusively prove with their next **Coasters** record: 'Searchin'' is about looking for the perfect girlfriend, and the flip-side, 'Young Blood', is about finding her. The double-sided Top 10 hit not only puts the label (Atco, a subsidiary of Atlantic) on the map, but establishes the Coasters and gives Leiber and Stoller enough money to move to New York, where they can set up in the Brill Building, the nerve centre of the music business. They really need to be in the middle of things, too: they've been approached about scoring the third **Elvis Presley** film (the

APR 11 : Singapore is granted self-government from Britain

1957 • HEADLINE NEWS

second, *Loving You*, is a full-scale colour production that shows Elvis to much better advantage than *Love Me Tender* and proves that the boy can actually act). Thanks in large part to their contribution, *Jailhouse Rock* is Elvis' finest cinematic moment so far and the title track becomes a huge best-seller.

June sees **Buddy Holly**'s career making an abrupt turnaround: the new version of 'That'll Be The Day' gets released on Brunswick Records, with the label identifying the artists as the **Crickets**, while Buddy signs a solo contract with Coral. (Both labels are Decca subsidiaries, and later in the year, Decca will try to cash in by releasing some of the Nashville recordings.) Thanks to a solid relationship with Norman Petty, who has gotten them the deal, none of this is too confusing: Norman records them, and they all make the decision as to what tape will be delivered to New York as by which artist. Thus, following 'That'll Be The Day' on to the charts is 'Peggy Sue' by Buddy Holly (despite the fact that the Crickets not only play on the record, but it's actually named after Cricket Jerry Allison's girlfriend), which in turn is chased up the hit parade by 'Oh, Boy!' by the Crickets. Buddy's 'nerdy' look (he wears glasses!) and hiccuping vocal style really hit home with the teens in America and Britain, turning tiny Clovis, New Mexico, into a major recording centre for Texan artists: among Petty's other successes this year is **Buddy Knox** of 'Party Doll' fame.

Black music is in a period of tumult: of the year's 12 Number 1

R&B records, an unprecedented seven are by white artists, including not only Elvis Presley and **Jerry Lee Lewis** but Canadian crooner **Paul Anka** and rock'n'roll's first 'fake' group, **Danny & The Juniors** (whose members actually do exist, but whose record is made by overdubbing lead singer Danny Rapp's voice again and again, a technique that West Coast rockabilly singer **Eddie Cochran** has been using with the instruments on his records). There's a generational change taking place, with many older established black acts failing to impress a new generation of black teenagers, who prefer vocal groups with minimal instrumentation to soloists fronting big bands. The change in the pattern of record buying is also down to the fact that the older groups almost all record for tiny independent labels, leading to a slew of regional hits that fail to coalesce into national ones. (A headline in *Billboard* notes that independent labels are forming on an average of one per day.) And when black teens *do* respond to solo singers, they are of a completely new kind.

Take **Sam Cooke**. Possessed of a meltingly beautiful tenor, Cooke has been the sensation of the gospel world for a couple of years, singing with the venerable **Soul Stirrers**. In a scene dominated by middle-aged homosexual men, he is a young heterosexual Adonis who can be heard riling up the young women on a remarkable recording of the Soul Stirrers at LA's Shrine Auditorium in 1954. After dipping a toe in pop music in 1956, he plunges in a year later with a song written by his broth-

er, 'You Send Me', which will become 1957's top-selling pop song, and a harbinger of a style that will become known as 'soul'. In Detroit, another singer who will help create soul, **Jackie Wilson**, has broken away from **Billy Ward & The Dominoes**, an old-fashioned vocal group with some hits in their past and will release his first record, 'Reet Petite', this year. It's a flop, but it's a beginning not only for Wilson, but also for the song's co-writer, Berry Gordy Jr, who will eventually found the Motown empire. Another rising star is **Larry Williams**, Specialty Records' second major black rock'n'roll singer after **Little Richard**, who will have two great hits this year, 'Short Fat Fannie' and 'Bony Maronie'. And, of course, there is Little Richard himself of whom, they say, there will only ever be one of his kind.

So much so that he makes the headlines in the US while touring way down under. Despite a considerable amount of worldly success, Richard has a vision of his own damnation and, standing up after his show in Sydney, he decides to chuck it all in and go to divinity school. He holds a

The great Sam Cooke, who scandalized his elders by leaving gospel to invent a new form of music that would be called soul, and who inspired everyone from Otis Redding to Rod Stewart.

Rock'n'Roll TV

In the film *The Girl Can't Help It* there is an amazing scene in which a black maid is discovered getting all excited watching **Eddie Cochran** perform 'Twenty Flight Rock' on a black-and-white television. It's been clear since **Elvis**' first appearances that this new medium can take the music where it's never been before and, in 1957, it hits the small screen with a vengeance.

One approach is the record-hop show, which has been popping up across the country. All it takes is a popular local DJ, some kids and some records: the DJ plays the records, the kids dance and the DJ usually has some local or national act on promoting a new release. The earliest of these is Philadelphia's *American Bandstand* which, since 1956, has had the youthful Dick Clark as host. On May 4, 1957, the *Alan Freed Show* on the ABC network becomes the first record-hop show to go nationwide, leaning heavily on live acts which, in turn, demand a big production budget. On August 5, ABC gives *Bandstand* a Saturday-morning slot and a hit show is born: Clark talks easily to teenagers and, for their part, the Philadelphia kids are eager to demonstrate the latest dances. The net result of all this (besides giving healthy plugs for acts in which Clark has an interest) is that rock'n'roll culture — clothes, hairstyles, dances — begins to become standardized. Before long, record-hop TV shows are in every city, providing a new network for the dissemination of the music and its artefacts.

Another development is the creation of a star *through* a show. Ozzie and Harriet Nelson were, respectively, a bandleader and his singer in the Thirties and, in the Fifties, they were among the first to try a weekly comedy series. Ozzie and Harriet play themselves as parents to David and young upstart Ricky, their actual children, and the show is a hit. Then, one night in 1957, 16-year-old Ricky brags to a date that he is about to make a record, a lie that he decides to make true. Ozzie pulls some strings and Ricky goes into the studio to make a one-shot single, 'Teenager's Romance', backed with **Fats Domino**'s 'I'm Walkin''. At the tail end of an April episode of the *Adventures of Ozzie & Harriet*, Ricky performs the songs and, all of a sudden, the record company finds itself with 60,000 orders, a Top 10 hit and eventual total sales of over a million. Ozzie, shrewd businessman that he is, realizes that Ricky doesn't have an ongoing contract with the label, Verve, and so he approaches Fats Domino's label, Imperial, about signing him. Bolstered by his weekly appearances on the family's show, with the loyalty of teenagers who had grown up watching him grow up on television and, performing with one of the best back-up bands of the era featuring guitar-whiz **James Burton**, **Ricky Nelson** starts a career that will span 25 years and will include a remarkable re-birth as one of LA's pioneer country-rockers in the Seventies.

Ricky Nelson, normal kid, TV star, inadvertent teen idol.

press conference the next day to announce his decision and, later on a ferry, he is challenged by his saxophone player over his sincerity, which Richard duly demonstrates by whipping off $8000 worth of diamond rings and chucking them in the harbour. Fortunately for all of us, Art Rupe at Specialty has a lot of recordings already in the can, and will continue to release them over the next year to make back his investment. Richard, however, is serious, and will not perform any rock'n'roll for many years to come.

If Richard's religious convictions are intense and **Jerry Lee Lewis**' has sublimated his while 'Whole Lotta Shakin' sears the airwaves, **Elvis**' become the subject of much controversy at the end of the year, as RCA readies the release of 'Elvis' Christmas Album'. Mixing Christmas standards with some bluesier material, it is banned on release in Canada, while clergymen everywhere debate the propriety of 'The Pelvis' dealing with sacred material. If Elvis is depressed that this completely sincere gesture is being taken wrongly, it can't help his mood to return to his new mansion, Graceland, to discover that he has been drafted: the letter orders him to report for induction into the Army on January 20, 1958. Colonel Tom immediately requests a 60-day delay so that Elvis can finish *Kid Creole*, the movie he's currently making, but the news is out and the legions of Elvis' fans are chilled by it. Without Elvis, what will happen to rock'n'roll?

DEC 19: The UK enquiry into the Windscale nuclear disaster blames insufficient staffing

1950s Crazes

If rock'n'roll turned teenagers into a new nation, it was one with not only its own music, but its own costumes, language, rites and even cuisine. Some of these things have become integrated into our culture to an extent we hardly even notice, while others seem as alien as they must have to the uncomprehending adults back in the Fifties.

The craze for Davy Crockett hats may have been the marketing model for many of the fads that came afterwards. Fashion came and went overnight in the Fifties: the poodle skirt, for instance was an ankle-length felt affair with a large poodle, usually white, appliquéed on it, while the minutiae of girls' hairstyles could provide a thesis for an aspiring cultural historian. As their mothers had done during the War,

girls began to wear pants, including a tight pair of jeans that stopped well above the ankle known as pedal pushers, and these cropped up in a **Carl Perkins** song. Boys' fashions were more conservative, although idols like **Elvis** and **Pat Boone** provided inspiration for haircuts (sideburns and the tapering bit at the back called the DA, for duck's ass) and shoes (Boone's white bucks were de rigeur for a while, although it was fiendishly difficult to keep them clean – a problem inherent in suede, as Carl Perkins implied when warning people not to step on his blue suede footwear). Some things never caught on: in parts of the US, boys suddenly started wearing their belt buckles on or near their left hips and, just as suddenly as they had started, they stopped.

Language, of course, was an important bond: much of the teenage slang of this era came from blacks, who were using words like 'cat', 'chick', 'cool' and 'hip' back in the Twenties. DJs were a vital source of slang, and when they weren't just passing on musician-speak, they sometimes made up their own languages. Murray 'the K' Kaufman, a New York DJ, invented Meusurray, which was something like Pig Latin, thus inserting the syllable 'eus' before the first vowel of a word – Meusurray Keusaufman was his own name modified. He also popularized a chant he'd found on an African recording: "B'daah-bay!" he'd yell, and the audience would reply "Ho!"

"B'daah-bay!" "Ho!" they'd repeat, and then "Kuwi sawa-sawaaa!" holding out the last syllable while the audience yelled back "Hooooooo!"

Teenage tribes tended to gather after school for a bit of refreshment and socialization, gravitating towards the malt-shop, an ice-cream parlour serving sundaes, banana splits, ice-cream sodas and floats, and the ubiquitous malted milk. However the food item that got launched into national prominence through its consumption by the Fifties teenager was the tautological 'pizza pie' (*pizza* meaning pie in Italian). Although pizza had been a staple of Italian bakeries in the Northeast since the turn of the century and California had pizzerias since 1934, the Americanized version of the dish, with its plethora of toppings which could be customized by the diner, came into its own during the early days of rock'n'roll. **Dean Martin**'s big hit 'That's Amore' begins with the words "When the moon hits your eye like a big pizza pie," and one of the most sought-after vocal harmony records of the era is **Norman Fox & the Rob Roys**' 'Pizza Pie' which, believe it or not, serves as a metaphor for the bond of true love.

And what about hamburgers? They were already well-entrenched in the American diet by the time rock'n'roll

▲ The hair just so, the clothes perfectly tailored. It's okay to kiss him.

▲ "Day-VEEE, Day-VEEE Crockett, King of the wild Frontier."

came along, but became part of rock-'n'roll culture via the automobile, which conveyed teens to the drive-in. Beginning in California, where the weather makes them a year-round affair, drive-ins were snack restaurants featuring the gamut of teen food, hamburgers, malts, and so on. You drove up to a box with a speaker, placed your order to someone inside, and were served on a tray that clipped on to your window by a waitress called a car-hop, who was sometimes, but rarely, on roller-skates to get the food to the customer quicker. Drive-ins were never about food though: they were about looking at other people's cars. Girls would drive their parents' cars, but boys had to have their own, so that they could not only work on the mechanics, but cus-

tomize them. The Fifties were the first great age of customized cars, with kids often spending hundreds of dollars on such cosmetic changes as fender skirts, pinstripes, and chrome details. Since the cars were never new, this was a way of making them new: first you would 'cherry' (restore) the car, then customize it. Boys who spent a lot of time on their cars were usually not the best students, of course, so a mysterious customized car pulling into a drive-in could have the same effect on a teenage girl's hormones as Marlon Brando had riding into town in *The Wild One*. Customization lives on today, particularly in the Mexican-American low-rider culture, which has elevated the practice into a fine art, with the cars on display in galleries and museums.

▲ The malt-shop was teen headquarters, and a bartender had to be an expert in order to mix the bewildering array of sodas his customers demanded.

◄ "What are you rebelling against?" "Whaddya got?" Marlon Brando's snappy comeback in The Wild Ones set the tone for a whole generation.

As 1958 dawns, it begins to occur to people in the non-creative side of the music business that the monster that is rock'n'roll can be brought to heel without losing the wild edge that makes it so popular with teenagers. The radio, for instance, is a place of anarchy: disc jockeys can simply play the records they like, which they do. This means that listeners are free to tune into one jockey's show and turn over to another as often as they like; radio stations have no firm hold over their audiences. Apart from an informal ban on indecent records, there's little control over what gets played. In 1957, a mini-revolution in programming had been launched in Omaha, Nebraska, where Todd Stortz, who owns a chain of radio stations in that part of the country, wired up a couple of jukeboxes in bars to test a theory he had: that there is a hard-core of about 40 records that people want to hear at any given time. Convinced he is onto something, he creates the Top 40, limiting the number of records played on his stations to precisely that number and, by 1958, the idea, despite resistance from DJs, is catching on nationwide.

In Philadelphia, another experiment is being conducted. Bob Marcucci and Bob DeAngelis of Chancellor Records have hit on the idea of manufacturing teen idols. Their first Frankenstein, **Frankie Avalon**, is a seasoned performer at the age of 19 and his innocuous 'De De Dinah' is a Top 10 hit at the start of the year. Shortly thereafter, Avalon introduces Marcucci to **Fabian Forte**, a darkly handsome, if vocally challenged, youngster from Frankie's Philadelphia neighbourhood. Marcucci starts Fabian on a strict regime of schooling for stardom, giving him diction lessons, singing lessons, the whole works. Although it doesn't happen overnight Fabian, too, is destined for a brief tryst with fame.

This sort of manipulation seems unavoidable: just as World War II cut off supplies of rubber from Southeast Asia and set the chemical industry searching for a substitute, **Elvis**' impending Army service seems to make everybody bar Colonel Parker think that an ersatz Elvis will soon be the most in-demand product for teens. *Kid Creole* finished, Elvis is tidying up his affairs in Memphis: he is inducted into the Army on March 24 and photographers crowd into the

barber's to immortalize the shearing of that famous hair.

Not that this leaves Memphis short of rock-'n'roll stars: in February, **Carl Perkins** has signed with Columbia to begin a long career of putting out superb rockabilly records. Sadly, the label is unprepared to promote them and as a result they don't sell although they still stand the test of time. And **Jerry Lee Lewis** seems unstoppable: after 'Whole Lotta Shakin'' comes the even more frantic 'Great Balls Of Fire' and the darkly sexual 'Breathless'. In February, he goes back into the studio to record 'High School Confidential', the title track to a movie about high-school dope dealing that remains a goofy classic and which opens with Jerry Lee and his band performing the song on the back of a flatbed truck. Lewis is a frequent visitor to *American Bandstand*, which is now the top-rated daytime television show in the US thanks to its new daily just-after-school time-slot and he also makes an appearance on the first *Dick Clark Show,* a weekend night-time all-rock'n'roll variety programme. A British tour is planned for May: this should be Lewis' crowning success.

On the R&B side, amazing records just keep on coming. Some are one-shots, like the **Monotones**' 'Book of Love', a primitive, but appealing song based around a hook stolen from a toothpaste commercial.

Pop Frankenstein Fabian, perhaps puzzling over his elocution lessons or wondering how to tie his shoes.

PFC. Elvis Aaron Presley (533010761) prepares to defend the Free World in a blizzard like they never had in Memphis.

The Boston Riot

At the beginning of 1958, Alan Freed is the king of rock'n'roll radio, appearing on New York's top pop station, WINS, promoting package shows of popular artists, syndicating a show to outlets all over the world and, in April, announcing that he is opening a nightclub in Miami Beach. To be called Alan Freed's Sugar Bowl, the club will cater to teens and book rock'n'roll exclusively. Buoyed by the success of his New Year's Day show at the Brooklyn Paramount Theatre, he begins organizing the spring package show, Alan Freed's *The Big Beat*, which would feature the acts that had made the Brooklyn show so successful: **Fats Domino**, the **Crickets** and **Jerry Lee Lewis**, along with a plethora of other performers including, fatefully, the **Cadillacs**. Despite warnings in the trade press that America's teens aren't as well-heeled as they had been in previous years, Freed puts the show on the road.

May 3 is supposed to be just another show: the Boston Arena. But Boston, for all its intellectual sophistication and concentration of prestigious universities, is also a town where racial tension simmers just below the surface even today. In 1958, the idea of an integrated show featuring purveyors of wild jungle music playing to an audience of integrated teenagers is sure to raise some hackles and, sure enough, as Freed comes into the venue, a Boston policeman shoves him and tells him "We don't like your kind of music here". Still, Freed is a veteran of this sort of situation and continues unfazed.

While the Cadillacs are on stage, a white girl pushes herself up there, and grabs lead singer Earl 'Speedo' Carroll by the crotch. That does it: within seconds, the stage is a swarming mass of blue and the audience is being pushed outside. The house lights come on as Freed takes the stage and announces "The police don't want you to have any fun here." In the street, it's no fun at all: police are beating teenagers and rumours begin to spread about gangs of teenagers on drugs, rape, hundreds of arrests.

In the end, there's only one person in trouble with the law, and that's Alan Freed who is indicted for inciting a riot. The rest of the tour is cancelled and Freed returns to New York, where he's in more trouble: Elroy McCaw, who owns WINS, wants to talk to him. McCaw is angry at the publicity Freed's bringing to the station and lets it be known that Freed's contract will not be renewed. While they're meeting, the promoter of the suddenly-cancelled show in Newark runs into the station waving a gun and looking for Freed, but can't find him and leaves.

The next day, Freed announces he's leaving WINS because they won't "stand behind my policies and principles." WINS says the departure is a "complete surprise" and wish him luck. A few days later, WABC, which has always trailed WINS in the New York rock radio sweepstakes, announces that they've hired Freed for a prime-time evening slot but, although nobody realizes it at the moment, Freed is beginning a descent from which he will never recover.

▲ "They call me, they call me the Fat Man," sang Antoine "Fats" Domino, who would grow to even more spectacular proportions.

George Goldner, inspired by the **Teenagers**' success (although **Frankie Lymon** has split off for a disastrous solo career and started the downward slide that will end with his death due to a drug overdose in his grandmother's apartment in 1968, aged 25), has been recording groups on End, including a quintet of teenage girls who call themselves the **Chantels**, led by 14-year-old Arlene Smith, who is possessed of an incredibly powerful voice for one so young and small. February sees

their 'Maybe', a distillation of teenage angst, climbing up the charts. **Chuck Berry**, too, is thinking about teenage girls when he writes 'Sweet Little Sixteen', celebrating the lengths these girls will go to in order to enjoy their favourite music, rock-'n'roll. It's another million-seller.

Fuelled by worries about a worsening American economy, another one-shot storms the R&B charts. 'Get A Job' by the **Silhouettes** is about a problem many teenagers who have just graduated are facing,

particularly black teenagers: there just aren't any jobs out there. With its complex vocal arrangement, sharp harmonies and shouted vocal, it probably would have been a hit no matter what its lyrics dealt with, but its straightforward treatment of a social issue hits a chord with the public. Naturally, it spawns an answer record, 'Got A Job', from a Detroit group, the **Miracles**, whose new Motown label has to sell the master to Goldner to get it any kind of distribution. It flops anyway, and

APR 7 : The Church of England gives its moral backing to family planning

Little Richard

The moral watchdogs of the Fifties who claimed rock'n'roll was dangerous not to mention degenerate, had no further to look than **"Little"** **Richard** Penniman for proof. Oddly, and perhaps fortunately, they never did: although his homosexuality was an all but open secret, he was beloved by millions, and his wild, shrieking records remain classics of the era, often imitated but never matched.

Born to a Pentecostal family in Macon, Georgia, Richard was kicked out of his home as a young teenager when his parents discovered his sexual proclivities. Already a seasoned gospel performer, he began a career as a blues singer. Around this time, he met another flamboyant performer, Esquerita, who influenced both his piano and hair styles. Moving to Houston in 1952, he recorded for the powerful Peacock label there, without success. Not even a 1955 session with the **Johnny Otis Orchestra**, one of the era's most popular bands, got him anywhere.

As a last ditch effort, he sent a demo-tape with a heart-rending appeal on it to Art Rupe's Speciality Records in LA. Unknown to Richard, their staff producer Richard "Bumps" Blackwell had been looking for a blues singer with a gospel edge, and Blackwell immediately arranged for a recording session in New Orleans with the cream of the city's musicians. Shy and nervous, Richard produced nothing Blackwell liked until he ripped into a filthy song he'd picked up on the blues circuit, 'Tutti Frutti'. Cleaned up by local songwriter Dorothy LaBostrie, opening with the immortal words "Awop bop a lu bop, alop bam boom!" it quickly entered the charts in late 1955, and Little Richard became a star.

▶ 'The Bronze Liberace' in the 70s with his mouth characteristically, open, probably delivering yet another scathing comment.

The next couple of years saw a slew of hits: 'Long Tall Sally', 'Rip It Up', 'Lucille' and 'Good Golly, Miss Molly' all sold over a million copies. But the tension between gospel and worldly music that made these full-tilt screamers hits was also preying on Richard's mind, and in the middle of a 1957 Australian tour, he had a vision of his own damnation after a frightening plane ride, and, after throwing $8,000 worth of diamond rings into Sydney harbour, announced that he was quitting rock'n'roll for divinity school. Richard kept his word, and received a degree from the Seventh Day Adventists.

By the time he cautiously attempted to re-enter the pop world in 1964, things had changed too much, even though the very **Beatles** who were ruling the roost at the time idolized him and had recorded his songs. He made some more brilliant records but he never recaptured his popularity, although he continued to tour and at one point had a young guitarist in his band named **Jimi Hendrix**.

He seems to have accepted this with equanimity, and he wound up a regular on television talk-shows, older but no less outrageous. **Little Richard** continues to perform,

and fittingly enough was one of the first inductees into the Rock And Roll Hall Of Fame.

▼ Little Richard and his band performing in the unforgettable film The Girl Can't Help It. Most of the time, neither could Richard.

Little Richard

The Plane Crash

On January 22, 1959, **Buddy Holly** is ensconced in the bedroom of his Greenwich Village apartment with a great new toy: a personal tape-recorder. He's in a bit of a rush because he's got to get ready for the tour, but there are a few songs he's got that he really needs to get down so that he can work on them when he gets back. 'Peggy Sue Got Married' is a natural idea, but some of the others, particularly 'Crying, Waiting, Hoping' and 'Learning The Game', show he's become a mature pop songwriter. As if sensing this, the vocals he records are much better than demos normally demand.

The Winter Dance Party tour is probably something Holly was forced to do because of financial problems: Norman Petty, feeling betrayed by Holly's new aspirations and his move to New York, may have been withholding royalties. But it's only going to be a two-week gig, then back to New York and some serious work. He and his band (guitarist **Tommy Allsup**, a crazed Lubbock DJ Buddy had produced, **Waylon Jennings**, on bass, and **Charlie Bunch** on drums) are billed as the **Crickets**, which they certainly aren't. Headlining the package is one **Frankie Sardo** (who never charted a record), newcomers from the Bronx, **Dion & The Belmonts**, are on board, as is the **Big Bopper** and an inordinately talented Mexican-American kid, Ricardo Valenzuela, who records as **Ritchie Valens**.

The tour is a disaster from the start, playing small dates in frozen towns in the upper Midwest, all of the musicians crammed into a drafty bus. By February 1, Bunch has already gone home with frostbitten feet and a mood of rebellion is overtaking the tour. They play two shows that day and head on to Clear Lake, Iowa, for the next evening's performance. By the time they get there, everyone is in a bad mood and Holly tells Allsup and Jennings that after the show he's going to hire a plane so they can fly to Fargo, North Dakota, ahead of everyone and get their laundry done: they've been wearing their stage-clothes to keep warm and they're sort of ripe.

Clear Lake's charter air service, Dwyer's Flying Service, consists basically of Jerry Dwyer and he's not there, but a young pilot named Roger Peterson sometimes fills in for him and agrees to make the trip. The weather outside is not getting any better but the show must go on. There are flying advisories out, ones any instrument-trained pilot could handle, but the Dwyer planes aren't licensed for instrument flying, plus there's the fact that Peterson has failed his instrument test recently. But he must figure it's best not to mention this so, after the

show, Holly calls his wife in New York and starts rounding up the guys to head off to the airfield.

Then there are some changes. The Big Bopper, tired of wedging his oversized frame in tiny bus seats, begs Waylon Jennings to let him have his seat and Waylon agrees. When Valens asks Allison to let him have his, though, he's not so agreeable. They decide on a coin-toss, the loser riding the bus. Allison loses. Holly, JP and Ritchie pile into the four-seat Beechcraft Bonanza, Peterson guns the engines and they're off. By this time, Jerry Dwyer is back in the office, and notices that the take-off is shaky. A few minutes later, he gets on the radio to see if everything is all right. No answer. He calls the Fargo airfield to see if the Beechcraft has landed. It hasn't. Finally, worried, he climbs into another plane and goes in search of Peterson and his passengers. He finds them, eight miles from Clear Lake, crashed in a cornfield, the bodies strewn all around. All of them are dead on impact.

Although folksinger **Don McLean** will subsequently dub this 'the day the music died' it is, of course, no such thing. Both Buddy Holly and Ritchie Valens become posthumous best-sellers (sadly, JP Richardson's surviving body of work doesn't come close to legendary status) and Holly in particular becomes the centre of a cult: when, some 25 years later, his trademark glasses are found in an Iowa sheriff's evidence room, they are sold to a British Holly fan who has moved to Lubbock to be closer to the source of his inspiration. A statue of Buddy in bronze, holding his beloved Fender Stratocaster, stands today in downtown Lubbock, and his grave is the destination for pilgrimages by the Buddy Holly Memorial Society.

Ritchie Valens (born Richard Steve Valenzuela) was the first major Hispanic-American rock star. ▶

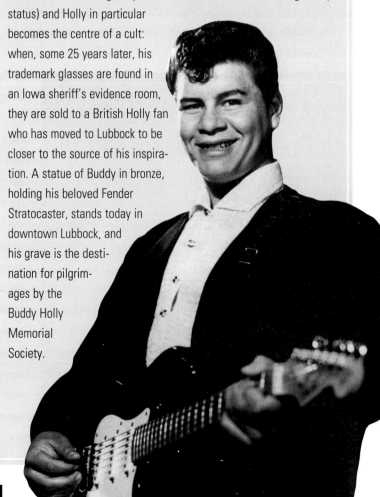

JANUARY 9: First recording session by the Shadows (then known as the Drifters).

JANUARY 16: Sade is born, as Helen Folasade Adu, in Nigeria.

FEBRUARY 3: On tour in the mid-West, Buddy Holly hires a private plane with the Big Bopper and Ritchie Valens. All three are killed when the aircraft crashes.

JUNE: Influential TV pop show Juke Box Jury begins on the BBC.

MAY 14: Cliff Richard's first film, Serious Charge, debuts in cinemas.

JULY 17: Billie Holiday dies.

AUGUST 31: 'Shout (Parts I and II)' by the Isley Brothers is issued.

NOVEMBER 16: '50,000,000 Elvis Fans Can't Be Wrong' LP is released.

DECEMBER 23: Chuck Berry is arrested on a charge of transporting a minor across a State line for immoral purposes.

his daughter. Neither side sells too well but both, particularly 'Memphis', become classics.

If the trend is towards softer records, beginning with the **Teddy Bears**' 'To Know Him Is To Love Him', continuing through the **Skyliners**' silky 'Since I Don't Have You' and the **Fleetwoods**' 'Come Softly To Me', the summer sees one incredible blast of sheer energy and power. **Ray Charles** has been recording since the beginning of the decade, the blind singer starting out as a poor man's blues crooner in the **Charles Brown** tradition, but over at his label, Atlantic, they expect great things from him even though his success has only been moderate and confined to the R&B charts, at that. This summer sees his breakthrough, a searing five-minute blast of passion based around an insanely simple riff played on a Wurlitzer electric piano, called 'What'd I Say'. With Charles and his back-up singers, the **Raelettes**, trading licks in a style taken straight from gospel, this is the first full-fledged dose of the music that Atlantic's Jerry Wexler calls 'soul'.

Still, it can't be denied that the old energy is waning (so much so that by the spring of 1960, there will be the first 'oldies but goodies' revival with five-year-old records suddenly slipping back into the charts), much of it due to the influence of Dick Clark's American Bandstand show, which spends a lot of its time promoting the local Philadelphia teen idols like **Frankie Avalon**, **Bobby Rydell** and **Fabian**. One of the year's hot new artists is **Bobby**

Darin who, after a couple of rock'n'roll novelties like 'Splish Splash', has turned to a mature crooning style, his Sinatra-esque 'Mack The Knife' from the Brecht-Weill version of the Threepenny Opera becoming one of the biggest hits of the year, leading to Darin, in October, being the youngest headliner at Las Vegas' Sands Hotel at the age of 22. Supporting this new wave of old-style singers is a younger generation of songwriters at New York's Brill Building, where songwriters — many of them teenagers or just past teen age — like **Neil Sedaka**, **Carole King**, Gerry Goffin and Bert Berns are providing material for the new artists, and, in the case of Sedaka and King, sometimes recording it themselves.

All along, people have been wondering how some stuff gets into the charts and, towards the end of the year, the government begins to take an interest in finding out. The new word on legislators' lips is 'payola', paying a disc jockey to play a record he might not ordinarily play — or so it is assumed. In November, a Senate subcommittee announces an investigation and hearings to start in the new year and suddenly radio stations start stumbling all over each other in the rush to appear more virtuous than Caesar's wife. Alan Freed refuses to admit to never taking payola and, on November 20, he is fired

Neil Sedaka, one of the new rock professionals on Tin Pan Alley.

from his TV show by WABC. On the 21st, WABC radio tries to make him sign an affidavit clearing himself of the charge and, when he refuses, he is fired there, too. And on the 28th, he is summarily dismissed from his spot on WNEW-TV in New York. Although he will struggle manfully on for a while longer this is, in effect, the end for Freed.

In December, the **Platters** are acquitted on their prostitution-abetting charges but they, too, are effectively ruined. Meanwhile **Chuck Berry** makes headlines with his arrest on Mann Act charges for transporting a minor across state lines with the intent of engaging in prostitution. Shooting has begun on the next **Elvis** film, GI Blues, so that he can get to Hollywood in March when his Army service is over, but everybody wonders if the experience of army life might not have changed him so much that he'll be unrecognizable.

It might be a cliché to say that a new decade will bring sweeping changes, but in this case it's the truth. The wonder is that rock'n'roll will survive.

DEC 4 : A monkey returns safely to earth from 55 miles out in space

'Hope I die before I get old'

The Sixties

opened and closed with rock music in the doldrums but, in between, lay The Golden Age. Before that, the youthquake of Fifties rock had been first absorbed and then tamed by the music industry, before being harnessed for the marketing of Philadelphia teen idols and instantly forgettable one-hit wonders. The deaths of **Buddy Holly**, **Richie Valens**, the **Big Bopper** and, soon after, **Eddie Cochran**, seemed to set the seal on the end of an era. But in the coffee houses of Greenwich Village, in the ghetto of Detroit and in the suburbs of Liverpool, new musical fusions were already underway which would take the styles of the past and blend them for the new decade.

As fast as the new musics were developing, so was the technology and the means of acquiring it. The arrival of the Dansette auto-changer meant that virtually every home could afford a record player and collections of the new 45 rpm record were swiftly compiled by an increasingly affluent teenage generation.

The appearance of the **Beatles** and **Bob Dylan** galvanized what became known as the Beat Generation into kick-starting the swinging Sixties. At first Liverpool's Merseybeat and London's R&B scene had it all, packaged in the brightest finery that Carnaby Street and King's Road could provide. Television soon latched on to pop shows as a way of reaching the young audience and specialist pop-rock radio stations came into being to cater for increasing demand.

As Britain's mods and rockers gave way to America's hippies in the mid-Sixties, the youth drugs of choice switched from amphetamines to marijuana and LSD, and the music changed accordingly. America's West Coast psychedelic scene dominated briefly, until the cross-fertilization of folk with rock bred the hybrid that saw the decade out — the singer-songwriter. By 1969, the energy had dissipated again and rock was dabbling its way towards the Seventies, with interminable guitar solos, concept albums and inept experiments with sitars and primitive instruments as the most obvious symptoms of its malaise.

In retrospect, it's obvious that the Sixties' biggest contribution to youth music was freeing pop performers from the tyranny of the professional songwriters of Tin Pan Alley; enabling them for the first time to sing about whatever mattered most to them, just as blues and folk artists had always done.

1960s

Johnny Black

◄ The Who: 'My Generation'

Although 1960 sees a vogue for guitar instrumental hits on both sides of the Atlantic, the year's most successful single is a lush, orchestral, film-related, middle-of-the-road instrumental, 'Theme From A Summer Place' by Canadian **Percy Faith** (US Number 1/UK Number 2). However, more typical of the prevailing instrumental sound is Seattle band the **Ventures** with the tremolo-heavy 'Walk Don't Run' (US Number 2/UK Number 8). The track is a simplified copy of a tune on a **Chet Atkins** album but, according to the Ventures' Bob Bogle "If you put Chet's version next to ours, you wouldn't recognize it as being the same song. He played in a very advanced style."

Other hit singles in this genre are **Duane Eddy**'s twangy theme from the teen movie *Because They're Young* (US Number 4/UK Number 2), and 'Apache' by British combo the **Shadows** (UK Number 1), charting without frontman **Cliff Richard** for the first time. The Shadows also instigate a new marketing initiative by starring in the first colour promotional film to be specially made for the new-fangled video juke boxes which have begun to appear in European holiday resorts.

A vocalist even more squeaky-clean than Cliff, **Pat Boone** picks up a gold disc on February 12 for 'Pat's Great Hits', which includes homogenized covers of **Little Richard**'s 'Tutti Frutti' and 'Long Tall Sally'. Boone is the man who, when recording **Fats Domino**'s 'Ain't That A Shame', had questioned the grammatical accuracy of the title and suggested to his producer that he would rather sing "Isn't that a shame."

Eddie Cochran Dies In Car Smash

At midnight on April 17, 1960, a Ford Consul taxi skidded and smashed backwards into a concrete lamp-post on the A4 road near Chippenham, Wiltshire, England. Rock star **Eddie Cochran**, thrown out onto the tarmac, died from head injuries at 4pm the next day in Bath Hospital. Travelling in the same taxi, rocker **Gene Vincent** suffered minor injuries, as did Cochran's songwriter-girlfriend Sharon Sheeley.

the roadway. Nearby Sharon Sheeley lay moaning and crying 'Eddie, where's Eddie?'"

While recovering in a London hospital, Sheeley maintained that Cochran was not dead but merely, "Away on a long tour and it won't be long before I see him again."

In the words of the *Daily Mail*, "Twenty-one-year-old Cochran, whose latest record, 'Three Steps To Heaven', was due for release, had just completed a 12-week tour of Britain. The passengers were thrown out, and confetti, Cochran's guitar and photographs were scattered on

Cochran, whose hits included 'Summertime Blues', 'C'Mon Everybody' and 'Hallelujah, I Love Her So', was born Edward Ray Cochranson in Oklahoma on October 30, 1938 and started his recording career in 1954. An accomplished musician, it was not unknown for Cochran to play all of the instruments on his records and sing his own vocal harmonies, using multiple-recording techniques which he developed himself.

'Three Steps To Heaven' was ready for release, but instead Eddie Cochran drove straight there in a Ford Consul. Gene Vincent, also in the car, sustained only minor injuries.

"The most publicized soldier since General McCarthy'. Demobbed from the US Army, a sideburn-free Elvis tells the press there's still room for him in rock despite the new breed of Philadelphia teen idols.

Nevertheless, Boone is among the favourite singers of "the most publicized soldier since General MacArthur", Sgt **Elvis Presley**, who, on March 5, is demobbed from the US army at Fort Dix, New Jersey. "I hear that trends have changed," he tells a press conference, "so it might be pretty difficult for me." He also declares his romance with 16-year-old Priscilla Beaulieu to be "nothing serious." Asked about teen idols **Frankie Avalon** and **Fabian** who have come along in his absence, Presley appears unconcerned. "I don't consider them rivals. There's room for everyone. If other people can make it, good luck to them." It is, however, his announcement that he will probably not grow back his famous sideburns, shaved off for military service, which sends reporters scurrying for the telephones.

An indication of changing times for the industry comes later when, on March 10, the British weekly, *Record Retailer*, publishes the UK's first album chart, showing the **Explosive Freddy Cannon** at Number 1. The fact that rock artists are not yet dominating the album scene is, however, obvious from the year's best-selling UK album, the soundtrack to the film *South Pacific*, while the US album charts are led by 'The Lord's Prayer' from the **Mormon Tabernacle Choir**.

The church, via gospel music, is also a mainstay of the developing soul music scene, whose increasing importance is underlined when **Barrett Strong** enjoys a US national hit with 'Money' on the Anna label owned by Gwen Gordy. On May 16, encouraged by his sister's success, young black entrepreneur Berry Gordy

British album charts began in March 1960 but rock was not yet the dominant force. The Mormon Tabernacle Choir outsold every US rock act, while the soundtrack to the movie South Pacific was the year's top album in Britain.

Jr announces plans to start his own label, Tamla, with a re-issue of Strong's hit.

Later in May, across the Atlantic, Liverpool's Cavern Club overturns its jazz-only policy, initiating Wednesday as its regular 'beat' night. The first rock gigs feature **Cass & The Cassanovas** and **Rory Storm & The Hurricanes**.

Soul music continues its ascendancy when, on August 1, gospel singer **Aretha Franklin** records her first pop tracks for Columbia Records and, a week later, 21-year-old **Tina Turner** makes her recording debut with husband **Ike** on the single 'A

Fool In Love', which only peaks at Number 27 in the US but still sells a million copies.

This large figure seems less surprising in the light of a *Seventeen* magazine survey in the same month which reveals that the average American teenage girl spends four and a half hours each day listening to the radio and playing records.

Her wall would almost certainly also be covered in coloured pictures torn from glossy teen magazines, fea-

turing cleancut young Italo-American stars like **Dion** DiMucci. Despite still being perhaps the most popular of the white doo-wop bands, New York's Dion and his group the **Belmonts** are reported to have "ankled one another's scene" (split up) on October 17 when group member Angelo D'Aleo is conscripted into the US army. Dion plans a solo career.

Ben E King of the **Drifters**, having also recently embarked on a solo career, offers an atmospheric ballad he has composed to his old band. The Drifters' manager, George Treadwell tells King, "It's not a bad song, but we don't need it." So, on October 27, after failing to sell 'Stand By Me' to his former group, King records it in New York himself, with Jerry Leiber and Mike Stoller producing, assisted by newcomer Phil Spector.

No ballads yet, though, for **Chubby Checker**. With three Top 40 dance hits already under his belt, 19-year-old Chubby hears, on December 24, that the Philadelphia Orphans Court has raised his weekly allowance from $150 to $200. Just in time for Christmas.

The construction of the Berlin Wall was probably the most concrete manifestation of how, as the Cold War escalated, the international atmosphere grew chillier. Folk artists openly criticized international governments but it would be some while before rock acts moved into the political arena.

The dance sensation that was shakin' the nation was former comedy impressionist Chubby Checker, whose Twist records sparked a craze that soon had movie stars, fashion gurus and politicians shakin' a tail feather in New York's fashionable Peppermint Lounge.

ROCK'N'ROLL record

Payola

Alan Freed (centre), the DJ who taught America to rock'n'roll.

Growing concern about music biz corruption peaked in May 1960, when a Manhattan Grand Jury indicted America's most influential DJ, Alan Freed, on charges of accepting $30,650 in payola (bribes) to play records on the radio. At the same time, *Billboard* magazine reported that many US radio stations were now excluding rock'n'roll from their broadcasting formats. Earlier in the year, US Congressman Emanuel Celler claimed that without payola "the cacophonous music called rock'n'roll" would not be popular. Another Congressman, Thomas O'Neill, called rock "sensuous music unfit for impressionable minds." Anti-payola legislation was introduced, urging fines and jail sentences for anyone found guilty of receiving or giving payola.

At Congressional Committee hearings in April, Dick Clark, host of the influential TV show *American Bandstand*, admitted having a financial interest in 27% of the records played on his show. A clean cut, softly spoken and persuasive personality, Clark's sober demeanour and his willingness to co-operate with the Committee led its chairman to describe him as "a fine young man". No action was taken against Clark.

Freed, whose *Moondog Rock'n'Roll Party* on Cleveland's WJW radio introduced black rhythm and blues to a predominantly white audience, is also acknowledged as the man who first used the term 'rock-'n'roll', formerly slang for sexual intercourse, to teenage music. He was identified with what Congress saw as the "corrupting influence" of rock'n'roll and therefore became the scapegoat in the drive to clean up the music business. When black singer **Frankie Lymon** was seen jiving with a white girl on Freed's CBS-TV show *Rock'n'Roll Dance Party*, the show was cancelled.

Freed further prejudiced his chances by stating that he would not co-operate with payola investigators.

The trial opened on 19 September.

1960s Trash

That unholy trinity, sex, drugs and rock'n'roll, are such standard fare in the music biz that, to qualify as a bona fide scandal, things have to go seriously off the rails. And, from the first days of the Sixties, they did.

In February 1960, while the Alan Freed payola scandal was making national headlines, black R&B singer-songwriter **Jesse Belvin**, composer of the **Penguins**' hit 'Earth Angel', died in a car crash near Fairhope, Arkansas. Rumours that the local chapter of the Ku Klux Klan had tampered with the car's steering wheel were never proved. Further violence erupted a year later, when **Jackie Wilson** was shot in his New York apartment by Juanita Jones, described at the time as "a deranged female fan".

Drugs discreetly entered the picture on October 13 1962, when Don Everly collapsed during rehearsals on the stage of the Prince Of Wales theatre in London, leaving his brother Phil to continue the **Everly Brothers** UK tour alone. Don had overdosed on the amphetamines to which he had become addicted, after being prescribed them to help overcome his exhaustion. He later attempted suicide.

The decade's first significant plagiarism suit arrived in March 1963, when **Chuck Berry** successfully sued Brian Wilson for appropriating the melody of Berry's 'Sweet Little Sixteen', as the basis for the **Beach Boys**' hit 'Surfin' USA'. **Sam Cooke**'s career came to a sudden end when he was shot dead by the manageress of the Hacienda Motel in Los Angeles on December 10 1964, after apparently attempting to rape a Eurasian girl he'd picked up earlier that evening. Coincidentally, Cooke's death followed rumours that the Mafia had taken out a contract on the singer, when he refused to become involved with them.

There was a violent end too for British impressario Reg Calvert, who had masterminded many pop careers, including the **Fortunes** and **Pinkerton's Assorted Colours**. On June 21 1966, he died from exposure to the wrong end of a shotgun in Saffron Walden, during an argument over a pirate radio station he owned. Less than a month passed before **Bobby Fuller**, who had reached the US Top 10 in March with 'I Fought The Law', was found dead in his car in West Hollywood. Although his body smelled of gasoline and he had been badly beaten, the precise circumstances of his death have never been clearly established.

Five months later, in Boston, **Ray Charles** was fined $10,000 and given a five-year suspended prison sentence for possession of heroin and marijuana. Illegal substances were also the cause of the **Rolling Stones**' biggest headaches in 1967. Following up a recent drug bust involving folk singer **Donovan**, salacious British tabloid the

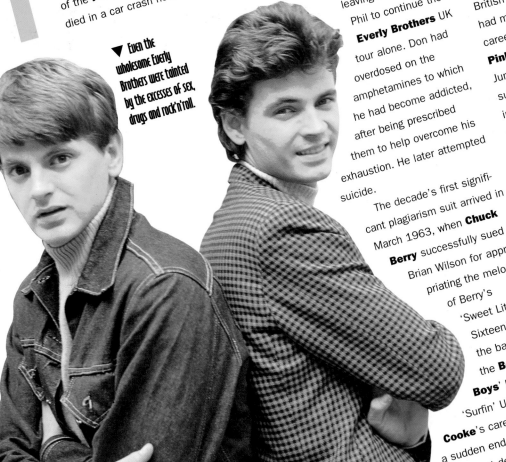

▲ Reactionary forces are often pitted against rock'n'roll. Did the Ku Klux Klan have a hand in the death of Jesse Belvin?

▼ Even the wholesome Everly Brothers were tainted by the excesses of sex, drugs and rock'n'roll.

News Of The World ran a story on February 5 under the headline Pop Stars And Drugs - Facts That Will Shock You. The report revealed that the **Moody Blues** had hosted parties at which LSD was taken by Pete Townshend of the **Who** and Ginger Baker of **Cream**.

The story started off a feud within the **Stones** by claiming Mick Jagger had participated at one such party when, in fact, it had been Brian Jones. A week later, tipped off by a News Of The World informant, police raided Keith Richards' home. Finding Jagger and **Marianne Faithfull** with Richards, they took away samples to be tested, but arrested no-one. Brian Jones' first dope arrest came in early May, followed by charges against Jagger and Richards but, when the pair received lengthy jail sentences in June, it became apparent that the establishment was using the group to set an example, a warning to wayward British youth in general. A storm of media protest resulted in the sen-

▼ Folk-pop pixie Donovan was embroiled in a classic tabloid nude girls and drugs scandal during 1967.

tences being quashed on appeal on July 31. It was clear, for the first time, where public sympathies now lay.

The summer of 1967 was also notable for the furore that followed John Lennon's comment that the **Beatles** were now more popular than Jesus. The remark was largely ignored in Britain, but provoked a wave of Beatle-record burnings across America.

A heroin overdose took the penniless former child star **Frankie Lymon** out of play in February 1968, when he was found dead on his grandmother's floor in New York. Another 1968 drug casualty was Syd Barrett who, on April 6 was finally obliged to quit **Pink Floyd** because his continual consumption of LSD rendered him virtually unable to function as a working musician.

Doors' frontman, Jim Morrison's on-stage obscenity busts enlivened the spring of 1969, but the controversy in July over the naked pubescent girl on **Blind Faith**'s debut album cover was overshadowed by the mysterious death of **Rolling Stone**, Brian Jones. Having been ousted from the group just weeks earlier, Jones was found dead in his swimming pool during the night of July 3. His death has never been satisfactorily explained.

The paranoid megalomaniac son of a teenage prostitute, Charles Manson brought the decade of peace and love to an ironically grisly end in Los Angeles. Utilizing sex, drugs and

rock'n'roll effectively as implements of brainwashing, he manipulated a group of impressionable young women and men whom he called The Family. Desperate to be a rock star, Manson pressed his attentions on **Beach Boy** Dennis Wilson and the **Mamas & the Papas**' John Phillips. He also endeavoured to secure a contract with Terry Melcher, son of Doris Day and successful record producer for the **Byrds**.

When Melcher rejected him, Manson initiated a killing spree which ended in the massacre of several innocent victims, including film director Roman Polanski's pregnant wife, actress Sharon Tate. Manson's delusions had led him to believe that messages were being sent to him in Beatles song lyrics, such as 'Helter Skelter' and 'Revolution'. Indeed, the words "Helter Skelter" were written in blood on the walls at the scene of a second Manson-inspired massacre on August 10.

Just as it seemed things could not get bleaker, on December 6, Hell's Angels engaged as security staff for the Rolling Stones concert at Altamont Speedway, California, killed a young black fan, Meredith Hunter, in full view of the stage. The Sixties were over.

▼ The Mamas and the Papas were unwittingly taken in by the psychotic Charlie Manson.

▼ The massacre of actress Sharon Tate and her house guests brought the hippie era to a violent close.

Frank Sinatra, who once described rock'n'roll as "the most brutal, ugly, vicious form of expression" unveils plans on January 13 1961 for his own label, Reprise Records. "I want to avoid having bad rock'n'roll records associated with Reprise," he announces, "and the policy in the main will be to concentrate on quality performers."

Another new company arrives on January 30 when Jerry Leiber and Mike Stoller, a top songwriting and production duo for over a decade, announce plans to form their own independent production company, providing finished masters for such labels as Atlantic and RCA Victor.

February finds the **Platters**, one of the world's most successful vocal combos, suing Mercury Records. The legal action stems from Mercury's refusal to accept new Platters' tracks for release, because they do not feature lead vocalist Tony Williams. The group's manager and chief songwriter, Buck Ram, points out that Williams left the group last June and that the group's contract does not specify Williams as the featured solo voice. Group members themselves point out that, even when Williams was with them, it was normal practice for lead vocals to be shared.

Later in February, **Jackie Wilson**, whose hits include 'Reet Petite' and 'Lonely Teardrops', is shot in the chest by a 'deranged female fan' Juanita Jones who invades his New York apartment.

Elvis Presley, whose early stage act borrowed much from Wilson's erotic performing style, is having a better time. Across the Atlantic, on March 9, he scores a British first by reaching Number 1 with three consecutive ballads, 'It's Now Or Never', 'Are You Lonesome Tonight?' and 'Wooden Heart', underlining his transformation from sexy rocker to wholesome family entertainer.

The even more wholesome British balladeer **Craig Douglas** pays the price for venturing into dangerous territory on April 8, when his UK cover version of **Gene McDaniels**' US hit '100 Pounds Of Clay' is banned by the BBC for blasphemy on the grounds that its lyric suggests that God might have created woman out of building materials. Potentially offensive lines such as "He created a woman and lots of lovin' for a man" are re-recorded as "He created old Adam – then he made a woman for the man". Both versions are available

> An early inspiration to Elvis Presley, dynamic singer Jackie Wilson was also an early victim of obsessive fan-mania. He was shot during February by a deranged female admirer in his New York apartment.

Folknik Signed For Unprecedented Royalty

Barely 20 years old, Bob Dylan was spotted early in 1961 playing autoharp and singing at the Folklore Centre in Greenwich Village, by a writer from the *Village Voice*. His report described Dylan as "extraordinary" and predicted his emergence within the year as a major talent to be reckoned with.

Dylan's offical New York debut came at Gerde's Folk City in Greenwich Village on April 11, opening for bluesman **John Lee Hooker**. Just over a fortnight later he made his recording debut, earning $50 for playing harmonica on **Harry Belafonte**'s recording of 'Midnight Special'.

On September 29 noted *New York Times* music critic Robert Shelton lent weight to the *Village Voice* opinion when he gave Dylan his first major press review. Raving over a Dylan slot at Gerde's, Shelton described him as "a cross between a choirboy and a beatnik" who was "bursting at the seams with talent." Shelton ended his

review with the words "Mr Dylan is vague about his antecedents and birthplace, but it matters less where he has been than where he is going and that would seem to be straight up."

That same day, Dylan had played harmonica on a recording session for his friend, folk singer **Carolyn Hester**, through whom he had met veteran record producer John Hammond. Hammond, whose previous signings included **Billie Holiday**, **Count Basie** and **Aretha Franklin**, was so impressed by Dylan's talent and Shelton's review that he offered a contract with a $1000 advance.

Columbia Records' faith in the young folknik's potential was underlined by the fact that he was signed to the label for five years at an unprecedented royalty rate of four percent.

On November 20 and 22, Hammond and Dylan recorded his debut album at a cost of $400. With the working title, 'Bob Dylan', it was set for release early in 1962.

FEBRUARY 4: Johnny Burnette cancels a UK tour when he is rushed to hospital for an emergency appendectomy.

MARCH 25: Elvis Presley performs his last live show for eight years at Block Arena, Pearl Harbour, Hawaii.

APRIL 7: Rockabilly guitarist Charlie Shivers dies in a gas explosion at his farm in Kentucky.

JUNE 2: First successful conviction of record bootleggers takes place in Hackensack, New Jersey.

JULY 4: The Platters' musical director Rupert Branker is beaten to death in Los Angeles.

OCTOBER 30: Phil Spector's Philles label releases its first disc, 'Oh Yeah, Maybe Baby' by the Crystals.

NOVEMBER 10: Britain's biggest ballroom chain, Mecca, announces plans to replace some live music events with 'disc sessions'.

in the shops, but the BBC insists on playing only the re-recording.

Ray Charles, also in the throes of a stylistic transformation, from blues shouter to soulful crooner, achieves a tour-de-force, scooping up four US Grammy Awards on April 12, for Best Vocal Peformance (male), Best Single ('Georgia On My Mind'), Best Album ('The Genius of Ray Charles') and Best Song ('Let The Good Times Roll').

Chuck Berry finds a different route into family entertainment on May 31 when he opens Berry Park, his thirty acre outdoor amusement park in Wentzville, Missouri. The park

includes a Ferris Wheel, swimming facilities, miniature golf, a children's zoo and various themed rides. The park also features a ballroom at which Chuck will be performing from time to time.

Like Chuck, Ray and **Elvis**, British rocker **Billy Fury** signals his intention of appealing to more mature audiences when he charts with a Goffin/King big ballad, 'Halfway To Paradise' in May. In June, he tells the *New Musical Express*, "I'm growing up and I want to broaden my scope. I just can't write the rock stuff like I used to. My aim now is to write catchy, easy-paced songs after the

style of 'You Made Me Love You'."

Fortunately, reports of the death of rock'n'roll are proving somewhat exaggerated. In Liverpool, on July 6, the first issue of a new music newspaper, *Mersey Beat*, is published. It contains an article by local beat group musician **John Lennon**, entitled "Being A Short Diversion on the Dubious Origins of Beatles". Lennon's group the **Beatles**, fast becoming Liverpool's favourite act, begin a residency at the city's Cavern Club on August 2. Rock's flame, though dim, burns on.

Two weeks later, on August 14, **Gene Vincent** collapses from exhaustion during his first UK tour since he was injured in the 1961 car crash which killed **Eddie Cochran**. It is reported that he has still not fully recovered from his injuries, or from the mental strain of the crash.

In mid-September it is reported that **Little Richard**, who withdrew from the rock world in 1957 to become a preacher, has returned to recording with an album of gospel material, arranged by Quincy Jones. The album is called 'Little Richard –

Ailing Johnny Burnette cancels UK tour.

King Of The Gospel Singers'.

Further signs of change surface later in September when **Dave Brubeck** puts the distinctively modern jazz sound of 'Take Five' into the US pop charts. Meanwhile, in Britain, the revived New Orleans style of Dixieland Trad Jazz is making inroads on the charts with such London-based performers as **Kenny Ball** and **Acker Bilk**.

Up north in Liverpool, after being asked for a **Beatles** disc by customers in his store during November, record shop owner Brian Epstein goes to the Cavern Club to see the group. Impressed by their potential, he wastes no time in securing their signatures on a management contract on December 13.

Meanwhile, the band destined to become the Beatles' biggest American rivals, the **Beach Boys**, have released their first single. California's teenage beach culture is documented for the first time on record when their debut single, 'Surfin'', is released by Candix Records in Los Angeles on December 8. The surfing scene has, in the past, generated guitar instrumental hits, but the Beach Boys seem to have found a new slant.

1961 closes with a pair of novelty records dominating the US charts. First, **Gene Chandler**'s 'Duke Of Earl' is released on Vee Jay and, despite being a throwback to the doo-wop sound of the Fifties, it soars to Number 1. Finally, on December 24, 'The Lion Sleeps Tonight' by the **Tokens**, based on the traditional melody 'Wimoweh', sells a million and becomes the first African song to reach Number 1 in the US.

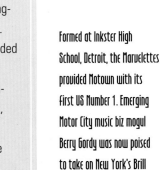

It's trad, dad! While cool modern jazz was taking great strides in America, Britain indulged in a brief love affair with a homogenized New Orleans jazz revival led by the likes of Mr. Acker Bilk (above), Chris Barber and Kenny Ball.

Motown on the Map

By scoring its first US Number 1 on December 10 1961 with the **Marvelettes**' debut single, 'Please Mr Postman', the Detroit-based Motown Record Corporation moved into the major league. Earlier, on February 12, the **Miracles**' 'Shop Around' had become Motown's first million seller, and so the Marvelettes' Number 1 wrapped up a spectacular year for the company.

Motown, with its sister label Tamla, was based at 2648 West Grand Boulevard in Detroit, and had been founded by former record shop owner Berry Gordy Jr just 18 months earlier. Another Gordy venture, the music publishing company Jobete Music, had thrived after Mr Gordy had composed and produced over 20 US Top 100 entries, including 'Reet Petite' for **Jackie Wilson**, 'You Got What It Takes' for **Marv Johnson** and 'Money' for **Barrett Strong**.

Having already earned the nickname Mr Hitsville, Gordy was now hoping that his expanding Detroit operation could give New York's Brill Building songwriters a run for their money.

Motown's year was rounded out by the signing of a gifted young blind singer and instrumentalist, Steveland Judkins, just 11 years old, who was scheduled to release his first disc in 1962, under the name of **Little Stevie Wonder**.

Formed at Inkster High School, Detroit, the Marvelettes provided Motown with its first US Number 1. Emerging Motor City music biz mogul Berry Gordy was now poised to take on New York's Brill Building hit factory.

The **Beatles** open the year with an audition for Decca Records' A&R man Dick Rowe. He is not impressed and turns them down, preferring to sign another band at the same audition, Dagenham

"I'm so young and you're so old". Teen millionaire Paul Anka's vast fortune was founded on his international hit, 'Diana', a promise of undying devotion written when he was 15, for 20-year-old Diana Ayoub who babysat ▶ for his younger siblings.

five-piece **Brian Poole & The Tremeloes**.

British pop's reluctance to acknowledge its continuing reliance on cover-versions of American hits is underlined later in January when former merchant seaman **Karl Denver** claims to have first heard his UK Top 5 hit, 'Wimoweh', sung by a native tribe in South Africa as part of a ceremonial dance. It is presumably no more than a curious coincidence that, six months ago, the song was a US Number 1 for the **Tokens**, under the title 'The Lion Sleeps Tonight'. The melody is genuinely South African but it has been in the repertoire of American folk singers such as **Pete Seeger** for several years.

A sure indication that the latest dance craze, The Twist, has not peaked comes in February when producer Sam Katzman

reveals that his film, *Twist Around The Clock*, made on a budget of $250,000, has grossed $6 million in six months. Unimpressed, the Bishop of Buffalo, New York, bans The Twist from being heard or danced in his diocese.

With thousands of American boys on military service in Vietnam, the **Shirelles** score their biggest hit to date with the highly topical tale of divided lovers, 'Soldier Boy', reaching the US Number 1 position on May 5.

In Britain, the power of the European station Radio Luxembourg is displayed in May when **B Bumble & The Stingers** take the instrumental 'Nut Rocker' into the UK Top 10 without a single play on BBC radio.

Undaunted by their Decca rejection, the Beatles audition for George Martin at EMI and, on May 31, Liverpool's *Mersey Beat* newspaper carries a front page story revealing, "Impressario Brian Epstein has secured a recording contract with the powerful EMI organization for the Beatles to record for the Parlophone label."

As the Beatles step onto the ladder, veteran **Paul Anka** can already look back at a career in which, since 1957, he has sold over 30 million records. Apart from his income as a performer, Anka also earns royalties for writing many of his hits. His composition 'Diana', for example, has been recorded in 320 versions, totalling 10 million sales.

Incredibly, all of this has been achieved while he is still, legally, a minor. On July 30 1962, Paul Anka turns 21 and can finally take full control of his vast wealth.

Brill!

When **Neil Sedaka**'s 'Breaking Up Is Hard To Do' became the artist's first Number 1 and ninth consecutive hit, the music business knew it had to sit up and take notice of a significant new phenomenon: the Brill Building.

Sedaka was one of a close-knit group of songwriters and performers whose work was becoming known as Brill Building Pop, after the building at 1619 Broadway, New York, where many music publishers had offices.

It was said in the Thirties and Forties that Tin Pan Alley was located just across the street from the nearest dollar. This new Tin Pan Alley could be located more precisely because, in effect, the Brill Building had become a production line for quality pop music, much of it under the guidance of one man, Don Kirshner, whose first experience of the music industry had been in an unsuccessful songwriting partnership with the equally unknown Robert Cassotto.

Neil Sedaka — cornerstone of the Brill empire.

Things brightened up for Kirschner in 1957 when he founded Aldon Music at 1650 Broadway with an older, more experienced partner, Al Nevins, former guitarist with the **Three Suns**.

The objectives of Aldon Music were simple. With rock music having lost its initial momentum, Kirshner decided to take its energy and re-apply the old-fashioned Tin Pan Alley disciplines of craft and professionalism to the art of making hits for the youth market.

One of the first signings to Aldon Music was the writing duo of **Neil Sedaka** and Howie Greenfield, whose 'Stupid Cupid' provided a hit for **Connie Francis** in July 1958, and secured the pair a long-term contract. As a solo performer, Sedaka then turned out 'Oh Carol',

Barry Mann and Cynthia Weil at work in the Brill Building.

'Calendar Girl', 'Happy Birthday Sweet Sixteen' and a string of others.

Kirshner's first partner, Robert Cassotto, suitably re-named **Bobby Darin**, scored a hit with 'Splish Splash' (US Number 3 in 1958). Seeking further talent, Aldon was impressed by 'Oh Neil', an answer record to Sedaka's 'Oh Carol', written and sung by Sedaka's former girlfriend, **Carole King**. On a wage of $75 a week, and mostly partnered by her current beau Gerry Goffin, she was soon pumping out hits including 'Will You Love Me Tomorrow' for the **Shirelles**, 'Take Good Care Of My Baby' for **Bobby Vee**, 'Crying In The Rain' for the **Everly Brothers**, and 'The Loco-Motion' for their babysitter, **Little Eva**.

Kirshner's next coup was a liaison with **Barry Mann**, writer and performer of the hit 'Who Put The Bomp?' Teamed up with Cynthia Weil, Mann quickly scored with 'Bless You' for **Tony Orlando** and 'Uptown' for the **Crystals**. Describing conditions in the Brill Building, Mann revealed how "Cynthia and I work in a tiny cubicle, with just a piano and chair, no window. We go in every morning and write songs all day. In the next room Carole and Gerry are doing the same thing, with Neil in the room after that. Sometimes, when we all get to banging pianos, you can't tell who's playing what."

And Aldon Music wasn't the only publisher in and around The Brill Building. Successful songwriting teams Leiber and Stoller, Pomus and Shuman, Bacharach and David, as well as individuals like Phil Spector and **Gene Pitney** could all be found plying their trade at the Brill or nearby.

the piano just before I left for rehearsal and, to help me remember it, I just fitted a lyric to the melody very quickly. I hummed it in the car all the way over to keep it in my head. To my surprise, everybody liked the lyric, so we kept it." Named after their favourite New Jersey Bowling Alley, the Four Seasons specialize in close harmony vocals, featuring the keening falsetto of **Frankie Valli**, which soon becomes one of the most characteristic sounds of the early Sixties.

The equally distinctive harmonies of the **Everly Brothers** are shattered five days later, on Sunday October 13, when Don Everly collapses during rehearsals at London's Prince of Wales theatre. He is rushed to hospital, and, two days later, is flown home to America for medical treatment, leaving brother Phil to complete their headlining tour alone.

▲ Named after their favourite New Jersey bowling alley, the Four Seasons' aggressive harmonies provided a hip, hard-edged East Coast counter-blast to the laid-back warmth of California's Beach Boys. Leader Frankie Valli is second from the left.

Another 21-year-old millionaire, producer Phil Spector, buys out his partners at Philles Records on October 6, making him the youngest record label chief in history.

Further proof that rock belongs to the young and the fast comes from composer Bob Gaudio. "'Sherry' took fifteen minutes to write," he reveals after the **Four Seasons** soar to the US Number 1 position for the first time on September 15. "I wrote it at

Possibly the UK's most soulful female vocalist, Dusty Springfield eventually earned the title "the white negress", but her career began in the Springfields, a folksy trio that ▶ racked up several hits.

Yeah, Yeah, Yeah.

"There is no such thing as a Liverpool Sound," insisted the **Beatles**' record producer George Martin, responding to the pop press' enthusiastic adoption of the terms Merseybeat and Liverpool Sound. "I prefer to talk of the Beatles' sound.

After all, they started it. I'm not suggesting other groups copy the Beatles. Quite the contrary, for their styles are wholly different. That's why you can't lump them together under the heading of a Liverpool Sound."

Martin's words, however, merely confirmed the trusty maxim that nothing should ever be believed until it has been officially denied. The British music scene had been turned upside down in 1963 by the Beatles and by Merseybeat, defined by socialist newspaper the *Daily Worker* as, "the voice of 80,000 crumbling houses and 30,000 people on the dole."

With one minor hit single, 'Love Me Do', behind them, the Beatles were virtually unknown at the start of the year but, by its end, they were household names and international stars.

Their second single, 'Please Please Me', fared rather better than 'Love Me Do', reaching Number 2 in the UK on January 17 but, chart positions notwithstanding, as the support act on **Helen Shapiro**'s February tour, they were unceremoniously ejected from an English Midlands hotel for wearing leather jackets in the restaurant.

By now, however, the momentum was beginning to build. During March, having started another tour as the support act, it became obvious that the fans who queued for days to secure tickets did so to see the Beatles, rather than headlining American stars **Tommy Roe** and **Chris Montez**. The Beatles were quickly promoted to the top of the bill.

Across the Atlantic, however, Vee Jay Records of Chicago released 'Please Please Me' to no great effect. It can't have helped that the record's centre credited the group as 'The Beattles'.

Brian Epstein, the Beatles' manager was quick to follow up the Beatles' UK success with his other Liverpudlian protégés **Gerry & The Pacemakers**, whose first single, 'How Do You Do It?', became the first Merseybeat Number 1. Ironically, 'How Do You Do It?', written by established pop tunesmith Mitch Murray, had been rejected by the Beatles before being passed on to Gerry Marsden's Pacemakers.

The Beatles finally made the coveted Number 1 slot on April 18 with 'From Me To You', just as Brian Epstein unveiled **Billy J Kramer & The Dakotas** who, by May 2, had taken a Lennon-McCartney song, 'Do You Want To Know A Secret', to Number 1 themselves. Kramer was, of course, Liverpudlian but his backing band, the Dakotas, hailed from nearby Manchester, another Northern city fast developing as a rival to Liverpool.

Manchester's rock comedy act, **Freddie & The**

The Beatles on Juke Box Jury. America had not yet fallen to the Mop Tops, but in Britain they had already made the transition from mere pop stars to household names. They were the first rock band whose Christian names alone were enough to identify them, even to the older generation.

Liverpool record shop owner Brian Epstein was thrust into the limelight as manager of the Beatles. When he first saw them, in the Cavern Club, he predicted that managing the group "shouldn't take me more than half a day a week". Before long it was taking eight.

AUG 28 : Martin Luther King delivers his 'I have a dream' speech on the steps of the Lincoln Memorial, Washington DC

1963 - HEADLINE NEWS

Yeah, Yeah, Yeah.

The dilution of the hard-rocking Mersey Sound was as fast as it was predictable. Former Manchester milkman Freddie Garrity and his Dreamers typified the second wave, replacing musical energy with childish humour.

Dreamers illustrated just how fast the city was moving when their cover of **James Ray**'s US hit 'If You Gotta Make A Fool Of Somebody' reached Number 3 on May 9, while close harmony quintet the **Hollies** weighed in with 'Just Like Me' at the end of the same month, at which point **Gerry & The Pacemakers** scored their second Number 1 for Liverpool with 'I Like It'.

By now, public and media interest in the Liverpool Sound was overwhelming but national newspapers still overlooked a small news item in the *Liverpool Echo* on June 21. The paper reported that, at a party in Liverpool to celebrate Beatle **Paul McCartney**'s birthday, his songwriting partner **John Lennon** punched DJ Bob Wooler in the face after Wooler loudly proclaimed that Lennon and Brian Epstein were lovers.

As the year unfolded, every self-respecting London-based record company talent scout started to spend much of his week in Liverpool or Manchester, hoping to grab a piece of the fast-developing action. The close-harmonies and distinctive jangling guitars of long established Liverpool quartet the **Searchers** took a cover of the old **Drifters**' hit 'Sweets For My Sweet' to Number 1 on June 27 and by August the first edition of a new magazine, *Beatles Monthly*, was on sale.

Gerry & The Pacemakers became the first act ever to notch up three Number 1s with their first three releases, on October 10, with the powerful ballad 'You'll Never Walk Alone' from the musical *Carousel*. Three days later, 15 million viewers tuned in to the **Beatles**' first performance on the ITV variety series, *Sunday Night At The London Palladium*. Thousands of fans jammed the streets outside, battling with police for a glimpse of the mop-tops.

On television again in November at the Royal Variety Command performance, in front of the Queen Mother, Princess Margaret and Lord Snowdon, **John**

Like Freddie, Gerry Marsden and the Pacemakers slotted neatly into the role of all-round entertainers rather than real rockers, but they formed the vanguard of Brian Epstein's empire as he sought to extend his domination beyond the Beatles.

Lennon found it impossible not to make fun of the audience. Half-way through the set he quipped, "On the next number, would those in the cheap seats clap their hands? The rest of you, rattle your jewellery."

Along with their mop-top hair cuts, Cuban-heeled boots and collarless jackets, this vein of cheeky Scouse humour was becoming a distinguishing characteristic of the Beatles. Asked by one reporter why he wore so many rings on his fingers, drummer **Ringo Starr** retorted "Because I can't get them through my nose."

As December opened, the Beatles had seven records in the Top 20 and their name was enough to sell substantial quantities of an eighth one, 'All I Want For Christmas Is A Beatle', by comedienne **Dora Bryan**.

By the end of the year the seal was set on their acceptance by the establishment when the *Times*' music critic William Mann succinctly nailed their importance with the words "for several decades, England has taken her popular songs from the United States ... but the songs of Lennon and McCartney are distinctly indigenous in character" before indulging himself in intellectual raptures over their "chains of pandiatonic clusters ... submediant key switches ... and Aeolian cadences".

Two days later, Richard Buckle in the *Sunday Times* put it even more plainly, declaring the Beatles to be "the greatest composers since Beethoven". Yeah, yeah, yeah. And amen.

NOV 22 : John Fitzgerald Kennedy is assassinated in Dallas

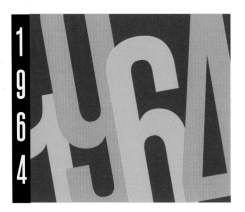

1964

Based in a converted Manchester church, a new weekly chart-based BBC TV show, *Top Of The Pops*, begins broadcasting to the UK on the first day of the year. Hosted by peroxide blond Jimmy Savile, it stars the **Rolling Stones**, **Dusty Springfield** and the **Dave Clark Five**.

Just three days later, the British Board of Trade announces that the highest record sales ever were achieved in October 1963, making it a boom year for the music business. It was also a year dominated by just three acts – the **Beatles**, **Bob Dylan** and the **Rolling Stones**.

Following up their *Top Of The Pops* appearance, the **Stones** are quick off the mark, on January 6, with the Group Scene 64 tour. Their first headlining tour, it kicks off at the Granada Theatre, Harrow, and also features the **Ronettes**, the **Swinging Blue Jeans**, **Johnny Kidd & The Pirates** and **Marty Wilde**.

FEB 6 : Channel Tunnel project is jointly announced by the UK and France

1964 - HEADLINE NEWS

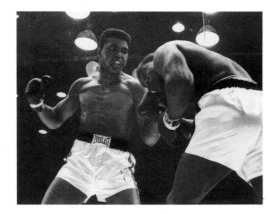

Still in the vanguard, the Beatles fly into New York's Kennedy Airport on February 3 for their first American tour, to be greeted by thousands of screaming fans. In the same week, Matthew Welsh, the Governor of Indiana, asks local radio stations not to air the **Kingsmen**'s hit song 'Louie Louie' because of speculation that its near-unintelligible lyrics may be obscene. Governor Welsh claims his "ears tingled" when he heard the song. The song's publisher, Max Firetag, responds on February 8 by offering $1000 to anyone who can find obscene lyrics in the number.

Seventy-three million American viewers watch the Beatles' national television debut on the influential *Ed Sullivan Show* on February 16, and two days later they play their first US concert, at Washington Coliseum, Washington DC, headlining over **Tommy Roe**, the **Chiffons** and the **Caravelles**.

In Miami, the Beatles take time out to visit Cassius Clay who, on March 7, emerges as an unlikely candidate for Chubby Checker's crown as king of the dance scene. "I'm better and prettier than Chubby Checker," boasts Clay. Since defeating Sonny Liston for the World Heavyweight Boxing Championship on February 25, demand for Clay's 1963 album, 'I Am The Greatest', has rocketed.

Irrefutable evidence that British pop has finally shaken off its subservience to America comes on March 21 when, for the first time

Jimmy Savile hosts the first edition of Top Of The Pops.

ever, the *NME*'s UK Top 10 Singles chart features only British artists. As if in confirmation, a week later the renowned Madame Tussauds Waxworks announces that the Beatles are to become the first pop stars to be immortalized in wax.

Bob Dylan's first UK pop chart entry comes on April 3 with 'The Times They Are A Changin'', and a day later it is reported that the **Beatles** hold all Top 5 positions in the US singles chart with 'Can't Buy Me Love' at Number 1.

The direct involvement of musicians in politics escalates on April 24 when folk singer **Joan Baez** refuses to pay 60% of her income tax as a protest against US military spending.

Following an RCA announcement in April that **Elvis Presley** has sold over 100 million albums for them in eight years, an indication of the vast sums being earned by the

World heavyweight contender Cassius Clay composed one of his celebrated doggerel verses when he met the Beatles at his gym in Miami on 18 May. "When Liston picks up the papers/And sees the Beatles came to me/He will be angry/And I'll knock him out in three." On the night, it took six.

Phil Spector

Known as "The Tycoon of Teen", Spector was the first rock producer whose ability to achieve a distinctive sound in the studio came to be regarded as the defining quality of the records he worked on. Known as his "Wall of Sound", Spector applied it to recordings by the **Crystals**, the **Ronettes**, the **Righteous Brothers** and more, often effectively relegating the artists' performances to a secondary role in the architecture of the music.

In essence, to create what he termed his "little symphonies for the kids" he packed large instrumental ensembles into tiny studios, and employed previously unknown multiple-echo techniques to build up a huge sound, unrivalled in its day.

It is often forgotten, however, that Spector was also an accomplished songwriter, having contributed to the penning of **Ben E. King**'s 'Spanish Harlem', the **Drifters**' 'On Broadway' and the **Teddy Bears**' million-seller 'To Know Him Is To Love Him' as well as many others. His particular forte was simple, irresistable hooks, for which his criterion was the question "Is it dumb enough?", by which he meant, was the hook simple enough to cut through everything else and sell the record? Classic Spector hooks are the heartbeat drum intro to the Ronettes' 'Be My Baby', the mesmeric guitar lick that opens the Crystals' 'Then He Kissed Me' and the insidiously repetitive piano of 'He's A Rebel'.

Born Harvey Phillip Spector on December 26, 1940 in the Bronx, New York, he became involved in music only after moving to Fairfax, California in 1953. There he joined a group of aspiring musicians including **Sandy Nelson** – who was later to play drums on 'To Know Him Is To Love Him'. His career really started when **Lee Hazelwood** recommended him to the New York production team of Jerry Leiber and Mike Stoller. He then tasted success with his own group the Teddy Bears, before moving wholeheartedly into production.

The Tycoon Of Teen, Phil Spector, contemplates the creation of yet another of his "little symphonies for the kids". And no, that's not the Wall Of Sound he's sitting on.

At a time when whole albums were made in a day, Spector would spend a week perfecting just one single. His success peaked in 1966 when **Ike & Tina Turner**'s 'River Deep Mountain High', a UK Top 3 item, flopped completely in America, not because of the record itself which has since become a classic, but because the industry had had enough of Spector's self-aggrandizing, dismissive arrogance and simply refused to get behind the record.

Even so, he went on to work with the **Beatles** on the 'Let It Be' album, although his melancholic orchestration on 'The Long And Winding Road' infuriated the song's composer, **Paul McCartney**, who cited Spector as a reason for the Beatles' break-up.

After the end of his marriage with his former protégée, Ronnie Spector of the Ronnettes, his behaviour grew increasingly erratic, reclusive and unfathomable. But his latter work nothwithstanding, his influence on successive generations of rock musicians has never been doubted.

Beatles comes from news on April 30 that they have received a cheque for $140,000 – their share of Beatles Chewing Gum profits in America, where it has been on sale for just four months.

When **Bob Dylan** plays his first UK gig at London's Royal Festival Hall on May 17, the way has been paved for him by the Beatles' admiring words. "I like his whole attitude," enthuses **George Harrison**. "The way he dresses, the way he doesn't give a damn ... the way he sends up everything."

The discontent so often expressed by rock stars seems to be mirrored when the worst youth violence of the year flares up on the English south coast, where gangs of Mods and Rockers riot on the streets and beaches. Seventy-six are arrested in Brighton and 51 in Margate where two teenagers are stabbed.

On June 1, the **Rolling Stones** arrive at Kennedy Airport for their first US tour, which kicks off at Lynn, Massachussetts. Two days later, the Beatles are obliged to start a world tour without Ringo, who has collapsed from exhaustion. Fellow-Liverpudlian Jimmy Nicol fills in. The Stones fly back from the USA on June 16 to play one date at Magdalen College, Oxford. The gig was arranged before their sudden success for a fee of £100, less than a tenth of the cost of their air fares.

Roy Orbison's 'It's Over' is knocked off the UK's top spot on June 25 by Newcastle R&B quintet, the **Animals**, with 'House Of The Rising Sun', formerly recorded by **Bob Dylan**. At four minutes long, EMI

Records were reluctant to release it but the fans are not put off. "I saw Ringo a couple of days ago," bass player Chas Chandler boasts to *Record Mirror*, "and he told me how much he liked it. John Lennon too admires it, and that's nice to know."

There is moral indignation in the British press after all five Rolling Stones (the show usually only accomodates four) appear on July 4 as panellists on BBC TV's *Juke Box Jury*, where their irreverent attitude angers many viewers. "The producer was happy with it," bassist Bill Wyman explains to the *New Musical Express*. "And the audience were OK too. If some of the viewers didn't like it, they should have switched off. Some people take these programmes too seriously."

The July 6 Royal Premiere of the Beatles' movie *A Hard Day's Night* with Princess Margaret and the Earl of Snowdon in attendance, comes in the wake of news that the soundtrack album has sold 1.5 million copies in nine days, making it the fastest-selling album in UK history.

One side-effect of the beat group explosion is revealed on August 29 with a report that sales of guitars

have reached a new peak in both Britain and America. The last high point was in 1957 after the arrival of **Elvis Presley**. An even stranger side-effect can be observed on September 4 when the Indonesian government bans Beatle-style haircuts.

The most serious American challenge to the Beatles in 1964 seems to come from the **Four Seasons**. Having notched up their fourth US Number 1 in June with 'Rag Doll', they are invited by US President Lyndon B Johnson, on September 5, to perform at the upcoming Democratic Party National Convention.

George Harrison forms his own publishing company, Harrisongs, on September 11, the day before raw North London rockers the **Kinks** go to Number 1 in the UK with their third single, 'You Really Got Me'. "There's nothing kinky about us though," explains leader Ray Davies. "Maybe we do wear frilly shirts, but so do many other groups. Kinky is just such a fashionable word that we knew people would remember it."

The Beatles move overtly into the political arena when they refuse to take the stage for a concert at the

Clashes and pitched battles between the UK's two rival youth factions, Mods and Rockers, became annual events. They first made headlines in the summer of 1964 when riots broke out in several towns along the south coast of England.

But Would You Let Your Daughter Marry One?

"They look like boys whom any self-respecting mum would lock in the bathroom!" yelped Judith Simons in the *Daily Express*, early in 1964. "But the Rolling Stones – five tough young London-based music makers are not worried what mum thinks...The Stones have taken over as the voice of the teens!"

Vocalist **Mick Jagger** was unworried when confronted with Simons' opinion by *Melody Maker* on March 7. "I don't particularly care either way whether parents hate us or not," he said. "I can tell you this much – my parents like me."

Four singles into their career, the Stones finally topped the *Melody Maker* charts with 'It's All Over Now' on July 2 despite, or perhaps because of, their unsavoury public image.

"Some groups give performances," explained **Stones**' guitarist **Brian Jones**. "We have a rave. A mad, swaying, deafening, sweating half-hour of tension and excitement which gives us just as big a kick as the kids."

Fortuitously, the Stones arrived on the scene just as the British media switched from overkill into backlash against the **Beatles**. Almost as soon as Tottenham's **Dave Clark Five** had crashed into the charts with 'Glad All Over', the *Daily Express* was running the headline 'Tottenham Sound Has Crushed The Beatles!'

Soon after this, a cartoon in the *Daily Mail* showed a group of schoolchildren pointing at a girl of about 16, saying "She must be really old ... she remembers the Beatles." Another cartoon, in the London *Evening Standard*, showed the British Prime Minister berating his Cabinet, all sporting Beatle hair cuts, with the words "How can I say you're with it, with old-fashioned haircuts like that?"

Every possibility was leapt at in the attempt to find the new trend likely to displace Beatlemania. When **Millie Small**'s UK hit, 'My Boy Lollipop', went to Number 2 in the US in May, the media predicted a ska explosion but, despite a Millie Small Day at the New York World's Fair in August, the ska boom never materialized.

The **Rolling Stones**, however, were in with a genuine chance. Their debut album, released on April 16, hit the Number 1 spot in the UK just two weeks later. Under the astute management of former Beatles PR man Andrew Loog Oldham, the Stones were carefully given a deliberately contrived young rebel image to take the fullest possible advantage of the Beatles' increasing sophistication and family appeal. When Dick Tatham of *Showtime* magazine asked if the Stones could topple the Beatles, Oldham replied, "No, that's not their aim. The Beatles have built a general appeal. It takes in parents and fringe fans. The Stones are on a teen kick – period."

Nor was it unknown for Oldham to tip journalists off about the latest Stones outrage, or to suggest an angle by which an enterprising soul might take advantage of the Stones penchant for attracting attention. Even the shock headline "Would You Want Your Sister To Marry A Rolling Stone?" was allegedly invented by Oldham and fed to a willing Fleet Street hack.

Outraged headlines followed the Stones wherever they went. It was hardly surprising then that, in early April, Wallace Scowcroft of the British National Federation of Hairdressers was fretting in print that Brian Jones "looks as if he has got a feather duster on his head" and offered the whole group free haircuts.

Under the headline 'Rolling Stones Gather No Lunch', the *Daily Express* reported on May 12 that the group was refused service at the Strand Hotel, Bristol, for not wearing ties. "But ties would get in the soup," protested Jagger.

They were "The ugliest group in Britain" according to the *Daily Mirror* on May 29, not to mention "Dirtier and streakier and more dishevelled than the Beatles" in America's *Associated Press* just three days later.

"A lot of people say we're scruffy and don't wash," retorted Jagger. "So what? If they don't like me, they can keep away."

Other stars fell obediently into line with Mr Oldham's publicity-raising master plan. On June 3, when middle-aged crooner **Dean Martin** introduced the Stones on his *Hollywood Palace* TV show, he could not resist a string of jibes. After an appearance by a trampoline artist, Martin quipped "That's the father of the Rolling Stones. He's been trying to kill himself ever since."

But on June 20, former London School of Economics student Jagger revealed more common sense than his image suggested. "I give the Stones about another two years," he predicted. "I'm saving for the future. I bank all of my royalties for a start."

Such precautions were hardly necessary. When Richard Green of *New Musical Express* reviewed the final date of the Stones' summer UK tour at the Granada, East Ham, he pointed out that it was becoming "even more obvious that the Stones are approaching the Beatles' popularity and could even overtake it."

Asked if there was animosity between London and Liverpool bands, Brian Jones tactfully said "It's all a big thing invented by the newspapers. We are on very friendly terms with the Northern beat groups, and there's a mutual admiration between us. Obviously, we prefer the Americans, but there hasn't been anything beatier in Britain for a long time."

Supreme Supremes

When the **Supremes** hit the road with **Gene Pitney**, the **Shirelles** and **Brenda Holloway** on Dick Clark's Caravan of Stars tour in June 1964, their presence was denoted only by the words 'and others' at the bottom of the tour posters. Six months later, they were set to become Motown's most successful group ever, notching up three US Number 1s before the year was out.

In the now well-established girl-group tradition, the **Supremes** provided the glamorous icing on a cake that was baked by a team of backroom boys, in this case the songwriting and record producing team of Lamont Dozier in tandem with brothers Eddie and Brian Holland.

Credited on Supremes records as Holland-Dozier-Holland, this trio offered one of their songs, 'Where Did Our Love Go?', to the **Marvelettes**, but the group turned it down. The Supremes didn't care for it either but, with a string of eight flops behind them, lacked the muscle to hold out for something better.

To their amazement, it soared to the Number 1 position in the US on August 22 to become the first of five consecutive chart toppers. The sound, as *Record Mirror* pointed out, was smoother than most Motown offerings and 20-year-old lead singer **Diana Ross** accurately described it as "somewhere between rock'n'roll and typical popular music. We reckon it's sweeter than just

rock'n'roll. It's just kinda built up with us, because we've always lived in the same neighbourhood and sang together in school and church choirs."

That neighbourhood was the Brewster Projects, a run-down housing estate in Detroit's ghetto area, where Diana first sang with the other Supremes, Mary Wilson and Florence Ballard, in an earlier group the **Primettes**. "I was planning to be a music teacher," recalled Mary, "but my music teacher got pretty annoyed because I used to skip lessons to attend rehearsals with the group."

Until the success of 'Where Did Our Love Go?' they had been known around the Motown offices as the "No-Hit Supremes" but when 'Baby Love' went to Number 1 on October 31, they became the first Motown group to score two chart toppers.

The field was wide open for the Supremes, as none of 1963's successful new girl groups maintained their popularity. New outfits were vying to replace them. The **Dixie Cups**, a New Orleans-based trio, reached Number 1 with 'Chapel Of Love', and the **Shangri-Las** from New York also hit the top with 'Leader of The Pack', but with their third Holland-Dozier-Holland single, 'Come See About Me', rocketing to Number 1 in November, the Supremes lived up to their name and were confirmed as the most successful girl group ever.

The Supremes confirmed their status as the Sixties' most successful girl group when they notched up three Number 1s in a row, but lead vocalist Diana Ross would eventually outstrip even their achievements.

Gator Bowl in Jacksonville, Florida on September 11 until they are assured they are playing to a non-segregated audience.

On September 25, Brian Epstein turns down an American business-man's £3.5 million offer to buy out his contract with the Beatles. The following day, **Herman's Hermits** reach the Number 1 spot in the UK with their single 'I'm Into Something Good'. It is their first hit, but marks the third chart success for independent record producer Mickie Most, who previously drew blood with the **Animals**' 'House Of The Rising Sun' and the **Nashville Teens**' 'Tobacco Road'.

With the girl group phenomenon peaking in America, Britain sees an upsurge in home-grown female solo

Sandie Shaw broke into show business by talking her way backstage to sing for UK pop idol Adam Faith in his dressing room. With her long straight hair and longer legs, Shaw epitomized the classic British 'dolly' bird.

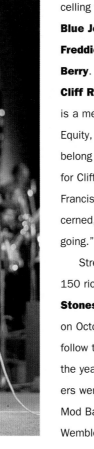

singers. The mini-skirted, barefoot **Sandie Shaw**, who reaches Number 1 on October 8 with 'Always Something There To Remind Me', has followed in the footsteps of Scottish raver **Lulu** who took 'Shout' into the Top 10 in May, and **Dusty Springfield**'s biggest hit so far, 'I Just Don't Know What To Do With Myself', which reached Number 3 in July. And, although she has not yet proved herself, former convent girl **Marianne Faithfull** must stand a good chance of success. Her debut single, released on August 13, is 'As Tears Go By' written by Mick Jagger and Keith Richard of the **Rolling Stones**.

After talks with the Musicians Union, which is fiercely opposed to the apartheid system, the **Stones** cancel a proposed South African tour on October 9. Other MU bands cancelling tours there are the **Swinging Blue Jeans**, the **Four Pennies**, **Freddie & The Dreamers** and **Dave Berry**. There is speculation about **Cliff Richard** because, although he is a member of the actors' union, Equity, his group the **Shadows** belong to the MU. "We can't speak for Cliff," says MU secretary Harry Francis, "but as far as we are concerned, the Shadows won't be going."

Street violence flares again when 150 rioting fans are arrested during a **Stones** concert at the Paris Olympia on October 20. Violence seems to follow the Stones whose first riot of the year came in April, when 30 bikers were arrested outside the Mad Mod Ball at the Empire Pool, Wembley, while police tussled with

fans inside. There were fist fights at Hamilton, Scotland on May 19, and on July 31 their concert at the Boom Boom Room in Belfast was stopped after 12 minutes to remove hysterical girls who had to be restrained with straight-jackets. There was trouble too at the Hague in the Netherlands, on August 8 where two girls had their clothes ripped off amid scenes of hooliganism.

There is more trouble for the Stones on October 24 when their conquest of America receives a setback. Their *Ed Sullivan Show* appearance sees the switchboard jammed with complaints. The following day Sullivan tells the press, "Frankly, I didn't see the Rolling Stones until the day before the broadcast. I was shocked when I saw them. I promise you they'll never be back on my show if things can't be handled. We won't book any more rock'n'roll groups and we'll ban teenagers from the theatre if we have to. It took me 17 years to build this show. I'm not going to have it destroyed in a matter of weeks."

Nicknamed 'the Great Stoneface', Sullivan is virtually a living anachronism, left over from the days of variety and vaudeville, but his Sunday night show is one of the highest rated on American television, making him a powerful figure. His tastes are predictably middle-American. He took to the **Dave Clark Five** and immediately re-booked them, describing them as "nice, neat boys who perform well". Unlike the Rolling Stones.

The *TAMI Show* airs on US TV on October 28, featuring **Chuck Berry**,

Pirates of the Airwaves

"Hello everybody. This is Radio Caroline, broadcasting on 199, your all-day music station."

With those words, on March 29, 1964, disc jockey Simon Dee ushered in a new era for British radio. He was speaking from a small studio aboard former 702-ton passenger ferry 'Frederica', known to its listeners as Radio Caroline.

Caroline was owned by Ronan O'Rahilly, a former record plugger, whose difficulty in securing radio plays for a **Georgie Fame** single, led him to consider emulating the Dutch pirate radio station, 'Veronica', with his own ship.

As was the case with most European countries, British law only forbade commercial radio broadcasting on land. By basing itself in the North Sea, Caroline was able to exploit this legal loophole, providing British teenagers with all-day rock-'n'roll fun, while simultaneously providing O'Rahilly with all-day profit from advertizers.

Even before Caroline took to the air, moves were afoot to stop it. In the House Of Commons on February 6, Postmaster General Ernest Bevins had been questioned following rumours about the impending launch of Radio Caroline. Bevins replied that legislation would be introduced to deal with it.

Because of 'needletime' restrictions, it was difficult for the BBC's Home Service and Light Programme to play as many pop records as teenagers might like. There was a prevailing fear that, if records took over, live music would all but disappear. 'Needletime' restrictions existed to ensure that performing musicians could make a living. As a result, the best thing available was an unsatisfactory weekday lunchtime show on the Light

Programme featuring dance bands more familiar with the swing of **Glenn Miller** or the strict-tempo of **Victor Sylvester**, and always struggling to come to grips with the latest sounds. Things were slightly better at the weekend, when two shows, *Saturday Club* and *Easy Beat*, played new records and featured live rock groups.

Even so, teenagers hungry for pop tended to tune to Radio Luxembourg, broadcasting from the tiny Duchy of Luxembourg in Europe, after dark. Luxembourg's formula of non-stop pop records became the model for the new pirate stations which sprang up in the wake of Caroline. Radio Atlanta was anchored off Frinton-on-Sea, Essex, although most pirate activity was in the Thames Estuary, where Radio London, Radio Invicta and Radio City all competed for the huge London-area teen audience.

There was even, briefly, Radio Sutch, owned by and starring the eccentric rocker, the self-styled Lord David Sutch (later Screaming Lord Sutch), broadcasting from Shivering Sands Tower, off the Kent coast.

Although new to Britain, pirate radio had existed since at least 1958, when Radio Mercury began broadcasting to Denmark and Sweden. A year later, Radio Veronica was serving Holland and, on 16 February, 1961, Veronica made its first transmissions in English, covering an area along the eastern coast from the northern port of Hull to the seaside resort of Margate.

Teenage reaction was almost unanimously in favour of the pirates but, before long, the police had paid visits to several stations, even though proposed anti-pirate legislation had not yet been formulated.

ROCK 'N' ROLL
record

JANUARY 7: British blues harmonica star Cyril Davies dies of leukemia.

MARCH 2: The Beatles start shooting their first feature film, A Hard Day's Night.

MAY 4: The Moody Blues form in Birmingham.

JUNE 5: 'Liza Jane', first single by Davy Jones (later to become David Bowie) & The Kingbees.

AUGUST 1: Rockabilly star Johnny Burnette drowns in a boating accident in California.

SEPTEMBER 10: Rod Stewart records his first single, 'Good Morning Little Schoolgirl'.

SEPTEMBER 16: A new all-rock music show, Shindig, is premiered on ABC TV in the US, featuring Sam Cooke, the Everly Brothers and the Righteous Brothers.

OCTOBER 22: EMI rejects the audition tape by the High Numbers, later to become the Who.

The British Are Coming

The **Stones** might have been hogging headlines in Britain but the February 15 music charts published by *Billboard*, the bible of the American music trade, showed that the **Beatles** not only had five songs climbing the US Hot 100 singles but they also had three albums on the albums chart. The same issue carried a story headlined 'US Rocks and Reels From Beatles Invasion – Beatles Begin New British Artist Push', quipping that the last time Britain had as much influence on American affairs was during the American Revolution way back in 1775. A month later, *Billboard* reported that Beatles releases were accounting for 60% of total singles sales.

Around this time though, the British anti-Beatles backlash finally arrived at the other side of the Atlantic. *Billboard* reported that "just about everyone is tired of the Beatles. Disc jockeys are tired of playing the hit group, writers of trade and consumer publications are tired of writing about them, and manufacturers of product other than Beatles records are tired of hearing about them. Everyone's tired of the Beatles, except the public."

Tired of them or not, the media couldn't deny the facts. By April 4, *Billboard's* Top 5 singles ('Can't Buy Me Love', 'Twist and Shout', 'She Loves You', 'I Want To Hold Your Hand' and 'Please Please Me'), were all by the Beatles. A week later they held down a record-breaking 14 positions in the Top 100 while the album 'Meet The Beatles' sold over 3.5 million, making it one of America's all-time best sellers.

And in their wake came the British Invasion, a flood of UK acts including the **Dave Clark Five**, the **Searchers**, **Peter and Gordon**, the **Animals** and the **Nashville Teens** storming up the charts as American record companies scrambled to sign anything with long hair and an English accent. Some, like **Chad Stewart** and **Jeremy Clyde**, were significantly more successful in America than they had ever been at home.

---

the **Beach Boys**, the **Supremes**, the **Rolling Stones**, **Marvin Gaye**, **James Brown**, **Smokey Robinson**, **Billy J Kramer** and more. An eventful month ends with **Roy Orbison**'s ninth Top 10 single, 'Oh Pretty Woman', being awarded gold record status.

Having shown up late for two UK radio programmes, *Top Gear* and *Saturday Club*, the **Rolling Stones** are banned from live shows by the BBC on November 23. Wild man Jagger seems tactfully restrained when he announces, "If the BBC are upset, we're sorry. We don't want anyone to be upset with us. If necessary we will apologize. The contract must have been signed for us while we were in the States. I didn't know anything about it."

On December 12, **Brian Jones** denies rumours that he is to leave the Stones. During the band's recent US tour he spent several days in hos-

pital with what was reported in England as pneumonia, although American media sources suggested a drug overdose.

Bluesy keyboard virtuoso **Georgie Fame**, whose lack of BBC radio play was said to have inspired the birth of pirate radio, finally goes to Number 1 in the UK with 'Yeh Yeh' on December 17.

Hundreds of distraught fans break down the doors of the A R Leake funeral home in Chicago, on December 18, when **Sam Cooke**, probably the most influential R&B vocalist of his generation, is buried. Cooke was shot dead in Los Angeles on December 11 after allegedly attempting to rape a young woman he had taken to a motel.

The Christmas season is only a little kinder to **Brian Wilson**. Following a nervous breakdown, the first of three in a two-year period, during a flight from Los Angeles to

Houston, he announces that he will not tour or perform with the **Beach Boys**. He will, instead, concentrate on songwriting and production.

Nor is the season's traditional goodwill overflowing in London on Christmas Day itself when female Beatle fans attack **George Harrison**'s girlfriend Patti Boyd at the *Beatles' Christmas Show*. The girls are apparently angered that actress/model Patti has stolen George from them. The pair have been dating since they met on the set of *A Hard Day's Night*.

Having gained popularity with several *Shindig* appearances, Phil Spector's latest proteges, the **Righteous Brothers** end the year in grand style by taking Phil Spector's epic production, 'You've Lost That Lovin' Feelin'', written by Brill Building duo Barry Mann and Cynthia Weil, to the top of the US charts on Boxing Day.

Elvis really made his own tribute to his career in the film, *Elvis On Tour*; "When I was a boy, I was the hero in comic books and movies. I grew up believing in that dream. Now I've lived it out. That's all a man can ask for." What he didn't count on was the invasion of privacy.

NOV 17 : The British Government imposes an arms embargo on South Africa

1960s Underground

"Underground music," declared rock promoter Bill Graham, "is just any band that ain't had a hit yet." Working in San Francisco, the heart of the Sixties West Coast underground, Graham was well placed to pontificate. He dealt on a daily basis with underground icons like the **Grateful Dead** and **Jefferson Airplane**, but he tempered their hippie idealism with his hard-nosed financial sensibility. The rock underground, with which businessmen like Graham frequently found themselves at loggerheads, had not developed in isolation. It was one part of a larger social organism, advocating a revolution in literature, theatre, film and lifestyle.

This early Sixties underground culture, evolving out of the Fifties beatnik movement,

first sowed its seeds by creating its own press. the *Oracle* in San Francisco, the *Village Voice* in New York and *International Times* in London all spread the anti-establishment word. M Preston Burns, writing in the Boston alternative paper *Avatar* in June 1967, attempted an early definition of the underground by linking it to subversive activists and communities throughout history, including Jesus and the Christian movement but, for most hippies, the precedents were irrelevant. What mattered was that the hippie lifestyle offered an alternative to a society which seemed to have become obsessed with materialism. Although London

and New York each had developing underground cultures, it was San Francisco's Haight-Ashbury hippies who first gained international attention and, along the way, hit records. Haight-Ashbury offered communal living, free love and dope smoking as alternatives to family, fidelity and alcohol. The bands who espoused the lifestyle did so via extended guitar-based experimental rock, played at free open-air concerts, or in ballrooms featuring complex light-shows. Their song lyrics, much influenced by Bob Dylan, rejected militarism, capitalism and conformity in favour of peace, love and understanding.

As disaffected teens from all over America flocked to San Francisco, the record industry saw a new marketing opportunity and, before long, the reputations of established acts like the **Four Seasons** and the **Beach Boys**, were rendered quaintly obsolete by the hits of **Jefferson Airplane**, the **Electric Prunes**, **Strawberry Alarm Clock** and other surrealistically titled outfits. The West Coast rock music underground started as an alternative to the mainstream pop and rock that dominated the charts, was now overground, and in bed with the money-making machinery it purported to despise.

Another, less easily assimilable, underground was developing in New York's Greenwich Village. Directly descended from the folk music scene and the beat poets, a café society thrived in the folk clubs of The Village, revolving around Bleecker St and MacDougal St. Out of this cultural melting pot came the **Fugs**, a trio of ranting poets who, after hearing the **Beatles**, adopted rock as a vehicle for the theatrical dissemination of radical ideas. Like the Haight Ashbury hippies, they were anti-war, pro-love and pro-dope, but they dealt in short sharp songs with heavy intellectual and philosophical ramifications, not to mention blasphemies and obscenities, which made them virtually unplayable on the radio. Fêted by the New York arts cognoscenti, including Andy Warhol, the Fugs were doomed to remain influential cult heroes.

Almost simultaneously, the **Velvet Underground** and **Nico** appeared, operating in the same New York arts milieu and with Warhol as their apparent mentor. Just as the

Beach Boys had chronicled the sun-kissed California surf scene, so the Velvets performed the same function for New York's sophisticated, decadent social circus. But in stark contrast to the soft focus Technicolor hippie ideals of San Francisco, frontman **Lou Reed** presented stark black and white cinema-vérité reports of heroin addiction, violence and sexual deviation. Like the Fugs, the Velvets were adored in New York, but despised almost everywhere else. Their timing was all wrong, and their uncompromising attitude didn't sell records. Two decades would have to pass before Lou Reed's influence would be widely acknowledged, and before his songs would take on the veneer of prophecy. In fact, there was no prophecy. He was recording what he saw around him.

In London, centred on the UFO Club, a third underground explosion was underway. Taking its cues more from San Francisco than New York, the English underground had the **Pink Floyd** as its flagship, turning rock towards an exploration of electronics, space travel, mysticism and whimsical tales of goblins and witches. New York's influence on London was seen in politically active bands like Mick Farren's **Social Deviants** but, as in America, the time was still too soon. The Sixties youth revolution was fuelled by a glorious mass delusion that war, racial hatred and greed could be banished not through confrontation

but by waving banners, chanting slogans and pushing flowers down the barrels of guns.

Even so, the underground was far from ineffectual. By Bill Graham's simplistic definition, the Beatles, the Beach Boys and the **Rolling Stones** were all underground bands until they started having hits. In fact, the opposite was nearer the truth. All three bands adopted underground values long after they had acquired mass popularity. Without the underground there could not have been, to take just one example, 'Sgt Pepper'.

By the end of the Sixties, much of the underground had been absorbed into the system. In the process, however, it had not only obliged the music business to re-think its corporate strategies and widen its musical horizons, but also provided a new set of social priorities for a generation.

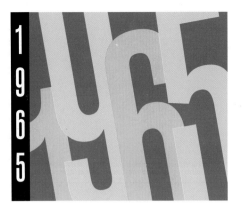

The year is ushered in with the *NME* chart entry of **Them**, a Belfast R&B quintet, performing the **Big Joe Williams** standard, 'Baby Please Don't Go', with a powerful vocal from **Van Morrison** and featuring session-man **Jimmy Page** on guitar.

The **Who**'s first appearance on *Ready Steady Go* comes on January 28, just a day before **Elvis Presley**'s former demo-singer **PJ Proby** splits his velvet pantaloons during a performance at the Castle Hall in Croydon, on tour with **Cilla Black**. The story breaks in the UK media, PJ's act is described as "obscene" and three days later Proby finds himself banned from all ABC theatres. His protestations that the incident was an accident seem far-fetched in the light of several previous close calls of a similar nature.

On February 7, **George Harrison** has his tonsils removed at University College Hospital, London, but is sufficiently recovered by February 11 to join **John Lennon** as a guest at **Ringo Starr**'s wedding to childhood sweetheart, Maureen Cox, in London.

Meanwhile, across the Atlantic, Motown's flag is being flown by **Jr Walker & The All-Stars**, scoring their first hit single with the rousing, rasping 'Shotgun', featuring Walker's primitive but unusually-

distinctive sax style.

Flying out to the Bahamas on February 22, the **Beatles** begin filming a second movie, provisionally titled *Eight Arms To Hold You*. While the group is in the Bahamas, EMI Records announce that the Beatles have sold over 100 million records in less than three years, a feat which took Elvis Presley eight.

After several minor chart entries, Motown's **Temptations** finally secure a Number 1 US hit with 'My Girl' on March 6.

Written by **Smokey Robinson**, the song was originally intended for his group the **Miracles**, but when the Temptations heard the demo, they convinced him to let them cut it.

Still seemingly unable to find trousers which can actually remain in one piece throughout an entire performance, PJ Proby is ordered off the stage at Watford Town Hall, just outside London, on March 9. Having also been banned from BBC TV appearances and from America's *Shindig* show, it seems more than just coincidence that his current single is titled 'I Apologise'.

Proby's splitting trousers are briefly eclipsed in the music press on March 13 when it is revealed that **Eric** 'Slowhand' **Clapton** is quitting the **Yardbirds** just before the release of their latest single, 'For Your Love'. "Eric did not like our new single", explains vocalist Keith Relf. "He should have been featured, but he did not

Clapton is God (and Keith is Buddha). Yardbirds' vocalist Keith Relf reserves a seat on the astral plane, the better to transcendentally meditate on the real reasons why Slowhand quit the band.

The Kinks Are Well-Respected Men

The **Rolling Stones** sold more records but, despite a largely disastrous year, **Ray Davies** of the **Kinks** still emerged as 1965's likeliest contender for Lennon and McCartney's crown as the UK's top songwriter.

When the year opened, the Kinks from London's Muswell Hill district looked like classic flash-in-the-pan material. Although they had a Number 1 hit in 1964 with 'You Really Got Me', their stage outfits of frilly shirts and red hunting jackets gave them a decidedly dated look, and their follow-up single, 'All Day And All Of The Night', was virtually identical to 'You Really Got Me'.

'Tired of Waiting For You', a slower version of the same formula, became their second UK Number 1 on January 21, but the raving follow-up, 'Everybody's Gonna Be Happy', stalled embarrassingly at Number 17.

"We have not really changed our sound, only our style," acknowledged Davies. "But we have learned that it is futile to go on recording the same sort of records. If we want to keep hitting the charts, we must make sure everything is different."

Before that objective could be achieved, however, disaster struck again. On May 25, Ray's brother Dave, who played lead guitar for the group, careened into drummer Mick Avory's cymbals during a London gig and was knocked unconscious. The remainder of their UK tour had to be cancelled.

In July, they were beset by yet another problem. While the group was touring America, release of their latest UK single, 'See My Friend', was delayed because of a legal dispute between their manager, Larry Page, and their record producer, Shel Talmy. Fortunately, when it did see the light of day the sound featuring a hypnotic, drone-like quality was distinctively different from their earlier releases.

But it was the release of an EP, 'Kwyet Kinks', just in time for the Christmas market, which caused critics and public alike to acknowledge that Davies was now in a class of his own. The EP's most radio-played track, 'A Well Respected Man', with its caustic yet whimsical analysis of the British class system, marked a dramatic stylistic leap for the Kinks.

Although their December hit single, 'Til The End Of The Day', was in their earlier hard-rocking style, every track on 'Kwyet Kinks' was restrained and sensitive. The distinctively different sound Davies had been seeking was now clearly evident.

Not a bad year for a band whose second single, 'You Still Want Me', reportedly sold just 127 copies.

The Kinks kame over kwite kwyet as 1964 ended.

1965 · HEADLINE NEWS   Feb 7 : American aircraft begin bombing North Vietnam

The Who

"There's a sort of vicious strangeness about these four beatsters from Shepherd's Bush," wrote Alan Smith of the *NME* in June of 1965, assessing the impact of the **Who**. "They talk quite happily about the way guitarist Pete Townshend smashes his guitar against an amplifier when the mood takes him."

With their hair styled by Robert James and their Carnaby Street clothes, the Who had emerged as the perfect Mod band, but the enthralling energy which propelled them into the Top 10 three times during the year also threatened to tear the group apart.

It was in February that their debut single, 'I Can't Explain', entered the UK charts, giving the wider public a taste of what London's Marquee Club had been billing as the Who's 'maximum R&B' sound.

TV exposure on *Ready, Steady, Go!* and *Top Of The Pops* revealed the band as an unusually dynamic outfit, with guitarist Pete Townshend flailing away at his instrument while drummer Keith Moon's arms and legs pounded wildly at his kit.

They followed the Top 10 success of 'I Can't Explain' with 'Anyway Anyhow Anywhere' maintaining their profile into June, at which point Roger Daltrey described Townshend as "very political, a right Bob Dylan," and revealed for the first time that the group's internal rela-

tionships were as violent as their stage image. "We've all got explosive temperaments. It's like waiting for a bomb to go off."

The bomb went off on September 22, during a short Scandinavian tour when Daltrey punched out Keith Moon and found himself nearly thrown out of the band.

When their third single, 'My Generation', was released in October the Who's managers Chris Stamp and Kit Lambert declared "The field is wide open for new managers, now that Epstein has become a remote millionaire and Andrew Oldham has gone respectable."

Lambert and Stamp's plan was that the Who should be perceived as anything but respectable. The habit of smashing their equipment on stage led to musical instrument shops closing up whenever the band came near. "We have to get new guitars and drums every month or so," confirmed Daltrey. "It's costing us a fortune."

Rumours of a split flared up again when Daltrey stormed off stage at the Glad Rags Ball in London on November 19, during a set plagued with PA problems. "The Who will never split up," Daltrey told the *NME*. "We have arguments all the time but it gives us an extra spark. The Who thrives on friction." Nevertheless, Boz Burrell, leader of the **Boz People**, was thought the likely replacement if Daltrey was given the push.

Pete Townshend of the Who fails in yet another attempt to die by electrocution before he gets old. With their onstage antics mirrored by equally violent behaviour offstage, the Who positioned themselves as the Kinks' wicked alter egos, just as the Stones had previously done with the Beatles.

ROCK'N'ROLL Record

JANUARY 3: The Fender Guitar Company, makers of the Stratocaster and Telecaster models, is bought by CBS for $13 million.

JANUARY 12: A new US TV music show, Hullaballoo, premieres on NBC featuring the Zombies, Gerry & The Pacemakers and the New Christy Minstrels.

JANUARY 20: America's most successful DJ, Alan Freed, dies in poverty in Palm Springs.

FEBRUARY 8: Pye Records signs "the British Bob Dylan", Glasgow-born singer/songwriter Donovan.

FEBRUARY 15: Nat 'King' Cole dies of cancer.

AUGUST 27: The Beatles meet Elvis Presley at his Bel Air mansion. They chat and sing together for four hours.

NOVEMBER 22: Bob Dylan marries former model Sara Lowndes.

want to sing or anything, and he only did that boogie bit in the middle." Clapton's comment is rather more terse, "They are going too commercial." His replacement, **Jeff Beck**, from London R&B band the **Tridents** has been recommended by session guitarist **Jimmy Page**. Jim McCarty of the Yardbirds raves, "Jeff gets so many weird sounds out of his guitar, you'd think he trained as an effects man." Clapton is to join **John Mayall's Bluesbreakers**, a combo he considers more authentic.

As April begins, a row which has been brewing since the beginning of the year, when the US Department of Labor announced it would not issue British rock bands with work permits or visas, has reached a ludicrous stage. Although at Number 1 in America with their single 'Game Of Love', **Wayne Fontana & The Mindbenders** have been refused permits on the grounds that "The artists are insufficiently well-known in America to warrant them working here." Other groups suffering similar treatment include the **Hollies**, the **Zombies**, the **Nashville Teens** and the **Animals**. Although the Department of Labor refuses to admit it, this action is widely interpreted as an attempt to protect the careers of America's star acts.

Two years after its UK success, novelty act **Freddie & The Dreamers** finally secure the US Number 1 position with 'I'm Telling You Now' on April 10. As a result, advance demand for their Mercury Records US debut album tops 142,000, the highest in the label's history.

With even more staggering advance orders of 600,000, **Herman's Hermits** soar to the US Number 1 spot on May 1 with 'Mrs Brown You've Got A Lovely Daughter', while another of their singles, 'Silhouettes' occupies the Number 5 position. A former child actor in Britain's long-running TV soap opera, *Coronation Street*, toothy Herman (Peter Noone) is now more popular in America than he is at home. This has been achieved by capitalizing on his quintessential cheeky Englishness, so beloved of American audiences that the band release markedly more 'English' singles in America than they do in the UK.

The **Beatles** are among the crowd on May 9 when **Bob Dylan** plays the first of two nights at London's Royal Albert Hall. Other celebrities turning out include **Donovan**, **Paul Jones** singer with **Manfred Mann** and **Eric Burdon** of the **Animals**.

In the same week, the Animals' organist **Alan Price** cites fear of flying as his reason for quitting the group. "My nerve broke just a few hours before we were due to fly to Scandinavia," he reveals. "Then there was Japan and everything coming up. I just had to leave." He is to be replaced by former **Mike Cotton Sound** keyboardist Dave Rowberry, of whom Price says, "He's a friend of mine. He knows his stuff inside out. There's no loss with me out."

The *Daily Telegraph* reports on May 28 that London's Carnaby Street, formerly "a dreary thread of a street" is now the Mecca of bright young things who want to keep ahead of fashion. "You can bump into people, as I did, such as **Mick Jagger** buying a sports jacket. The Duke of Bedford, Peter Sellers, Lord Snowdon, Marlene Dietrich, Sean Connery and **Cilla Black** all shop here."

In America, as the month ends, the **Beach Boys** clinch their second Number 1 with 'Help Me Rhonda'. Although he does not play on the single, former session-man Bruce Johnston is now a full-time Beach Boy, having been asked to fill-in for leader/songwriter Brian Wilson on live dates.

It is announced on June 12 that the Beatles are to be awarded MBEs (Member of the Most Excellent Order of the British Empire) for their services to Britain. The ceremony is to take place at Buckingham Palace in October.

Manchester's Hollies achieve their first UK Number 1 hit, 'I'm Alive', on June 24 and two days later in America an equally distinctive vocal harmony sound ascends to the top as the **Byrds** first single, a close-harmony cover of Dylan's 'Mr Tambourine Man', featuring a jangling 12-string guitar, takes over the US Number 1 slot. The Byrds leader, former folk singer Jim McGuinn, took up 12-string guitar after seeing **George Harrison**'s Rickenbacker in *A Hard Day's Night*. "Dylan is a friend of mine," reveals McGuinn. "I've been singing in the same Greenwich Village coffee houses as him since 1961. But I don't want the Byrds to be called a folk group. Folk is what we came from. We're somewhere between folk and rock."

On July 22, with their current sin-

MAR 21 : Martin Luther King leads 25,000 protestors in a 54-mile Civil Rights march from Selma to Montgomery

1965 - HEADLINE NEWS

APR 6 : British actress Julie Andrews wins an Oscar for Best Actress at the annual Academy Awards for her lead role in Mary Poppins

gle, 'Satisfaction', topping the US charts, **Rolling Stones Mick Jagger**, **Brian Jones** and **Bill Wyman** are fined £5 each on charges of "insulting behaviour" arising from an incident that occured in March. At the end of their British tour, after having been refused use of the toilets at the Francis Garage, West Ham, east London, Jagger, Jones and Wyman had shown their contempt by urinating against the garage wall. "Just because you have reached an exalted height in your profession," the magistrate rebukes them, "it does not mean you can behave in this manner."

Despite having not yet released a record, when the **Lovin' Spoonful** play the Night Owl coffee house in New York's Greenwich Village on July 24, their reputation is such that the audience includes the **Byrds**, Phil Spector and **Bob Dylan**.

The following day, evidently inspired by the Byrds' electric treatment of his songs, **Dylan** plays a live electric set for the first time, backed by members of the **Paul Butterfield Blues Band**, at the Newport Folk Festival in Rhode Island. He is promptly booed off, allegedly in tears, by the crowd of folk purists.

Phil Spector's former production assistant, Salvatore Bono, and Cherilyn LaPier, a session singer he met while she was performing backup vocals on the **Ronettes**' 'Be My Baby', make an appealingly odd couple in their tight striped bell bottom trousers and Afghan jackets. The image is exactly right for the times when, as **Sonny and Cher**, they croon 'I Got You Babe' into each other's eyes, and hog the US and UK Number 1 spot for most of August. "With us," says Sonny, "I think the universal message is really just love."

The **Beatles** perform at Shea Stadium, New York, on August 15, before 56,000 hysterical fans – the largest crowd yet for any rock show. The screaming is so loud and continuous that when group members come offstage they tell friends that they literally could not hear themselves play. The following day, equally over-enthusiastic fans drag **Dave Clark Five** organist Mike Smith from the stage of the Avalon Theatre in Chicago, and he breaks two ribs.

Rolling Stones' manager Andrew

Whereas the Who adopted the trappings of the Mod movement to find an audience, the Small Faces were authentic Carnabetian mods from day one. In Steve Marriott they were blessed with one of the great vocalists and teen hearthrobs of the era.

Loog Oldham announces on August 20 that he is starting a new record label to be called Immediate. Under the motto "Happy to be part of the industry of human happiness", the label's first release is 'Hang On Sloopy,' by American beat group the **McCoys**.

After only six weeks together, London's second successful mod band, the **Small Faces**, achieve their first hit with 'Whatcha Gonna Do 'Bout It' when it enters the UK charts on September 2. Carnaby Street clothes-horses to a man, the Small Faces, unlike the **Who**, were mods before they formed their group.

One of the year's most alarming trends, the censoring of pop by ban-

ning tracks from radio or TV broadcast, is thrown into sharp relief in September when the BBC TV show *Juke Box Jury* refuses to play the **Hedgehoppers Anonymous** single 'It's Good News Week' because it mentions birth control. The liberalization of pop song lyrics that came along with the protest movement means that more artists now find themselves in conflict with the establishment. Earlier this year the **Shangri Las**' 'Leader Of The Pack' was banned by both BBC radio and the TV show *Ready, Steady, Go!*, which had previously banned 'Terry' by **Twinkle**. Both records were judged to be 'sick'.

Ironically, the **Rolling Stones**'

'Satisfaction', banned in June by many US stations, went on to become their first Transatlantic Number 1. And when the BBC banned gravel-voiced **Barry McGuire**'s 'Eve of Destruction', he joked to *Melody Maker*, "The ban doesn't worry me too much. I hear this is the latest way to get a hit in England."

The most impressive new voice of the year undoubtedly belongs to **Scott Walker** (Scott Engel) of the heart-throb **Walker Brothers** who take their third single, the Bacharach-David ballad 'Make It Easy On Yourself' to Number 1 in Britain on September 23. Having failed to find success in their native California, the Walkers reasoned they would stand out from the crowd if they moved to England. The ploy appears to have worked.

After returning from headlining ten shows in Czechoslovakia, the first of which was on October 2, **Manfred Mann** become the first rock band to perform behind the Iron Curtain. "We went as a sort of jazz group," explains vocalist Paul Jones. "The Ministry of Culture said we could come if we were a jazz group. In fact, the kids didn't want jazz. They're mad on rock'n'roll. They can't get records over there, but they listen to Radio Luxembourg, so they knew a few of our hits."

In the teeth of establishment disapproval, the **Beatles** are awarded their MBEs in a ceremony at Buckingham Palace on October 26. The Queen is reported to have asked them "How long have you been together now?" to which Ringo imme-

The Walker Brothers moved from Los Angeles to London to find success. None of them were brothers, none of them were called Walker, and their combination of good looks and tear-jerking ballads was something the men didn't know but the little girls certainly understood.

diately responded "Forty years." Several MBE holders have returned their insignia in protest. "I have been proud to wear my decoration since 1942 when it was pinned on my chest by King George VI," says MBE holder James Berg, "but now the whole thing has become debased."

But nothing like as debased as **PJ Proby**. "I'm flat broke, penniless, destitute, call it what you like," he reveals in mid-November, a claim he will make several times over the years. Since his trouser-splitting scandal, things have gone from bad to worse for the outrageous singer. He has cancelled many live shows, postponed others and changed his management company several times.

His neighbours in London's Chelsea have signed a petition complaining of the noise he makes in his flat and, to cap it all, his work permit expires on December 4.

November, however, gives San Francisco's many fledgling rock bands a reason to celebrate. A $20,000 advance from RCA Records has been scooped by **Jefferson Airplane**, whose debut gig was as recent as August 13, at a club owned by group member Marty Balin. The largest advance ever paid to any rock band, this suggests that the major labels are beginning to see San Francisco as a possible home-grown challenger to the British Invasion. The city's Haight-Ashbury district has

become a recognized centre for alternative youth culture activity, with bands such as the **Warlocks**, **Great Society** and the **Charlatans** establishing a thriving local rock scene.

The oldest song lyrics ever in a pop hit, are featured in the **Byrds'** second US Number 1, which hits the top on December 4. The song, 'Turn Turn Turn', was adapted by folk singer **Pete Seeger** from Chapter 3 of the Book of Ecclesiastes.

The year ends with **Dusty Springfield** being voted the World's Top Female Vocalist in the annual *NME* poll, although **Sandie Shaw** has racked up more hits, five in all, during 1965 including the Number 1 hit 'Long Live Love'.

The Eve of Protesting

Largely in the wake of **Bob Dylan**'s first real chart success, 'Like A Rolling Stone', which made Number 2 in the USA in August, a raft of so-called 'protest-singers' sprang out of nowhere, most prominent among whom was **Barry McGuire**. A gruff-voiced former **New Christy Minstrel**, McGuire's 'Eve Of Destruction' topped even Dylan's achievement by soaring to the US Number 1 spot on September 25.

Despite writing such obvious protest songs as 'Blowin' In the Wind' and 'The Times They Are A Changin'', Dylan denied being a 'protest' singer. "Don't put me down as a man with a message," he insisted. "My songs are just me talking to myself. I have no responsibility to anybody except myself."

British folkie **Donovan**, who had recently recorded **Buffy St Marie**'s anti-war anthem 'The Universal Soldier', seemed equally reluctant to be seen as part of a bandwagon. "'Universal Soldier' isn't politics to me. I don't know anything about politics or protest. I'm just singing songs that are written." But **Manfred Mann**, whose version of Dylan's 'With God On Our Side' had attracted much attention, disagreed. "Anyone who records a song has a certain responsibility. We wouldn't record a protest song unless every member of the group agreed broadly with the message."

Despite 'Eve Of Destruction''s controversial condemnation of war and racism, Barry McGuire was as reluctant as Dylan and Donovan to accept the protest tag. "It's not exactly a protest song," he said. "It's merely a song about current events." Nevertheless, the song was banned by Los Angeles radio stations during the Watts Riots, and suffered a similar BBC ban in the UK. Its chart success in Britain was down exclusively to being championed by pirate radio stations Caroline and London.

Accused of copying Dylan, Eve of Destruction's 19-year-old composer, PF Sloan, acknowledged a debt, "Dylan is the greatest writer I've ever heard. I don't mean to copy him. He just started me off into examining my own thoughts, which I had never done before." A more cynical view on the subject, however, was supplied by hit maker and producer Jonathan King. "'Eve Of Destruction' is a hit because it is a great sound," he said. "Why should it be sincere? Since when has pop music been a vehicle for sincerity?"

Mick Jagger seemed to agree, slamming the song as "not sincere in any way" and "written because it's commercial". McGuire quickly leapt to Sloan's defence, saying "I can't change what Mick Jagger thinks or feels, but I know how I feel about the song, and how I felt when I first heard it. Tell him to listen to the record again."

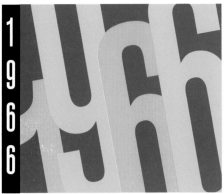

Birmingham's Golden Eagle pub lacked the legendary status of Liverpool's Cavern, but that's where the Spencer Davis Group were spotted. Fronted by prodigiously-gifted 18-year-old multi-instrumentalist Stevie Winwood they provided 1966 with its first major smash.

The year's first new Number 1 in the UK is 'Keep On Running', the fourth single by Birmingham's **Spencer Davis Group**. On 20 January it finally displaces the **Beatles**' 'Day Tripper' which has dominated the top slot since the week before Christmas. The song introduces the public at large to the talents of 18-year-old vocalist **Stevie Winwood**.

It is announced in the same week that with three million-selling singles last year by the **Supremes**, and others by the **Four Tops**, **Temptations** and **Jr Walker**, the Motown Record Corporation has outsold all other US companies during 1965.

The news from Liverpool is less heartening. 100 youths barricade themselves in the Cavern Club, home of the Beatles, as a protest following its closure on February 28 due to financial problems. Six days later, a 5000 signature petition is sent to British Prime Minister Harold Wilson demanding that the club be re-opened.

British duo **Chad Stewart** and **Jeremy Clyde**, almost unheard of in their home country of England, apply for US citizenship in February, following two years of hit records, sold-out concerts and the imminent possibility of their own TV series.

The situation is mirrored in

Britain by the **Walker Brothers**. Starting a four week run atop the UK charts with 'The Sun Ain't Gonna Shine Anymore', the Walkers announce that they are applying for British nationality. The trio moved to England from California in 1965 and established themselves with a string of hits including 'Make It Easy On Yourself' and 'My Ship Is Coming In'. "It takes a long time for the whole thing to become finalized," says Scott Walker, "but even if we are not still at the top in Britain when everything is completed, it will make no difference. We like it here and intend to stay for good. We are essentially British stars."

There are legal niceties to be ironed out for another well-known British band. Reaching Number 5 in the UK with their single 'Substitute', on April 4, it appears that the **Who** have not suffered unduly as a result of court proceedings following the song's release. 'Substitute' first appeared on March 4, with 'Instant Party' on the B-side, via the Reaction label under the group's new deal with

Polydor Records. Immediately afterwards, the Who's former label Brunswick released a single fittingly called 'A Legal Matter', which was also backed with 'Instant Party'. As 'Instant Party' had been recorded with their Brunswick producer, Shel Talmy, he served an injunction on March 9 to stop Polydor marketing the track. Polydor counter-attacked by issuing a second version of 'Substitute' with a new track, 'Waltz For A Pig' credited to the Who Orchestra, on the B-side.

A bizarre accident which seems to echo the lyric of surf duo **Jan and Dean**'s hit song 'Deadman's Curve', occurs on April 12 when Jan Berry's Corvette collides with a truck on Whittier Boulevard, Los Angeles. Berry is rushed to hospital with serious head injuries. Coincidentally, it is understood that the singer had received his call-up papers just before the accident.

Despite achieving her first UK Number 1 with 'You Don't Have To Say You Love Me' on April 28, **Dusty Springfield** is adamant that she will

Simon and Garfunkel

When **Simon and Garfunkel**'s 'Sounds Of Silence' went all the way to Number 1 in America on the first day of 1966, the duo were no longer in existence.

The twosome had gone their separate ways in 1965 after their Columbia Records debut album failed to sell more than a handful of copies. Arthur Garfunkel was back at Columbia University in New York, and Paul Simon was working as a solo performer in Britain, the country he considered his spiritual home, when he heard that the single, 'The Sounds of Silence', was racing up the US charts.

Paul and Art had known each other since schooldays, and even released a single, 'Hey Schoolgirl', which scraped into the US Top 50 under the name **Tom and Jerry**, but they did not become Simon and Garfunkel until early 1964 when they started working New York's Greenwich Village coffee house circuit. It was as Simon and Garfunkel that they recorded the debut album 'Wednesday Morning, 3 am', which contained 'The Sounds of Silence' arranged for voice and acoustic guitar only.

When the folk-rock explosion led by the **Byrds** began to take off, a Boston radio station picked up on 'The Sounds of Silence' and

gave it regular airplay. Columbia Records producer Tom Wilson had some extra studio time on June 15 1965, immediately after recording **Bob Dylan**'s 'Like A Rolling Stone', so he asked guitarist Mike Bloomfield and organist Al Kooper if they would mind adding some electric backing to the Simon and Garfunkel single to make it more contemporary.

It was this version, amended and released without Simon and Garfunkel's knowledge, which was moving up the US charts late in 1965, when Simon told the *New Musical Express*, "This record industry, it encourages freaks ... I hope I never get to that scene where people will be just looking rather than listening. I'd prefer not to be known at all."

When the song went to Number 1, it was no longer possible for Simon or Garfunkel to avoid fame. Before the end of the year, they'd notched up four more hit singles ('Homeward Bound', 'I Am A Rock', 'The Dangling Conversation' and 'A Hazy Shade Of Winter') and released two more albums, 'Sounds Of Silence' and 'Parsley Sage Rosemary and Thyme', which showed they were going to be around for some time.

"Even at 22," said Simon, "I think I've got quite a lot to say. Just the physical act of sitting at a typewriter gives me an intense thrill."

not record again for her record label, Philips, until she is released from the American part of her contract. Dusty has received many letters from American fans asking why it is so difficult to find her records in the States and the singer feels that Philips are not adequately representing her interests over there.

The **Mamas & The Papas**, a close harmony quartet who did well with their debut single, 'California Dreamin'', achieve their first US Number 1 when 'Monday Monday' hits the top on May 7.

On May 13, the distinctive sound of the classical Indian instrument the sitar, played by **Brian Jones**, is heard in the **Rolling Stones** new release 'Paint It Black'. **George Harrison** of the **Beatles** has also been experimenting with the sitar,

and plans to visit India for lessons from Indian virtuoso **Ravi Shankar**.

Another contract dispute hits the headlines later in the month when it is revealed that producer Phil Spector is suing the **Righteous Brothers** for $3.5 million. He claims they were in breach of contract by leaving his label, Philles Records, and signing to Verve. "If they can get out of this contract," he seethes, "then no con-

From the same Greenwich Village folk scene that nurtured Bob Dylan, came Simon and Garfunkel. Without telling the duo, the record producer added rock guitar, organ and drums to their song, 'Sounds Of Silence'. Transformed from a haunting folk song into a contemporary folk-rock item it stormed the charts.

American-style open air rock festivals were becoming established in Britain by 1966. The National Jazz and Blues Festival at Windsor on August 1 provided not only the live debut of Eric Clapton's new band, Cream, but also a riot by Who fans.

tract in the record business is worth the paper it's printed on."

The flamboyant Spector's career is, however, in crisis. Having spent a staggering $22,000 to record **Ike and Tina Turner**'s 'River Deep Mountain High', and having then over-hyped the track to a point where the US music industry was sick to death of his continual self-aggrandizement, the song flops in America. It makes Number 3 in the UK but its failure at home is seen as a turning point in Spector's fortunes.

Bob Dylan plays the Royal Albert Hall in London on May 26, the day before the **Who**'s manager Robert Stigwood announces that wild **Keith Moon** has returned to the group after leaving for a week. His brief departure came about when he turned up so late for a show at Newbury's Rikki Tik club that an enraged **Pete Townshend** struck him over the head with his guitar.

Eric Clapton's departure from **John Mayall's Bluesbreakers** is more permanent. He is replaced on June 17 by the relatively unknown

Peter Green. British rock paper, *Melody Maker*, reports a week later that Clapton has formed a new trio, **Cream**, with **Ginger Baker**, acclaimed drummer in the **Graham Bond Organisation**, and **Jack Bruce**, highly rated bassist with **Manfred Mann**.

Local authorities accuse the **Rolling Stones** of desecrating the American flag, after an incident at their concert on July 6 in the War Memorial Hall, Syracuse, New York, where the group reportedly dragged the flag across the stage. This follows on from controversy late in June when 14 New York hotels banned the group from their premises.

Mystery shrouds the death of Texan rocker **Bobby Fuller** whose badly beaten body is found in his car in Los Angeles on July 18. The cause of death is given as asphyxiation. As leader of the **Bobby Fuller Four**, the dead man had found great success with a US Top 10 position in January this year for his single 'I Fought The Law'.

Georgie Fame scores his second UK Number 1 on July 21 with 'Get Away', a song which started life as a jingle for a petrol company. Three days later the Cavern re-opens in Liverpool with Prime Minister Harold Wilson in attendance.

Bob Dylan is reported to have been seriously injured in a motorcycle crash on July 29 near Woodstock, New York. He is rushed to Middletown Hospital with broken vertebrae, concussion and lacerations to the head.

The latest in a succession of group membership shuffles comes

with the announcement on July 6 that **Paul Jones** is leaving Manfred Mann to pursue a solo career. He is to be replaced by **Mike D'Abo**, formerly with **A Band Of Angels**. As well as remaining signed to HMV Records as a solo act, Jones is to star in a film, *Privilege*, about a rock idol who becomes the focus of a power-seeking religious cult. Other bands suffering personnel changes include the **Hollies** who have sacked 'unreliable' bass player Eric Haydock, the **Searchers** who have lost drummer Chris Curtis, and the **Nashville Teens** whose drummer Barry Jenkins left in March to replace John Steel in the **Animals**.

Cream make their live debut at the UK's National Jazz and Blues Festival at Windsor on the first day of August. Considerable damage is caused by fans who riot during the equipment-smashing section of the Who's performance. The **Yardbirds** should also have appeared but new guitarist **Jeff Beck** has contracted severe tonsillitis.

Just four days after topping the US charts on July 30 with their first hit 'Wild Thing', the **Troggs** have scored their first UK Number 1 with the equally primitive follow-up, 'With A Girl Like You'. The group, from Andover in Hampshire, reached the UK Number 2 position with Chip Taylor's song 'Wild Thing', and the follow-up has been written by Troggs' vocalist Reg Presley, who tells *Music Echo* "I write most of my stuff on buses and in taxis ... anywhere where I'm alone, yet surrounded by people." The Troggs' sound is characterized by simple chord progressions

MAY 6 : Moors murderers Ian Brady and Myra Hindley are sentenced to life imprisonment for the brutal killing of at least three children

1966 – HEADLINE NEWS

Byrds Flying High

Having closed 1965 with their second US Number 1, 'Turn Turn Turn', the **Byrds** were conspicuous by their absence from the Top 10 in 1966. Their biggest hit, the controversial 'Eight Miles High', stalled at 14 in America and 24 in the UK, while its follow-up 'Mr Spaceman' made even less impact.

But despite declining singles sales, poor live reviews and membership fluctuations, the Byrds could make a strong case for being the world's most influential band.

Having almost single-handedly invented the folk-rock genre with their jangling 12-string guitar and close-harmony version of 'Mr Tambourine Man', they stunned audiences at Hollywood's The Trip club in January 1966 by introducing jazzy elements and innovative eastern flavourings to their set.

Evolving almost faster than the fans could keep up with, the Byrds then introduced the notion of raga-rock via the unique guitar sounds on 'Eight Miles High'. Writing about their third album, 'Fifth Dimension', reviewers were tripping over themselves to coin new terms, including space-rock and jazz-rock, for the cornucopia of unusual sounds, styles and effects it contained.

And if imitation is the sincerest form of flattery, there's little doubt that the Byrds were flattered by the deliberately Byrd-like style of 'And Your Bird Can Sing' on the **Beatles**' album 'Revolver'.

However, a serious threat to the Byrds' future lay in the group's inner friction. It was well known that the quick-tempered **David Crosby** had threatened to leave on a number of occasions, and that studio sessions had ended in fist-fights. The first casualty of this turmoil was **Gene Clark**, who left the group in March. A surprisingly frank press release explained that he was "Tired of the travel, the hotels and the food. Tired of the pursuit of the most relentless autograph hunters, weary of the constant screaming. Bothered by the photographs and interviews and exhausted by the whole punishing scene."

Unless the Byrds could resolve their bitter internal rivalries, no matter how influential they had become, they were primed to implode before much longer.

and a solid thumping beat, noticeably out of step with the more sophisticated pop currently dominating the charts but, as **Graham Nash** of the **Hollies** observed, "They're so far behind, they're in front."

The **Lovin' Spoonful** finally make it to the US Number 1 slot on August 13 with 'Summer In The City', but the song gives them problems in live performance. "It turns out that while Steve is playing organ, poor John has to play piano, which he can only do by concentrating," explains guitarist Zal Yanovsky. "So Joe sings lead when we do it live."

September opens with yet another group, the **Kinks**, set to lose an original member. Bass guitarist Pete Quaife is quitting after injuries sustained in a road accident left him unable to perform for three months. Meanwhile **Georgie Fame** is parting company with his **Blue Flames**, and

Eric Burdon is left with little choice but to completely reform the **Animals**, now that guitarist Hilton Valentine and bassist Chas Chandler are moving into record production work.

Decca has unveiled a new label, Deram, which is described as a "hip label for groovy people". Deram's first release, on September 30, is 'I Love My Dog', the debut single of young singer-songwriter **Cat**

◀ Most significant among the bands re-asserting America's rock'n'roll credentials was the Byrds. Their late 1966 album 'Fifth Dimension' married the close harmonies of folk-rock to the distorted guitars of psychedelia, then threw in jazzy nuances, spacey electronics, taped sound samples and Indian scales for good measure.

Hey, hey we're the corporate puppets. When the Beatles hit their stride, the balance of power shifted from record companies to artists. Corporate rock'n'roll struck back with the creation of the Monkees. The Monkees were manufactured to be obedient Beatle robots, producing revenue without rocking the boat.

Stevens. Soon afterwards, another young singer-songwriter, **Neil Diamond**, makes his debut in the American Top 10 singles when 'Cherry Cherry' peaks at Number 6.

A new London-based underground newspaper, *International Times*, is launched on October 15 with a party featuring little known psychedelic band **Pink Floyd**.

The next day, **Joan Baez** is arrested and jailed for her participation in an anti-Vietnam demonstration at Oakland, California. Rather more positive news for women comes with the announcement that, after two Number 1 singles this year, their current LP release, 'Supremes A Go Go', has made Motown's **Supremes** the first girl group to top the album chart.

The banning of rock records,

Too Much Monkee Business?

The advert in *Variety* proclaimed "Madness! Auditions. Folk and rock musicians-singers for acting roles in a new TV series. Running parts for four insane boys, age 17-21".

Hollywood TV producers Bob Rafelson and Bert Schneider placed the ad late in 1965 as the first step towards a weekly series recreating the winning chemistry of the **Beatles**' *Hard Day's Night* movie.

437 hopefuls attended the auditions and, when a suitable four had been selected, they were taught how to act, how to improvize and, most importantly, how to mime to rock records. After an initial attempt to let the quartet create its own music, it was realized that though they each possessed a modicum of musical talent, they were a long way from being a group.

Fortunately, Don Kirshner, the entrepreneur who had virtually invented the Brill Building system of assembly-line pop hit manufacture in the late Fifties, had been put in overall control of the show's musical output. In June 1966, Kirschner flew out from New York with a dozen demo recordings by reliable songwriters including Goffin and King, **Neil Diamond** and Tommy Boyce and Bobby Hart.

The song chosen as the **Monkees**' first single, 'Last Train To Clarksville', was said to have been written by Boyce and Hart during a 20-minute coffee break. In the studio, during recording, Kirshner devised its distinctive "No-no-no" wails as a deliberate echo of the **Beatles**' famous 'Yeah-Yeah-Yeah'.

Despite a $100,000 launch campaign preceding the August 16

release of the single, it didn't dent the US Top 10 until a week after the first screening of *The Monkees* TV show on September 12. Eight weeks later, 'Last Train To Clarksville' was at Number 1.

The chosen four, **Michael Nesmith**, **Peter Tork**, **Mickey Dolenz** and **Davy Jones** became instant stars, and shops were flooded with Monkee merchandising from woolly hats like the one Mike wore in the show, to talking Monkee dolls, bracelets, lunch boxes, shirts, watches, chewing gum and pencil cases.

But it wasn't all plain sailing. Initial audience ratings were poor, largely because conservative middle America didn't immediately take to the idea that long-haired youths playing loud rock music deserved a regular weekly TV series. On top of which many TV critics panned the blatant plagiarism at the show's heart. A *Newsweek* critic observed, "Television is a medium which thrives on thievery ... Beatlemania has been exchanged for Monkeeshines."

Nevertheless, the show was soon attracting 10 million viewers across America every Monday evening, and the teenage audience responded to the anarchic spirit which came from much of the show being improvised. "We don't learn scripts," said Nesmith. "Hell, we don't even read 'em."

One of the biggest challenges facing the Monkees at the end of 1966 was whether the appeal of a pre-fabricated American-style Beatles could be exported back to Britain, where the TV series was not scheduled to be transmitted until early 1967.

which caused so much concern in 1965, hits headlines again in October when **Dave Dee, Dozy, Beaky, Mick & Tich**'s single 'Bend It' is banned by several American radio stations for being too suggestive. In Australia, the **Troggs**' 'I Can't Control Myself' has hit censorship problems because of the lyric "Your slacks are low and your hips are showing." Finally, the controversial novelty disc, 'They're Coming To Take Me Away Ha Haaa!' by **Napoleon XIV** has been banned by radio stations on both sides of the Atlantic because its lyric treats insanity in a manner regarded as tasteless.

Bob Dylan, who has been in hiding since his motorcycle accident in August, is tracked down in early November to a remote house in the wilds of Cape Cod, Massachussetts, where he is being visited regularly by

beat poet Allen Ginsberg.

Meanwhile, the good news that bassist Pete Quaife is rejoining the **Kinks**, is balanced by the bad news that **Jeff Beck** and **Jimmy Page** are both planning to quit the **Yardbirds** when their US tour ends on November 27.

The **Beach Boys**' new single, 'Good Vibrations', has reputedly been six months in the making at a cost of $16,000. It must be an enormous relief for the song's creator, **Brian Wilson**, when it tops the British charts on November 19, and repeats that success in his homeland by reaching the US Number 1 spot on December 10. 'Good Vibrations' is the first new material to have emerged from Wilson since the ground-breaking 'Pet Sounds' album in June. A complex multi-tracked studio creation, the album is said to be

impossible to perform live. "Brian Wilson lives in a world of flowers, butterflies and strawberry flavoured chewing gum," fumes the **Who**'s **Pete Townshend**. "His world has nothing to do with pop. Pop is going out on the road, getting drunk, meeting the kids."

Flamboyant American guitarist **Jimi Hendrix** releases his first single, 'Hey Joe', on December 16. Formerly based in New York, Hendrix moved to London on September 21 on the advice of former **Animal** Chas Chandler who has become his manager. His newly formed band, the **Experience**, plays its first London gig at the Bag o' Nails club on November 25.

The final edition of the UK's most exciting pop TV show, *Ready, Steady, Go!*, is broadcast on December 23. The UFO, formerly an Irish folk club, opens in London on the same night, featuring the increasingly popular cult band **Pink Floyd**.

Progressive rock and psychedelia dominate the scene in 1966, but it is sobering to note that, just as **Jim Reeves** hogged the UK Number 1 spot with the sentimental country ballad, 'Distant Drums', throughout October, so **Tom Jones** closes the year with a five-week run at the top for a similar composition, 'The Green Green Grass Of Home'. Jones is also said to be considering a 'substantial offer' from Motown to become their first UK artist. However, as 'Green Green Grass Of Home' is Decca's first million-selling single by a British artist, it is highly improbable that they will release Jones, whose contract runs until 1970.

JANUARY 21: George Harrison marries model/actress Patti Boyd.

FEBRUARY 7: The first edition of US rock mag Crawdaddy is published.

FEBRUARY 17: Nancy Sinatra, daughter of Frank, goes to Number 1 in the UK with 'These Boots Are Made For Walkin''.

MARCH 5: Staff Sgt Barry Sadler's patriotic Vietnam tribute, 'The Ballad of the Green Berets', ascends to the US Number 1 slot.

APRIL 15: The Rolling Stones LP, 'Aftermath', is the first to feature only Jagger and Richard compositions.

MAY 22: 16-year-old Bruce Springsteen makes his first recording, 'That's What You Get', with his group the Castiles in New Jersey.

OCTOBER 9: John Lennon meets Yoko Ono for the first time.

▲ The Aberfan disaster brought death to 144 children in a tiny Welsh mining village.

Beatles Not Bigger Than Jesus (Or Even Beach Boys)

1966 was not kind to the **Beaties**.

The year started well with 'Day Tripper' topping both the American and British singles charts, but dark clouds loomed on March 4 when the London *Evening Standard* published an interview in which **John Lennon** declared "Christianity will go. It will vanish and sink. I needn't argue about that, I'm right and will be proved right. We're more popular than Jesus Christ right now."

Plans for their next American tour were well advanced when, on June 15, Capitol Records in America issued their latest album, 'Yesterday and Today'. Its cover showed the four Beatles dressed as butchers holding meat-cleavers, with headless dolls and lumps of meat completing the image. Reaction in England, where the picture had been seen in both *New Musical Express* and *Disc*, was muted.

In America however, record distributors and retail outlets were horrified. The day after release, Capitol hastily recalled all 750,000 copies, abandoning a $250,000 advertising campaign and planning to re-issue the album in an innocuous sleeve.

John Lennon's observations on religion sparked Beatle burnings across America.

Ironically, on American Independence Day, July 4, the Beatles were attacked by angry crowds after accidentally snubbing the wife of President Marcos during a visit to Manila in the Phillipines.

Hardly had the butcher cover fuss died down, when Lennon's remarks in the *Evening Standard* were reprinted in *Datebook*, an American teen magazine. The response was immediate, especially in the deeply conservative Bible Belt. Local radio stations not only banned Beatle records, but actively promoted burnings of Beatle records, books, magazines and memorabilia. In South Carolina, the Grand Dragon of the Ku Klux Klan nailed Beatles' albums to burning crosses and vowed vengeance on the group if they played in America. In Cleveland, the Rev. Thurman H Babbs threatened to excommunicate members of his congregation who attended a Beatles' concert.

On August 3, the reaction spread worldwide when the South African Government banned all sales of Beatle records. The Vatican newspaper warned sternly that "some subjects must not be dealt with profanely, even in the world of beatniks." Across America, concert promoters were threatening to cancel shows.

That the affair could damage not only the Beatles but anyone associated with them became clear on August 10 when Capitol Records' share prices fell sharply on the New York Stock Exchange.

The next morning, on the first day of their US tour, a Beatles' press conference was hastily convened in Chicago. John Lennon began by attempting to explain that his comments were taken out of context and that "If I had said television was more popular than Jesus, I might have got away with it." It wasn't enough. The assembled mob demanded, and finally got, an apology from a deeply reluctant Lennon. "I'm not anti-God, anti-Christ or anti-religion. I was not saying we are greater or better ... I apologize, if that will make you happy."

That night's show went ahead, thankfully without incident, and three days later the Roman newspaper *Observatore Romano* ran an item accepting Lennon's apology. London's *Catholic Herald*, although branding the remark as "arrogant", even acknowledged that there was potentially some truth in it.

The Memphis concert proved the Beatles' most harrowing. Extra police were drafted in following reports that snipers would infiltrate the theatre, and bomb threats delayed the start of the show. In the event, the group suffered no greater harm than being pelted with rotten fruit and rubbish.

By August 29, the date of the final American show at Candlestick Park, San Francisco, it was being reported that the Beatles were threatening never to play live again.

It must have been some comfort when their next album, 'Revolver', topped the US charts in October, but the year still had another shock in store. Having acknowledged earlier in 1966 that 'Paperback Writer' was Paul's attempt to write something as complex as a **Beach Boys**' song, the Beatles had to face the fact that the Beach Boys had beaten them into second place as the World's Top Vocal Group in the annual *New Musical Express* Readers Poll.

1960s Crazes

Of all the fads, foibles and crazes that swept the Sixties, few caught on as universally as The Twist.

It started when Detroit R&B singer, **Hank Ballard**, devised a song to accompany the twisting movements of his backing band, the **Midnighters**. Ballard's version was not a hit, but when **Chubby Checker** performed his cover version on Dick Clark's influential American *Bandstand* television show, The Twist took off and went to Number 1 in September 1960.

Unlike almost any dance before it, The Twist required that partners did not touch. In Chubby's own words, it went like this: "Imagine you've just stepped out of the shower and you're drying your back with a big towel. At the same time, you're stubbing out a cigarette with your foot."

The craze moved out of the teen arena when actress Zsa Zsa Gabor was seen dancing to Chubby's hit at New York's celebrated Peppermint Lounge. On July 11 1961, an article in *Billboard* magazine revealed that The Twist was now popular among adults at dance club contests in Philadelphia.

Twist records quickly became a musical sub-genre of their own. There was 'The Peppermint Twist', 'The Latin Twist', 'Soul Twist', 'Ya Ya Twist', 'Twist And Shout', 'Twist Twist Senorita' and countless others. And it initiated a slew of new dance crazes from The Watusi to The Pony, The Hully Gully, The Fug, The Shake and The Jerk, to name only a few. Even the Addams Family butler had a dance, The Lurch, named after him.

But not everybody was convinced. Bishop Burke of the Catholic diocese at Buffalo, New York, banned The Twist on January 26 1962, ensuring it could not be heard or danced to in any Catholic school, parish or youth club. A community dance centre in Tampa, Florida followed suit soon after.

Journalist Beverley Nichols put his finger on what disturbed the establishment about The Twist when he wrote, 'The curious, perverted heart of it is that you dance it alone.'

As the decade closed, however, it became clear that The Twist had changed forever the way young people danced. Nobody waltzed at Woodstock. Nobody sambaed to the **Stones**. Virtually all subsequent free-form rock'n'roll writhing is clearly descended from The Twist.

Most of the crazes of the Sixties, however, were more ephemeral. The Hula Hoop, internationally omnipresent in the late Fifties, barely limped into the Sixties and passing fads such as bed-racing (1961), piano-smashing (1963), tab-collar shirts and hair-ironing (1965), lapel badges (1966) and granny glasses (1967) arrived in the heat of the summer only to disappear as the nights grew longer. A certain amount of body heat could be generated in those chilly evenings, however, by participating with as many like-minded spirits as possible in the craze for telephone booth cramming, which also evolved into a sub-category of cramming as many people as possible into a Mini car.

The success of the **Beatles** launched countless fashion trends, including long hair for boys, collarless Beatle jackets, cuban-heeled boots, the Royal Guardsmen look from 'Sgt the Royal Guardsmen look from 'Sgt Pepper' and the aforementioned granny glasses, popularized particularly by John Lennon.

The cult television series, *Batman*, almost rivalled the Beatles by spawning short-

▼ The Jerk was just one of the myriad bizarre dance crazes inspired by The Twist.

▲ In the Sixties the Batman myth became the epitome of high camp.

lived crazes for a hairstyle called the Bat Cut, a dance called The Batusi, and even discotheques modelled on the Batcave.

Some crazes remained locked within specific sections of society. Britain's clothes-crazy Mods, for example, exhibited an extraordinary fascination for decorating their motor scooters, most noticeably by the addition of several, or in some cases dozens of, extra mirrors.

Even hippie culture, whose motto 'Turn on, tune in, drop out' emphasized its origins as an alternative to fashion-conscious popular culture, ironically spawned a host of fashions, worn by teens who worked through the week and then became 'weekend hippies'. Paisley pattern shirts and dresses, body paint, beads, bells, flowers and Afghan jackets were hippie uniform, best seen en masse at free rock festivals.

The essence of a craze is that it arrives, enjoys a brief period of exceptional popularity, and then disappears whence it came. Some crazes, however, enjoy a different curve. They arrive, peak, and then settle in. The skateboard, for example, appeared in 1964 as a landlubber's version of the California-based surfing craze, but then took hold, especially among preteens, and still hasn't gone away.

The trend that skateboarders' older brothers seem keenest to see maintained is the miniskirt. The

New York Times pointed out in 1966 that the phrase 'nearly reaching the limits of decency' had been coined in 1927 for that year's knee-grazing skirts, but mothers across the free world were united in shrieking, "You're not going out wearing that pelmet!" at long-legged daughters who saw the Sixties mini as a symbol of women's liberation. When the clothing industry

tried to launch the midi in 1968, opinion polls revealed that as many as eight out of ten women had no intention of ditching their minis.

One fashion craze which was perceived as simultaneously erotic and liberated was the knee-length white boot. **Nancy Sinatra**'s 1966 hit record 'These Boots Are Made For Walkin'', with its line 'one of these days these boots are gonna walk all over you' must take some credit for this curious state of affairs, although sales were also given a huge boost by Jane Fonda in the 1967 movie *Barbarella*.

"These are crazy times," said New York fashion designer Norman Norell, as the decade ended. "We are searching for something. Women want change, and clothes can change."

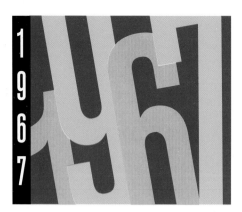

This is a turbulent year, a period of conflict for rock. The news is almost all bad, starting on January 3 when **Beach Boy Carl Wilson** refuses to join the US army after receiving his call-up papers. Just two days later, folk songwriter **Jesse Winchester** flees to Canada, also to avoid being drafted.

Florence Ballard quits the **Supremes** soon after, claiming to have been forced out. She is replaced by Cindy Birdsong, and the group name becomes **Diana Ross & The Supremes**. Ballard sues Motown, claiming she'd never been properly paid, but loses the case.

On January 13, British superstar **Cliff Richard** reveals his intention of retiring from showbusiness to teach religious instruction in schools and, on America's *Ed Sullivan Show,* two days later, **Mick Jagger** is obliged to mumble the lyrics of the new Stones' single 'Let's Spend The Night Together', because the network considers the song obscene.

The news isn't much better on the **Beatles**' front. On January 27, press reports state that they have turned down a $1 million offer from American promoter Sid Bernstein to play a single date at Shea Stadium.

Even the ever-smiling **Monkees**, with their debut album topping the

Billboard chart for the eleventh consecutive week, seem in despair. Guitarist Mike Nesmith unburdens himself to the *Saturday Evening Post*, "The music had nothing to do with us. It was totally dishonest. Do you know how debilitating it is to have to duplicate other people's records? That's what we were doing."

Acclaimed by many as the UK's Phil Spector, Joe Meek is found dead on February 3, with a bullet wound in the head, at his home studio in London's Holloway Road. Meek produced hits for **Lonnie Donegan**, the **Honeycombs**, **John Leyton**, **Mike Berry** and others but his single greatest achievement lay in writing and producing the **Tornados**' 'Telstar', a US and UK Number 1 hit in 1962. He is known to have been depressed

about his recent lack of success. A devoted **Buddy Holly** fan, it is seen as significant that his probable suicide coincides with the eighth anniversary of Holly's death.

The following Sunday, UK scandal sheet the *News Of The World* carries a story claiming that the **Moody Blues** have hosted drug parties attended by **Pete Townshend**, **Ginger Baker** and Mick Jagger. A week later, Mick Jagger and **Keith Richard** of the **Rolling Stones** plus **Marianne Faithfull** are busted for drugs at Redlands, Richard's home in West Wittering, Sussex.

Disgraced trouser-splitter **PJ Proby** has, meanwhile, returned home to Los Angeles where he is obliged to file for bankruptcy in Los Angeles, listing debts of £180,000

Turn on, tune in, drop out. San Francisco's hippie counter-culture was exported worldwide in 1967, and became a dominant force not only in rock music but in shaping the morality and philosophy of an emerging generation.

Mick Jagger and Marianne Faithfull run the paparazzi gauntlet as they leave court after their drug bust.

Haight Spells Love

While 'Swinging London' vibrated to the mod sound of the **Who** and the **Small Faces**, an entirely different youth scene had developed half a world away. It was all Love and Peace on the west coast of America.

The hits of 1967, including 'San Francisco (Be Sure To Wear Flowers In Your Hair)' by **Scott McKenzie**, 'Let's Go To San Francisco' by the **Flowerpot Men** and 'San Franciscan Nights' by **Eric Burdon**, advertised a counter-culture which had been evolving since 1965.

Centred on San Francisco's Haight Ashbury district, nicknamed The Hashbury, with its elegantly crumbling wooden Victorian houses, a new generation inspired by the beatniks of the Fifties came into being. They called themselves hippies, and their gurus were rock bands with idiosyncratic names such as the **Grateful Dead**, **Jefferson Airplane** and **Quicksilver Messenger Service**.

One striking feature of this counter-culture was its rejection of traditional American consumer society ethics. Hippies didn't work, except in their own communes. They took drugs openly and some indulged in group sex. Many hippie rock concerts were free. Held either outdoors, or in huge ballrooms heavy with marijuana smoke, and illuminated by complex projections of slides and films known as light-shows, these concerts could be traced back to October 16 1965. This was when the Hashbury's Family Dog commune held its first show at Longshoreman's Hall featuring the **Charlatans**, said to have been San Francisco's first hippie band, plus the **Great Society** and Jefferson Airplane.

Just over a month later, author Ken Kesey and his entourage, known as the Merry Pranksters, held the first Acid Test at The Longshoreman's. While the Grateful Dead played and the light-show flashed, the hallucinatory drug LSD (known as acid) was given out to the audience. "Quite often several things would be going on at once," explained **Jerry Garcia**, guitarist with the Grateful Dead. "There was this incredible cross-interference and weirdness."

On January 14 1967, 20,000 hippies showed up for the first Human Be-In and Gathering of the Tribes, an open-air event at the Polo Grounds in Golden Gate Park. Opened by LSD-advocate Timothy Leary chanting his notorious slogan "Turn on, tune in, drop out", it featured music by Jefferson Airplane, **Big Brother & The Holding Company** and Quicksilver Messenger Service.

Responding to the new attitude on April 7 veteran DJ Tom 'Big Daddy' Donohue initiated 'progressive FM radio' on the city's KMPX station. Ignoring the current pop charts and favouring album tracks, regardless of length. The format proved popular.

A week later the area's increasing celebrity status was confirmed when the Greyhound Bus Co announced plans to run tourist trips through Haight Ashbury. Inevitably, media attention also turned hippie culture into a fashion. Soon, many of the kids attending the expensive shows at the Fillmore or Avalon Ballrooms, supposedly palaces of psychedelic rock culture, were "weekend hippies", holding down steady jobs throughout the week, and dressing up when Friday night came around.

Writing in the *New York Times* magazine on May 14, journalist Hunter S Thompson declared, "The Hashbury is the new capital of what is rapidly becoming a drug culture ... Love is the password, but paranoia is the style." In other words, hippies saw drugs as a passport to bliss, but they were also a ticket to jail. Thompson went on to suggest that the Hashbury was merely the tip of an iceberg because "drugs, orgies and freak-outs were almost as common to a much larger and more discreet" cross-section of "respectable" San Franciscans.

Even though **George Harrison** visited Haight Ashbury on August 8 and conferred the **Beatles**' stamp of approval on the scene, the end was already in sight. In October, disillusioned flower children held the Death of Hippie event, featuring a mock funeral to protest at the commercialization of their way of life.

As 1967 drew to a close, many of the first generation hippies had moved out of the San Francisco area. Ed Denson, manager of rock band **Country Joe & The Fish** captured the mood when he said, "I'm very pessimistic. Most of the hippies I know don't really understand what kind of a world they're living in. If they were more realistic, they'd stand a better chance of surviving."

MAR 18 · liberian oil tanker, the Torrey Canyon, runs aground off the southern English coast causing the most severe ecological disaster of the era

1967 · HEADLINE NEWS

including £50,000 to the UK tax authorities.

There's a happier return home for singing group the **Bee Gees**, led by the brothers Barry, Maurice and Robin Gibb. Already stars in their adopted home, Australia, they returned to the UK earlier this month to be signed up by impressario Robert Stigwood on February 24. Things look good too for former **Yardbird Jeff Beck** who unveils his new **Jeff Beck Group**, featuring vocalist **Rod Stewart**, bassist **Ron Wood** and drummer **Aynsley Dunbar**, at their UK debut in London on March 3.

It is revealed on March 11 that **Lennon and McCartney**'s 1965 song 'Yesterday' has become the most covered number ever with 446 different recordings by other artists. A week later their composition

'Michelle' picks up the Ivor Novello Award for most performed song of 1966. In America, though, the **Beatles**' 'Penny Lane' is ousted from the top of the US charts by the **Turtles**' 'Happy Together' on March 25, the same day on which the **Who** and **Cream** both arrive in America for their concert debuts.

In the wake of 'I'm A Man', their biggest US hit yet, brothers **Stevie** and **Muff Winwood** quit the **Spencer Davis Group** on April 2, at the Empire Theatre, Liverpool. Winwood is already forming a new band, as yet unnamed, with Jim Capaldi, Chris Wood and Dave Mason.

With 'Hi Ho Silver Lining' climbing

the UK singles charts, **Jeff Beck** admits on April 14 that he is embarrassed by his vocal performance, especially when compared with his usual frontman, **Rod Stewart**. This day also sees Polydor release 'New York Mining Disaster 1941', the debut single by the Bee Gees. The accompanying press release proclaims them to be 'The Most Significant Talent Since The Beatles'.

Guided by the LSD-induced visions of Syd Barrett, the band that mattered most in London during 1967 was Pink Floyd. For a few brief months they made avant-garde experimental psychedelic rock that was also acceptable chart material. Inevitably, though, Barrett was heading for disaster.

Sgt Pepper

Even before it was released on 1 June, the **Beatles**' long-awaited new album, 'Sgt Pepper's Lonely Hearts Club Band', was causing controversy. On May 27, the album's final track, 'A Day In The Life', was banned by BBC TV because of presumed drug references.

Three days after 'Pepper' hit the record store shelves, journalist Derek Jewell observed in his *Sunday Times* review that "There won't be much dancing done to 'Pepper'. The Beatles are now producing performances, not music for frugging to. Will the kids follow?"

John Lennon hoped they would. "The people who have bought our records in the past must realize that we couldn't go on making the same type forever," he said. "We must change. and I believe those people know this."

Group members were said to be concerned about reactions to the album which, with its array of unusual new sounds, caused some critics to wonder if the Beatles were moving too fast for their fans. Richard Goldstein in the *New York Times* came down hardest, finding it "busy, hip and cluttered."

"Whether the album is their best yet," mused Allen Evans in the *New Musical Express*, "I wouldn't like to say ... Whether it was worth the five months it took to make, I would argue."

In fact, 'Sgt Pepper' took six months to record at a cost of £25,000, and involving over 700 hours of studio time. It was EMI's most expensive production to date. Even the album's cover was a marathon creation. A life-sized three dimensional collage featuring the real Beatles surrounded by dozens of their heroes, it was assembled and photographed by artist Peter Blake. Brian Epstein's assistant, Peter Brown, told the *Daily Express* "It took me weeks of telephone calls to celebrities all over the world to get permission to use their photographs. Most were surprised but quite happy when I approached them. Stockhausen, for instance, turned out to be quite a fan of the Beatles."

But neither the critics' doubts nor the Beatles' fears had an effect on sales. 'Sgt Pepper' entered the UK album charts at the top, having sold 250,000 copies in one week, and stayed there for 22 weeks.

Jimi Hendrix

Having entered the national consciousness at the end of 1966 with his stunning debut single 'Hey Joe', **Jimi Hendrix** went on to become 1967's most exciting new artist.

An already impressive live reputation was boosted immeasurably on January 24 when no less an authority than **Mick Jagger** declared that Hendrix's stage show was "the most sexual thing I've seen in a long time." *Rave* magazine was a little more specific when it said, "Jimi is a wild player to watch on stage. He plays guitar with his hands, his feet and his teeth. What's more, he can play two guitars at once. They're calling him the negro Bob Dylan round the clubs."

On March 31, a week after releasing his second single, 'Purple Haze', Hendrix hit the headlines again when he climaxed a blistering show at London's Finsbury Park Astoria by setting fire to his guitar, sustaining burns to his hand in the process.

By May 20, Hendrix had signed a US deal with Reprise Records, securing an advance of $50,000. The company chose to market him in America as "the greatest talent since the Rolling Stones."

Such heady acclaim did him no good on June 10, however, when he was refused admittance to Kew Gardens in London because, according to a spokesman, "people in fancy dress are not allowed."

In July, hardly had Hendrix started his first American tour – oddly enough supporting the **Monkees** – than he found himself the focus of a conservative backlash in the media. The Daughters of the American Revolution attacked his stage performance for exactly the same reasons as Jagger had praised it.

Just seven dates into the tour, on July 22, Hendrix quit. His manager, former Animal Chas Chandler, explained, "There had been many protests and a lot of parents were up in arms because the Monkees audience is primarily in the 7-12 age group. He was asked to cool his act but felt he could not co-operate, as it was like asking him to play with one hand. He talked it over with the Monkees and decided to quit."

He remained in America headlining club dates. His third single, 'The Wind Cries Mary', was another Top 10 hit in the UK and although he would never emulate his British singles success at home, by the end of the year it was beginning to move up the US charts.

▲ Arguably the most innovative rock guitarist who ever lived, it is too often overlooked that Jimi Hendrix was also an intelligent lyricist, a fine tunesmith and a consummate showman whose flair for self-promotion brought him immeasurably more attention than his musical virtuosity.

An all-night underground concert, *The 14 Hour Technicolor Dream*, draws 10,000 groovers to London's Alexandra Palace on April 29 with **Pink Floyd**, the **Move**, the **Pretty Things** and **John's Children** among the 41 bands performing. The event, including poetry readings, a helter-skelter and films, is a benefit for the underground newspaper *International Times* which was recently raided by police.

On May 2, Capitol Records announce that the **Beach Boys** have abandoned their long-awaited new album, 'Smile'. The following day Beach Boy **Carl Wilson** appears in court on draft evasion charges.

It is also announced on May 3 that the **Walker Brothers** are splitting to pursue solo careers. The revelation ends a period of confusion. **Scott Walker** claimed a month ago that the next Walker tour could be their last but **John Walker** immediately denied it. Now, the band's agent Harold Davidson says, "They have accomplished as much as possible as a group, and their future progress lies in the freedom to exploit their individual talents."

There seems to be more harmony around in California on June 10, when **Jefferson Airplane**, the **Doors**, the **Byrds**, **Smokey Robinson**, **Country Joe & The Fish** and others attract 15,000 fans to Mount Tamalpais, California for the *Fantasy Faire and Magic Mountain Music Fest*.

The biggest festival of the year must be Monterey Pop. Organized largely by **John Phillips** of the **Mamas & The Papas**, it opens on June 16, filling three days of California sunshine with music by **Jimi Hendrix**, **Janis Joplin**, the **Who**, the Byrds, **Otis Redding**, the **Animals**, **Canned Heat**, **Simon and Garfunkel**, **Buffalo Springfield**, Country Joe & The Fish and more.

The **Young Rascals** return to the US Number 1 spot with 'Groovin'' on June 17, after being ousted for two weeks by the success of **Aretha Franklin**'s version of the Otis Redding song 'Respect'. 'Groovin''

1967 - HEADLINE NEWS | JUN 5 : The Six Day War between Israel and Egypt begins

Prior to skipping the light fandango and turning cartwheels across the floor, Procul Harum had been a no-nonsense Southend R&B band. The move from R&B to psychedelia was shared by countless musicians of the era, including Pink Floyd, Jimi Hendrix Experience and Cream.

first went to Number 1 on May 20, was knocked off on June 3, then re-appeared to regain its crown.

On June 19, **Paul McCartney** admits to having taken LSD and six days later the **Beatles** perform 'All You Need Is Love' on TV as part of *Our World*, the first international television link-up. Seated beatifically at their feet in the studio are **Mick Jagger**, **Brian Jones** and **Marianne Faithfull**.

Understandably, Mick Jagger looks less content on June 29 when he and **Keith Richard** are sentenced to three months' imprisonment for drug offences. This prompts an editorial, headlined Who Breaks A Butterfly On A Wheel?, by William Rees-Mogg of the *Times*. "It should be the particular quality of British justice to ensure that Mr Jagger is treated exactly the same as anyone else, no better and no worse," writes Rees-Mogg. "There must remain a suspicion in this case that Mr Jagger

received a more severe sentence than would have been thought proper for any purely anonymous young man."

Before Jagger and Richard are freed on appeal on the 29, July sees a string of classic chart toppers. The **Association** take over the US Number 1 spot with 'Windy' for four weeks starting on the first day of the month. **Procol Harum** end a six-week run at Number 1 in the UK with 'A Whiter Shade Of Pale' on July 15. In the last week of the month, 'Light My Fire' by the **Doors** begins a three-week run at the top of the US charts.

Pink Floyd's first album, 'The Piper At The Gates Of Dawn', is released on August 5. Its title, chosen by leader **Syd Barrett**, comes from Kenneth Graham's children's novel *Wind In The Willows*.

Another singer who revels in literary allusion, **Van Morrison**, releases his first solo single, 'Brown Eyed Girl', in America on August 5. Four

days later, having played their first major date two weeks before at the Village Theatre in their native New York, **Vanilla Fudge** find success in the UK when their heavy version of the **Supremes**' hit, 'You Keep Me Hanging On', enters the charts.

The legal loophole which allowed pirate broadcasters to transmit from waters off the UK is plugged on August 15 by the new Marine Offences Act. When Radio London closed down the previous day, it chose the Beatles' 'A Day In The Life', banned by the BBC, as its parting shot. Radio Caroline continues to broadcast.

At Patti Harrison's suggestion, on August 26 the Beatles, Mick Jagger and Marianne Faithfull go to Bangor in Wales to meet the Maharishi Mahesh Yogi, an Indian guru preaching the benefits of transcendental meditation. Their visit is cut short the following day by news that Beatles' manager Brian Epstein has been

 Viva Las Vegas! Elvis marries Priscilla.

FEBRUARY 2: The Bee Gees return to England, after achieving stardom in Australia.

FEBRUARY 8: Peter and Gordon split after a career which has generated 14 US hits.

FEBRUARY 27: Pink Floyd's debut single, 'Arnold Layne', is released.

MAY 1: Elvis Presley marries Priscilla Beaulieu in Las Vegas.

JULY 24: The Times runs a full-page ad advocating the legalization of marijuana, signed by all four Beatles and other celebrities.

AUGUST 12: Fleetwood Mac make their debut at the National Jazz and Blues Festival, Windsor, England.

NOVEMBER 9: America's first national rock music periodical, Rolling Stone, is published.

DECEMBER 10: The Steve Miller Band signs a record $750,000 contract with Capitol Records.

found dead in bed at his home In Chapel Street, Belgravia.

Like Jagger before him, **Jim Morrison** of the **Doors** is asked to amend the lyric of a song for its September 17 airing on the *Ed Sullivan Show*. Morrison ignores Sullivan and the offending line "Girl we couldn't get much higher" in 'Light My Fire' is transmitted live and intact.

The launch of Radio 1, the BBC's new pop music station, arrives on the last day of the month. The new station, designed to replace the recently outlawed pirate radio stations, is based on American radio formats. Former pirate DJ Tony Blackburn opens proceedings by playing the **Move**'s latest single, 'Flowers In the Rain'. "The BBC have succeeded to a certain extent," admits Ted Allbury, of pirate station Radio 390, "but Radio 1 is like seeing your mother dancing the frug. She may do it perfectly well, but you wish she wouldn't behave like that."

The **Bee Gees**' 'Massachusetts'

takes the Number 1 slot in the UK on October 14. In the same week, Bee Gee **Barry Gibb**, reviewing the new **Troggs** single 'Love Is All Around' for *Melody Maker*, declares, "I think the Troggs have got themselves into a bit of a rut and they're trying to get out of it. Their image is fading, the sexual bit has had it."

According to their producer Lou Adler, the **Mamas & The Papas** are on "an indefinite leave of absence." Having unexpectedly cancelled live dates in London and Paris, the group have also abandoned their half-completed new album. Adler says they are taking a break to seek inspiration and will not record "until they feel more creative." Industry speculation is rife that vocalist Denny Doherty is leaving the group and may be replaced by **Scott McKenzie**, whose recent hit 'San Francisco' was written by Papa John Phillips.

Author Norman Mailer is among those arrested when Greenwich Village anarchist rock poets the **Fugs** lead a massive peace march on the Pentagon on October 21. Aided and abetted by beat poet Allen Ginsberg and underground film-maker Kenneth Anger, the Fugs attempt to exorcize evil spirits from the Pentagon by chanting 'Out Demons Out' and by placing flowers in the barrels of the rifles brandished against them by National Guardsmen.

A more whimsical brush with authority comes on November 2, when the **Move** appear in court in

London, following a suit filed by British Prime Minister Harold Wilson. To promote their single 'Flowers In The Rain', they had used a postcard showing the PM naked in bed.

During a concert by the Doors in New Haven, Connecticut on December 9, a security man, mistakes singer Jim Morrison for a fan and manhandles him. When Morrison strikes out in retaliation, he is maced. Later, on stage, Morrison begins a lengthy tirade against police brutality, which causes police to turn on the house lights, and drag him off. He is arrested and charged with breach of the peace and resisting arrest.

Otis Redding and four of his group the **Bar Kays** perish on December 10, when their plane crashes into Lake Monoma, Wisconsin. Redding's friend and Stax label-mate **Eddie Floyd** says "I can only say that I've lost my brother. We, as soul brothers, are as one."

The **Beatles**' *Magical Mystery Tour* is screened by the BBC on December 26 to disappointing reviews. Even devoted Beatle fans are confused by the seemingly plotless travels of a psychedelically painted bus through the south of England.

On December 29, only weeks after the release of 'Mr Fantasy', the debut album from Stevie Winwood's new group **Traffic**, it is revealed that Dave Mason has quit the band. The year closes with **Gladys Knight** reaching the Number 2 position in the US with 'I Heard It Through The Grapevine', held from the top by the Beatles' 'Hello Goodbye'.

DEC 3: Dr. Christian Barnard performs the first heart transplant

1967 - HEADLINE NEWS

Unquestionably the most successful and influential group of the 1960s, the **Beatles** radically changed the way popular music was made.

After several years of learning their craft in the rock clubs of Liverpool and seedy strip joints of Hamburg, the Beatles signed to Parlophone Records in 1962. By adding their uniquely British gifts to elements learned from the American rock'n'roll and soul records they'd grown up with, the group's songwriting team of **John Lennon** and **Paul McCartney** fashioned a sequence of pop hits which were hard-edged but always melodic, swathed in close harmonies and shot through with catchy guitar hooks from **George Harrison**.

They became the first British group to sell rock music back to America. Indeed, their records sold so well abroad that Prime Minister Sir Alec Douglas-Home dubbed them "my secret weapon", and in 1965 they were awarded MBEs for their contribution to the British economy. Their influence by now had extended beyond the realm of music into fashion, humour and even lifestyle for Sixties teens. They gave up performing in late 1966 when audiences at their concerts were so large and noisy that the group could not hear itself perform.

The innovative 'Sgt Pepper's Lonely Hearts Club Band' (1967) is usually considered to be their greatest recording, but the peak of their song-writing, performing and arranging skills probably came earlier on albums like 'Rubber Soul' (1965) and 'Revolver' (1966). The influence of their record producer, George Martin, is however most evident on 'Sgt Pepper'. Unlike the Beatles, Martin was musically trained, and years of producing comedy records for EMI had made him adept at devising unusual new sounds, a skill which proved invaluable when turning the Beatles' experimental ideas into sonic reality on 'Sgt Pepper'.

After Pepper, their music became deliberately less complex, seeking a return to roots values. As the Sixties ended, the group had grown apart, a process speeded by drug excesses, personal disagreements, jealousy and the inevitable pressures of success. Their final albums contained flashes of individual brilliance, but the group was no more.

When Tony Palmer wrote in *The Observer* in 1969 that they were "the greatest songwriters since Schubert", it was almost their epitaph. McCartney quit in April 1970, and the others agreed to call it a day, although bitter legal squabbles contin-

▼ The Fab Four rescued British rock from oblivion.

ued for years after.

Their legacy, apart from a catalogue of classic songs, could be seen in the imitative work of groups like **Electric Light Orchestra**, the **Raspberries** and scores of others who aspired to be the new Beatles. After the Beatles, most rock artists wrote their own material, because it was considered distinctly second-rate to be merely an interpreter of songs written by others. The stranglehold of Tin Pan Alley and the Brill Building was ended.

McCartney and Harrison remained successful in solo careers, as was Lennon until his murder in 1980.

◀ With perfect timing, the Beatles ended when the decade did.

The Beatles

The Rolling Stones

From being white R&B imitators in small London clubs, the **Stones** have rolled on to become the self-proclaimed "greatest rock'n'roll band in the world".

The minimal success of their raw, early singles was massaged into wider popularity by a carefully planned image of being wilder than the **Beatles**. The image was first lent credence by a number of contrived publicity stunts, and later by genuine drug busts. Nevertheless, like the Beatles, the group pursued a recording career of increasing musical sophistication, dabbling in ethnic sounds and psychedelia until the death of rhythm guitarist **Brian Jones** in 1969. Soon after, they returned to an earthy simplicity which has been their trademark ever since. When Jones' successor, Mick Taylor, proved too flashy, he was replaced by former **Faces** member **Ron Wood**, whose chunky rhythmic sense perfectly complemented **Keith Richard**'s.

Whereas the core of the Beatles' music was usually melodic, the classic Stones sound is built primarily on Richard's endless rhythmic variations of the three chord trick at the heart of dance party hits like 'Brown Sugar' and 'Honky Tonk Women'. Around these patterns, occasionally shaded by country stylings, he and vocalist **Mick Jagger** construct functional melodies, to carry lyrics often infused with primitive sexuality, driven on a metronomic dance beat by drummer **Charlie Watts**.

The group's continuing popularity with successive generations is founded on its ability to provide a spectacular and enjoyable live show, teased along by a seemingly endless public appetite for the latest sexual indiscretions of Jagger and drug excesses of Richard.

▼ Have we seen your mother, baby! If so, one of us may be your father.

▲ Quite why these five neat, tidy lads provoked such outrage in the mid-Sixties remains a mystery.

'We're so pretty, oh so pretty'

The Seventies

1970s
Lloyd Bradley

It seems remarkable that in just 10 years music could develop from the innocence of **Herman's Hermits**' 'Years May Come, Years May Go' and the **Jackson 5**'s 'The Love You Save', to the future shock of **Gary Numan**'s 'Are Friends Electric' and the **Sugarhill Gang**'s 'Rapper's Delight'. Yet it happened. During the Seventies, popular music continued to evolve with all the frantic energy it had shown in the decade before, though its progress was obscured by the way that it fragmented in myriad directions. Rock'n'roll came of age, shucked off its hippie associations and become accepted as part of the fabric of modern society. A western economy that allowed artists to shift phenomenal amounts of records made the Seventies a time of colossal growth for the music industry, and acts were afforded unlimited freedom to explore their art. If the result was sometimes wanton self-indulgence, it was also a time of great creative ferment.

Curiously, much of this turmoil was a reaction to one aspect of rock that refused to change. The intense, rather humourless, heads-down approach so common at the decade's start provoked glam rock: a jubilant escape from seriousness, patched jeans and too many joints on a Saturday night. Then came punk, reclaiming music for 'the kids' by putting attitude and exuberance before expertise. Both glam and punk regenerated rock as a saleable commodity by adding flash and sting to pop music and it was the lasting effects of both styles that produced such durable acts as **Queen**, **Rod Stewart**, **Elton John**, the **Police** and **U2**. With its theatrical excess and gender-bending posturing, glam also inspired the 'new romantics' who emerged at the dawn of the Eighties. Rap, too, was reactive — an urban backlash against the disco music which, thanks to the likes of Gamble & Huff, had once appeared to be rescuing soul music from the Motown rut, but had then hi-jacked it completely, steering it towards a void called **Boney M.**

More than anything, the Seventies was littered with brief fads that created entertainment categories all of their own. **Marvin**'s 'What's Going On', **Bowie**'s 'Aladdin Sane', 2-Tone, pub-rock, **Marley**'s 'Catch A Fire', the novelty records of TV stars, the plethora of Christmas records. You could almost forgive the Seventies for flared trousers.

◄ The Sex Pistols: 'Pretty Vacant'

JAN 1 : The age of majority in the UK is reduced from 21 to 18. • JAN 23 : The first Jumbo Jet flies from New York to London

1970 - HEADLINE NEWS

Change was the key word as the new decade rolled around – having survived the growing pains of the Sixties, rock music was finally coming of age. Understandable really. America's first teenagers were now thirtysomethings, and a new generation of teenagers had grown up with wall-to-wall music, accepting it as a natural part of their lives. Now they wanted something different.

At the beginning of the Seventies, pop music too was about to enter adolescence, torn between taking itself too seriously and the need to let off steam. Perhaps the biggest single difference between rock music in the years 1960 and 1970 was that, post-Woodstock and post-Altamont, it had become established as a serious art form and means of social expression, part of the soundtrack to modern life. And this was in spite of the credibility-threatening presence of **Rolf Harris** at Number 1 in the UK singles chart all through January with the excruciating Christmas singalonga 'Two Little Boys'.

Immediate evidence of a new 'this is grown up music'-type approach appears in January, with the release of **Deep Purple**'s album 'Concerto For Group And Orchestra'. Every bit as pompous and overbearing as the title suggests, it is a recording of the Purps in concert with

Diana Ross and the Supremes were no more by the end of January.

the Royal Philharmonic at London's Royal Albert Hall, recorded for BBC Radio the previous September. The suite was written by organist Jon Lord, apparently a frustrated classicist and never altogether happy living in the shadow of guitarist Ritchie Blackmore's more-prolific but less-complex songwriting. The album is intended as a one-off, to demonstrate just how far rock is capable of progressing – 'the new classical music' as many people believe – but it sells in sufficient quantities to give the group their first chart LP. Elsewhere the traditional guitar/ bass/drum combo comes under threat from new technology when, in January, an American electronics engineer puts on sale to the public the device that has been available professionally, in prototype form, for a year. Suddenly the entire sound and structure of rock music-as-we-know-and-love-it is under threat: **Dr Robert Moog** has invented the synthesizer.

Line-up changes figure too. At New York's Fillmore East on New Year's Eve, **Jimi Hendrix** takes the stage with the **Band Of Gypsies**: Buddy Miles (drums), Billy Cox (bass). As the guitarist's first all-black unit, it's widely assumed to be some sort of exploration of his jazz/blues roots, but the group only lasts as long as the second number of the next night's show at a peace

Jimi Hendrix's Band Of Gypsies didn't make it past their second show.

rally in Madison Square Garden. With the words "Sorry, we just can't get it together", Hendrix stalks off stage and later announces he is dissatisfied with Miles. He will re-recruit drummer Mitch Mitchell for subsequent concerts and his last officially sanctioned studio recording, 'The Cry Of Love', naming the group the **New Experience**.

In Las Vegas, **Diana Ross** plays her last show with the **Supremes** and introduces her replacement Jean 'Sister Of Heavyweight Boxing Champion Ernie' Terrell. In Los Angeles, **Eric Burdon** is hoping to break into the movies but happens across the Long Beach funk band Night Shift. He renames them **War**, they record two albums and tour Europe together, then he splits. Soon, like so many musicians Burdon once worked with, they're doing much better than the one-time Animal. In the UK, **Blind Faith** break up after one LP, one UK show and one very lucrative US tour. **Eric Clapton** goes on the road with **Delaney & Bonnie**, while **Steve Winwood** starts work on his Mad Shadows solo project. He calls in Jim Capaldi and Chris Wood for session work, which is so successful that the threesome formalize their reunion with the album 'John Barleycorn Must Die', **Traffic**'s finest hour.

Some things never change though. **Keith Moon**'s extracurricular activity continues to attract attention: after being attacked outside a nightclub in the UK, drummer Moon – who never learned to drive – tries to escape in his Rolls Royce, running

The Voice Of Young America: The Jackson 5's first four releases sold a total of 15 million.

The Jackson Five

Given pop stars' built-in obsolescence, it seems remarkable that the singer who made the biggest impact in 1970 would still be making world headlines almost a quarter of a century later. But **Michael Jackson**, the 11-year-old frontman of the **Jackson 5**, was no ordinary pop star. During that first year with Motown Records the group spent 13 weeks at Number 1 in the US singles charts as their four releases – 'I Want You Back', 'ABC', 'The Love You Save' and 'I'll Be There' – sold in excess of 15 million copies. Each of their three 1970 albums went Top 10 in the USA. And they re-established the company as the Voice Of Young America.

In 1970 the group consisted of Sigmund Jackson aka Jackie (then 19), Toriano aka Tito (17), Jermaine (16), Marlon (13) and Michael, but the three oldest boys had already been performing for eight years – known as the Jackson Family, their three-part harmonies were augmented by cousins Johnny Jackson and Ronnie Rancifer. Managed and coached by their father Joe, a crane driver who once played guitar with the **Falcons** (the Detroit R&B band that at one time or another featured **Eddie Floyd**, Levi Stubbs' brother Joe and a teenage **Wilson Pickett** as lead singers), the quintet made a living in the bars and clubs around their hometown of Gary, Indiana. It wasn't until 1964 that Marlon and Michael – at seven and five, respectively – were judged ready to enter showbusiness and joined

the vocal line-up, relegating their cousins to pianist and drummer. The name was changed to the Jackson 5 and, by winning talent contests, they started to establish themselves beyond Gary's city limits.

Although legend has it that **Diana Ross** 'discovered' the Jackson 5, credit for such scouting actually goes to **Gladys Knight**. In 1967, after they had supported her and the **Pips** at a concert in Indiana, she wrote to label owner Berry Gordy suggesting he check them out. A year later – after the Jackson 5 had performed as far afield as New York City, where they won Amateur Night at Harlem's Apollo Theatre and released an unsuccessful single, 'Big Boy', on a local label – the group were noticed by another Motown act, **Bobby Taylor & The Vancouvers**, who also recommended them. In June 1969, Berry Gordy and Diana Ross attended a fund-raising concert for Gary's mayor, the brothers were on the bill and Gordy was sufficiently impressed to sign them on the spot. Within weeks, the family had moved to California for 'grooming' and rehearsals; in October their first live performance as a Motown act was at the Hollywood Palace as special guests of headliners **Diana Ross & The Supremes**. Hence the confusion – a mix up that was compounded by their first album being called 'Diana Ross Presents The Jackson 5'. The corporate thinking was that they'd need this glamour-by-association factor to give them a leg-up.

MAY 4 : Four students at Kent State University, Ohio, are shot dead by National Guardsmen during an anti-Vietnam demonstration

1970 - HEADLINE NEWS

over and killing his chauffeur. Likewise rock's ability to offend the Establishment remains intact: **John Lennon**'s exhibition of erotic lithographs at the London Arts Gallery is confiscated by the police as obscene (in April, magistrates will reject the police case); **Led Zeppelin** are refused entry to Singapore because their hair is too long, then they have to rename themselves to play in Copenhagen after Count Von Zeppelin objects to their use of his family name – they perform as the Nobs.

As one teen sensation fades, so another takes its place. Mike Nesmith follows Peter Tork's lead and quits **Monkee**-in' around; Davy Jones and Mickey Dolenz continue recording but, when the aptly-titled 'Changes' album flops in June, they too will call it a day. The end of the Monkees signifies the end of the first post-hippie mainstream teen idols – when the group hit big three years previously, they were the earliest high-profile example of hippie values made presentable for television and marketed for a younger generation of record buyers. The wait for their replacements isn't too long either. As

Nesmith is handing in his notice, the first Motown single by the **Jackson Five**, 'I Want You Back', is Number 1 in the US. It will stay there for a month, selling over one million copies. A black group who appeared to be breaking the traditional, slick Motown mould with their hippie clothes and afros – the fact that they are accepted so readily by mainstream America illustrates how the country is slowly coming to accept its own cultural diversity.

Meanwhile, at the other end of the spectrum, the idea of the deep and meaningful, intensely-musical supergroup has survived the demise of **Blind Faith**. Greg Lake has quit **King Crimson** to form **Emerson, Lake & Palmer**, with the **Nice**'s Keith Emerson and Carl Palmer, late of **Atomic Rooster**, their mission to continue to advance the cause of rock-as-serious-music with quasi-classical displays of virtuoso musicianship; and **Crosby, Stills, Nash & Young**'s debut album 'Deja Vu', an over-elaborate set of melodic country rock (Stephen Stills had been taking guitar lessons from Jimi Hendrix), is released to become the best-selling

US album of the year. Relying less-heavily on 'brilliant' musicianship, but definitely a lot more fun is **Black Sabbath**'s eponymously-titled first album. Allegedly recorded over two days as opposed to CSN&Y's reported 800 studio hours, its instant success further consolidates the breakthrough into the mainstream for this hard rockin' music soon to be known as heavy metal. During this year, the Sabbs, Led Zeppelin and Deep Purple will all have albums in the end-of-year Top 20.

It really is all over for the **Beatles**, too. **Ringo Starr** releases his first solo album, 'Sentimental Journey', in March; **Paul** follows suit with 'McCartney' in April and, next month, sessions for **George Harrison**'s triple disc debut 'All Things Must Pass' begin in earnest. Against such a background, the Beatles release 'Let It Be', the LP and title of the film of the recording sessions. None of the group attend any premieres, lending credence to the documentary, which is about the band falling apart. Guitarist **Peter Green** quits **Fleetwood Mac**, citing the intolerable pressures of stardom and the desire to devote more of his time to religious pursuits as reasons – presumably in an attempt to live the blues rather than merely play them, he instructs the group's record company to stop paying him royalties. In November, Green will put out an unsuccessful solo album. Other casualties of the time include a school of south London fish – when **Pink Floyd** perform a concert at the Crystal Palace Bowl, they play so loud that the music kills many of the

Led Zeppelin in long-hair-at-airport drama; Singapore, 1970.

New York accountant Allen Klein: the man who triggered the Beatles' breakup?

Let it lie

The Sixties were officially laid to rest on December 6, 1969, when the disaster that was Altamont – where Hell's Angels stabbed a fan to death within sight of the stage where the **Rolling Stones** were performing – expunged the last vestige of optimism lingering from the pop music of the previous 10 years.

However, the epitaph for the decade that more than any other shaped popular-music-as-we-know-it, was really written in the break-up of the **Beatles** almost a year later. The dissolution of the group marked the loss of one of the last remaining links between the original UK rock'n'rollers and the post-hippie practitioners who were shaping the new era. The Beatles themselves had ploughed a furrow through beat, pop and acid and, in so doing, had transformed their career into a microcosm of rock's development. By seeking high-profile involvement in social, political and cultural agendas, the Fab Four's career had become the perfect embodiment of the Spirit Of The Sixties. But the pressures that brought the decade to an end, also inevitably brought the Beatles to an end too.

When, on New Year's Eve 1970, Paul McCartney filed suit in the High Court in London to end the partnership trading as the Beatles & Co and appointed a receiver to wind up its affairs as well as to finish its association with New York rockbiz accountant Allen Klein, it was little more than a formal conclusion to a process of disintegration that had been going on for years. Indeed, during the preceding 12 months, the problem had scarcely been hidden from the public – when Paul released his debut solo album 'McCartney' in April, tucked into the advance copies sent out to the media was a self-penned 'interview' including the statements:

Q   Are you planning a new single or album with the Beatles?
A   No.
Q   Do you foresee a time when Lennon-McCartney becomes an active songwriting partnership again?
A   No.
Q   Do you miss the Beatles and George Martin? Was there a moment, e.g., when you thought "Wish Ringo was here for this break"?
A   No.
And if anybody still had any doubts, the album's press release made it clear that "Paul McCartney has left the Beatles because of personal,

business and musical differences. They do not want to split up, but the present rift seems part of their growing up."

From a creative standpoint, this was hard to dispute: it had long been obvious that the Beatles – a unit formed over 10 years earlier, during rock's infancy, by three musically unsophisticated teenagers – was not large enough to contain the spectrum of ideas produced by four rapidly-developing talents. At the time of the writ, each Beatle appeared to be approaching his solo work with greater gusto than the group venture – as the film *Let It Be* suggested. And artistically, their individual projects went far beyond the ambitions of most groups.

Businesswise, Apple Corps, another personification of Sixties ideals, was in tatters. The operation was famous for its generous arts development budgets and extravagant multi-media entertainment projects, as well as badly run offices and boutiques that became paradises for kleptomaniacs. The Beatles' attitude to record company A&R had also been distinctly hands-off and so this area of operations duly suffered a night of the long knives at the hands of Allen Klein. By this time, Apple existed on a purely functional level as little more than the group's management company and low-yield record label – thus stripping away another common bond between the four.

It was Klein's involvement in the group's affairs that sparked the Lennon-McCartney explosion. Klein was brought in at John's suggestion (on Mick Jagger's recommendation after Klein had made sense of the Stones' tangled financial affairs during the late-Sixties) because he believed the group was going broke; George and Ringo were amenable, but Paul wanted his affairs and 25 per cent of the company administered by his new in-laws, the powerful New York law firm, Eastman and Eastman. Whereas in the past the bickering between John and Paul had often been petty, Paul's mistrust of Klein concerned enormous amounts of money and this was something that could be translated into legal language. It was assumed by many at the time, and has never been denied by McCartney, that dissolving the Beatles was the only way he could remove Klein's influence from his business affairs.

Whatever the reason, the band that had played the major part in giving 'that pop racket' an acceptable, vastly lucrative face in the Sixties was no more. Although the writing had been on the wall for some time and each member would go on to prolific solo careers, it would take rock music years to get over the loss.

▲ Eric Clapton, a solo success but not so lucky as Derek and the Dominoes.

occupants of the lake in front of the natural amphitheatre's stage. Ten years into his musical career, **Elton John** at last gets noticed in May when his second LP, 'Elton John', is a hit.

On May 23, the **Grateful Dead** play their first ever gig outside the USA at the Hollywood Rock Music Festival, Newcastle-Under-Lyme, a minor open-air show at a small town in the centre of England. Did Jerry, Pigpen and the boys think they were going to play in Los Angeles? Maybe that would've been for the best, as in the heart of Merrie Englande their four-hour set is upstaged by a boisterous performance from the virtually unknown support act **Mungo Jerry**. Later in the year, that group will have the hit of the summer with 'In The Summertime', a record featuring the less-than-road-safety-conscious rhyming couplet "have a drink have a

drive/do a ton twenty-five". Twenty three years on, this same song will be chosen by the government to spear-head an anti-drinking and dri-ving campaign on British TV.

In June, **Eric Clapton**'s first solo album ('Eric Clapton') charts on both sides of the Atlantic, so he drafts **Allman Brother** Duane into the band that have just quit backing **Delaney & Bonnie** and renames himself and them **Derek & The Dominoes**. The group's first LP, 'Layla & Other Assorted Love Songs', will not feature the guitarist's name on the sleeve because he's deter-mined to succeed on merit rather than because of his reputation – 'Clapton is God' is a major piece of graffiti at this time. The LP fails in the UK but reaches the Top 20 in the US. The title track, which goes on to become something of a Clapton theme song, is dedicated to "the wife of my best friend", which proves to be **George Harrison**'s other half, Patti Boyd. Next month she sits with Clapton at the gala opening of Ken Tynan's nude stageshow *Oh Calcutta!* and will soon move in with him, opening a rift between Clapton and Harrison that will take years to heal.

Elsewhere, **James Brown** dis-bands the **Famous Flames** to put together one of the Seventies most influential soul music groups, the **JBs** – notable recruits at this stage includ-ed Fred Wesley, Bootsy Collins and Pee Wee Ellis. Their stripped-back,

rhythmic style will set a standard for streetfunk that will dominate US black music during the decade. The **England World Cup Squad** sets what becomes a far more tiresome trend, for soccer teams to record beery, terrace-anthem-type songs, with the template beery, terrace anthem 'Back Home', intended to rouse the English players into action during the World Cup in Mexico. The **Dave Clark Five** go their separate ways – remarkably, the North London stompers who had their first hit in 1963 are still chart regulars, racking up two hits this year.

In July, a callow 19-year-old, who had a brief career as a child actor in TV commercials and used to help out at the Marquee Club after school, answers an advertisement for a drum-mer in UK weekly rock magazine *Melody Maker*. The audition goes well and Phil Collins is suddenly a member of **Genesis**. Following Maureen Tucker's recent maternity leave from the **Velvet Underground** – she will not return – **Lou Reed** quits. Although the band soldiers on for one more album with Willie 'Loco' Alexander on vocals, everybody knows it's all over. It never really gets going for Dib Cochran & The Earwigs. This ad hoc group is comprised of **David Bowie**, **Tony Visconti**, **Marc Bolan** and **Rick Wakeman** and, although their hastily-recorded, high-camp pop single 'Oh Baby' doesn't happen, it will later become a much-prized collectors' item. During the last weekend in August – a British public holiday – the UK's biggest-ever rock audience assembles for the second Isle Of Wight Pop Festival, a three-day event featuring the **Doors**, the **Who**, **Jethro Tull**,

ROCK'N'ROLL
record

MARCH 7: Lee Marvin tops the UK singles chart with 'Wand'rin' Star', from the movie Paint Your Wagon – of particular interest is a B-side featuring a wistful-sounding Clint Eastwood crooning 'I Talk To The Trees'.

MAY 11: Cliff Richard turns serious thespian, treading the boards in a repertory production of Peter Schaffer's Five Finger Exercise in a small theatre in the London suburb of Bromley.

JUNE 9: Bob Dylan is awarded an honorary Doctorate Of Music by Princeton University.

JULY 28: In the space of one week, Mick Jagger opens in two films: Ned Kelly, the tale of the legendary Australian armoured bandit with the Stone in the title role; and Performance (a release delayed since 1968 due to concerns about the movie's violence), in which he plays a slightly mad ageing rock star.

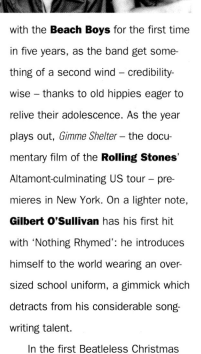

▶ The Partridge Family and their amazing performing teeth. A televisual sensation.

Procul Harum, Kris Kristofferson, Joni Mitchell and Joan Baez, and headlined by Jimi Hendrix. His set takes place at 3.00 am and is recorded for release in 1971 as 'Jimi Hendrix At The Isle Of Wight'. It turns out to be his last performance in front of a big crowd.

Marc Bolan shortens the name of his group to T Rex, makes the most of the electric guitar he's been dabbling with for over a year and cranks out the single 'Ride A White Swan', a complete change in musical direction that owes more to soul and heavy metal than it does it to the gentle folk music he's been associated with in the past. The song is the first in a long line of hits for the group. David Bowie, meanwhile, signs with manager Tony DeFries and, although his 'Man Who Sold The World' album fails to make an impression in the US, where it is first released, this is the partnership that will make Bowie a superstar.

Would you buy a pop song from this man? Many did, Gilbert O'Sullivan became one of the era's most influential and ▼ successful writers.

Both these events will come to be acknowledged as the official birth of glam-rock.

In the USA, NBC airs the first episode of a teen-oriented sitcom following the adventures of a family rock group – The Partridge Family propels minor league actor David 'Son Of Jack' Cassidy to musical megastardom around the world. Although the TV show will not reach the UK for nearly two years, the Partridge Family's records, featuring Cassidy as lead vocalist, are still hits there. Curtis Mayfield quits the Impressions, with his debut solo album, 'Curtis', ready for release. A 19-year-old Billy Joel checks himself into New York's Meadowbrook Psychiatric Hospital – the man who will one day marry model Christie Brinkley is suffering from acute depression, apparently brought on by a failed romance. Or maybe it has something to do with the resounding flop made by his first album, 'Atilla' – the one with him dressed as a barbarian for the sleeve photo.

Myra 'Mrs Jerry Lee' Lewis, now aged 26, files for divorce to end her 13-year marriage. This action so shocks her 'devoutly Christian' husband – nickname 'Killer' – he forsakes liquor, cigars and other women for all of two months. At the Whisky A-Go-Go in Los Angeles, Brian Wilson performs

with the Beach Boys for the first time in five years, as the band get something of a second wind – credibility-wise – thanks to old hippies eager to relive their adolescence. As the year plays out, Gimme Shelter – the documentary film of the Rolling Stones' Altamont-culminating US tour – premieres in New York. On a lighter note, Gilbert O'Sullivan has his first hit with 'Nothing Rhymed': he introduces himself to the world wearing an oversized school uniform, a gimmick which detracts from his considerable songwriting talent.

In the first Beatleless Christmas since 1961, George Harrison releases the epic album 'All Things Must Pass'. Co-produced by Phil Spector and featuring Eric Clapton, Ringo, Ginger Baker, Badfinger and Billy Preston, it hits the UK Number 4 spot and US Number 1, selling over 3 million copies. On New Year's Eve, Paul McCartney files suit against the Beatles & Co, to dissolve the partnership, to end its relationship with manager Allen Klein and to have a receiver take over the Fabs' affairs.

NOV 27 : The UK Gay Liberation Front holds its first public demonstration

As part of rock's absorption into mainstream culture, the age band of record buyers widened both upwards and downwards and the music market became fragmented. It was no longer a case of 'rock music just selling to teenagers' and 1971 was the year when this increasing spread of consumers first became visible in the end of year best-selling album and singles charts. Older fans were buying the album-oriented likes of **CSN&Y**, **Led Zeppelin**, **ELP** and **Deep Purple**,

while younger singles buyers were going for less-cerebral groups such as **T Rex**, the **Sweet**, **Mungo Jerry** and **Middle Of The Road**. 1971 also marked the peak of progressive rock – **ELP**'s 'Tarkus', a pompous, lyrically incomprehensible, grandiose and flashy 'concept' album – from which point it could mercifully only decline.

Any notion of the Spirit Of The Sixties lingering on into 1971 is quelled almost immediately – as soon as the Charles Manson murder trial gets underway. **Beatles** records are played to the court, so the jury can assess their potential for influencing people into acts of evil – a key element in Manson's defence is his claim that he was led to do what he did by listening to the Fabs' 1968 track 'Helter Skelter'. This is the first time rock records have been cited in

court, by either defence or prosecution. It won't be the last. Elsewhere, indications of things to come can be seen when **David Bowie** arrives in the US to promote his album, 'The Man Who Sold The World'. Due to work permit problems, he can't perform, but makes headlines when, in Texas of all places, he appears in public wearing a dress. The 36-year-old, former rebel **Elvis Presley** receives a Jaycee Award as one of America's Ten Outstanding Young Men Of 1970 – he is the only entertainer amongst the chosen few. And **Van Morrison** establishes himself as one of America's most respected live acts thanks to extensive touring with his Caledonia Soul Orchestra.

Frank Zappa isn't so fortunate on his tour in the UK, when he is forced to pull out of a proposed show

Stevie Wonder came of age, gained artistic independence and started making proper albums.

The Beatles Apart

Judging by the glut of solo material the ex-**Beatles** put out directly after the break-up, it seems that, once the group was out of the way, the floodgates were opened and a great creative flow was released. Either that, or they'd been keeping back their best work over the last couple of years.

John Lennon, who had hinted at what he was capable of doing outside the group with his singles, had been making albums as part of the **Plastic Ono Band** but these tended to be so personal they verged on the impenetrable. Then, in October 1971, came 'Imagine'. A far more direct record than its predecessors, it is his best-selling solo work and the LP that is also held to be his most creative, ranging as it does from beautiful love songs to barely-veiled attacks on **Paul McCartney**.

Paul's 'McCartney' had some excellent moments, but largely suffered from its unsophisticated recording process – it was made in Paul's home studio – while 'Ram', a huge hit on both sides of the Atlantic, demonstrated his consummate skill with a melody. Meanwhile, the formation of **Wings** came as no real surprise, as

Paul had always enjoyed being part of a group. What was a shock though was Wings' debut album, 'Wildlife': unadventurous to the point of being twee, it was critically trashed and didn't sell nearly as well as McCartney's previous offerings. Opinion was that, with three LPs in 18 months, McCartney had stretched himself too thin.

Ringo Starr's 'Sentimental Journey' in 1970, a collection of popular standards produced by George Martin, was more or less what was expected from the least promising Beatle. Then he surprised many by taking off to Nashville to record 'Beaucoups Of Blues' with a crew of top notch country sessioneers. The results were enjoyable and entirely credible, sales were reasonable and managed to allay fears that his solo career would soon falter.

George Harrison provided the real surprise with the triple album set 'All Things Must Pass', a three million-selling US Number 1. Never a big contributor to the Beatles' writing credits, his solo effort is thought to contain all the songs the others rejected. True or not, it was also hailed as a masterpiece and achieved a degree of success he was never able to repeat.

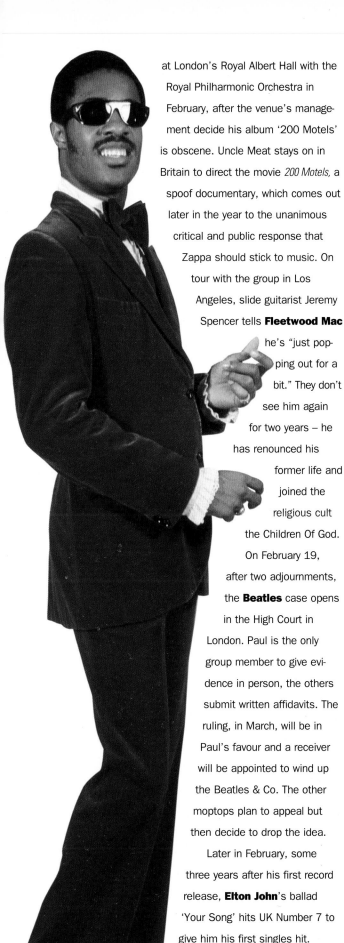

at London's Royal Albert Hall with the Royal Philharmonic Orchestra in February, after the venue's management decide his album '200 Motels' is obscene. Uncle Meat stays on in Britain to direct the movie *200 Motels,* a spoof documentary, which comes out later in the year to the unanimous critical and public response that Zappa should stick to music. On tour with the group in Los Angeles, slide guitarist Jeremy Spencer tells **Fleetwood Mac** he's "just popping out for a bit." They don't see him again for two years – he has renounced his former life and joined the religious cult the Children Of God.

On February 19, after two adjournments, the **Beatles** case opens in the High Court in London. Paul is the only group member to give evidence in person, the others submit written affidavits. The ruling, in March, will be in Paul's favour and a receiver will be appointed to wind up the Beatles & Co. The other moptops plan to appeal but then decide to drop the idea.

Later in February, some three years after his first record release, **Elton John**'s ballad 'Your Song' hits UK Number 7 to give him his first singles hit. Another career milestone happens when Gordon Sumner, bass

player in semi-pro bands and training to be a teacher, is nicknamed '**Sting**' by a fellow member of the Newcastle Big Band. Apparently his favoured yellow and black hooped jumper makes him look like a giant bee.

The **Rolling Stones** decamp to France as tax exiles. This is the start of an exodus that marks the Seventies as British rock stars leave their home shores in droves to make the most of the decade's enormous record sales incomes and to avoid the pain when the British government raise the upper-bracket income tax to a crippling 95%. Less financially concerned are **Led Zeppelin**, who embark on a particularly punter-friendly UK tour by way of saying "thank you" to their fans. They perform at the clubs and dance halls they first started at in 1968, charging 1968 prices for tickets and paying themselves a 1968 fee. Also on tour, but with a slightly higher profile are **Black Sabbath**, who are fast becoming a byword on both sides of the Atlantic for archetypal rock'n'roll excesses – drugs, drink, groupies and exhausting tour schedules. A reputation that will serve their leader Ozzy Osbourne well for more than 20 years.

David Bowie's 'The Man Who Sold The World' is at last released in the UK, but with a racy new sleeve showing Bowie reclining on a chaise longue, again wearing a dress. When it doesn't chart (it didn't in the US either), the record is withdrawn and the sleeve changed to show the singer in more conventional attire. Although this alteration has no discernible effect on sales, it means original copies of the frock sleeve will

become highly collectable in years to come. Another rock oddity finds the **Beach Boys** sharing a Fillmore East bill with the **Grateful Dead** – this coupling is an indication of the US progressive rock crowd's adoption of the group after its reformation a year ago, and is explained as being late-twentysomethings' attempt to revisit their pre-Summer Of Love teens. **Alice Cooper** breaks through in the US with a Top 20 single, 'Eighteen', and a Top 30 album, 'Love It To Death'. Income generated from this success allows his stage set to be expanded into a gore-soaked theatrical spectacular and the group quickly become an enormous live draw in the US.

In May, the **Rolling Stones**' first release on their own label (Rolling Stones Records) is 'Brown Sugar'. On the B-side of the single, as a bonus third track, is a cover of **Chuck Berry**'s 'Let It Rock'. To this day you can't find the track anywhere else – recording it was such an impromptu decision there wasn't even a master tape of it kept in the vaults. The new label's first album, 'Sticky Fingers', comes out later in the month, gaining massive publicity from its Andy Warhol-designed sleeve of a jeans-clad male crotch complete with fully functioning zip fly. In certain quarters it's considered outrageous.

On May 13, **Stevie Wonder** turns 21 and not only receives his accumulated childhood earnings, but can now renegotiate all his contracts with Motown. The fact he is paid only $1 million of a horde worth an estimated 20 times that means Wonder will never fully trust the company again. He now only enters contractual

discussions with Motown, having first very publicly approached other record labels. Eventually he re-signs to them under what is a ground-breaking agreement for that company: under it, he sets up his own production and publishing companies – Taurus Productions and Black Bull Publishing – and also wins total creative freedom to deliver finished product at a new, favourable royalty rate. His new situation allows him increasingly to divorce himself from the Motown way, and put songs together as albums instead of as chart fodder singles. Arguably, this will prove to be the biggest single factor in the collapse of Motown as a creative or cultural force.

On a more boisterous note in the UK, **Slade** have their first chart hit with 'Get Down And Get With It', while **Dave & Ansil Collins** shoot to Number 1 with 'Double Barrel'. In fact 1971 proves quite a year for reggae in Great Britain. The Collins duo finish fifth in the year's Top 10 singles sellers (they also have a hit with 'Monkey Spanner'), and the **Upsetters**, **Bob & Marcia**, the **Pioneers**, **Greyhound** and **Jimmy Cliff** all have hits.

When **John and Yoko** join **Frank**

Zappa & The Mothers Of Invention on stage at New York's Fillmore East (recorded and included on 'Some Time In New York City'), it is Lennon's first stage performance since 1969 as well as one of the last concerts at the venue.

Bill Graham, the influential concert promoter for the last five years, is going out of business, blaming rock's recent over-commercialization – a remarkable complaint, given that his name is synonymous with the late-Sixties exploitation of rock as a cash generating machine. As rock-'n'roll becomes part of the tourist circuit, the two-room shack in which Elvis Presley was born is opened to the public in June.

On the strength of the 'Hunky Dory' demo tapes, Tony DeFries negotiates a lucrative deal for **David Bowie** at RCA Records. As if to demonstrate that groups are capable of running their own affairs, the **Rolling Stones** instigate a $7.5 million lawsuit against business manager Allen Klein for 'mismanagement of funds', and later they'll also file a writ against their original management team of Andrew Oldham and Eric

Easton for 'royalty deprivation'.

July 31 marks the first of two charity concerts at Madison Square Garden organized by **George Harrison** to raise money for the victims of the war and famine in Bangladesh – the former-Beatle took on this task in response to a personal plea from his friend, sitar player **Ravi Shankar**. On the bill are Shankar, **Harrison**, **Ringo Starr**, **Bob Dylan & The Band**, **Eric Clapton**, **Klaus Voorman**, **Leon Russell** and **Billy Preston**. The shows become the most successful charity events to date but sadly huge tax demands in the UK and US prevent a great deal of the money raised from going to those for whom it was intended. George Harrison writes a personal cheque to boost the Bangladesh Relief Fund, and the concerts became a valuable lesson for future fundraisers of the need to avoid being crippled by bureaucracy. The shows are recorded as a triple-album box set which, released in December, tops the UK charts and gets to Number 2 in the US.

Later in August, after months of opposition from his record company, **Marvin Gaye** releases 'What's Going On'. Motown boss Berry Gordy believes the LP and its radical depar-

Bob Dylan and George Harrison.

Jonathan King

Now best known as a broadcaster, TV presenter and newspaper columnist in America and Great Britain, **Jonathan King** was once a one-man UK pop industry. It began in 1965 when, as a 19-year-old Cambridge undergraduate, he wrote and recorded 'Everyone's Gone To The Moon', Number 4 in the UK and 17 in the US. Three months later he wrote and produced a similarly transatlantic hit in 'It's Good News Week' by **Hedgehoppers Anonymous**, a group of young Royal Air Forcemen. Two years later, after a spell of music journalism and a minor US hit with 'Where The Sun Has Never Shone', he produced **Genesis**' first single 'The Silent Sun' (King was at Charterhouse School with the group's founder members) and hosted a music and chat show on UK television.

Undeterred by critics of his music, King returned to recording in 1970 with the UK Top 30 hit 'Let It All Hang Out' and, even by his own hyperactive standards, the next year was particularly full. In February, calling himself the **Weathermen**, he reached the UK Top 20 with a cover of 'It's The Same Old Song'. He repeated this success in May as **Sakkarin** with a heavy metal version of the **Archies**' 'Sugar Sugar' – his po-faced treatment of such a silly song

was, apparently, a statement of enormous irony. Next month, he had a hit under his own name with 'Lazybones' and, in July, wrote and produced that popular singalong of the day 'Leap Up And Down And Wave Your Knickers In The Air' for **St. Cecelia**. In December, King was in the British charts twice, once as himself with 'Hooked On A Feeling' and also at Number 3 as the creative force behind the **Piglets**' 'Johnny Reggae', a cod-Caribbean knees-up featuring TV actress Adrienne Posta on chirpy Cockney lead vocals. At the same time as all this, in September, he produced 'Keep On Dancing' for unknown Scottish group the **Bay City Rollers**. It got to Number 9, and was their only hit until 'Rollermania' three years later.

Although Jonathan King continued to have deliberately daft hits under questionable pseudonyms – One Hundred Ton & A Feather, Shag, Athlete's Foot, Bubblerock, Father Abraphart and so on – when he started his own label in 1972, UK Records, his roster possessed considerable credibility – among others, **10cc**, the **Kursaal Flyers** and **Kevin Johnson**. Seems strange that the man, whose last hit under his own name was the Costa Del Sol disco anthem 'Una Paloma Blanca', could have such hitherto unrevealed good taste.

---

ture into social and ecological concerns set to jazzy, almost ambient music, will ruin the singer's career. The record sells two million almost immediately, establishes Gaye as a serious artist and remains one of the most talked about Motown albums.

In the same month the *Sonny & Cher Comedy Hour* debuts on US TV and this highly successful sketch'n'singing show will run for three series. With her profile thus boosted, **Cher** has a Number 1 in the US later in the year with 'Gypsies, Tramps & Thieves' – the record will go on to sell a million, reach the UK Top 5 and is to this day one of her best known songs. An animated series, the *Jackson 5*, also airs on US TV – years later, it is speculated that seeing himself as a cartoon at this impressionable age (12) is a significant step on the way towards

Michael's odd behaviour in later life. Adding to the rock/televisual crossflow, on September 17, *The Partridge Family* debuts on the British airwaves.

Lemmy joins **Hawkwind** on bass with a six-month contract. After Dave Anderson leaves, he stays four years. A security guard is stabbed to death during disturbances at the **Who**'s concert in Forest Hills, New York, and rioting at a **Motley Crue** show at London's Albert Hall leads to a ban on rock at the venerable venue. And **Rick Wakeman** joins **Yes**, to give their music a more flamboyant style.

After Glenn Frey, Randy Meisner, Don Henley and Bernie Leadon complete a spell as **Linda Rondstadt**'s backing group, they decide to stay together as a unit and call themselves the **Eagles**. Spotted by Asylum Records boss David Geffen, they are

booked to play for a month as resident band in a bar in Aspen, Colorado, to tighten their act. Thus prepared, Geffen signs them to his label the following spring.

Shaft opens at US cinemas in September, the theme song and soundtrack LP top both US charts and earn **Isaac Hayes** two Grammies, an Oscar and a Golden Globe award. It also kicks off a string of 'blaxploitation' movies – featuring sex, violence, low production values and successful soundtracks by top black artists: 'Superfly' (**Curtis Mayfield**); 'Trouble Man' (**Marvin Gaye**); 'Black Caesar' (**James Brown**); 'The Mack' (**Willie Hutch**); 'Together Brothers' (**Barry White**); 'Truck Turner' (Isaac Hayes) and so on.

The **Bay City Rollers** have their first UK hit – 'Keep On Dancing' – but

Sonny and Cher: she got a new body and became a film star; he put on weight and became a mayor.

1971 – HEADLINE NEWS   FEB 4 : UK car manufacturer Rolls Royce is declared bankrupt

won't have another for three years. In London, a rock'n'roll veteran has one more stab at stardom, when he and his producer blag some free studio time and record 'Rock'n'Roll Parts One and Two'. After considering such names as Vicky Vomit, Terry Tinsel and Stanley Sparkle, said old timer – he is 31 – settles on **Gary Glitter** and nearly a year later the record will be a massive UK hit. In return for an advance large enough to pay the plane fare back home to Jamaica, Chris Blackwell signs the **Wailers** – who are stranded in London, penniless and cold – to Island Records. On returning home, they immediately begin recording 'Catch A Fire'.

On November 4, the **Who** play the inaugural concert at the Rainbow, in north London's Finsbury Park. Formerly the Astoria, an Edwardian musical hall turned cinema, the listed art deco building – its stage is housed in a huge mock fairy castle with twinkling 'stars' set in the ceiling – is consecrated to rock music and will be the capital's most prestigious mid-sized (capacity, approx 4,000) venue. As their solo careers tail off, the **Mamas & The Papas** attempt a reunion but it doesn't last long. **Genesis** release the 'Nursery Cryme' album, with Phil Collins singing lead on one track. The accompanying live shows attract much attention thanks to Peter Gabriel's elaborate masks and props as well as an on-stage raconteur – Gabriel says the latter is there to cover up stage fright and the group's perpetual retuning of instruments.

In time for the Christmas market, **Yes**' fourth album 'Your Move' is the first to feature the distinctive logo and

cod sci-fi artwork of Roger Dean. Another first-in-a-series concerns **Slade**'s single 'Coz I Luv You', a prime example of what is to become their trademark creative spelling. 'Led Zeppelin 4' breaks a few rules too, when its sleeve carries no band name and no title, just four Runic symbols. It also contains 'Stairway To Heaven', a song which becomes so entrenched as a rock standard that guitar shops carry notices prohibiting it being played on the premises.

Guitarist Robert Fripp sacks Pete Sinfield from **King Crimson**, meaning he is the only original group member left. In the US, **Melanie**, a low-profile folk singer, releases 'Brand New Key'. The song, which apparently took a quarter of an hour to write, was meant for use as uptempo light relief during her acoustic concerts but its lyrics are open to misinterpretation – Melanie maintains it has no smutty hidden meaning – and it gets banned by several American radio stations. It still tops the charts there for three weeks, will make the Top 5 in the UK, eventually selling over a million and is a success she never quite manages to repeat. Less Top 40-friendly is **David Bowie**'s 'Hunky Dory' LP: although critically acclaimed – often hailed as his best ever – it doesn't sell in vast quantities until after 'Ziggy Stardust' becomes a hit in a couple of years' time.

During **Frank Zappa**'s set at the Montreux Casino on the shores of Lake Geneva in Switzerland, on December 3, an audience member, seeking to enhance the band's special effects, fires a flare gun into the wings and starts a fire that completely

Genesis. Well brought up boys from a good school. Mostly.

destroys the building. While Zappa plays a major part in shepherding the crowd to safety, the **Mothers**' $50,000 of equipment is destroyed and **Deep Purple**, at the show because they are waiting to start recording in the venue next day, retire to the terrace of their nearby hotel to watch the flames. Downdrafts from the mountains push the fire out over the lake, inspiring the Purps to pen 'Smoke On The Water', one of hard rock's most enduring anthems. Zappa's problems though are only just beginning: a week later, on stage in London, the jealous boyfriend of an ardent female fan jumps on stage and shoves the bandleader into the orchestra pit. Zappa fractures his skull, breaks a leg in several places and has to spend nine months in a wheelchair.

To close the year, an embryonic **Roxy Music** – Ferry, Eno, Mackay and Thompson – play two tiny gigs at Reading University as well as the Friends Of The Tate Gallery's Christmas Party, while **Sly & The Family Stone**'s 'There's A Riot Goin' On' album is Number 1 in America. The LP, widely acknowledged as the group's creative highpoint, is their only album to make it to the top.

Marc Bolan and the Birth of Glam

ROCK 'N' ROLL record

FEBRUARY: Eric Clapton retires from public life in a bid to combat his drink and drug problems.

MAY 12: Mick Jagger marries Bianca Rosa Perez-Mora Marcia in St Tropez, in the south of France.

JUNE: Carole King's 'Tapestry' album hits the top in the US. It'll stay there for four months and sell 15 million copies.

JUNE 3: After three months writing poetry, Jim Morrison dies of a heart attack in the bath at his apartment in Paris.

SEPTEMBER 3: John Lennon and Yoko Ono leave London for New York. John will never return to the UK.

OCTOBER: Rod Stewart, becomes the only artist to top the UK and US album and singles charts simultaneously with 'Every Picture Tells A Story' and 'Maggie May'.

OCTOBER 29: Allman Brother Duane is killed when he crashes his motorcycle in Macon, Georgia.

In 1971, **Slade**'s singer Noddy Holder declared, "the fans are fed up with paying to sit on their hands, while watching musicians who clearly couldn't care less about the customers. What's wanted is more of a party atmosphere."

What Holder objected to was the pompous self-indulgence of so-called progressive rock – where, avoiding all contact with their audience, men with long hair and beards put their heads down and played elongated, dull solos. While this approach may have shifted millions of albums and prompted much 'deep and meaningful' thought, what about the instant gratification of your classic three-minute pop song?

Lumpen, ex-skinheads Slade understood the mood of their time. As they began a five-year run of enormously successful singles – each as easy to stomp along to as its phonetic title was to spell: 'Cum On Feel The Noize'; 'Gudbuy T'Jane'; 'Look Wot You Dun' and so on – they sparked off a craze that took music back to basics and clothes in the direction of glam-rock. Over the next few years, in Britain if nowhere else, acts such as the **Sweet**, **Mud**, **Wizzard** and **Alvin Stardust** dressed up like Christmas trees and demanded that the nation dance even if they seldom challenged its intellect. The exception to this rule was a man who retained his musical integrity throughout his two-year reign as the undisputed king of glam. In sequined top hat and satin tailcoat, **Marc Bolan**, was that rarest of creatures, a glam rocker with credibility, and the only artist to genuinely straddle the gap between the hippie Sixties and the brash, platform-soled Seventies.

An ex-mod and one-time model, it seemed inevitable that Bolan should have gone the glam route – his first band, the mid-Sixties psychedelic outfit, **John's Children**, overdressed sufficiently for him to talk about them later as the first ever glam act. But the sensitive artist side came to light when, as half of acoustic duo **Tyrannosaurus Rex**, he made albums with mystical titles like 'My People Were Fair And Had Sky In Their Hair ... But Now They're Content To Wear Stars On Their Brows', 'Beard Of Stars' and 'Prophets, Seers And Sages', and topped off the gentle folkie music with lyrics centring on mythology, magic and mumbo jumbo in general. The hippies loved it, but when Bolan went all-electric in 1971 (having already shortened the name), he found a new teenage following attracted to his pumping rock, coy sexuality and elfin good looks. Of course, he was always careful to make sure his lyrics had a large element of ambiguity to them – 'Metal Guru', 'Ride A White Swan', 'Get It On (Bang A Gong)', 'Solid Gold Easy Action' ... what did they all mean?

The original glam rocker, Marc Bolan.

No matter. 'T Rextasy' swept the UK. In 1971 and 1972, T Rex were the best-selling singles band, finishing among the Top 10 album sellers too. By the middle of 1973, the band had had 10 UK Top 10 hits – three of them spending a total of 11 weeks at Number 1 – three Number 1 albums and three others in the Top 20. But then it all collapsed just as quickly: Bolan got fat; left his wife; sacked band members; baited the press; went into tax exile, and stopped having hits as his young fan base grew up. Later on in the Seventies, he was hailed by the new British punks as something of a pop prophet, but there was no revival in his chart fortunes. Sadly, Marc Bolan was killed in a car crash in 1977.

JUN 15 : Education Secretary Margaret Thatcher discontinues free milk to British schoolchildren

1971 - HEADLINE NEWS

1970s Trash

▲ Slade succinctly summed up the Seventies approach to booze 'n' birds.

If ever a decade was made for rock-'n'roll trash it was the Seventies. Look in the textbooks under 'Rock Stars Misbehaving' and it's a safe bet you'll find a seven, a nought and a small 's'. While these 10 years may be best remembered for platform shoes, the concept album, punk and *Saturday Night Fever*, don't forget it was also the decade that opened with **Jimi Hendrix** choking on his own vomit and ended with Sex Pistol **Sid Vicious** stabbing his lover Nancy Spungen to death.

It was always destined to be like that – once the peace'n'love'n'wanting to change the world of the Sixties had faded into the post-Woodstock distance. Soon records were selling as never before and rock's wealthy new aristocracy felt free to do as they wished. Herpes hadn't even been thought of yet, let alone AIDS, and accurate research into the debilitating long term effects of the rock-'n'roll lifestyle had yet

▲ Alice Cooper: You wonder where he had room to hide his snake.

to be conducted. In other words, it was an era belonging to a bunch of people with diminished social responsibilities, too much money and not enough hard evidence that hedonism can damage your health. Hardly a recipe for the quiet life.

As the Sixties mutated into the Seventies, the old, comparatively introverted icon was being replaced by the if-you've-got-it-flaunt-it type of role model who was determined to enjoy himself on and off stage. "Sex sells" claimed **Alice Cooper**, whose first four albums averaged sales of a million each and one of them even came complete with a free pair of frilly knickers. But sex lost its shock value as the decade progressed. In fact Cooper himself took to dressing in drag – maternity wear and school-girl uniform – and dangling his pet snake, Gloria, between his legs before the press sat up and took notice. And although **Bowie**'s dress-wearing initially made headlines, with-in a few years bisexuality was almost regulation on the more sensitive side of glam-rock.

At the other end of the scale, the likes of **Slade**, **Gary Glitter** and **Rod Stewart** were reintroducing the idea of the British "lad" into rock, featur-ing beer, football, sex and Saturday Night's Alright For Fighting. In fact, salacious stories involving hairy-chest-ed pop stars and blondes became so run-of-the-mill that only well known fundamentalist **Keith Moon** could regularly command headlines – espe-cially when a tale broke about him and his binoculars. Apparently, while

on tour, he'd stand on his hotel room balcony and, using the aforemen-tioned optical aids, pick out likely objects of lust from the crowd of girls outside. Then, with gestures both lewd and directional, he'd instruct his man on the ground to bring her up. The manic drummer later adapted this scheme to take advantage of fans outside the London apartments of fellow rock stars. According to one, "he would just turn up, having bribed his way past the doorman, with a cou-ple of the girls from outside and dis-appear into a spare bedroom. He used to say they would just go to waste otherwise."

Despite the vast amounts made in the Seventies, some stars were spending money faster than they were making it. **Marvin Gaye** was rumoured to have debts of over $7 million and as a result tried to com-mit suicide by overdosing on freebase cocaine, while living in a trailer on Hawaii. **Sly Stone**, another promi-nent pipe user, filed for bankrupt-cy in 1976 and **Isaac Hayes** – apparently no stranger to con-trolled substances either – put his business in the hands of the receiver a year later. And even though Seventies funk

▲ Marvin Gaye — voice of an angel, debts of a Third World country.

▲ Jagger and Hall, rock's very own Richard and Liz.

▼ Isaac Hayes, yet another casualty of expensive Seventies recreational habits.

before he divorced her, and by then he had faced a paternity suit from **Marsha Hunt**, been cited in **Marianne Faithfull**'s divorce proceedings, been suspected of involvement with **David Bowie**'s wife following speculation as to whether she was the subject of his 1973 hit 'Angie', and was finally to take up with **Bryan Ferry**'s ex, Jerry Hall, begging the question of what went on before she was an ex. **Keith Richard**'s drug and weapons arrests kept his name in the news; his most spectacular headline appeared after he accidentally set fire to a London hotel room while, apparently, in a considerably relaxed frame of mind. Even the normally invisible, media-wise, Charlie Watts was involved, when his wife Shirley was arrested at Nice airport for thumping a customs officer.

Then there was punk. Even without the **Sex Pistols**, punk was a tabloid headline waiting to happen. With its S&M-style sleazy-sexy clothes, photogenic coiffures and well-rehearsed scowls, it was impossible to keep this media-friendly 'evil' out of the news.

At this time, fighting became par for the course. **Nick Lowe** began a fruitful working relationship with the **Damned** after a fight with **Rat Scabies** on a bus; the **Jam** once took on and held their own against a rugby team staying at the same hotel as them in Leeds in England. Meanwhile, **Siouxsie** and her drummer Kenny Morris spent a night in the cells following a disturbance after a **Johnny Thunder & The Heartbreakers** show. Indeed, even when punks tried to do the right thing it often fell apart in a welter of violence – at the end of a show Siouxsie & The Banshees played for charity, the group was presented with a bill for £2,000 worth of damaged seats.

The **Clash** were seldom out of court for offences ranging from theft to shooting pigeons with an air rifle. Crowd disturbances at gigs were regu-

dictated lavish productions with a lifestyle to match, it wasn't just the soul stars that were finding themselves in the red: Denny Laine, co-writer of the 2.5 million selling 'Mull Of Kintyre', was only one of many examples of mainstream bankruptcy. But **Gary Glitter** was rock's highest profile insolvent after he continued to live like he was selling a million records when he was virtually retired. "It was ridiculous – I was staying down at my country house, thinking up ways to spend money – £6,000 on motorized curtains, a machine that dispensed champagne automatically from a fridge by my bed and an open air swimming pool kept so warm all the year round that in winter you could see steam rising from it. And all the time I was enjoying life down there I wasn't making any records."

Of course the **Rolling Stones** never strayed too far from their Bad Boys Of Rock image either. Bianca may have made an honest man out of Mick, but it was only a few years

lar newspaper fodder, as drunken pogoing fans became increasingly frenzied. Local authority bans frequently prevented groups playing under their own names. The **Stranglers** had the power turned off mid-set when the management of the Roundhouse in London noticed singer Hugh Cornwell's T-shirt was a corruption of the Ford Motors logo reading 'Fuck'. But the high point of punk misbehaviour came on December 1, 1976: on the nationwide, early evening, British TV show *Today*, venerable presenter Bill Grundy taunted the Sex Pistols and some chums (Siouxsie among them) into trying to shock him. They responded with a volley of abuse so comprehensive that it dominated the next day's print media, got Grundy fired and earned the Pistols a place in rock legend.

To many, the Seventies represented the decline of Civilization As We Know It. And they could have had a point ... The writing was on the wall as early as January 1971, when long hair on men was made legal in the Soviet Union.

1972 was the year the teenies took over. The **Osmonds**, **T Rex**, **Slade**, **Gary Glitter**, **David Cassidy** and so on all dominated rock during those twelve months. It wasn't only in the singles charts either. While artists like **Led Zeppelin** and **Deep Purple** were still shifting respectable quantities of albums, the teenie groups had started outselling them. It was a shift that signified the decline of the long player as a 40-minute concept with integrated artwork and philosophy, and marked the format's return to those simple days of being nothing more challenging than a collection of singles.

Notwithstanding such theories, the year opens with one of the ultimate singles bands, **Status Quo**, in limbo. Undaunted by the lack of a recording contract, the group concentrate on playing live, building up a strong following as they develop the heavier, heads-down, blues-based boogie approach that remains their trademark. The triple album recorded at **George Harrison**'s *Concert For Bangladesh* hits UK Number 1 and US Number 2. In a similarly concerned frame of mind, **Bob Dylan** revives his old protest song ways with the single 'George Jackson' – devoted to the black militant who was killed in prison. And while **David Bowie**'s single 'Changes' isn't at all successful, the singer starts what becomes another UK pop music trend over the coming years when he declares his bisexuality in an interview with the British music weekly *Melody Maker*.

At the more wholesome end of things, **Cliff Richard**'s TV show *It's Cliff Richard* begins a 13-week run on British TV. **Wings** begin an, apparently, entirely spontaneous tour of British universities – they simply turn up and ask the college concerned's social secretary if they'd like Wings to perform in their hall that night. If any college turns them down, it's not on record. But while they're 'bringing their music to the kids', the BBC and the Independent Broadcasting Authority announce an airplay ban on the group's apparently pro-Republican debut single release, 'Give Ireland Back To The Irish', a record written as a reaction to the Bloody Sunday massacre when British troops opened fire on Catholic protestors in Northern Ireland.

In February, one-time **Pink Floyd** member the reclusive **Syd Barrett** reappears, albeit briefly, as part of a Cambridge-based trio called Stars. After three local gigs, they split up and Barrett goes back into hiding. The UK Number 1, 'Son Of My Father' by **Chicory Tip**, is the first big British hit to make extensive use of the synthesizer. **Alice Cooper** consolidates his US success of last year, when his 'Killer' LP goes Top 30 in the UK. In August, comes 'School's Out' – both the album and title track will sell a million copies each – which becomes an all-time international teen anthem.

On March 31 the Official Beatles Fan Club closes down but by then Britain is in the grip of what the tabloid press calls 'T-Rextasy'. After the group's single 'Telegram Sam's' rapid ascent to the top the previous

The fun-loving Wings, toured university campuses as a way of bringing their music to the kids. Or something.

FEB 9 : A state of emergency is declared in the UK as the month-old miners' strike leads to power cuts • MAY 2 : J. Edgar Hoover, founder of the FBI, dies

FEBRUARY 23: Elvis and Priscilla Presley separate.

MARCH 16: John and Yoko are served with deportation orders based on John's 1968 conviction for possessing cannabis.

APRIL 15: 'Amazing Grace', a bagpipe piece by the Royal Scots Dragoon Guards, tops the UK charts and goes on to be the best-selling British single of the year.

AUGUST 2: Brian Cole of the Association takes a fatal heroin overdose in Los Angeles.

SEPTEMBER: Bob Dylan plays the outlaw Alias in Sam Peckinpah's western Pat Garrett And Billy The Kid. He also composes the movie's soundtrack.

NOVEMBER 3: James Taylor and Carly Simon marry in her Manhattan apartment.

NOVEMBER 11: Berry Oakley, the Allman Brothers bass player, is killed in a motorcycle accident in Macon, Ga, three blocks from where Duane Allman was killed.

▲ They're bold! They're experimental! They're ELO.

month, the band play a series of sell-out shows at the Empire Pool Wembley, filmed by Ringo Starr as the Apple Films 'rockumentary' *Born To Boogie*. The Tyrannosaurus Rex double LP 'My People Were Fair...' and 'Prophets, Seers And Sages' is reissued to top the UK albums chart and their 1968 tracks 'Deborah' and 'One Inch Rock' are reactivated on a double 'Å' sided single which goes Top 10. Later, their 'Metal Guru' will be another Number 1, while 'Bolan Boogie' – the singles collection up to the end of last year – will become a best selling album.

Stevie Wonder releases 'Music Of My Mind'. Recorded with synthesizer experts Robert Margoleff and Malcolm Cecil, it is the first of five LPs that establish the former child prodigy as a grown-up, album-oriented talent, capable of appealing to both the black-funk and white-rock markets – later in the year the **Rolling Stones** take him on tour with them as opening act. In November, 'Talking Book' continues Wonder's musical direction and goes Top 20 on both sides of the Atlantic, while 'Innervisions' (1973)

'Fulfillingness First Finale' (1974) and 'Songs In The Key Of Life' (1976) complete the set and bring him a total haul of 11 Grammy awards. Also redefining himself is **Paul Simon**, whose first, eponymously-titled solo album, goes Top 5 in America, before he reunites with **Art Garfunkel** for a one-off concert at New York's Madison Square Garden the following month.

After a show in Zurich, **Mott The Hoople** call it a day, until long-time fan **David Bowie** offers them one of his songs provided they stay together to record it as part of an album – they reject 'Suffragette City' in favour of 'All The Young Dudes'. Produced by Bowie, it's a hit in the UK and the US (their first on either side of the ocean) and the album of that name (featuring Bowie and guitarist Mick Ronson) makes the UK Top 20. Meanwhile, Bowie himself finally achieves some sort of breakthrough: 'Hunky Dory' staggers to 176 in the US album listings, a mere five months after it was released. Strange to say, it is Bowie's fourth LP, yet his first album chart placing anywhere. **Gilbert**

O'Sullivan's 'Alone Again Naturally' is top of the US charts for six weeks, his biggest international hit. As part of his approach to the US he ditches the school uniform in favour of a preppy sweater and college scarf. "The boy is growing up" he tells journalists at the time. The single is quickly followed by the US Top 10 LP 'Gilbert O'Sullivan – Himself', and the erstwhile Raymond O'Sullivan is firmly established as an international artist, selling records all over the world for the next five years. Memorable efforts include 'Clair', 'Why Oh Why Oh Why', 'Get Down', 'Ooh Baby' and 'I Don't Love You But I Think I Like You'. On a more cerebral note, the **Electric Light Orchestra** debuts in a London pub, to play, as leader Roy Wood puts it, "jazz and classically influenced free-form music". Consisting of Wood, Jeff Lynne and other ex-**Move** members, plus assorted cellists and violinists, they don't go down too well with critics or crowd.

Remarkably, the band destined to become the archetypal American country rock group, the **Eagles,** record their first album, 'The Eagles', at a studio in Barnes, an affluent London suburb. The LP and its singles provide the band with the first of nearly a decade of huge US hits. Similarly displaced are the **Beach Boys** who in May decamp to Holland, where, at considerable expense, they have studio equipment flown in from America so they can spend the rest of 1972 making an album over there. It seems a long way from Californ-i-a and their record company refuses to release the resultant LP, 'Holland', until the group add 'Sail On Sailor', a track recorded in Los Angeles. When the album does come out, in the spring of 1973, its minimal commercial and critical success will not appear to have justified the cost.

The **Grateful Dead** take something of a sabbatical over the summer as **Jerry Garcia**'s first solo album 'Garcia', **Bob Weir**'s 'Ace' and **Mickey Hart**'s 'Rolling Thunder' are released. Pigpen is less productive though, as he is forced to rest and give up drinking after a serious liver complaint is diagnosed. **Barry White** produces 'Walking In The Rain With The One I Love' for girl trio **Love Unlimited**, during which he groans down a telephone line as part of the lyrics – the first time the syrupy bass tones of the future Walrus Of Lurrrve have been captured on wax.

In June, **Lou Reed**, who signed a solo deal last year, releases his debut album, 'Lou Reed'. Recorded in London and including among its backing musicians **Yes** members Rick Wakeman and Steve Howe, it is not a hit. What is a hit though, four months after its release, is **Gary Glitter**'s

'Rock And Roll Parts 1&2' which makes the UK Number 2 spot to kick off a three-year run of chart successes that establish him as one of Britain's best loved entertainers – the record is also his sole US hit, reaching Number 7.

Yet to release a record, **Roxy Music** play on the influential BBC TV show the *Old Grey Whistle Test*, then a couple of weeks later support **Alice Cooper** at Wembley Arena to excellent press reviews. 'The Rise And Fall Of Ziggy Stardust And The Spiders From Mars' finally gives **David Bowie** a hit in the UK, getting to number 5. In its wake, 'Hunky Dory' climbs to Number 3 and by the end of the year 'The Man Who Sold The World' and 'David Bowie' (now retitled 'Space Oddity') are re-released. Both go Top 20 in the UK, while only the latter charts in the US. Meanwhile in Sweden, a single comes out entitled 'People Need Love', the group is called Bjorn, Benny, Agnetha & Frida and they will soon become that well-known acronym, **ABBA**.

'The London Chuck Berry Sessions', an album of studio tracks featuring the legendary rock'n'roller backed by members of the **Faces** and supplemented by live material from the Lanchester Arts Festival, all recorded earlier in the year, gives Berry his biggest-selling album ever. By the end of the year, he will enjoy enormous singles success too with 'My Ding A Ling', a mildly risque, double-entendre million-selling novelty record. Sales were not harmed by formidable UK

public morals campaigner Mary Whitehouse trying to get it banned. Five months later, in June, she will urge the BBC to ban the **Rolling Stones**' 'Exile On Main Street' on the grounds of obscenity – interestingly, when the Corporation's Chairman, Lord Hill gives it a spin, he can't see anything wrong with it, in spite of its litany of swearwords.

Blue Oyster Cult release their debut album, establishing their unique loud and heavy sound, and they soon begin extensive touring as **Alice Cooper**'s resident support band. The **Kinks**' 'Supersonic Rocket Ship' proves to be their last UK hit for over ten years. At this time, the band are working almost exclusively in America where the Sixties nostalgia industry is already in full swing. The McCartneys, on tour with **Wings** in Sweden, are arrested for drug possession. This is the first of a series of much-publicized busts, abroad and even at their farm in Scotland, which culminates in Paul's brief spell in a Japanese jail in 1980. The Maccas seem so careless about concealing their herb that people wonder if they are trying to make some sort of oblique socio-political statement.

Lou Reed's debut solo album was called, interestingly, 'Lou Reed'.

Chuck Berry and his Ding A Ling left Mary Whitehouse all in a tizzy.

Rock'n'Roll Suicide?

It took a long time for the public to catch on to **David Bowie**. The media had sung his praises for a number of years but it wasn't until the album 'Ziggy Stardust' came out in 1972 that Bowie's sales figures started to reflect his reviews – his back catalogue too began to do brisk business. 'Ziggy's follow-up was the LP 'Aladdin Sane', which appeared in April and, though unable to match its predecessor, got to Number 1 in the UK as well as the Top 10 in the US. Dramatically, at the height of his new found fame, on July 3, 1973, on stage with the Spiders From Mars at London's Hammersmith Odeon, David Bowie announced "Not only is this the last show of the tour, but it's the last show we'll ever do."

Music papers held front pages, legions of teenagers with recently-dyed red hair went into shock and the record company rush-released 'Sorrow' from the 'Pin-Ups' LP. But for Bowie himself, it was all part of a calculated decision. What he was doing was setting the pattern

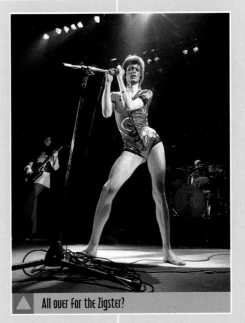

All over for the Zigster?

for the next 20 years – re-inventing his public persona as often as he felt it necessary to keep his audience interested. While any rock star's change of image is good for a few column inches, Bowie had worked out the career advantages of moving the goal posts so often and so skilfully that he remained an enigma. His strategy kept everybody on their toes: his audience had to keep guessing who he was; his contemporaries could never out-Ziggy him, or beat him at his own game, because he'd just re-write the rules and move on to Eurogloom or blue-eyed soul, leaving the wannabes behind like dinosaurs. Bowie was also gee-ing himself up to stay at the cutting edge of his own career rather than become a slave to it, cranking out the same old riffs as the law of diminishing returns set in.

It wasn't Bowie who'd retired, it was Ziggy. And anybody who had listened to the album would have known what was happening.

John Lennon releases 'Some Time In New York City,' a double album that teams him up with local band **Elephant's Memory** for one record of overtly political songs, while the other disc features live recordings with the **Mothers Of Invention**. Also doing well in the Big Apple is **David Bowie** who, five dates into his first US tour, has sold out five nights at

Ringo Starr (left) and David Essex hope an audience suspend disbelief as they play rock'n'rollers in That'll Be The Day.

Carnegie Hall New York. Having less luck closer to home is **Led Zeppelin** manager Peter Grant: his attempts to organize a concert by the group at Waterloo Station, London are cancelled by an unsympathetic British Rail.

In August, **ELO**'s first album 'Electric Light Orchestra' reaches the UK's Number 32 spot, following the Top 10 success of their first single '10538 Overture', but in America the LP is issued under a brilliant new title, 'No Answer' – it turns out that the US record company telephoned their UK counterpart to find out the album title and a secretary had rung Roy Wood to ask him what it was but he wasn't in. She told the US office "No answer". Next month though, Roy Wood will quit ELO to set up the pop-oriented **Wizzard** and ride the

glam-rock wave. Another debut album is **Roxy Music**'s 'Roxy Music': recorded in a month for less than £5,000 and produced by Pete Sinfield, late of **King Crimson**. It receives rave reviews and enters the UK chart at Number 10. In October, the band embark on a triumphant tour that shudders to a halt when vocalist Bryan Ferry has to have his tonsils removed midway through. Considerably less smooth role models for pop fans are school friends Paul Cook, Steve Jones and Wally Nightingale who have put together an as yet unnamed band that is, in fact, a very early incarnation of the **Sex Pistols**.

That same month, shooting begins for the film *That'll Be The Day* starring **Ringo Starr** and **David**

Those Troggs Tapes

1972 - HEADLINE NEWS   SEP 5 : 11 of the Israeli Olympic squad are killed by Arab terrorists following an attack and hostage-taking at the Olympic Village in Munich

Little Jimmy O checks out Elvis' tailor.

The Troggs: lively debate on the finer points of the creative process.

The Osmonds, clearly out-dentisting The Partridge Family.

Four years after the **Troggs**' last hit and two years since their split, a bootleg tape began to circulate of the Wiltshire-bred former flower children at work in a London recording studio. It's thought that the well produced cassette was marketed to coincide with a revival of interest in the band as they regrouped to play a British club and university tour. However, interest in the tapes themselves had little or nothing to do with the Troggs as a force in popular music, more as some sort of dry run for the UK comedy duo Peter Cook & Dudley Moore's infamous, foul-mouthed 'Derek & Clive' records or as the inspiration for *Spinal Tap*.

During a 1970 recording session, the band were experiencing difficulties and, while giving vent to their frustrations in loud West Country accents, the microphones were left open and the tape kept running just in case somebody produced something useable. 'The Troggs Tapes' are the bits when they weren't playing any music. This recording did the rounds among people in the rock business as a prime example of how a group of pretty basic guys goes about the creative process. You have to hear it to believe it. Their lively debate included the following:

Reg Presley (vocalist): You had it there at the beginning, Ron. It was sounding good, Ron ... Ronnie?
Ronnie Bond (drums): You can say that all fucking night, but I just cannot feel it any other way than what I've been fucking doing it.
Presley: You have played it tonight.
Bond: Don't expect fucking miracles.
Presley: It's fucking there. I can't fucking hear it any other way than that.
Tony Murray (bass): Play duh-duh duh-duh duh chuh.
Presley: No, play more beats.
Murray: Play duh-duh duh-duh duh chuh on whatever drum you were playing it on originally.
Bond: You can say that all fucking night, but you won't listen.
Murray: We can keep trying.
Bond: Yeah. Well just shut your fucking mouth for five minutes and give me a fucking chance to do it ... Just fuck off.
Presley: Well just fucking think then.

And so on.

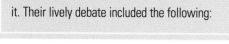

Essex (on sabbatical from *Godspell)* as an aspiring rock'n'roller Jim McLean on the Isle Of Wight during the Fifties. The movie will be a huge success and provide the exposure that propels

Essex to pop stardom. After years of building a solid live following, **Genesis**' fourth LP, 'Foxtrot', becomes their first chart success. In November, the BBC and IBA announce an airplay ban on **Wings**' 'Hi Hi Hi', believing it to contain drug references, so radio DJs 'flip' the record, with 'C Moon' becoming the A-side. In the US, **Diana Ross** makes her movie acting debut in the starring role in *Lady Sings The Blues*, a dramatization of the life of jazz singer **Billie Holliday**. Ross' performance is widely perceived as lacking true depth but that doesn't stop her receiving a Best Actress Oscar nomination.

In time for the festive season, **T Rex**'s film *Born To Boogie* is premiered; their 'Solid Gold Easy Action' single hits UK Number 3 and a reis-

sue of 'Unicorn' and 'Beard Of Stars' peaks at UK Number 44. The group finish the year as the UK's best-selling singles act and third in the LP listings. **John Lennon**'s 'Happy Christmas (War Is Over)', recorded over a year ago but held up by a dispute over writing credits, will make its first of many seasonal chart appearances. Britain's Christmas Number 1 though belongs to a well-nourished **Little Jimmy Osmond** and 'Long Haired Lover From Liverpool', a record that was a minor hit in the US six months previously. The nine-year-old, who admits in interview he has no idea where Liverpool is, is the youngest ever UK chart topper and the song – which shares the Top 10 with 'Crazy Horses' by his brothers and 'Why' by **Donny** – will become 1972's biggest selling single.

A Family Affair

The singing siblings who became the **Osmonds** performed together for nearly 10 years before they caught the eye of a record company astute enough to realize that the **Jackson 5** in white would be a good earner. As soon as the ink on their contract was dry, the Osmonds were packed off to Muscle Shoals studio to record the 'Mama's Pearl' soundalike, 'One Bad Apple'. The single had an

entirely Jackson-style reception too – Number 1 in America for more than a month, selling over a million. It was shortly afterwards, that the solo potential of the group's 11-year-old lead singer, **Donny**, was recognized, and while the Osmonds racked up five gold albums between 1971-73, Donny's parallel career scored four gold albums, seven Top 10 singles, including five million sellers. Then off the production line came **Marie** and **'Little' Jimmy** who, with or without

brothers, appeared to dominate the UK charts until the mid-Seventies and had a home on BBC TV's light entertainment schedule until the end of the decade. Curiously, after the initial flush was over, the Osmonds did much better in Britain where 'Osmania' got a grip in July 1972, when 'Puppy Love' topped the charts for five weeks.

By 1979 though, 'Little' Jimmy was no longer so small or cute, Donny and Marie's material had descended into the worst type of countrified mawk – it was something they'd always threatened, notwithstanding Donny's ill-advised forays into disco – and then Donny did the worst thing possible. He grew up. The altogether rather sensible LP 'Donald Clark Osmond' got no further than the Top 160 in America and bombed in the UK. No one loved him anymore.

1972 – HEADLINE NEWS • SEP 12 : The Cod War breaks out as an Icelandic gunboat sinks two British trawlers in the North Sea • DEC 25 : An earthquake in Nicaragua kills 10,000

1970s Underground

Although UK punk declared itself to be unique – something which swept away everything that had gone before – it had a clear blueprint in the left-field Detroit rock scene of the late-Sixties and early-Seventies which produced bands like the **MC5**, the **Prime Movers**, the **Iguanas** and the **Stooges** (the latter three bands each featured **Iggy Pop** in their line-up). During 1977, all the Stooges' LPs were re-released in the UK in response to demand from domestic punks: they professed to have no

heroes, but they turned Iggy Pop, with his depraved, self-lacerating behaviour, into an icon. Strangely, while the Detroiters' shock-tactics agenda of drugs, high octane rock 'n'roll, onstage outrage and violent revolutionary ideology pointed the way for the UK movement, a truly overground US punk scene never developed.

Perhaps this particular side alley of US rock culture represented the end of an era – the death throes of the Sixties idea of music as an instrument of revolution – rather than a Brave New Dawn, as punk in the UK was perceived. Or perhaps punk failed to take hold (either before or after 1976) because it was diametrically opposed to the American Dream. US rock audiences liked a working class hero, as long as he behaved like a star. **Elvis Presley**, with his 23-room mansion and assortment of Cadillacs, was perhaps the ultimate symbol of a national culture

of self-improvement so strong it was practically enshrined in the Constitution. In the US of the mid-Seventies, there weren't many takers for the notion of well brought-up, middle class kids ripping perfectly good clothes and pretending to have been born in the gutter.

The closest thing to UK punk in the US during the mid-Seventies was the new wave in New York, at the new wave in New York. The city CBGB's club in particular. The city had already given Britons some punk prototypes in the hugely influential form of the **Velvet Underground** and, later, the **New York Dolls** (briefly managed by Malcolm McLaren and starring the classically self-destructive **Johnny Thunders**) as well as hip figureheads like **Patti Smith** and **Richard Hell**. By 1976 the scene had evolved into something older and more considered than London's, but for a while the two cities nursed a jealous rivalry, quietly pilfering whatever they could of the other place's style and vigorously denying they'd done so. Apparently, CBGB

stood for 'Country, Bluegrass, Blues and Music For Urban Gourmets'. The people at this venue were part of the New York art scene rather than impoverished inner-city dwellers – a post-Warhol crowd. They were used to acts like **Talking Heads**, **Blondie** and the **Ramones** and were more devoted to high-concept, passionate

pop music than to kneejerk anarchy. At this time, overtly stylized presentation was de rigeur in Manhattan and the scene was much more glamorous

than the UK's. By decade's end the best hardcore punk action was to be found over on the West Coast, home to a new underground breed that included the **Dead Kennedys**, **Black Flag** and **X**.

Back in the spring of 1977 the **Damned** became the first UK punk band to perform in America – at CBGB's, naturally. It was the start of a small-venue 'toe in the water' tour that provoked a healthy response among college kids, but it failed to convince record companies and mainstream radio that punk had anything significant to offer. Early in 1978, the **Sex Pistols**' highly publicized and ultimately self-destructive US tour of bigger venues was a shambles. Undoubtedly, another reason punk never took off in America, aside from the fact that the conventional music business chose to ignore it, was the sheer size of the country: independent record companies couldn't reasonably expect

anything more than a local hit. American or British, the full impact of punk's underground influence would not become evident until the Nineties, and the commercial triumph of punk's inheritors **Nirvana** and **Guns N'Roses**.

The US industry might well have misjudged punk, though. CBS, to whom the **Clash** were signed worldwide, felt the group's 1977 debut album, 'The Clash', was unsuitable for the market and refused to release it. By the time the band arrived to play live dates in the US two years later, the LP had sold over 100,000 copies as an expensive import item.

1973

1973 saw trends from the previous year gathering pace. Glam-rock progressed from merely being about **Marc Bolan** to becoming a bona fide 'movement': **Gary Glitter**, **Slade** and the **Sweet** continued on an upward curve, while their glittering ranks were swollen by new chart regulars such as **Wizzard**, **Mud** and **Suzi Quatro** – the latter two were the sharp end of pro-

ducer Mickie Most's RAK Records empire, built on rock'n'roll-ish teen-oriented hits penned by Nicky Chinn and Mike Chapman. The new lighter pop sensibilities weren't confined to the pubescent market either. **David Bowie** and **Elton John** established glam-rock's credibility in the albums market, the former with 'conceptual' LPs and lavish multi-media stage presentations, and the latter with good honest songwriting. Likewise, Sixties rock-derived pop spilled over into the MOR market, as **Donny Osmond**, **Paul McCartney**, **Simon & Garfunkel** and **Gilbert O'Sullivan** became the new generation's **Perry Comos** and **Andy Williamses**. Early disco burst into life as Gamble &

Huff's Philly Sound began to replace Motown and, in that groove, more and more soft soul began appearing in the charts on both sides of the Atlantic. But early in the year, it was nostalgia that ruled.

On January 13, **Eric Clapton** is coaxed into returning to live performance when **Pete Townshend** organizes a comeback show for the guitarist at the Rainbow Theatre. Participating are Ron Wood, Steve Winwood and Jim Capaldi, but the success of the event is not enough to stop Clapton from disappearing into the night afterwards. The next day, the **Elvis Presley** TV special *Aloha! From Hawaii* is beamed live from Honolulu to Japan and the Far East. America and

Glitter Over England

Glam-rock came into being during 1971, but it was two years later that its most endearing, and enduring, figure stamped his personality on the British psyche – **Gary Glitter**, probably the most unlikely teen idol ever. Paunchy, past 30 and with a bouffant quiff, he took glam-rock's job description to its giddy limit with a stage persona that wore the tallest platforms, the widest shoulders and the brightest sparkliest sequins of all. Terry Tinsel, Stanley Sparkle and Vicky Vomit were all rejected before Gary Glitter came up with a name to match his tongue-in-cheek image. But kids of all ages couldn't resist his act and, between 1972 and 1975, Glitter's far-from-complex songwriting technique garnered a string of 11 consecutive UK Top 10 singles – three Number 1s, including the million-selling 'I Love You Love Me Love' which went in at the top, and four runners up – and three Top 10 albums.

Analyzing this success years later, Glitter claimed he knew exactly what was required, "It was all a matter of getting that live show feel on to a record – a simple beat that anybody could follow, and to get the crowd involved I'd write every song around the bits where I

▲ Gary Glitter, getting the crowd 'involved'.

could punch the air and shout 'Oi!'. And with lyrics about love it was tough enough for the boys and still romantic enough for the girls. It was just like the old rock'n'roll songs."

He probably knew what he was talking about too, as Glitter's numerous previous incarnations stretch back to the original London rock'n'roll scene where, under the name of **Paul Raven**, he was a regular at the 2Is and the Safari Clubs. Then came a long exile honing his stagecraft in Hamburg (just after the **Beatles**), arriving back in the UK to catch the butt end of psychedelia and trying his luck under the names of Paul Monday and Rubber Bucket. 'Rock 'N' Roll Parts I & 2' recorded in late 1971 was, he admits, pretty much a last-ditch attempt.

But the most remarkable aspect of Gary Glitter's varied career is his incredible capacity for survival. He has come through drug addiction, alcoholism, bankruptcy, numerous youth culture revolutions, baldness and a suicide attempt to become the darling of the advertising and late night TV industries and, in recent years, he has consistently sold out 10,000 capacity venues with his annual Christmas tour.

MARCH 9: Lou Reed marries a New York waitress named Betty.

JUNE 23: Peter Noone rejoins Herman's Hermits for a British Sixties nostalgia concert at New York's Madison Square Garden. Also on the bill are Gerry & The Pacemakers and Wayne Fontana & The Mindbenders.

JUNE 26: Keith Richard and Anita Pallenberg are arrested on firearms and drugs charges.

JULY 28: The Grateful Dead, the Allman Bros and the Band share top billing at The Watkins Glen Festival at the Watkins Glen Raceway, New York State, which draws a record crowd of 600,000.

OCTOBER 9: Elvis and Priscilla are divorced.

OCTOBER: John and Yoko split up. He decamps to Los Angeles, to embark on what he later referred to as his 'lost weekend' – a hazy, alcohol and vitriol-fuelled state of affairs that lasts until the end of 1974.

Europe get a recorded broadcast the next night and the total estimated audience is 1.5 billion, the largest TV viewing figures ever for a single event. That's without a screening in Britain! For reasons never made completely clear, both ITV and the BBC refuse to take the show. However, the UK proves its own taste for nostalgia as the year opens with the **Moody Blues**' 'Nights In White Satin' 10 places higher in the charts than when it was first released five years previously.

Genesis start 1973 as they intend to continue – on the road: their first headlining tour of large UK venues is followed by their debut US tour. After a couple of months off, the band keep going, having released a live album – 'Genesis Live', recorded in the States – along the way. Their hard work pays off when both their live set and their studio album 'Selling England By The Pound' make the charts in Britain.

Despite a particularly unhappy relationship with his record company, **Bruce Springsteen**'s debut album 'Greetings From Asbury Park' is released. CBS had perceived him as a folkie-type, solo performer – 'the new Bob Dylan' – but the recordings contradict this notion with a horn section and girl backing singers. A somewhat confused marketing campaign reflects this misunderstanding and initially the record sells a mere 25,000. Elsewhere, the original **Byrds** reform but, although the reunion produces the successful 'Byrds' album, they don't stay together any longer than it takes to make the recording.

On March 23, **Yoko Ono** is granted permanent residence in the USA

John and Yoko and uncharacteristic April Foolery.

but partner **John Lennon** is ordered to leave the country within 60 days. A week later, the couple announce the founding of Nutopia, a new country with no laws and no borders, though no one can find it on any map. The press conference is held on the morning of April 1 – on John's November-released album, 'Mind Games', there will be a silent 'track' entitled 'The Nutopian International Anthem'. Meanwhile, the **Grateful Dead** set up Grateful Dead Records for themselves and Round Records to release other acts. The labels are the beginnings of a Dead business empire that will grow to include music publishing, studio, booking agency and travel company but it will only last four years before being dismantled. At **Lou Reed**'s concert in Buffalo, NY, a particularly enthusiastic (male) fan leaps on to the stage and bites the singer on the backside. His fortunes change next month though, when the 'Transformer' album – recorded in London, produced by Mick Ronson and David Bowie – yields the single 'Walk On The Wild Side', the old groaner's only solo chart hit and his future signature tune.

The **Wailers**' seminal 'Catch A Fire' album is released and, for the first time, a reggae album is given the same marketing support as a top rock album. Produced from tapes the band recorded in Jamaica in 1971/72, it is tickled up by Island Records owner, Chris Blackwell, with extra guitars and keyboards, and the original uncompromising arrangements are toned down and layered to make them more accessible to rock/pop-oriented (i.e. white) ears. The sleeve too is highly unusual for a reggae album – a two-piece cardboard arrangement constructed to look like a huge Zippo lighter, that opens on a rivet hinge to reveal a flaming wick with the record peeping out from behind it. This packaging attracts almost as much comment as the music but it helps break a reggae band to a mainstream audience. At least in Europe, if not yet in the US.

Elsewhere in spring, EMI Records launches **Queen** and the band plays a set at London's Marquee Club, remarkable mainly because of vocalist Freddie Mercury's subdued performance – his flamboyant style as frontman for the group will take a couple of years to fully develop. The **Rolling Stones** go to Kingston, Jamaica, to record in reggae producer Byron Lee's Dynamic Sound Studios, which comes as no real surprise as Jagger's fondness for authentic dub reggae is well known. The sessions will eventually become 'Goat's Head Soup', released in September. **Tom Waits**, a regular on the LA club circuit, releases his first LP, 'Closing Time', a rough-hewn blend of fractured jazz and beat-type lyrics. It doesn't sell too well, but

Dark Side of the Moon

In March 1973, **Pink Floyd**'s 'Dark Side Of The Moon' LP came out to mixed reviews. The Floyd's new album was deliberately gloomy, a thematically linked homage to madness, stress and the problems of everyday life. When it was first performed live as a prelude to the recording sessions, the title was 'Dark Side Of The Moon – A Piece For Assorted Lunatics'. The music was destined to be bleak: recorded over eight months on Abbey Road's then unused 24-track facility, it made much of sound effects and spoken soundbites. Although the suite was excellently constructed and engaging if not exactly entertaining, it couldn't be described as another 'Sgt Pepper' or 'Electric Ladyland'. In fact even the band couldn't put a finger on what made it so special. To date it has sold 25 million copies worldwide (when it came out on CD, one factory in Germany pressed nothing else for several months) and spent over 14 years in the US album charts. This record alone transformed the Floyd into a big league creative force and remains The Concept Album against which all others are judged.

Frank Zappa is sufficiently impressed to take Waits on tour with him as opening act.

Less adventurously, two **Beatles** compilation albums, 'The Beatles 1962-1966' and 'The Beatles 1967-1970', occupy the top two positions in the US chart and Numbers 2 and 3 in the UK during April. This success, undeniable proof of the continuing demand for moptop product, fuels the Beatles-to-reform rumour mill, which goes into overdrive in May as **Ringo Starr** starts recording his third album, 'Ringo', in Los Angeles. Each of the other three Beatles contribute to it, but never all together on the same track – on one song, the John Lennon-penned 'I'm The Greatest', only Paul is missing form the original Fabs' line-up. The resulting album, released in November, will go Top 10 in both the USA and UK and, with no small justification, be held to be the drummer's career best.

In May, **Mike Oldfield**'s 'Tubular Bells' is the first release on the Virgin Records label, the brainchild of Virgin Records Shop owner Richard Branson. Almost totally instrumental, the hour of intricate, ambient music has been built up almost note by note over six months and has literally hundreds of studio overdubs from 'one man orchestra' Oldfield who plays all the instruments except the flute and some drums. The album is destined to sell over 10 million copies; to become the basis of the score of the blockbuster movie *The Exorcist;* to win a Grammy Award (Best Instrumental 1974); to stay on the UK charts for a total of nearly six years; to earn Oldfield an entry in *Who's Who* and to provide the financial cornerstone of the embryonic Virgin empire. 10 years later, Oldfield will sue Branson over royalty irregularities, but he will never repeat this success with any of his future releases.

Joan Baez devotes one side of her 'Where Are You Now, My Son?' album to an audio documentary about the American bombing campaign in Vietnam. **Paul Simon** goes on tour for the first time since the split with Art Garfunkel. Donald Fagen and Walter Becker decide on the name **Steely Dan** – the name of a steam-powered dildo in William Burroughs's drug culture classic *Naked Lunch* – and recruit Denny Dias, Jim Hodder, David Palmer and Jeff Baxter on an ad hoc session basis as work begins on what will be the 'Can't Buy A Thrill' LP. Also starting out are Carnie (5) and Wendy (4) Wilson and Chynna Phillips (5), the trio that, 17 years later, will become **Wilson Phillips**, but now going under the name of the Satellites. They record their first single 'Take Me Out To The Ball Game', which is never released. Meanwhile, 56,800 people attend **Led Zeppelin**'s stadium show in Tampa, Florida, breaking a US attendance record set by the Beatles at Shea Stadium in 1965. **Jethro Tull** announce they're quitting touring, and keep their word for three years.

In tribute to **Gary Glitter**, and to while away the time waiting for EMI to release **Queen**'s finished debut album, **Freddie Mercury** gives himself the name Larry Lurex and puts out a hi-camp cover of the **Beach Boys**' 'I Can Hear Music'. In common with the LP 'Queen', and the single, 'Keep Yourself Alive', which come out in July, it fails to impress record buyers. Faring better though, is 'Ring

Gloomy, bleak, stressful, 25 million-selling? It must be a new Pink Floyd album.

Ring', **Abba**'s first single since they shortened their name – the record goes to Number 1 in all Scandinavian countries, with an English version topping charts in Austria, Belgium, Holland and South Africa. However, released in the UK in October, it will not chart.

Ian Gillan and Roger Glover quit **Deep Purple**. Phil and Don Everly quit each other in spectacular fashion: when on stage at the Los Angeles amusement park Knott's Berry Farm, the stage manager stops the second of three sets, announcing he is unhappy with Don's performance. Phil, in turn, smashes his guitar on the floor and storms off. Don plays the third set solo, announcing to the crowd that the duo will not perform together any more: "The **Everly Brothers** died ten years ago." Ray Davies quits his wife and children, takes two overdoses – thought to be half-hearted suicide attempts – announces he is retiring but within a week is back in the studio working on new **Kinks** material. In happier circumstances, **Paul McCartney & Wings** (now a threesome since Henry McCullough and Denny Seiwell's departure) quit Britain for Lagos, Nigeria, and Ginger Baker's ARC studios for six weeks of sessions

Abba came a disappointing third with 'Ring Ring' in the Swedish heats for the 1973 Eurovision Song Contest. One year later they won the chance to represent their country at the finals in Brighton with 'Waterloo'.

for the 'Band On The Run' album.

On August 6, **Stevie Wonder** is seriously injured in a car crash while on tour in North Carolina and remains in a coma for four days. Bizarrely, given the singer's virtually scandal-free image, his six weeks' convalescence sparks rumours of the car crash story being a front for hospitalization to overcome heroin/cocaine addiction. In September, David Coverdale leaves his job as a menswear shop assistant in a small Yorkshire town to join Deep Purple as vocalist. He answered a music paper ad, which requested a photo be sent – he submitted the only one he had, of himself aged 12 in a boy scout uniform. Riding in **Roxy Music**'s slipstream, **Bryan Ferry**'s first solo album hits UK Number 5. 'These Foolish Things' is a collection of covers of his favourite songs (the single 'Hard Rain's Gonna Fall' goes Top 10), an approach that will serve the singer well over the next 20 years. **King Crimson** play their last gig of the decade – following the internal upheavals of the last couple of years, Robert Fripp is the only original member left. Recordings intended to be **Jonathan Richman & The Modern Lovers**' first album are rejected by Warner Bros., after both the group and the company are unhappy with John Cale's production.

Following **Bob Dylan**'s very public falling out with CBS, the record company puts out a hastily knocked together set of out-takes and cover versions rejected from 'Self Portrait'. Entitled 'Dylan', the critics hate it and Bob himself is so disgruntled he signs to Asylum Records, where he will release two albums during the next year before

making up again with CBS chief, Clive Davis. Also in November, **Bruce Springsteen**'s second album, 'The Wild, The Innocent And The E Street Shuffle', comes out and its poor sales in no way reflect the excellent reviews it receives from America's critics.

The **Who**'s 'Quadrophenia' goes to Number 2 in the US and UK. A 'Tommy'-style concept album (the story of Jimmy The Mod), it features a wealth of sound effects which all had to be specially recorded as the group wanted the whole record in stereo but most SFX libraries only keep mono recordings. This quest for authenticity nearly costs the lives of the sound crew taping the swoosh of genuine waves when their boat capsizes. The band's Keith Moon has his own brush with danger in November, when he collapses on stage, apparently due to a pre-show drink spiked with horse tranquillizer. A teenage audience member takes over the drum stool to complete the set.

In time for Christmas, Wings' 'Band On The Run' is released. Critically acclaimed and all set to spend two years on both the US and UK charts selling over 6 million copies worldwide, it is a post-**Beatles** highpoint Paul McCartney has yet to surpass. Meanwhile, **Slade**'s 'Merry Xmas Everybody' (a hardy perennial that will rechart several times during the festive period over the next two decades) is the UK Christmas Number 1, the first time a seasonal song has got there since **Harry Belafonte**'s 'Mary's Boy Child' back in 1957. It also marks the end of rock stars' snobbery about seasonal songs – **Steeleye Span**, **Wizzard** and **Elton John** all have Christmas-type singles in the shops.

FEB 5 : Patty Hearst is kidnapped by the Symbionese Liberation Army

Clutching on to the coat tails of the cod rock'n'roll revival of the previous year, ersatz rockers such as **Alvin Stardust**, **David Essex** and **Cozy Powell** swelled glam-rock's ranks in 1974 but they couldn't keep the trend from slipping out of fashion when the UK caught a bad dose of 'Rollermania'. Half-mast trousers, bum-freezer jackets and tartan scarves replaced more sparkling items in the well-dressed teenager's wardrobe and the **Bay City Rollers** were king.

Later in the year, the concept album came back. Perhaps it was all down to new technology. Or maybe it was the unqualified success of what must be the ultimate muso album 'Tubular Bells' – still hanging around in the charts from last year – that left artists figuring virtuosity for virtuosity's sake was still cool. 1974 duly produced two of the decade's most portentous works, **Pink Floyd**'s 'Dark Side Of The Moon' and **Rick Wakeman**'s 'Journey To The Centre Of The Earth'.

Rock's lack of good new ideas was thrown into sharp relief when the **Beatles** figured in the Top 5 album selling acts of 1974 (five years after they split up!), but this was still to be the year that punk first raised its spiky head. However, it wasn't quite ready to start spitting yet.

As the new year dawns, **Steve Miller**'s 'The Joker' is US Number 1 in the album and singles chart. It is not the first time the song will be a hit. Another long-lasting pop item about to be established is the **Meat Loaf**/Jim Steinman partnership, as the former takes two roles in the off-Broadway musical *More Than You Deserve*, which is written by the latter. **Alice Cooper**'s star, however, begins its descent – the new album, 'The Love Muscle', barely scrapes into the Top 10 – and he fires his original band. **Led Zeppelin** announce the formation of their own record label, SwanSong.

And, as 'Sunday Bloody Sunday', **Black Sabbath**'s most successful album to date, epitomizes their steamroller sound, former manager Jim Simpson serves a breach of contract subpoena on the group, virtually forcing them into a two-year sabbatical while the legalities are sorted out.

After a nine month long US tour, the **Moody Blues** opt for a temporary split. Justin Hayward and John Lodge immediately start recording together at the group's nearly completed London recording studio, the first quadrophonic set-up anywhere in the world. **Genesis** get their first US chart placing as 'Selling England By The Pound' reaches Number 70 and, two months later, a year and a half after release, the LP shows up in the UK charts. The **Band** reunite with **Bob Dylan**, to record his 'Planet Waves' LP and later in the year they will tour with him resulting in the double live album 'Before The Flood'.

Kiss' debut album, 'Kiss', is promoted in the US with a nationwide series of kissing contests but only reaches Number 87 – December's follow-up, 'Hotter Than Hell', doesn't even do that well, peaking at Number 100. Other newcomers (second time round) are the Bay City Rollers whose 'Remember (Sha La La)' gives them their second UK Top 10 hit, two and a half years after the first. However, this time they're here to stay and, by the time the band tour in October, they've had two more hits and 'Rollermania' has the UK in its grip. During the next three years, the Bay City Rollers will have 10 Top 10 hits, including three Number 1s, five

 Black Sabbath formed in 1967 as Polka Tulk but quickly changed their name to Earth. They became Black Sabbath in 1969, the title of one of their early songs inspired by bassist Terry Butler's interest in black magic novelist Dennis Wheatley.

The Bay City Rollers were not from Bay City in Utah, as their name would suggest, but from Edinburgh in Scotland.

Early Queen gigs included a support slot on a Mott The Hoople tour and a show at London's Marquee club with quirky American duo Sparks.

best-selling albums and a clutch of US hits, including one Number 1. These days, the group are probably best remembered for the anthemic single 'Shang A Lang', press speculation as to whether they actually played their own instruments either on stage or in the studio and scandals involving their original manager Tam Paton, who was jailed for three years on a charge of gross indecency.

Other teen idols in the news in February are T Rex, when the 'Teen-age Dream' single is the first to bear the name **Marc Bolan & T Rex**, and the **Jackson 5** who cut short a tour of Africa after a few days – they prove unable to adjust to the local food and water. Elsewhere, **Van Morrison** disbands the large Caledonia Soul Orchestra to tour Europe with a five-piece band. After leaving university, **Joe Jackson** joins his first band, specializing in cover-versions-of-current-hits on the pub circuit and called Edward Bear. **Jefferson Airplane** become **Jefferson Starship**. And **Brian Eno**'s first solo album, 'Here Come The Warm Jets', is released, featuring Robert Fripp and Phil Manzanera.

Boosted by their first head-lining tour, **Queen** finally break

through and both 'Queen' and 'Queen II' chart in the UK, the former almost a year after release, the latter staying there for six months. Their stock rises still further in May, when the group make an impressive debut on *Top Of The Pops* appearing at very short notice after a **David Bowie** promo clip fails to turn up at the BBC. In south London, Chris Difford answers Glenn Tilbrook's ad in a music paper, they recruit Paul Gunn and Jools Holland and call themselves **Squeeze** after the Velvet Underground LP. And **Ten Years After** break up, as Alvin Lee decides the band has achieved its potential.

In April, the original **Wailers**, Peter Tosh and Bunny Livingston, quit the group, upset by Island Record's decision to promote future releases as **Bob Marley & The Wailers**. Happier campers are **Lou Reed**, who earns his first gold disc for selling 500,000 copies of the live LP 'Rock n' Roll Animal', recorded at New York's Academy Of Music, and **Billy Joel** whose 'Piano Man' album goes gold in America. It is his debut for CBS Records after the label's chief executive, Clive Davis, spotted him perform-

ing in a Los Angeles piano bar and offered him a contract, so the story goes. Another new signing, to EMI in London, is 16-year-old schoolgirl **Kate Bush**. She's given a deal on the strength of demo tapes sponsored by **Pink Floyd**'s Dave Gilmour but the company decides to let her highly personal style – words, music, dance, mime, squeaky voice – develop in its own good time and it will be four years before she makes a record. In the meantime, she continues to play tiny London venues with her group The KT Bush Band.

Marc Bolan leaves the UK for tax exile in Monte Carlo. David Bowie departs for America where he will spend the next two years. This summer, he'll tour the US with the spectacular *Diamond Dogs* show, a lavishly choreographed and highly theatrical staging of the album, which, when released in June, arouses controversy due to the half-man-half-dog sleeve painting by Belgian artist Guy Peellaert. Plans to take the tour to the UK are unviable from a financial point of view – but, rather shrewdly, a live album recorded during the tour will appear

Captain Fantastic Gets Paid

In July 1974, **Elton John** re-signed with MCA Records in the US for a five-album deal worth $8 million to the singer. At the time, it was the most lucrative contract in rock's history but no more than the former Reginald Dwight deserved. Less than 15 years previously, at 16 years old, he had been earning the princely sum of £1 per night for knock-ing out such bar room favourites as 'Roll Out The Barrel' and 'Down At The Old Bull & Bush' in a local hotel. Elton John started playing as a schoolboy, then to supplement his earnings as a tea boy in a London music publishing company, saving up to buy an electric piano so he could join the semi-pro **Bluesology**.

In the early days, Reg Dwight earned the meagre sum of £15 per week – out of which came con-tributions for petrol and van maintenance – as Bluesology backed a roster of singers including vis-iting US acts **Doris Troy**, **Major Lance**, **Patti LaBelle & The Bluebelles**, the **Inkspots** and **Billy Stewart**. Apparently the band were once due to do a show with **Wilson Pickett** but the Wicked One sought alternative musicians after hearing them rehearse. By the end of 1966, they'd become **Long John Baldry**'s regular backing band but disbanded less than a year later as Baldry's work became increas-ingly cabaret-oriented. However, not before Reg had

changed his name to Elton John, his inspiration coming from Bluesology's sax player Elton Dean and Long John himself.

Elton John concentrated on writing – together with lyricist **Bernie Taupin** – until 1969, when his first album, 'Empty Sky', failed to make an impression.

The shy, retiring Reginald Dwight. No one sold more records in America in the Seventies.

However, next year the follow-up, 'Elton John', got to Number 4 in the USA and 11 in the UK, setting off a chain reaction that didn't see him out of the US album charts for the entire Seventies – 'Tumble-weed Connection' (Number 5), 'Friends' (36), '11-17-70' (11), 'Madman Across The Water' (8), 'Honky Chateau' (five weeks at Number 1), 'Don't Shoot Me I'm Only The Piano Player' (Number 1, two weeks), 'Goodbye Yellow Brick Road' (Number 1, eight weeks), 'Caribou' (Number 1, four weeks), 'Greatest Hits' (Number 1, 10 weeks), 'Captain Fantastic And The Brown Dirt Cowboy' (the first LP to go straight in at Number 1, where it stayed for seven weeks), 'Rock Of The Westies' (Number 1, three weeks), 'Here And There' (2), 'Blue Moves' (3), 'Greatest Hits Vol 2' (21) and 'Single Man' (15). With the exception of 'Don't Shoot Me, I'm Only The Piano Player', which was top of the UK charts for six weeks, each of these albums was a bigger hit in the US than in his home country.

ROCK'N'ROLL record

APRIL 25: Pamela Morrison, the Lizard King's widow, succumbs to a heroin overdose.

APRIL: On the 20th anniversary of its original release, Bill Haley's 'Rock Around The Clock' re-enters the singles charts on both sides of the Atlantic.

JULY 29: 'Mama' Cass Elliott dies in London from a heart attack sustained after choking on food.

AUGUST14: Willie Russell's satirical play about the Beatles, John, Paul, George, Ringo ... and Bert, opens in London's West End after an initial run in Liverpool.

SEPTEMBER 23: The Average White Band's Robbie McIntosh dies after snorting heroin at a Los Angeles party. He believed it to be cocaine.

OCTOBER: Ted Nugent wins the US National Squirrel Shooting Archery Contest. The guitarist's passion for hunting has been well documented, his albums 'Call Of The Wild' and 'Tooth, Fang And Claw'.

The young Prince started out in Alexander O'Neal's backing band.

in British shops just in time for Christmas.

Also in April, **Abba** and 'Waterloo' win the Eurovision Song Contest, which is held in the UK where the record goes immediately to the top of the charts. Up until this point, Britain has been one of the few European countries resistant to the singing Swedes. Shooting begins on the film version of *Tommy*, starring the **Who**, **Elton John**, **Tina Turner**, Oliver Reed, Ann Margaret and Jack Nicholson. At the same time, **Pete Townshend** makes his solo live debut with a concert at the Roundhouse in London. Equally out on his own but much more successful is **Rick Wakeman**, whose solo LP 'Journey To The Centre Of The Earth' makes impressive use of developing synthesizer technology to scale new heights of self-importance. Meanwhile **Rod Stewart** sings on the **Scottish Football Squad**'s World Cup disc, 'Easy Easy'. It is something of a dream-come-true for London-born Stewart, when he duets with all-time great striker Denis Law – at one point, football-crazy Stewart had a Scottish flag as his bed cover and he has often been given to kicking footballs into the crowd at his shows.

On May 26, at **David Cassidy**'s concert at the White City Stadium in London, the crowd runs out of control, resulting in over 1,000 needing medical attention and six girls being taken to hospital. One 14-year-old girl dies four days later from injuries sustained in the crush. On the same night,

Bruce Springsteen and the recently-christened **E-Street Band** are playing the first of three gigs at Charley's Club in Boston. In the audience for the first two shows is influential *Rolling Stone* music critic Jon Landau, who is so impressed by the song 'Born To Run' that he is moved to include the phrase "I saw the rock and roll future – and its name is Bruce Springsteen" in his review. Misquoted, the words become the focus of an intense re-marketing campaign by CBS, which prompts other glowing reviews as well as a long friendship and, eventually, business relationship between the 26-year-old critic Landau and the man who will become The Boss.

Meanwhile, another legend is about to be born – somewhere in the mid-west of America, the Minneapolis Sound is taking shape. A blend of funk and rock, known in the local clubs and bars where it's performed

as Uptown, it's practised by two teenage bands: Grand Central (later named Champagne) with Andre Cymone on bass, Morris Day on drums and **Prince** on guitar, and Flyte Tyme – Terry Lewis on bass, **Alexander O'Neal** on vocals and Jellybean Johnson on drums. All are products of Minneapolis Central High School.

This summer, **Steely Dan** retire from live work for three years. **Cliff Richard** plays Bottom in an amateur production of *A Midsummer Night's Dream*; and, in a completely unconnected incident, the Christian-flavoured International Cliff Richard Movement holds its first meeting in a church in London. Temporarily reformed, **Crosby, Stills, Nash & Young** start a 30-date US tour but internal strife, clearly still present, is revealed when Neil Young travels separately from the other three. Also back on the block are **Lou Reed**, **John Cale** and **Nico** who play an impromptu reunion show in Paris. And so is **Eric Clapton** with his single 'I Shot The Sheriff'. Clapton's cover of Bob Marley's song is the first single taken from his 'comeback recordings' and goes to the top of the US charts. These sessions are the guitarist's first recordings since taking a controversial electro-acupuncture drug/alcohol addiction cure late last year, and his first studio work since 1970 as **Derek & The Dominoes**. Next month, the LP '461 Ocean Boulevard' comes out – it's named after the address of the studio in Miami where it was recorded.

AUG 9 : Gerald Ford is sworn in as US President • NOV 12 : English lord Lucan goes missing after the murder of his family's nanny

Tickets for **Elton John**'s three shows in Los Angeles in August sell out in a matter of minutes, while during the same month the **Osmonds** do six nights of live shows on BBC television. If this is some sort of cultural exchange, then surely the Americans are getting the better of the deal. As **CSN&Y**, the **Band** and **Joni Mitchell** play to 80,000 people at Wembley Stadium, clear signs of a new world order are emerging. A newly-formed **Blondie** begin a residency at CBGB's, the New York nightclub celebrated as the cradle of American punk. Living in London and occasionally contributing to music paper *NME,* **Chrissie Hynde** is working in future **Sex Pistol**'s manager Malcolm McLaren's clothes shop *Sex.* Hugh Cornwell, Jean-Jacques Burnel and Brian Duffy (aka Jet Black) form the **Guildford Stranglers** to play minor gigs in Surrey. Back in New York, fellow Rhode Island School Of Design students **David Byrne**, **Tina Weymouth** and **Chris Frantz** form a trio and take day jobs while rehearsing. And Ex-Kent State students Mark Mothersbaugh and Jerry Casale get together and recruit Mark's two brothers Jim and Bob into what is an embryonic, nameless, four-piece version of **Devo**.

Meanwhile, it's also early days for another rather different artist. As a guest at a Cuban wedding in Miami, 17-year-old Gloria Farjardo, a psychology student at the local University, is invited on stage to sing with the band, the Miami Cuban Boys, who are led by Emilio Estefan. Her success on this occasion leads to a partnership with Estefan – both artistic and domestic – and a name change to **Gloria**

Estefan. Less enamoured with his partners is Robert Fripp, who announces that **King Crimson** will not get together again, no matter what the personnel might be. They don't for seven years, either.

Under the pseudonym of the Country Hams, **Wings** release the single 'Walking In The Park With Eloise', written by Paul McCartney's father (James). In spite of Paul picking it as his favourite record on BBC Radio's *Desert Island Discs,* the song fails to chart. Similarly received is 'She's My Lady', the product of a **Dave Dee, Dozy, Beaky, Mick and Tich** reunion that lasts not much longer than it takes the single to flop. 'You Ain't Seen Nothing Yet', sung with a 'humorous' stutter by **Bachman Turner Overdrive** and only added to their 'Not Fragile' album as an afterthought, hits Number 1 in the US and Number 2 in the UK, selling over a million worldwide.

In November, **Genesis** start their 102-date Lamb Lies Down On Broadway tour, while, after their own successful US tour, **Traffic** split to pursue solo careers. **John Lennon** makes his final concert appearance when he joins Elton John on stage at Madison Square Garden for three numbers. It is the result of a bet Lennon lost with Elton, as to whether the former's 'Whatever Gets You Through The Night' single would reach Number 1 in America: Lennon was sure it wouldn't, Elton John recognized the song's potential.

Christmas cheer this year is supplied by **Roxy Music** and the scantily clad models on the sleeve of 'Country Life' – they cause so much controver-

sy in the US that the album has to be sold in opaque green shrinkwrap. While the fuss is going on, **Bryan Ferry** plays three solo dates in the UK. By performing in a dinner jacket, backed by a group and orchestra in full evening dress, he establishes his own lounge lizard look as quite distinct from the military chic he sports in Roxy Music.

Also expanding his musical CV is **Todd Rundgren**, who forms **Utopia** to develop his more symphonic ideas and to take a free-flowing approach to music and lyrics. And the year ends with guitarist Mick Taylor quitting the **Rolling Stones**, claiming the pressures of being in that band are too much for him. Press speculation centres on the **Faces**' Ron Wood as the most likely replacement, but he strenuously denies any interest in joining the Stones.

The humorously stuttering Bachman Turner Overdrive.

Rod Stewart and Britt Ekland. He had a considerably less cosy relationship with the Inland Revenue.

While Rollermania continued unabated and glam-rock evolved into the high camp of **Queen**, **Elton John** and **Roxy Music**, disco came on in leaps and bounds – **Disco Tex**, **Gloria Gaynor**, **KC & The Sunshine Band**, **Hamilton Bohannon**, **BT Express** and **Silver Convention** were just a few of the acts to break big during 1975. It wasn't all primping and preening though, for this was the year punk and new wave began to genuinely establish themselves – their surly protagonists took great pains to announce themselves as an alternative to progressive rock, but what they were really providing was the other side of the coin to disco.

In January, while checking out Sound City Studios in Van Nuys, California, as a possible recording venue, Mick Fleetwood hears a track by ex-Fritz duo Lindsey Buckingham and Stevie Nicks. Vastly impressed, Fleetwood asks to meet Buckingham and invites the pair to join **Fleetwood Mac**. This addition brings about the Mac's tenth line-up in eight years. Equally fluid in terms of personnel are **T Rex**, now effectively **Marc Bolan**'s backing group and made up almost entirely of paid-by-the-day session players – Bill Legend is long gone, Jack Green and Mickey Finn never came back after Christmas and, although

Steve Currie is still hanging on, he will be on his way next year.

At the start of 1975, having already filled several exercise books with songs as a teenager, **Declan McManus** supplements his income as a computer operator by playing in Liverpool folk clubs under the name **DP Costello**. In two years time, he'll change the DP to Elvis. **Crosby, Stills, Nash & Young** have another crack at recording together but a huge row between Nash and Stills prompts Neil Young to walk out, muttering darkly that he will never return. Glam-rock officially passes its sell-by date as **Gary Glitter** 'retires' following a televised farewell concert. News of his abdication makes national headlines in the UK, but years later in his auto-biography Glitter reveals the move as a wheeze to boost flagging ticket sales and to allow him his first holiday in three years. Genuinely calling it a day is country rock band **Brinsley Schwartz**. Although maintaining a respectable following on the UK pub circuit, the group has never quite managed to live up to their £120,000 launch in 1970, which saw a plane-load of UK journalists flown out to New York to witness the band's brief set supporting **Van Morrison**.

With *The Partridge Family* finished on US TV, **David Cassidy** signs a solo recording contract, but he will only have musical success in the UK. In America, he will remain better known for his acting, winning an Emmy Award in 1978 for Best Actor in the TV drama *A Chance To Live*. Also treading the boards is **Meat Loaf**, who opens in two roles in the Broadway production of *The Rocky Horror Show*. **Stevie**

Wonder is awarded the NARM Presidential Award "in tribute to a man who embodies every facet of the complete musical artist: composer, writer, performer, recording artist, musician and interpreter through his music of the culture of his time." Another interpreter of the culture of his time – in this case lager, football and general laddishness – is **Rod Stewart** who begins a high-profile affair with Swedish actress Britt Ekland after meeting her at a Los Angeles party. To a background of reports that he owes the Inland Revenue £750,000, he announces he is permanently relocating to California, where he applies for US citizenship. Later this year, during a stopover in the UK on his way to continental Europe, he refuses to leave the airport's international departure lounge to avoid setting foot on British soil.

Elsewhere, **ELO** employ a 30-piece string section and breakthrough in the US with the Top 10 album 'Face The Music'. 60,000 tickets for three **Led Zeppelin** shows in New York's Madison Square Garden sell out in four hours – in two month's time, the band will sell out 51,000 tickets for three shows at London's Earl's Court in two hours. Tired of touring, **Humble Pie** split up. Meanwhile the **Monkees** meet to discuss reforming after the hamburger chain McDonalds want them for a TV commercial. Tork declines on the grounds that he is vegetarian and Nesmith says he's more interested in making films. Although the TV advert does not work out, Jones and Dolenz team up with the group's one-time songwriters Tommy Boyce and Bobby Hart to spend two years touring *The Golden Great Hits Of The Monkees Show - The Guys Who Wrote 'Em And The Guys Who Sang 'Em*. Rather surprisingly, this is a huge success. And London's Rainbow Theatre, closes with the *Over The Rainbow Concert*, headlined by **Procul Harum**.

Previously part of a duo, former law student **Joan Armatrading** signs a solo deal and has to write her own lyrics – her former partner Pam Nestor used to do the words – before she

releases her first album 'Back To The Night'. It's a year before she has a hit though. After the break-up of the less-than-successful **Grin** in 1973 and intermittent touring as part of Neil Young's band Crazy Horse, **Nils Lofgren** signs a solo deal with the same company, A&M. Claiming to be fed up with vocalists, **Jeff Beck** vows only to work in instrumental bands. The promise holds good for several years. Ritchie Blackmore quits **Deep Purple** to form his own band, **Rainbow**. Tommy Bolin, ex-**James Gang**, joins the Purps as replacement. Following last year's decision by Becker and Fagan to stop touring **Steely Dan**, Michael McDonald, Denny Dias and Jeff Porcaro follow Jeff Baxter's lead and seek alternative employment – McDonald joins Baxter in the **Doobie Bros**, Porcaro will form **Toto**. Nobody is replaced and Steely Dan will remain a duo, supplemented by session men as and when required. Also on the move are the **Jackson 5** who leave Motown for Epic

Records, much bigger royalty cheques and the freedom to write their own material. Motown sues for $20 million for breach of contract (this will be settled out of court for an undisclosed sum), retains the name 'The Jackson 5' (the group now have to call themselves the **Jacksons**) and hangs on to brother Jermaine who is married to

 Peter Gabriel quits Genesis.

Canvey Island Rock

By the mid-Seventies, progressive rock had run out of steam, glam had faded, punk had yet to occur and heavy metal couldn't decide if it was a poodle or a pit bull. While the big groups were filling the arenas, there was little for the fans at grass roots level. Into this gap, for a brief moment in 1975, came Canvey Island, Essex, England, birthplace of what came to be called pub rock.

The island itself is an annexe of the deeply unfashionable towns of Southend and Basildon, and the music that roared out of there was a throwback to a time before progressive rock. The direct, earthy sound emanated from the days when good honest rock'n'roll was a Saturday night soundtrack to a few beers, a bag of fish and chips and, if you were really lucky, a bit of a punch-up. Acts such as **Dr Feelgood**, the **Kursaal Flyers**, **Mickey Jupp** and **Eddie &**

The Hot Rods played tight, stripped-down R&B and put on storming shows fine-tuned by perpetual live performance. And, thanks to music media support, the bands got to perform way beyond the Essex borders touring the nation's colleges and the host of tiny live venues that seemed to open weekly at this time.

But whatever excitement Thames Estuary R&B generated, longevity was never on the agenda. While these bands could sell out shows, they couldn't sell too many records: their music's raw power was virtually impossible to capture on plastic. After seeing them play from five feet away in a heaving, sweaty club, any record was bound to be a let down – it's not by chance that the genre's biggest hit was a live album, **Dr Feelgood**'s 'Stupidity', which got to Number 1 in the UK. It remains the most faithful postcard from Canvey Island.

APRIL 23: Depressed for a long time over dwindling success, as well as management and financial problems, Peter Ham, Badfinger founder hangs himself in the garage of his London home.

JUNE 29: Tim Buckley, the avant-garde folk-rocker, dies in hospital in California after taking a fatal dose of heroin and morphine, believing it to be cocaine.

AUGUST 5: Robert Plant and his wife are seriously injured in a car accident while on holiday in Greece. Plant is flown to the UK for treatment, but must immediately be flown out to the island of Jersey for tax reasons.

OCTOBER 9: Sean Lennon is born — John's only child with Yoko Ono. Yoko fell pregnant when the couple reconciled after their separation.

DECEMBER: Curiously, the Twist is briefly revived in American discotheques, as a double A-side of Chubby Checker's 'The Twist' and 'Let's Twist Again' goes Top 10.

Motown boss Berry Gordy's daughter.

After rejecting wild names such as the Portable Crushers and the Vague Dots, David Byrne, Tina Weymouth and Chris Frantz opt for **Talking Heads** – apparently they saw the term in an issue of *TV Guide*. Their debut gig is next month, supporting the **Ramones** at New York's CBGB's club. **Aerosmith**'s third album, 'Toys In The Attic', provides the key to the charts in the US. Likewise **Earth Wind & Fire**'s 'That's The Way Of The World', produces sales figures to enhance their growing live following.

At the end of The Lamb Lies Down On Broadway world tour, in St Etienne, France, **Peter Gabriel** quits Genesis for what he'll later describe as "personal reasons". Robert Cray is changing his circumstances too, when, after two years on the road with Albert Collins, he forms the **Robert Cray Band**. It's two years before they make a record though. And, in spite of continuing denials that he's interested in joining the group, Ron Wood 'guests' on the **Rolling Stones**' US tour.

Island Records sponsor a series of Brian Eno-produced demo tracks by **Television**, then opt against signing the band. The newly-named **Van Halen** are establishing a reputation as LA's loudest, heaviest rock band and, throughout the summer, become the regular opening act for visiting big names.

Of rock's old guard, **Alice Cooper** falls from

the stage in Vancouver, breaking six ribs – the tour is, appropriately, titled *Welcome To My Nightmare*. After all those sell-out shows, **Led Zeppelin** have to leave the UK to go into tax exile in Switzerland. And, supporting **Elton John** at London's Wembley Stadium, the **Beach Boys** get such a thunderous reception from the 100,000 strong audience that the headliner very visibly finds it difficult to follow them. After being released from five days in a Canadian jail on drugs charges to find **Hawkwind** have sacked him, Lemmy announces plans for his new band, **Motorhead**. Originally going to be called Bastard, he boasts them to be the "kind of band that if we moved in next to you, your lawn would die." They make their debut at London's Roundhouse in July and nobody who sees them would argue against that description.

On July 18, **Bob Marley & The Wailers** play the Lyceum Ballroom in London. A show recorded for the

▲ Motorhead were going to be called Bastard.

album 'Live!' this is at once recognized as the seminal reggae show, the music's arrival as a bona fide rock style with Marley as the genre's superstar. Meanwhile, **Ten Years After** regroup for a successful 40-date US tour. **Abba**'s single 'I Do, I Do, I Do, I Do, I Do' takes three months to reach 38 in the UK charts. **David Bowie** begins filming *The Man Who Fell To Earth*. At Knebworth Park in Hertfordshire, **Pink Floyd** bolster a reputation for extravagant stage performances when they produce a show that features real Spitfire fighter planes and quadrophonic sound. And **Lou Reed**'s 'Metal Machine Music' is released – this double LP of white noise, whines, feedback and screaming so confuses critics and public that it is speedily withdrawn from sale.

In August the **Tubes**, formed earlier in the year by former drama student John Waldo – he renamed himself Fee Waybill – release their debut single and subsequent theme song, 'White Punks On Dope'. **Roger Daltrey** stars in the Ken Russell extravaganza *Lisztomania*. After a protracted legal battle, **Frank Zappa** settles out of court with Verve to regain ownership of all masters originally recorded for the company and $100,000 cash payment in lieu of unpaid royalties. The battle for full control over his early albums continues. And **Bob Dylan** wins no friends among bootleggers by sanctioning the official release of 'The Basement Tapes', record-

1970s Crazes

It seems almost impossible to believe that 20 years ago apparently sensible people would opt to spend leisure time bouncing vigorously on huge orange balloons until they fell over – usually after just a few seconds. But they did. Indeed Space Hoppers, like Clackers (two balls on rods, connected to a handle that allowed the balls to 'clack' against each other), Deely Boppers (two balls attached, antennae-style, on wire to a head band) and streaking (a very public, entirely unclothed sprint), were crazes that more or less summed up the Seventies: ostentatious; largely pointless; at times mildly risqué, but nevertheless a lot of fun. Pretty much like most of the more memorable music – **Gary Glitter**, **Blondie**, **Barry White**, **David Bowie**, **Rick Wakeman**, disco, punk et al.

However, to palm off some other Seventies obsessions such as hot pants, James Bond's increasingly sexual shenanigans, bean bag furniture, oversized afros and a distressingly frank approach to cinematic violence as a nothing more than a series of superficial fads, is to do the decade and its disciples a great disservice. The key to the Seventies was 'freedom' and some of its bizarre crazes were the real manifestations of the advancements made courtesy of the social revolution of the previous decade. The hippie era had created a young, pop literate culture – rebels with any number of ready made causes – censorship, dress coding, the war in Vietnam, racism, sexism and so on. But by the Seventies, the newly won freedoms were no longer an issue and the younger generation were calling all the shots. Even the new executive class of the Seventies were ex-hippies.

Which might prompt many to say the lunatics had taken over the asylum. And they might have a point too. Especially when considering such Seventies innovations as sideburns that should have been sanctioned by the forestry commission; supersonic flights on Concorde so prohibitively priced even the most conspicuous consumers thought twice, and soap on a rope. If, indeed, further proof is needed that the Seventies was the Decade Of Daftness, consider the less-than-subtle fashion items that abounded: shirts – with loud print designs and 'spread' collars that could be measured in acreage; the platform-soled or stack-heeled shoe, and a preponderance of corduroy. As part of this sartorial display, it was not surprising that suddenly it was 'cool' for men to wear jewellery and aftershave. Given that a lot of people missed out on being hippies in the previous decade, the Seventies provided the opportunity for certain people to prove that they were 'with it': a chance for paunchy thirtysomethings to emulate John Travolta, complete with late open-necked shirt and gold flares, open-necked shirt and gold medallion. It was little wonder that, later in the decade, punk seemed to have so much to kick against.

► Hot pants were once cited as a major contributor to traffic accidents.

► Deely Boppers. Has anybody yet worked out what the point was?

Of course there's a substantial school of thought that would file all of this in the drawer marked 'character'. And the Seventies were rich in character, stuffed with personalities that truly believed there was no other way to live life than to the giddy limits.

And discos, the sexual licence brought about by contraceptive advancements, cocaine as the drug of choice (as predicted in *Easy Rider* in 1969) and booming economies helped provide the wherewithal.

In the UK, pubs reinvented themselves as somewhere young people might actually want to 'hang out' in – instead of places to avoid – giving rise to lager-fuelled oafish behaviour that invented and sustained the idea of laddishness as a desirable quality. Other larger-than-life characters emerged on the sports field. The previous decade had elevated many sporting personalities, and their extramural activities, to pop star status: the Seventies contribution was a unique clutch of 'colourful' professional footballers with questionable hair-

▶ James Bond (Roger Moore) conducts an interrogation.

cuts – such as George 'Bestie' Best, Rodney 'Marshie' Marsh and Stan 'Bowlsie' Bowles.

Across the Atlantic, the most obvious recipient of a Seventies-style Character Award was a whole new generation of television detectives. Kojak, Starsky & Hutch and John Shaft led the way when it came to hip talking, sharp-dressing, hard-womaniz-ing gumshoes, with Banaceck and Cool Million close behind. Starsky & Hutch, it seemed, were going for the feminist vote in an attempt to be New Men that only just stopped short of hugging trees; all very post-Sixties enlightenment. The rest, McMillan, Columbo and the Harts, all worked hard to make sure they stood out from the ranks.

▶ Starsky & Hutch may have put the New Man into police procedure, but they still had a wicked car.

1976 – HEADLINE NEWS   JAN 21 : Concorde carries its first passengers • FEB 18 : Sculptor Carl Andre's controversial pile of bricks goes on show at the Tate Gallery

Despite an unpromising start, 1976 turned out to be a watershed year for rock. Mercifully, progressive rock seemed dead and buried but nothing overtly new was taking its place. Disco was bubbling under; as were **Motorhead**; so too **Bob Dylan** who had one of his most commercial years ever, as well as the teeny-bop likes of **Slik** and **Our Kid**. So open was the field of rock music that old-time groups such as the **Beach Boys**, **Manfred Mann** and the **Beatles** had hits, while novelty records by bands such as **Laurie Lingo & The Dipsticks** (BBC DJs Dave Lee Travis and Paul Burnett), the **Wurzels** and **Disco Duck** cleaned up. Actor **David Soul** from *Starsky & Hutch* was able to have caring, sharing hits, hell, even ancient oboist **Acker Bilk** and superthin model **Twiggy** could get a record in the charts (though thankfully not the same one). Until the **Sex Pistols** came along with their late bid to claim the year for punk, 1976's confused outlook was best summed up by a November touring bill that featured the **Damned** as **Marc Bolan**'s support act.

The year opens with Motorhead's record company rejecting the band's loud and aggressive debut album as unsaleable. The band splits up, but Lemmy and Taylor stay together and are joined by 'Fast' Eddie Clarke to comprise the definitive Motorhead line-up. However, the dispute means they will be without a manager, record contract or income for most of the year. Corporately acceptable though, after two years of gigging around Australia, are **AC/DC**. When they are signed by Atlantic Records, they move to London to capitalize on their strong UK following built up by almost perpetual touring and the publicity garnered by leader Angus Young in his oversized school uniform. This month's other debutants are **Foreigner**, formed when Mick Jones (ex-**Spooky Tooth**) meets Ian McDonald (ex-**King Crimson**) at a session in New York. The twosome recruit one more Englishman and three Americans, hence the group

Drummer Phil Collins takes over the vocal duties for Genesis.

name. And the five year-old **George Harrison**/Bright Tunes court case is finally resolved in favour of the plaintiff: the US District Court judges accepts that Harrison's apparent adaptation of the **Chiffons**' 'He's So Fine' for the former Beatle's 'My Sweet Lord' single could've been

Australia's finest, AC/DC.

subconscious, but still allows damages of over half a million dollars against the ex-Beatle.

Elsewhere, folk band **Fairport Convention** abbreviate their name to **Fairport**. **Elton John** is the first rock star since the Beatles to be reproduced in Madame Tussauds waxworks in London. In a re-promotion of the Fab Four's back catalogue, EMI releases a box set of all the group's singles. Available individually, several chart and the one song previously unissued as a single, 'Yesterday', goes into the Top 10. In one of rock's first high-profile product endorsement arrangements, **Status Quo** do a deal with Levis so that their album 'Blue For You' is promoted in 6,000 UK jeans outlets.

On **Genesis**' 'Trick Of The Tail' LP, drummer Phil Collins takes over lead vocals after an unsuccessful search to find a replacement for Peter Gabriel. On tour later in the year, ex-**Yes**/**King Crimson** drummer Bill Bruford will join the band to allow Collins to come out from behind the kit to carry out his new duties. The **Who**, however, have to cancel a US tour when their drummer Keith Moon collapses during an early gig in Boston, Mass. In March, **ZZ Top** commence their 100-date Worldwide

Texas Tour, a show that involves 75 tons of equipment including a Lone Star State-shaped stage, on which sand, cacti, longhorn cattle, snakes and a buffalo mingle. Such are the crowds the threesome are attracting – thanks to several years of virtually non-stop touring – the venture is financially successful.

In April, Motown Records announce a $13 million deal with **Stevie Wonder**, the most lucrative contract in rock history. **Bay City Roller** Eric Faulkner almost dies after taking a drug overdose at manager Tam Paton's house. Returning by train from Moscow, **David Bowie** is detained for several hours at the Polish border, after customs officers take exception to Nazi documents and memorabilia found in his luggage. It is

The rockin' grandmother, ▼ Tina Turner.

▲ A relatively clean-shaven ZZ Top. Now that was a long time ago.

claimed he is researching a film about Goebbels, Hitler's Minister Of Propaganda. Also in trouble with the authorities is **Bruce Springsteen**, when he is thrown out of Graceland after climbing over the wall of the Memphis mansion at 3.00am. Remarkably, the security guards fail to recognize the future of rock'n'roll.

In the East End of London, Steve ''Arry' Harris and Dave Murray are joining forces with Paul Di'anno (vocalist) and Doug Sampson (drums) to comprise **Iron Maiden**, a group determined to keep hard rock

going in the face of advancing punk and new wave. Ironically, in years to come, they are hailed as spearheading the New Wave Of British Heavy Metal, a style unique in the world of metal because of its obvious punk influences. On the other side of the tribal fence, **Depeche Mode** are formed at a school in Basildon, Essex. The name, meaning 'fast fashion' was gleaned from a French style magazine. **Aswad**, who have been playing together for a year, sign with Island Records as the first British reggae band to gain a major deal. And in response to a postcard on a Dublin school noticeboard, Paul Hewson, David Evans, Adam Clayton, Larry Mullen and Dick Evans meet and start practising at Mullen's house, calling themselves Feedback. They will play cover versions at local engagements, eventually changing their name to the

Hype and then to **U2**, during which time Hewson and Evans turn into Bono and The Edge, respectively.

Although his post-Creedence career is doing very well, both under his own name and as part of the **Blue Ridge Rangers**, **John Fogerty** pulls a proposed album out of the release schedule and quits the music business. For the next nine years he will run the family farm in Oregon. Also in quitting mode is BBC Radio 1 DJ, Johnnie Walker, who leaves the station after being told to pretend he likes the Bay City Rollers, and **Tina Turner** who finally walks out on Ike, later to tell tales of almost constant abuse and cruelty. With four children to support, the former Acid Queen and newly-converted Buddhist lives on state welfare for a while as she strives to rebuild a career through cabaret and work in Europe, where

1976 - HEADLINE NEWS ● APR 5 : Reclusive millionaire Howard Hughes dies ● JUL 4 : America celebrates its Bicentennial she is considered a bigger star than she is at home. The couple will divorce in July.

Neil Young joins Stephen Stills on tour as the **Stills-Young Band**, and they will release a fairly successful album, 'Long May You Run', later in the year. In Toronto, Canada, **Peter Gabriel** begins recording his eponymously-titled first solo album. Tim Scholz, who for years has been fooling around with musician friends in his home-made studio, produces demo tapes good enough for Epic to release them, with minimal re-recording, as **Boston**'s first album. The **Ramones** make their UK debut at The Roundhouse in London, also on the bill are the **Stranglers** and the **Flamin' Groovies**. **Deep Purple** split: Coverdale goes solo before forming **Whitesnake**; Lord and Paice become two thirds of **Paice, Ashton and Lord**; Hughes rejoins **Trapeze** and Bolin returns to the US to form the **Tommy Bolin Band**. And in Middle America a bizarre attempt at rock'n'roll hype is taking place. **John Mellencamp**, having struck a management deal with **David Bowie**'s former manager Tony DeFries, has recorded his first album, 'Chestnut Street Incident', which is released by DeFries in demo form with Mellencamp rechristened **Johnny Cougar**. By way of a launch campaign, the manager has organized Johnny Cougar Day in the singer's home town of Seymour, Indiana and a less-than-enthusiastic Mellencamp finds himself contractually obliged to take part in an open top Cadillac motorcade in his own honour. The album is not a hit, and the two part

company the following year.

Also on the move is Alan Parsons, after years as Abbey Road Studios engineer – where he worked on such albums as 'Abbey Road' and 'Dark Side Of The Moon', and produced records by **Cockney Rebel** and **Pilot**. He leaves to debut as a musician/producer with 'Tales Of Mystery And Imagination', intended as a one-off venture and credited to the **Alan Parsons Project**. Based on the Edgar Allen Poe book of the same name, it's actually the first in Parsons' series of 'concept' albums, and the US release is marked by one of rock's first specially commissioned laser shows at LA's Griffith Park Observatory. With Roxy Music 'in hiatus', **Bryan Ferry** assembles a band (largely ex-Roxy personnel plus the respected session guitarist Chris Spedding) and begins rehearsing, with the intention of live work early next year.

Elton John plays a series of seven sold-out shows at New York's Madison Square Garden, which breaks a venue attendance record set by the **Rolling Stones** one year previously. In Los Angeles, after the band give a performance on the roof of a building, Mercury Records signs teenage rockers the **Runaways** – the company is said to view them as a female **Ramones**. And in Paris, **Grace Jones**, fashion model and sometime actress, tries her hand at recording disco songs.

In September, having just left school in Islington, north London, Gary Kemp forms power pop band the Makers with friends Tony Hadley, John Keeble, Steve Norman and Richard Miller. Three years later, after Miller

The Ramones played London's Roundhouse, as part of punk's advance guard.

leaves, Kemp's brother Martin takes over on bass and they'll rename themselves **Spandau Ballet**. Meanwhile, just down the road in adjoining Kentish Town, Lee Thompson, Chris Foreman and Mike Barson form a trio, the **Invaders**, to play the bluebeat music they grew up listening to. Over the next couple of years, the line-up will expand to include Suggs McPherson, Mark Bedford, Daniel Woodgate and Carl Smyth, osmosing into **Madness**.

In a more venerable vein, to celebrate what would have been the singer's 40th birthday (September 7), Buddy Holly Week is inaugurated in the UK by **Paul McCartney**, a lifelong fan and owner of Holly's song catalogue. In the US, The Buddy Holly Memorial Society is formed. **Brian Wilson**, once again performing with the **Beach Boys** to mark the group's 15th anniversary, is inducted into the Rock'n'Roll Hall Of Fame. And September ends with promoter Sid Bernstein, who handled all the Beatles' New York shows between 1964 - 66, taking full-page advertisements in the *New York Times* and the *International Herald Tribune*, requesting the **Beatles** to get back together for a one-off charity show. He claims the

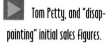

Tom Petty, and "disappointing" initial sales figures.

154

ROCK'N'ROLL record

MARCH 19: Founder member of Free and more recently Back Street Crawler, Paul Kossoff dies of heart failure on a transatlantic flight. He had a history of drug-related health problems.

JUNE: Elton John tops both the UK and US singles charts for the first time with 'Don't Go Breaking My Heart', a duet with Kiki Dee. He'll later perform the song with Miss Piggy on The Muppet Show.

JULY 27: John Lennon finally wins his four-year battle to stay in the USA when he is granted a green card.

SEPTEMBER 29: Jerry Lee Lewis accidentally shoots his bass player while firing at the door the musician is standing behind. The musician lives to sue his boss, who is also in trouble for drunk driving and waving a pistol outside the gates of Graceland, demanding to see Elvis.

DECEMBER 4: Tommy Bolin, ex-Deep Purple, dies as the result of a heroin overdose.

total revenue from TV sales could be as high as $230 million, but the call goes unanswered.

Boney M are put together in Germany by producer Frank Farian as the voices for his disco-oriented electronic compositions. All four members are West Indian in origin, working in Europe as session singers. Likewise experimenting with that dancefloor soundtrack are August Darnell and Andy Hernandez – the future nucleus of **Kid Creole & The Coconuts** – who join Darnell's brother's group **Dr Buzzard's Original Savannah Band**. The outfit fuses Thirties dance band music with disco beats to considerable club and chart success during the next three years. But the **B52s**, formed in Athens, Georgia, have no such modern aspirations – the name comes from the Southern US term for the exaggerated beehive-style hairdos favoured by the two female members, which is part of their whole kitsch early-Sixties approach.

The **Band** split – the given reason being because Robbie Robertson, their main songwriter, is more interested in establishing himself as a producer. In November, their final concert, *The Last Waltz*, will be a lavish affair staged at San Francisco's Winterland Ballroom (where they were discovered seven years previously), starting with a Thanksgiving Day Banquet and turning into a lengthy set featuring such illustrious guests as **Bob Dylan**, **Neil Diamond**, **Neil Young**, **Ringo Starr**, **Van Morrison**, **Joni Mitchell**, **Muddy Waters**, **Eric Clapton**, **Dr John** and **Paul Butterfield**. It is filmed by Martin

Scorsese for release in June 1978 and later universally recognized as the finest in-concert movie ever shot.

David Bowie moves to Berlin and becomes a near recluse. The city is cited as the main influence for the gloomy, European sound of 'Low' and 'Heroes'. More raucous but less successful, **Tom Petty & The Heartbreakers**' eponymously-titled debut album is released in the US to disappointing sales of a mere 6,500 copies in three months. Also having difficulties are **Kiss**, who fail to make an impact in the UK in spite of doing very well in the US – it's felt that the UK music press were somewhat underwhelmed by the band conducting interviews in full make-up. And things aren't going swimmingly for **Kevin Godley** and **Lol Creme** who have split from **10cc** to devote their time to developing a new musical instrument called The Gizmo – they claim it can create orchestral sounds from guitar notes and they announce they are working on a single called "Consequences" to showcase the device. Conceived as a three-minute track, during the next few months it

grows and grows into a triple album box set that gets no further than Number 52 in the UK. To add to their woes, very few customers purchase the revolutionary Gizmo.

As a mark of the changing times, **Marc Bolan & T Rex** go on tour in the UK with the **Damned** as support. On December 1, **Queen** are scheduled to appear on UK TV's topical magazine show *Today* but pull out at the last minute and the **Sex Pistols** are substituted. The band seize the opportunity to supply a live (and certainly direct) demonstration of the true Spirit Of Punk by abusing presenter Bill Grundy on air, with such venom it makes the front page of every UK newspaper the next day.

Two days later in Jamaica, politically connected gunmen burst into **Bob Marley**'s Kingston home, to fire volleys of shots that injure him, his wife and his manager. After that, and in genuine fear for his life, Marley will leave Jamaica to spend 18 months in Miami. On a happier note, **Genesis** are the first band to play the re-opened Rainbow Theatre. Despite its prohibitive pricing, a 4-LP box set of **Mike Oldfield**'s first three albums and a compilation of his singles reaches Number 22 in the UK. And the shoot for the cover photo of **Pink Floyd**'s 'Animals' LP goes horribly wrong when the 40ft inflatable pig slips its moorings and floats off into the sky above London. The city's airports warn pilots to be careful of a huge flying pig and, after one sighting at 20,000 feet over the Kent coast (50 miles from London), the plastic animal is never seen or heard of again.

When 1977 began, disco was showing no signs of letting up – even if it did sometimes seem to be getting perilously near the bottom of the barrel – but it turned out to be a year of revolution with punk establishing itself as the dominant force in rock culture. Punk spread its message of liberation – or 'evil tentacles', depending on which end of the media you read – beyond its immediate safety-pinned, bin-linered inner circle to influence emerging pop bands into taking a less precious approach to music. Evidence of how far this new wave of spiky British bands permeated the music business can be seen in the number of new groups that were hurriedly signed to major record labels after success with independent companies.

In an appropriate overture to 1977, **Joy Division** are formed in Manchester in January. Originally the Stiff Kittens, then Warsaw – they changed that name to avoid confusion with London punks **Warsaw Pakt** – the name they settle on comes from *House Of Dolls*, a novel about Nazi concentration camps. Similarly Teutonically-tinged is **David Bowie**'s 'Low', an album introducing his new, synthesizer-laden, living-in-Berlin, melodramatically gloomy sound. A path trod further with 'Heroes', released at the end of the year. Slightly jollier, but only just, is the **Eagles**' 'Hotel California' album, which tops the US charts selling seven figures immediately and going on to do much better than that. So well, in fact, that in later years Glenn Frey claims it precipitated the kind of "unbearable pressures of stardom" that led to the band's break-up.

Back in the UK, as a result of last year's **Sex Pistols** appearance on TV, the authorities appear to be taking no chances with punk as the plug is pulled on a **Stranglers** set at London's Roundhouse after someone notices Hugh Cornwell's T-shirt is printed with the word 'Fuck' in the style of the Ford logo. In May, dates on their UK tour are cancelled as many venues cannot get licences to

The Eagles. Hotel California. It's the beginning of the end.

The Stranglers had dates cancelled as local authorities failed to come to terms with punk.

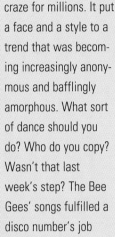

John Travolta and that suit. He was once the coolest man in the world. Apparently.

Saturday Night Fever

In December 1977, a little known singer/actor opens in a film about teenage angst and acrobatic dance. It's set among kids who hang out in a low-rent club in Brooklyn, and the soundtrack is by an Australian group who were big in the Sixties and who, though they made a comeback in the US in the Seventies, couldn't get arrested practically anywhere else. By January of the next year, *Saturday Night Fever* is a worldwide box office smash; the double LP of songs from the movie, headed by the **Bee Gees**, is on top of charts everywhere eventually shifting over 30 million copies as the best-selling soundtrack ever; **John Travolta** is a star, and the three-piece flared white suit is seen as the ulti-

mate expression of Seventies taste.

Saturday Night Fever defined the booming disco craze for millions. It put a face and a style to a trend that was becoming increasingly anonymous and bafflingly amorphous. What sort of dance should you do? Who do you copy? Wasn't that last week's step? The Bee Gees' songs fulfilled a disco number's job description – easy, upfront beat and untaxing lyric – yet were recognizably like pop songs. In other words, this was disco for beginners. And so many people entered through *Saturday Night Fever*'s strobe-lit portals that the genre gathered sufficient steam to dominate chart music until the end of the decade.

---

put on punk (or punk-type) groups and, two months later, the single 'Peaches' is banned by the BBC as the lyric "walking on the beaches/ looking at the peaches" is thought to be offensive. After building a strong London following, the **Jam** are signed to Polydor for £6,000. Their first album, 'In The City', will be out in

three months time to go Top 20 in the UK. Although they tend to be seen as part of the punk scene, their mohair suits, skinny ties and neat haircuts spark a minor Mod fashion revival. Likewise **Blondie**, whose first, eponymously-titled album is released in the UK, become the acceptable face of punk and quickly attract mainstream media attention.

Fleetwood Mac's 'Rumours' comes out and is widely taken to be a chronicle of the group's internal strife – the McVies have separated, Buckingham and Nicks are on the rocks and the Fleetwoods have filed for divorce.

But there's money in misery, as the LP will sell over 20 million worldwide, spending over 400 weeks on the UK charts and 130 in the US. In a harmony that borders on the paranormal, **ZZ Top**, exhausted by five years of almost constant touring, begin a two and a half year vacation, during which time, completely independent of each other, Gibbons and Hill will grow the trademark beards.

Sting, Stewart Copeland and guitarist Henri Padovani record the first **Police** single, 'Fall Out'. It will be released in May on manager Miles Copeland's Illegal label, selling over 2,000 copies and getting into the independent charts. Elsewhere, in spite of its much-vaunted mission to change the face of rock-music-as-we-know-it, punk continues to develop

Tough, uncompromising and the post punk face of the urban pop experience. In other words, The Jam.

along pretty familiar guidelines – with the usual talk of musical differences, albums markets and success in America: bass player Glen Matlock is fired by the **Sex Pistols**, to be replaced by John Ritchie, aka **Sid Vicious**; in March, reportedly recorded and mixed in eight hours, the Nick Lowe-produced 'Damned Damned Damned', by who else but the **Damned**, is the first punk LP; **Elvis Costello** signs to Stiff Records and, although his first two singles flop, by the end of the year his debut album, 'My Aim Is True', will be a hit on both sides of the Atlantic.

That same month, **Neil Young**'s room-mate, bass player **Rick James**, signs to Motown with his **Stone City Band** and his bristly brand of street soul known as 'punk funk'. Although James' music might at first seem a belated reaction to **George Clinton**, the **Ohio Players** and **Sly Stone**, by the end of the decade his thinly-veiled drug paeans bring him platinum status. Also fusing rock'n'soul are **Earth Wind & Fire**, whose stage show has by now expanded to include elaborate props, flamboyant quasi-Egyptian robes and added extras such as a levitating bass player, have their first UK chart hit with 'Saturday Night'. Meanwhile the 19-year-old **Prince** signs what is a groundbreaking deal for a debut artist at Warner Brothers, with a huge advance and total creative control for three albums.

Less rambunctious, **Peter Gabriel** releases his first solo LP entitled 'Peter Gabriel'; the first of four identi-

cally-titled LPs. The **Monkees** film *Head* is shown at the National Film Theatre in London. This is in response to popular demand and the movie achieves instant cult status as well as a long run at arthouse cinemas in the UK capital. Also destined to become something of a cult are the **Village People**, who are formed in April by French producer Jacques Morali. His inspiration comes from seeing the vogue in New York's gay discos for fancy dress costumes and the group he puts together represents an inver-

sion of archetypal American machismo, featuring a cowboy, a native American, a biker, a construction worker, a cop and a GI. Singing actors are hired to fulfil the 'roles' and initial success is limited. In Sheffield, UK, computer operators Martyn Ware and Ian Craig Marsh form a sythesizer duo called the Dead Daughters, a couple of months later Phil Oakey and Adrian Wright join and the band is, rather more sensibly, renamed the **Human League** after a computer game.

On the 8th of April, the Damned become the first UK punk group to perform in the US, with a show at New York's CBGB's. The **Clash** travel to Jamaica to record with legendary reggae producer **Lee Perry** – the band believe that punk and reggae music share a common bond as the voice of the oppressed. This feeling is not shared by their producer and, fed up with being treated in off-hand fashion, the Clash return home early with only one finished track, 'Complete Control'. The track will become part of their first album, 'The Clash', released in May to reach Number 12 in the UK.

Elvis Costello's first two singles were flops.

ROCK'N'ROLL
record

FEBRUARY: Cyndi Lauper loses her voice. Doctors say she'll never sing again but vocal therapy proves them wrong.

JUNE 15: Alice Cooper's boa constrictor dies when the rat it was breakfasting on bites back. Public auditions are held for a new co-star.

AUGUST16: Ginger Arden, the singer's girlfriend, finds Elvis Presley collapsed on the floor of a bathroom at his Memphis mansion, Graceland. After being taken to hospital, he is pronounced dead of heart failure at 3.30pm.

SEPTEMBER 16: Marc Bolan is killed when the car driven by his girlfriend Gloria Jones hits a tree in Barnes, southwest London.

SEPTEMBER: Six Elvis Presley albums are in the UK Top 30.

OCTOBER: Meat Loaf's 'Bat Out Of Hell' album is released in the US (in the UK next January). It will eventually sell 30 million and set a UK record by spending over 400 weeks in the British charts.

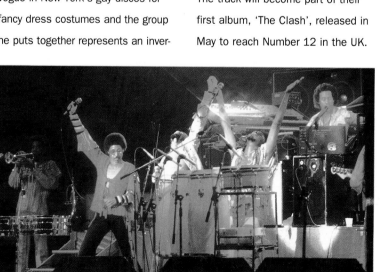

What We Did in 1977, by the Sex Pistols

1977 may have been the year in which punk lost its credibility, but it was also the **Sex Pistols**' finest 12 months. Maybe those two facts are not unconnected. The group had already introduced themselves to everybody in the UK by swearing live on nationwide television the previous December, but this year was the Queen's Silver Jubilee Year in the UK – what better time to make a strident political statement? Which is what the Sex Pistols' singer and manager, Malcolm McLaren or 'Talcy Malky', would have had you believe they were doing. The Sex Pistols' itinerary:

January: Their debut single, 'Anarchy In The UK', goes Top 40 in the UK, but EMI Records decide they can no longer tolerate the band on the label, withdraw the single and let them go. The company also lets them pocket a £40,000 advance.

Sid Vicious (left) and Johnny Rotten had a busy old year.

February: The band signs to A&M in a ceremony outside Buckingham Palace for an advance of £150,000. Less than a week later they are sacked by the label, following protests from other artists and pressure from head office in Los Angeles as well as reports of expensively-rambunctuous behaviour in the company's offices and a recording studio. A&M has already pressed 25,000 copies of the group's 'God Save The Queen' single, which have to be binned, and the band are allowed to keep half of their advance – which works out at £12,500 for every day they were on the label.

March: Bass player Glen Matlock is fired – apparently for being able to play guitar too well – and Sid Vicious joins. He is musically inept but attitudinally perfect.

May: The Sex Pistols sign to Virgin for £15,000. Later in the month, after a strike at the pressing plant has been narrowly averted when workers refuse to handle 'God Save The Queen' because of the picture of the Queen wearing a safety pin on its sleeve, the record gets to Number 2 in the UK...despite (or maybe because of) many shops refusing to stock it and the BBC banning it.

June: Virgin Records, who seem to be positively encouraging the band's shenanigans, hire a boat on the Thames, so 'Anarchy In The UK' can be performed outside the Houses Of Parliament. There are arrests when the vessel docks. That same month, Paul Cook and Johnny Rotten are attacked, in separate incidents, on London streets.

July: 'Pretty Vacant' goes Top 10 in Britain.

August: The band tour the UK, undercover, as the Spots – Sex Pistols On Tour.

October: 'Holidays In The Sun' goes Top 10 in Britain.

November: 'Never Mind The Bollocks – Here's The Sex Pistols' goes straight into the UK album charts at Number 1. In something of a test case, a London record retailer is warned that displaying the sleeve is an offence under the 1889 Indecent Advertising Act but magistrates rule this is not so.

December: The group sign to Warner Brothers in the USA, and finish up as the ninth best-selling singles act in Britain.

Earth, Wind And Fire acknowledge The Cosmic Pyramid.

In spite of punk's strong presence, traditional rock lives on. Six years after it was written, **Deep Purple**'s 'Smoke On The Water' is released in the UK and gets to Number 21. In Sydney, Australia, teenagers Tim, Andy and Jon Farriss, together with school friends Michael Hutchence, Kirk Pengilly and Garry Beers, form the Farriss Brothers. In a year's time, they'll rename themselves **INXS**. After protracted legal wrangling, **Bruce Springsteen** is free of his contract with producer Mike Appel – an agreement signed five years before on the bonnet of a car in a dark parking lot. Springsteen immediately renegotiates a far more lucrative deal with CBS and starts recording with Jon Landau. The resultant album will be 'Darkness On The Edge Of Town'.

Brian Eno meets **Talking Heads**.

After seeing the group support the **Ramones** in a London nightclub, he invites them back to his house and begins a long-lasting musical collaboration. **Iggy Pop** starts a successful summer of touring – with **David Bowie** on keyboards and **Blondie** as support – as punk bands covering **Stooges**' songs have given pop music a new lease of life. Annie Lennox and Dave Stewart record together, with Peet Coombes, as the **Catch** and have a minor hit in Holland with a single called 'Black Blood'. Andy Summers joins the **Police** – Henri Padovani will depart two months later, just as Steve Hackett will leave **Genesis** and the others opt to carry on as a trio.

On June 11th, in what will become a fairly regular occurrence, members of the **Clash** are in court. Joe Strummer and Topper Headon are fined £5 each for spray-painting 'Clash' on a wall. Twenty-four hours later, they are held overnight in prison in Newcastle for failing to appear in court the previous month charged with the theft of a Holiday Inn pillow-case, for which they'll be fined £200. It seems that being seen to be true to punk's outlaw philosophy is all important to this band. Similarly, **Led Zeppelin** drummer John Bonham and manager Peter Grant, who are arrested in the US and charged with assault on an employee of their concert promoter Bill Graham – the tour will later

be cancelled following the death of Robert Plant's son. And **Gary Glitter** has his own problems with the courts, when he is declared bankrupt while performing out of the country in *The Rocky Horror Show* in New Zealand.

After calling their jazz/rock fusion trio the Big Apple Band, then Allah & The Knife Wielding Punks, Bernard Edwards, Nile Rodgers and Tony Thompson add female vocals, opt for a disco style and rename their group **Chic**. After the personal intervention of the company president, they will be signed to Atlantic Records before the end of the year. Also starting out are **Dire Straits** – Mark Knopfler, his brother David, John Illsley and Pick Withers – who put aside £120 from their earnings playing in pubs to record a five-song demo (the group name is acknowledgement of their seemingly perpetual financial embarrassment). The gamble pays off within weeks when the tracks are played on BBC Radio resulting in a deal with Phonogram and a management con-

tract with Ed Bicknell. Looking to blend punk and reggae, Jerry Dammers, Lynval Golding and Sir Horace Gentleman form the Coventry Automatics, later the **Specials**. On the slide though are the **Bay City Rollers**, whose 'You Made Me Believe In Magic' is their last UK hit – they'll have one more, 'The Way I Feel Tonight', in the US before the end of the year, but otherwise that's it.

When **Bob Marley** is operated on at the Cedars Of Lebanon Hospital in Miami, in July, to remove a cancerous growth from his big toe, the media is told it's an old soccer injury which has been playing up. After a year studying dance at Michigan University, **Madonna** Louise Ciccone arrives in New York to take up a scholarship at Alvin Ailey's studio to work with prestigious choreographer Pearl Lang. **Adam & The Ants**, already big in London, are the first band on stage at the capital's seminal punk venue the Vortex. Also opening in the UK capital is trouser-splitting, Sixties rocker **PJ Proby**, in the title role of the lavish West End musical *Elvis* – the part of Presley as a young man is taken by an appropriately youthful **Shakin' Stevens**.

On September 16, the **Grateful Dead** play the first of three dates in front of the Great Pyramid Of Cheops in Cairo, an event scheduled to coincide with a total eclipse of the moon. Decidedly more down to earth, is the Stiff Live Stiffs UK tour, with a line-up of **Ian Dury &** the (specially formed for the occasion) **Blockheads, Elvis Costello, Nick Lowe, Wreckless Eric** and **Dave Edmunds**. The tour is the result of Stiff Records' massive

Debbie Harry of Blondie, a New Wave Pin Up.

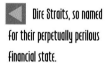
Dire Straits, so named for their perpetually perilous financial state.

Elvis

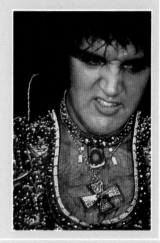

The official cause of **Elvis Presley**'s death was heart failure, but there was much speculation at the time over The King's unsparing approach to self-medication. The word was, that even if the drugs he took hadn't technically killed him, they'd certainly been keeping him alive for the last few years. The most remarkable thing about the Presley stash, though, was that it was completely legal. Everything in his famed travelling medicine chest – apparently it was like one of those multi-drawered cabinets on wheels that mechanics keep their tools in – was available on prescription. The only question mark hangs over what they were actu-

ally prescribed for.

Elvis's dangerous pharmaceutical cocktail cabinet consisted of:
Dilaudid: a powerful synthetic opiate, among the strongest painkillers.
Percodan: another major league painkiller, usually administered to serious burns victims.
Biphetamine: a strong stimulant, used in cases of dangerously slow heartbeat.
Dextroamphetamine: much the same.
Quaaludes: a strong sleeping pill.

▲ The King is dead.

mainstream success after being perceived as the polite face of punk – left-field and fiercely independent, the Stiff corporate ideology may have been born out of punk but its artists specialize in proper tunes, well produced sound and a traditionally disciplined rockist approach. The **Boomtown Rats** and the **Police** fall into the same category – pop music with attitude, that manages to attract both sales figures and credibility ratings.

Even more socially acceptable is an 11-year-old **Janet Jackson** who is

making her small screen debut in the US as co-star in the sitcom *Good Times*. Success in this leads to work in the series *Diff'rent Strokes* and *Fame*. Broadcast on September 9, **David Bowie** guests on **Marc Bolan**'s UK TV show *Marc* and duets with his host. Two days later, Bowie records an appearance for a Christmas TV show, singing 'Little Drummer Boy' in tandem with **Bing Crosby**. On September 16 Bolan is killed in a car crash and Bing Crosby will die of a heart attack in October.

In November, **Ozzy Osbourne** walks out on **Black Sabbath**, his disaffection with their musical direction – horns and a more delicate multi-layered production – having been common knowledge for a year. In spite of Savoy Brown's Dave Walker replacing him for some live work, the 'wild man of rock' will return after a couple of months. **ELO**'s 'Out Of The Blue' double LP is released to advance orders of over four million, bringing a suitably upbeat close to a year that had already grossed the group over $10

million from a world tour and record sales. **Elton John** starts his 'retirement' from live work, which lasts all of 18 months.

In a move to pep up **Leonard Cohen**'s rather sombre body of work, Phil Spector is engaged as producer. However, relations become strained when Spector takes to bringing an armed guard to the studio with him and the LP they end up with, 'Death Of A Ladies Man', is the Canadian's least successful LP to date. On December 15, the **Who** play at Shepperton Studios before a fan club members-only audience, the set is filmed for inclusion in the group's documentary film (and live LP) *The Kids Are Alright*. The year closes with **Wings**' 'Mull of Kintyre' at the top of the UK charts. The song is co-written by Denny Laine, who sells his rights to McCartney after being declared bankrupt, and it tops the UK charts for nine weeks, selling over 2.5 million to become the biggest selling UK single of all time until **Band Aid**'s 'Do They Know It's Christmas?'

▲ Adam (of the Ants) launches seminal punk club The Vortex.

David Bowie

▼ David Bowie: A psycho-sexual controversy for the people.

Shedding all previous incarnations, **David Bowie** came to earth in 1970 ready to try something new. He had studied mime and dance with the controversial Lindsay Kemp; co-founded *avant garde* performance venue the Beckenham Arts Lab; and recorded 'Space Oddity', a single way beyond the conventional boy-meets-girl parameters. But all this was merely an overture. Bowie went on to define the style of the Seventies with such force that no other artist had a bigger influence on the decade. In a way, Bowie re-invented himself so many times that he became the era in microcosm.

Always at the sharp end of the Seventies' psycho-sexual debate, Bowie courted controversy. He sparked off a minor media frenzy when, on a promotional visit to the US, he opted for women's clothing. The Bowie-in-a-dress outcry that forced one album to be withdrawn and re-sleeved, was just a warm-up for his *Melody Maker* interview in early 1972, when he told the world he was bisexual. Yet, despite such publicity, his early Seventies albums (the darkly ominous 'The Man Who Sold The World' and the melodic, introspective 'Hunky Dory') failed to stir the public as much as they did the critics, and were swiftly followed by his adoption of a futuristic rock posture for 1972's LP 'The Rise And Fall Of Ziggy Stardust And The Spiders From Mars'.

In 'Ziggy Stardust' and its follow-up 'Aladdin Sane', Bowie threw off the last vestiges of hippiedom and surfed the glam rock wave in the UK. Through a self-mythologizing storyline that put the very nature of his own rock stardom under scrutiny, he became one of the few glitter-loving glamour boys to make it in America. But then, with the stylistic agility that was becoming his trademark, he hopped off glam as it began to wane in 1974 and sent Ziggy Stardust into early retirement. He came back almost immediately with 'Diamond Dogs', an LP which embodied a maxim of the times, "nothing succeeds like excess". It was a concept opera of an album, complete with outrageous half-man-half-dog sleeve art and a stage show that made Busby Berkeley's productions look low budget.

By the mid-Seventies, movie stars were being left in the shadows as rock's big league became the showbiz aristocracy. One consequence was that more musicians tried their hand at acting: in 1975 Bowie began filming *The Man Who Fell To Earth*, a movie in which his role matched his image as an other-worldly pop star: the character's pose of cool inscrutability made only a modest demand on his acting talents.

Meanwhile, as the emergent disco trend pushed the pop/soul sound of Philadelphia towards the mainstream, Bowie latched on to the trend with 'Young Americans', an album of white boy soul mostly recorded in that city. Much of his next album, 'Station To Station', maintained a disco-funk feel, but at the same time explored a major late-Seventies rock trend, namely electronic music. From then to the end of the decade Bowie collaborated with **Brian Eno** to produce a trilogy of intense, synthesizer-based albums: 'Low', 'Heroes' and 'Lodger'. And he fully embraced the jet set lifestyle, becoming a model international rock star, flitting between New York, Berlin, Switzerland and London.

By his own reckoning David Bowie could be a shrewd exploiter of other people's ideas, as much as an instigator. But in his eclecticism, his brazen artifice and his abandonment of the Sixties' naive optimism, Bowie became the key figure of this new decade.

It was ironic that when his first album 'Greetings From Asbury Park' was released in 1973, **Bruce Springsteen**'s record company should have chosen to promote the singer as the "new **Bob Dylan**". True, the LP did have a heavy Dylan influence, but Springsteen's narrative style was inspired as much by **Chuck Berry** and the **Rolling Stones**, as well as reacting against the late-hippie folk boom. Springsteen's big, raucous **E-Street Band** – taken into the studio against the record company's wishes – was also a vociferous declaration of back-to-basic values in a time of "progressive" rock.

Bruce Springsteen's no-nonsense, R&B-based sound powered out of New Jersey – itself one of the least glamorous of US states – to reclaim rock'n'roll as part of traditional blue collar culture. Here in fact was the root of his appeal: Springsteen romanticized the everyday and sang about the things that really mattered to the majority of rock fans – girls, cars, dancing, fighting, pay-day and getting away with it. His notion of music was that it should could connect with life, be exciting, involving and immediate.

Though his earliest songs could be densely poetic, at full tilt Bruce Springsteen would leave the listener breathless – his wall of sound seemed to owe more to **Phil Spector** than it did to Bob Dylan.

And Bruce gave good honest sweat for his audience: his three-hours-and-upwards stage shows prompted the kind of energetic audience participation that had not been seen since the Stones back in the Sixties, before **Mick Jagger** picked up too many affectations.

Perhaps the most remarkable thing was Bruce Springsteen's progress – technically and artistically – within the parameters he'd set out in 'The Wild, The Innocent And The E-Street Shuffle' back in 1973. He became an incredible performer. The fateful, oft-misquoted remark, "I saw rock'n'roll's future", made by rock critic and soon-to-be Bruce Springsteen producer Jon Landau was inspired by a live show in Cambridge, Massachusetts in 1974. The release of 'Born To Run' the following year showed great musical sophistication and a maturity of lyric-writing that could be both visceral and poignant at the same time – just listen to the rock classic title track. The album 'Darkness On The Edge Of Town', three years later, portrayed Springsteen growing up: by now nearly 30, he concerned himself less with teenage frippery and more with the enduring problems of the working man. At this stage in the hedonistic Seventies, he was one of the few artists throwing light on the underside of the American dream.

In 'Born To Run' Bruce Springsteen had given the decade one of its pivotal rock'n'roll

anthems. But it's to the more measured tones of 'Darkness' that we look for first evidence of his most lasting achievement: he proved that rock'n'roll could express the doubts and the insights of maturity as much as the exuberance of youth.

▼ Good, honest, blue collar rock.

Bruce Springsteen

Bob Marley

By the time the **Wailers** – **Bob Marley** was just an ordinary band member at this time – released the 'Catch A Fire' LP in 1972, reggae had been lurking in the background of Britain's pop scene for more or less a decade. It had never been taken seriously as a genre and was considered as little more than ghetto music, with a second constituency among white working class skinheads. And this image might well have persisted had not Chris Blackwell, the independently wealthy white Jamaican owner of Island Records, decided to promote the Wailers using the same methods applied to major mainstream rock acts. Thus, 'Catch A Fire' was put together as an album rather than the collection of singles that reggae LPs had previously tended to be; the music was made palatable for a wider audience with the addition of acoustic guitar and keyboard overdubs on top of raw reggae tunes; and it was marketed in an elaborate flip-top Zippo lighter-style sleeve that became an instant collector's item.

The strategy succeeded brilliantly and it broke the Wailers (and reggae in general) through to a new, album-buying college audience. But it also presaged the end of the group as a unit. The original trio of Bob Marley, Bunny Livingston and Peter Tosh had come together as the **Wailin' Wailers** in 1964 and, before signing to Island in 1972, had evolved their music from rude boy ska to righteous rasta reggae, with every member of the band sharing equal billing. Island felt it would be easier to promote the group if the charismatic Marley became figurehead and so renamed the band **Bob Marley & The Wailers**. Within 18 months of 'Catch A Fire's release, Tosh and Livingston had left.

Marley however, repaid Island's long-term investment in him and went from strength to strength as the Third World's first superstar. His vibrant personality, his ability to project reg-gae into the global market-place and his good relations with the media, combined with his tireless recorded output, elevated him to a household name every-where. He became the only reggae artist to make any lasting impression on the US.

Back in the UK, Bob Marley proved a ready made icon as reggae reached new heights in the mid-Seventies, thanks to a bizarre alliance between punk and reggae – punks would claim to identify with black youths as fellow inner city warriors, though many thought this unlikely partnership had something to do with the average rasta's ready access to ganja. Marley approved of punk, though. In 1978, he showed the true spirit of co-operation, when he released the single 'Punky Reggae Party'.

Whether or not Bob Marley could have taken his celebrity to new heights in the following decade will, sadly, never be known. In 1980 while preparing for the biggest US dates of his career – opening for **Stevie Wonder** – he collapsed and was diagnosed as having cancer. On May 11, 1981, in hospital in Miami following treatment at a clinic in Switzerland, he died of lung cancer and a brain tumor. As a lasting testament, Bob Marley's birthday, February 6, is now a Jamaican national holiday.

▼ Bob Marley's birthday is now a Jamaican national holiday.

▲ The Wailers took reggae to a truly international stage.

Looking back, it's hard to believe that a group as self-destructive as the **Sex Pistols** could have gained so much fame and come to wield enormous influence on rock'n'roll and the music industry itself. To anyone who valued musical virtuosity, the Pistols and the punk movement they led were an abomination — though, in fact, their flair for powerful three-chord guitar rock was exemplary. But then again what the group actually played was only one small

com-
ponent
of their
story. The
Sex Pistols'
brief success
represented an
inspired marketing
operation by their manager
Malcolm McLaren, selling

an attitude – complete with sneering, snarling and spitting – which expressed contempt for everyone. You didn't have to like the music to like the attitude. The Pistols were punk icons for a new generation of rock fans and leaders of a street rebellion against the mid-Seventies' meaningless artistic values.

The Pistols' ethos can be traced back to 1974, when McLaren, managing drummer Paul Cook and guitarist Steve Jones in the Swankers, supposedly sacked third member Wally Nightingale for being "too musically proficient". McLaren's Svengali-like influence continued unabated until 1976 when, renamed the Sex Pistols and fronted by leering lead singer Johnny Rotten, the group got banned from venues all over the UK, more for their notoriety than anything they actually did. Examples of their infamy included swearing at a hostile TV interviewer Bill Grundy – generating so many column inches that they could be measured in miles – as well as the uproar over Jamie Reid's provocative sleeve design for 'God Save The Queen' (depicting the monarch, in her Jubilee Year, with a safety pin through her nose) which prompted the threat of strike action at a UK pressing plant. Bassist Glen Matlock, a talented writer, was replaced by the incompetent but iconic Sid Vicious. In topping the UK charts, 'God Save The Queen' surpassed the band's 1976 debut, the landmark single 'Anarchy In The UK'. They earned well over

£100,000 in advances from three different record companies as high jinks and constant press attention and condemnation got them sacked with remarkable frequency.

It's no wonder the group imploded in 1978 in a welter of good old fashioned rock'n'roll antagonism – it was public knowledge that apart from the Jones/Cook alliance they never really like each other, with the ill-fated Vicious's drug abuse and Johnny Rotten's intellectual pretensions only serving to exacerbate the situation. Neither did it come as any surprise when manager Malcolm McLaren unveiled a 1979 Sex Pistols documentary called *The Great Rock'N'Roll Swindle*. What was more of a shock was that the group actually managed to record an album, 'Never Mind The Bollocks'. The title serves as The Sex Pistols' epitaph: in their short, spectacular career the band created a combustible blend of music and attitude that has inspired their successors ever since.

▲ The Sex Pistols constantly courted controversy.

The Sex Pistols

1978

1978 was one of those years when rock styles that had come to the fore in the previous 12 months proved their staying power and became part of the establishment. Punk and new wave continued to thrive, with bands emerging and returning to obscurity on a monthly basis, while disco and disco-influenced pop continued to be well represented by **Donna Summer**, **Abba** and **Boney M** – the fact that these three acts had been the best-sellers of the previous year too goes to show how much pop music stood still in 1978.

The year commences with **Alice Cooper** being admitted to a psychiatric hospital for treatment of his alcoholism. Also going into exile, for tax reasons, are **Status Quo** who will spend the next 12 months touring Australia and recording in Holland,

making just one lightning visit to Britain for the Reading Festival. And on their way to making the tax man sit up and take notice are **Chic**, whose first release, the disco stomper 'Dance Dance Dance (Yowsah Yowsah Yowsah)' is a million seller. Starting out in less auspicious circumstances is **Gary Numan**, who dumps his day job in a shop the day **Tubeway Army**'s first single 'That's Too Bad' is released. It doesn't sell, however. And neither do the next two. **Simple Minds** – three of whom were once half of short-lived punk band Johnny &

The Self-Abusers – make their live debut in Glasgow. Later in the year they'll record a six-song demo which, thanks to UK music press enthusiasm, leads to a deal with Arista.

In February, the BBC bans **Tom Robinson**'s single 'Glad To Be Gay'. **David Coverdale**, ex-**Deep Purple** and thus avowedly heterosexual, returns to the UK from a year in Munich to put together a group to front his second solo LP, 'Northwinds'. A set of rock ballads like his 1976 LP 'Whitesnake', this is a pan-European affair with the singer in Germany adding his vocals to instrumentals recorded in the UK and flown over. When Coverdale decides he wants to go on the road, his band is called **David Coverdale's Whitesnake** but the tour fails to push the album into the charts and line-up changes will be frequent – something of a feature of this group in years to come. More successful in rocking the charts is **Van Halen**'s eponymously-titled debut album which sells 2 million copies after a cold start.

Boney M, one of the year's best-selling acts.

Chic freak out.

Gary Numan gave up his day job.

JUL 26 : World's first test tube baby born in Manchester, England

1978 · HEADLINE NEWS

Blue Oyster Cult had the Jam as opening act. Why?

Exercising the kind of clout that goes with those figures, when the band starts its US tour the next month, the contract rider insists all brown M&Ms be removed from the bowls of confectionery put out in the dressing rooms. In another contractual first, the band's recording deal also includes a paternity insurance clause.

The **Damned** split up; two months later they'll perform an equipment-trashing farewell gig at London's Rainbow Theatre then, in September, they'll play a reunion concert as Les Punks, with **Motorhead**'s Lemmy on bass, allowing Captain Sensible to stand in on guitar for Brian James who cannot be lured back. They decide to reform permanently, but as James owns the name, they have to appear as the **Doomed** while they involve m'learned friends in getting their old moniker back. The **Police** dye their hair blond for an appearance in a US TV advert and gain an immediate new punk credibility. In March, the **Clash**'s Paul Simenon and Topper Headon are fined a total of £800 for shooting racing pigeons with an air rifle in London. Record company patience seems to have paid off when **Kate Bush**'s debut single 'Wuthering Heights' is UK Number 1 for four weeks. **Chrissie Hynde** puts together her first regular backing band, dubbing them the **Pretenders**, after the **Platters**' song 'The Great Pretender'. **Dire Straits** play a short residency at London's Marquee club to great critical acclaim, but in spite off this and a sold-out tour, their first album, 'Dire Straits', only reaches 37 in the UK. Curiously, it does much better in Australia and New Zealand where it is a chart topper. In an odd combination of styles, the **Jam** support **Blue Oyster Cult** on a US tour. Maybe it's one of the reasons Paul Weller's trio will never have large-scale American success.

On April 22, during a violent general election campaign in Jamaica – supporters of rival candidates Michael Manley and Edward Seaga engage in nightly urban gun battles – **Bob Marley** returns to the island to host

That Chic Beat

Once Saturday Night Fever had got a grip on the entire population of the world, or so it seemed, there was room on the dance floor for a role model slightly hipper than the **Bee Gees** or **John Travolta** in his white suit. Enter **Chic**. The name was carefully chosen – obviously stylish, probably rather expensive and definitely cosmopolitan. Above all, it promised sophistication, which is exactly what many people were looking for at a disco, but band members were black as well, which made their music just that bit more authentic. With their clever combination of pounding rhythms and lush arrangements, the group were tailor-made for the upmarket-yet-still-gettin'-funky dancer. The sound became known as the Chic Beat.

When Chic scored that first million seller, 'Dance Dance Dance (Yowsah Yowsah Yowsah)', they didn't exist beyond the writing/production team of guitarist Nile Rodgers and bass player Bernard Edwards, plus vocalist Norma Jean Wright. When she left suddenly, the line-up was expanded to include drummer Tony Thompson and singers Luci Martin and Alfa Anderson. But the formula kept on working – distinctive of bass line, deceptively simple in structure and multi-platinum in sales terms: 'Everybody Dance', 'Le Freak' (with over four million sales, one of the biggest singles of the decade), 'I Want Your Love', 'Good Times' and 'My Forbidden Lover'.

As Chic the performers faded from view, Chic the backroom boys came into the spotlight. After weaving their writing/production magic on **Sister Sledge** in 1979, hit albums that had Rodgers & Edwards' handprints on them were, among others, **Debbie Harry**'s 'Koo Koo', **Madonna**'s 'Like A Virgin', **David Bowie**'s 'Let's Dance' and **Diana Ross**'s 'Diana' (she insisted on her own re-mix after feeling the duo had pushed her vocals too far back in the mix). The team also contributed individual songs to **Mick Jagger**, **Al Jarreau**, **Duran Duran** and **Aretha Franklin**.

1978 : HEADLINE NEWS   JUL 18 : South African authorities refuse to give Nelson Mandela the thousands of cards sent to mark his 60th birthday

Millie Jackson stretching the boundaries of good taste.

the *One Love Peace Concert*. Such is the musician's stature, he brings the two opposing candidates and their 'enforcers' on stage to shake hands. Under less fraught circumstances, publicity seeker **Jonathan King** stands as Royalist candidate in a British parliamentary election. He does not win but polls several thousand votes. In Athens, Georgia, Michael Stipe and Peter Buck meet in the record store where Buck works. They share an interest in left of centre, post-punk British music, two years later, they'll form **REM**. In May, the **Thompson Twins** – pre-Alannah Currie – arrive in London from Yorkshire, equipped with a van, a PA and a boast that they can play anywhere. What follows is two years of low-key gigs. **Scritti Politti** come to the capital too, a foursome that came together the previous year at Leeds Art School after singer Green Gartside

was inspired by a **Sex Pistols** show – they make their mark playing small punk venues. On a slightly larger scale, 90,000 tickets for **Bob Dylan**'s London shows sell out on the first day.

In June, what could have been the early emergence of Two Tone takes a blow when after supporting the **Clash** on the *On Parole* UK tour, the **Special AKA** – Jerry Dammers' Coventry Automatics, now with the addition of Terry Hall and Roddy Radiation – are approached by Bernie Rhodes with an offer of management. He moves the group to London, but, after they get fed up with an interminable period of rehearsal, Dammers takes his band back to Coventry severing ties with Rhodes, who is more interested in cutting a management deal with the newly-formed **Dexy's Midnight Runners**, so called after the street slang for a particular type of dexedrine.

Tommy Ramone leaves the **Ramones** – he will continue to produce them under his real name of Erdelyi and is replaced by Voidoid Marc Bell, who calls himself Marky Ramone. **Tom Waits** launches an acting career with a bit part in the Sylvester Stallone directed depression set melodrama *Paradise Alley*. The **Rolling Stones**' 'Some Girls' LP causes controversy over its use of photos of Raquel Welch, Lucille Ball and Farrah Fawcett Majors as part of

a camp wig advert-style sleeve illustration. The pictures have to be changed. Paul Simenon and Joe Strummer are fined £75 for being drunk and disorderly after a show in Scotland, which causes no controversy at all since it's now apparent that the **Clash** appear in court almost as often as they appear on stage.

Elsewhere, **Def Leppard** make their live debut playing at a school in Sheffield, Yorkshire, for the princely sum of £5. Shortly afterwards drummer Rick Allen will join – at 15, he is four years younger than Joe Elliot, the band's senior member. Meanwhile Virgin refuses to release the **Steve Jones/Paul Cook/Ronnie Biggs** single 'Cosh The Driver', until it is renamed 'No One is Innocent (A Punk Prayer By Ronnie Biggs)'. Another ex-Pistol **Sid Vicious** plays a 'farewell' show in London, under the title *Sid Sods Off*. He is backed by Rat Scabies, Glen Matlock and Steve New, calling themselves the Vicious White Kids. Johnny Rotten, now reverted to his God-given name of John Lydon, announces the formation of his new band **Public Image Limited** who are ex-Clash member Keith Levene (guitar), musical newcomer Jah Wobble (bass) and ex-**Furys** drummer Jim Walker. The group will play a live showcase in London on Christmas day in London. Noticeably more glamorous in the image stakes, a band called **Duran Duran** is formed in Birmingham UK. Taking their name from a character in the Sixties sci-fi movie *Barbarella*, the line-up consists of John Taylor (guitar), Nick Rhodes (keyboards), Simon Culley (bass and clarinet), Steven Duffy (vocals) and a

ROCK 'N' ROLL
record

APRIL: Such is the domestic demand for Boney M's single 'Rivers Of Babylon', that eight UK pressing plants can't keep up with it and copies have to be imported from the continent.

APRIL 21: Fairport Convention's Sandy Denny dies of a brain haemorrhage after a fall down a flight of stairs.

SEPTEMBER 1: Emilio Estefan and Gloria Fajardo get married.

SEPTEMBER 8: The Who's drummer, Keith Moon, succumbs to a drug overdose at the same London apartment where 'Mama' Cass Elliot overdosed in 1974.

OCTOBER 11: Sid Vicious calls the police to the Chelsea Hotel in New York, where he is living, reporting Nancy Spungen to have been stabbed. She is dead on arrival.

OCTOBER: All four members of Kiss simultaneously release solo albums, with sleeves featuring matching photos of the band.

drum machine. Significantly, at the same time as these first shoots of New Romanticism start to bud, the seminal punk fanzine *Sniffin' Glue* – the inspiration for a host of xeroxed and stapled imitators – folds.

In the UK in September, **Millie Jackson** tours and her way-past-the-knuckle approach to on-stage banter – cunnilingus seems to provide a particular fascination – excites considerable media discussion. Even with the resultant publicity, Jackson never really

appeals beyond the specialist market. *The Wiz*, a schmaltzy all-black disco-flavoured remake of *The Wizard Of Oz*, doesn't either. Co-produced by Motown, it stars Richard Pryor as the Wizard, **Michael Jackson** as the Scarecrow and a 33-year-old **Diana Ross** as Dorothy. The critical pummelling extends even to the sound-track album which is written and produced by Quincy Jones. Elsewhere, **Alexander O'Neal** joins **Flyte Time**, with Jimmy Jam and Terry Lewis. The

group becomes **Prince**'s full-time backing band, but O'Neal is soon fired, reportedly because he's openly unhappy about the discipline the wee fellow imposes on them.

Ozzy Osbourne walks out once more on **Black Sabbath** after disagreements over musical direction fail to be resolved – he can't reconcile himself with the Sabbs' new sensitivity and sophistication. After trying, unsuccessfully, to organize his own group, he will be back within months. Osbourne's polar opposite is loveman **Teddy Pendergrass** who, on September 2, plays the first of a series of highly successful *Ladies Only* concerts. When Bernie Rhodes is fired as the **Clash**'s manager next month, he manages to obtain a court order stating all the group's earnings must continue to be paid to him. Andy McCluskey and Paul Humphreys host an evening they consider to be a self-indulgent experiment in anti-music at a club in Liverpool. They call the session **Orchestral Manoeuvres In The Dark**, and it's such a success they realize they have a future doing this sort of thing on a more permanent basis.

Brian Eno releases his first fully ambient album, 'Music For Films'. Although critical reaction is mixed, the new approach finds a strong cult following almost immediately and he forms his own label, Ambient, on which 1979's 'Music For Airports' will be the first release. Also this year, the Eno-produced **Talking Heads** album 'More Songs About Buildings And Food', goes Top 30 on both sides of the Atlantic. **Captain Beefheart**'s comeback LP, 'Shiny Beast (Bat

▶ Brian Eno spends quality time in the dressing up box.

Chain Puller)', however, does not chart. Also possessing a nifty line in whimsy are the **Teardrop Explodes** – named after a caption in a Liechtenstein-type comic – who are formed in Liverpool, an earlier line-up included Julian Cope, Pete Wylie and Ian McCulloch.

In the USA, following five months work, **Prince**'s first album 'For You' is released. It sells 400,000 almost immediately. **Queen**'s Madison Square Garden shows are a big hit too, they feature unclothed female cyclists traversing the stage during 'Fat Bottomed Girls'. **Emerson, Lake And Palmer**, however, announce their official split.

In December, to coincide with the release of his 'Incantations' album, **Mike Oldfield** gives his first ever interviews. It is reported at the time that he has been taking assertiveness training. Not the sort of thing **Rod Stewart** requires as his future evergreen, 'Da Ya Think I'm Sexy', is top of the UK charts and two months later will repeat this success in the USA. **Boney M**'s 'Mary's Boy Child' is the seasonal UK Christmas Number 1, staying there into the New Year to sell into the seven figure bracket.

It's Fun at the YMCA

Or at least it was fun for the **Village People**, who were the most unlikely hit act of the year with three million-sellers out of three attempts. In January 1978, 'YMCA' went to Number 2 in the US and one place higher in the UK, selling over three million. The follow-up, in March, 'In The Navy' (which the US Navy considered using as a recruitment song until its full implications were pointed out), got to 3 and 2 in the US and UK respectively and managed one million. The hat trick of platinum singles was achieved, when this success galvanized the previous year's effort, 'Macho Man', back into life – it soon passed the seven figure sales mark.

The Village People: the cowboy, the construction worker, the Indian, the policeman, the biker and the G.I. - six stereotypes of the America male who took the sound of the New York gay discos to an unwitting, but not unwilling, public.

By 1979, new wave was turning into old wave, with acts like **Blondie**, the **Police** and the **Boomtown Rats** having been around for so long they were practically part of the furniture. The time was ripe for the punk backlash to get underway. First out of the Midlands – and North London's Camden Town – came the ska revival led by the **Specials**, which not only provided recognizable tunes for exuberant pogo-dancing but also gave the nation's youth an excuse to smarten themselves up in suits and ties. Further down the sartorial road, with clothes to put a peacock to shame, the New Romantics began to emerge from their closet in 1979. In what was touted as a glamorous reaction to five years of dressing down, this new movement came dressed up in velvet, lace, brocade, clouds of hairspray, the occasional tea towel and the music of **Spandau Ballet** and **Duran Duran**. Glamour and glitz was

The ska revival was led ▽ by the Specials.

▲ Spandau Ballet make the New Romantic cultural statement.

to influence much of the coming decade's music. But the longest-lasting influence came right at the end of the decade when an unknown group had a hit with an all-new style. It was black music's backlash against the apparently unstoppable onslaught of disco – **Boney M** were still chart regulars this year – and, once the **Sugarhill Gang** released 'Rapper's Delight', black American music would never be the same again.

One of the year's first major news stories concerns San Diego, California, where schoolgirl Brenda Spencer shoots dead several other teenagers at her school and gives as a reason "Because I don't like Mondays". A statement that makes a considerable impact on **Bob Geldof**, who pens a song about the incident. In July, it tops the UK charts for four weeks and is banned in the USA. On a gentler note, the year also opens with **Toto**'s debut single and album ('Hold The Line' and 'Toto', respectively) each selling a million copies, with the effect that their easy-action traditional rock approach becomes a genre title, Adult Orientated Rock. Or AOR.

As **John Travolta**'s 'Travolta Fever' album (a repackaging of his

musical highlights from *Saturday Night Fever* and *Grease*) barely scrapes into the US Top 200, he hangs up his microphone (and dancing shoes) to concentrate on 'serious' acting. Just as serious is **Bruce Springsteen** who is coming to the end of his first sold-out, large venue tour, and has established the far-from-flimsy reputation for sets lasting upwards of three hours. Elsewhere, **Sid Vicious** goes on trial in New York charged with the murder of Nancy Spungen. The **Invaders** play their last gig before changing their name to **Madness**. **Madonna** gets a job as a dancer with the *Patrick Hernandez Revue* – a disco stage show in Paris – but she soon leaves to start her first group in New York, the Breakfast Club: she plays drums. **Ozzy Osbourne** leaves **Black Sabbath** – this time for good, as he founds Blizzard Of Oz but soon gives the group up in favour of a very successful solo career. And the Canadian government name **Rush** as Ambassadors Of Music.

The **Clash** tour America: they'll return later in the year for more dates, but in spite of the shows being well received, they never will sell enormous amounts of records in that

MAR 26 : Egypt and Israel sign a peace treaty in Washington DC • MAR 29 : Idi Amin flees Uganda

Sid Vicious went on trial for murder. Of his girlfriend, not 'My Way'.

country. **Elvis Costello** has his problems in the US too, when touring with his 'Armed Forces' album, he gets into a heated argument in a hotel bar with Steven Stills and Bonnie (**Delaney & Bonnie**) Bramlett, currently in Stills' band. The dispute is reportedly about the relationship between race and music and it comes to an end when Bramlett punches Costello in the face. **Bob Marley & The Wailers** become the first reggae act to headline at New York's Apollo Theatre Harlem. Although rapturously received by New York's Caribbean community – and a legion of white reggae fans – it is not the start of Reggae USA the critics claim it to be. Still on the subject of reggae, **UB40** make their live debut in a pub in Birmingham. The group, all long-time reggae fans, have known each other since childhood and, since they are all jobless, they choose as their name the official Department Of Health And Social Security coding for unemployment benefit claim forms. The group continue to gig locally, where they are spotted by **Chrissie Hynde** who engages them as support act on her UK tour at the end of the year, exposure that results in much major record company interest. However, in keeping with the fierce spirit of independence that is to become the group's trademark, they sign with a local label owned by the couple who run their favourite record shop.

School music teacher and part-time rock band member **Howard Jones** buys a synthesizer using money he received as compensation for a road accident. It allows him to perform solo in south-east England pubs and clubs, where he teams up with mime artist Jed. On the strength of her vocal performances in the New York cabaret *Catch A Star*, **Pat Benatar** is signed to Chrysalis Records. After the group is dropped by Island Records, founder member John Foxx quits **Ultravox** to be replaced by Midge Ure. On April 3, **Kate Bush** plays her first large live gig at the Empire Theatre in Liverpool. **Van Halen** consolidate last year's success as 'Van Halen II' sells five million and the group undertakes a large-scale world tour, during which their reputation for on the road excess is equalled only by their over the top stage show – at their concert in the Anaheim Stadium, California, a David Lee Roth stunt double parachutes on to the stage.

Keith Richard avoids a custodial sentence on a Canadian drugs charge by playing a benefit concert for the Canadian National Institute For The Blind. For the purposes of the show, he puts together the **New Barbarians** – Ron Wood (guitar), Stanley Clarke (bass), Ian McLagan (keyboards), Zigy Modeliste (drums) and Bobby Keyes (sax) – who work so well together that, during the following month, they undertake a brief US tour.

In not such perfect harmony, **Joan Jett** leaves the **Runaways** as she and Lita Ford can no longer see eye to eye on the band's direction – Jett prefers straight rock'n'roll, Ford wants a more theatrical heavy metal-ish approach. Jett heads for London

The Pride Of Camden Town: Madness

MAR 31 : Children and pregnant women are evacuated as the nuclear plant at Three Mile Island, Pennsylvania, threatens to go into melt-down

After several years careful nuturing, Kate Bush bloomed.

Siouxsie of the Banshees.

to record with ex-**Sex Pistols** Cook and Jones. **Blondie** finally has a US hit with the disco-ish 'Heart Of Glass' (Number 1), the song occupies the equivalent spot in the UK for four weeks, selling over a million. The **Cure**, who have built a strong fan base through extensive touring get to Number 44 with their first album, 'Three Imaginary Boys'. **DeBarge** sign to Motown Records, five singing siblings – four boys and a girl – they are hailed as the New Jackson 5, a mantle that does them as much harm as good.

On May 21, when he begins a series of eight shows in Leningrad, **Elton John** becomes the first western rock star to tour the Soviet Union. As groundbreaking – in their own way – are **Iron Maiden** when they play at a London club in the *Heavy Metal Crusade*, a festival held to mark the emergence of the 'New Wave Of British Heavy Metal'. The term was coined by UK music magazine *Sounds* to describe an aspect of the music that is punk-influenced, harder edged and unique to the UK in the light of America's more flamboyant rock bands, or metal lite as they are sometimes rather scathingly described. After touring the UK supporting **Siouxsie & The Banshees** and Europe with **Iggy Pop**, the **Human League** are signed by Virgin Records.

Sting opens in the film of *Quadrophenia*, based on the **Who**'s double album, in a minor role as Ace, a supercool mod who has a day job as a hotel bellboy. **Ringo Starr**, **George Harrison** and **Paul McCartney** play at **Eric Clapton**'s wedding to George's ex-wife Patti, fuelling rumours that the **Beatles** are ready to reform. And, backed by a 50-piece orchestra and choir, **Mike Oldfield** undertakes his first tour, which is a critical if not financial success.

In June, after their first LP charts briefly in the UK, **Simple Minds** undertake a heavy schedule of live

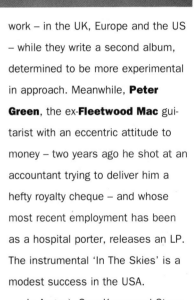

work – in the UK, Europe and the US – while they write a second album, determined to be more experimental in approach. Meanwhile, **Peter Green**, the ex-**Fleetwood Mac** guitarist with an eccentric attitude to money – two years ago he shot at an accountant trying to deliver him a hefty royalty cheque – and whose most recent employment has been as a hospital porter, releases an LP. The instrumental 'In The Skies' is a modest success in the USA.

In August, Gary Kemp and Steve Dagger revive an old school band, the Makers, as **Spandau Ballet**. The group takes its lead from the emerging New Romantics – an anti-punk, elaborately dressed, elite London nightclub scene, in many ways a kind of up-market, overdressed glam-rock. In December, after playing a series of highly publicized but strictly exclusive London shows, they turn down an offer from Island Records boss Chris Blackwell in favour of starting their own record label, Reformation. Less successfully, **Linda McCartney** releases the virtually unnoticed

'Seaside Woman' under the name of Suzy & The Red Stripes. **Bruce Springsteen** and CBS file suit against convicted album bootleggers, seeking almost $2 million in compensation. While a certifiedly genuine article on the market is *I, Me, Mine*, a hand-crafted, leatherbound book by **George Harrison**. Offered up at the wallet-lightening price of £148, it is the Quiet One's analysis of all the songs he has written, and includes hand-written copies of their lyrics. The limited edition of 2,000 personally signed copies sells out with surprising speed.

Six months after the release of the agonized 'Here My Dear' album – a tortured account of a marriage breakup, with royalties from it pledged as part of a settlement to his ex-wife – **Marvin Gaye**, beset by drug addic-

tion and a $2 million tax bill, is living in a caravan in Hawaii. Elsewhere, after two UK Number 1 singles ('Are Friends Electric' and 'Cars') and an album, 'The Pleasure Principle', entering the chart at Number 1, **Gary Numan** drops the Tubeway Army name – the group, he claims, was only put together for touring, never as a permanent fixture. 'In Through The Out Door' by **Led Zeppelin** goes to Number 1 in the UK and US. It will sell over five million copies and proves to be their last LP. A little belatedly, **Abba** begin their only US tour. **George Michael**, Andrew Ridgeley, Paul Ridgeley, future recording artist **David Austin** and some other fellow members of the same scout troop form ska revival band the **Executive**. While **Scritti Politti** are

on tour with **Joy Division** and **Gang Of Four**, Green Gartside collapses with a heart complaint – ill health will continue to dog him. **U2** release their first record, the EP 'U2:3'. On sale only in Ireland, it goes to Number 1. And ex-**James Gang**er, one time-**Eagle Joe Walsh** announces he is to run for President Of The USA in 1980. He doesn't.

Four months after release, **Michael Jackson**'s 'Don't Stop 'Til You Get Enough' gives him his first US Number 1 since 'Ben' in 1972 and the album it's from, 'Off The Wall', released in August, goes Top 5 on both sides of the Atlantic that month. The LP will eventually pass the 10 million sales mark and will be widely accepted as the first glimpse of Michael Jackson as a mature artist

1979 - HEADLINE NEWS • JUL 20 : Sandanista rebels overthrow the Nicaraguan government • SEP 2 : English serial killer, the Yorkshire Ripper claims his 12th victim

Post-Punk

Although, by the late Seventies, punk had pretty much sunk like a stone in the millpond of popular music, its ripples continued to spread across the surface as a generation of post-punk acts created a new mainstream. Influenced by punk's anti-rock star, anti-fashion DIY ethos, acts such as **Blondie**, the **Pretenders**, the **Boomtown Rats**, the **Police**, **U2**, the **Undertones**, the **Jam** and **Depeche Mode** were reinventing music as something new, fresh and vibrant. Despite being fans of punk, they played by

rock's traditional rules. Although they retained a bristly attitude, they respected the industry's artistic and commercial guidelines and, perhaps most importantly, didn't spit at anybody. They were the new wave, or punk for people who didn't like punk. And though some of the newcomers eventually evolved into caricatures of the rock stars they had intended to replace, at the time it was new wave which actually brought about the changes central to punk's ethos.

ROCK'N'ROLL record

JANUARY 13: Donny Hathaway falls to his death from a window in the Essex House Hotel, New York City.

FEBRUARY 2: At a party in New York, Sid Vicious collapses and dies from fluid on the lungs brought on by a heroin overdose.

MARCH: Kylie Minogue, aged 10, gets her first TV role in the Australian soap opera The Sullivans.

APRIL 6: Rod Stewart marries Alannah Hamilton, ex-wife of actor George.

JUNE: Meat Loaf stars in the title role of the rockbiz comedy movie Roadie. The film also features Debbie Harry, Alice Cooper and Roy Orbison.

JULY 10: Chuck Berry is jailed for three months on a six-year-old tax evasion charge.

AUGUST 18: Nick Lowe marries Johnny Cash's step daughter, Carlene Carter, in California.

NOVEMBER 2: Mick and Bianca Jagger are divorced.

Michael Jackson when he still looked like a proper person.

from the 'Slow Train Coming' album is booed when he opens the tour of the same name in San Francisco. This follows months of speculation as to whether Dylan has been born again into the Christian faith. Not so Christian in outlook are Dunstable council – a suburban local authority in the UK – who refuse to allow an **Iggy Pop** gig because his touring band includes ex-**Sex Pistol** Glen Matlock, and they have never lifted the ban they imposed on the punk group two years previously.

On December 18, the **Police** play Hammersmith Palais and Hammersmith Odeon in London on the same night. After much pre-publicity, they make the 600-yard trip from one venue to the other in an armoured car, while scores of police are employed to keep order among the enormous crowd lining the route. New York's influential *Village Voice* magazine names **Neil Young** 'Artist Of The Decade'. A dozen audience members are trampled to death in a rush to claim unreserved seats at a **Who** concert in Cincinnati. **Status Quo** reach Number 16 in the UK with *a ballad*! And as the year closes, **U2** play their first show on the UK mainland at the Hope & Anchor pub in north London (an important post-punk venue). Only nine people turn up, and the band are probably not helped by being billed as V2 on publicity material.

instead of the cute little kid who sang with the Jackson 5. **Soft Cell** are formed by Marc Almond and David Ball, who met at college in Leeds the previous year. They play their first show in December at the college, augmented by a slide show and projected special effects. **Paul McCartney** receives a commemorative medal from the UK Arts Minister as "the most successful composer of all time" – since 1962 his songs, including those he co-wrote, have sold 100 million singles and 100 million albums. Meanwhile the **Stranglers**, who don't get any medals at all, release 'The Raven' album in a 3D sleeve.

Next month, the **Sugarhill Gang**'s 'Rapper's Delight' is a huge hit on both sides of the Atlantic. Essentially a re-hash of **Chic**'s 'Good Times', it announces the commercial arrival of hip hop, a DIY funk style that involves talking in rhyme over drastic re-edits of samples from other people's records,

a style that has been simmering in US street culture for a few years. On the more melodic side of soul, **Stevie Wonder** releases the double LP 'Journey Through The Secret Life Of Plants', and launches it by performing it with The National Afro-American Philharmonic Orchestra at New York's Metropolitan Opera House. This delicately-crafted instrumental album purportedly explores the botanical kingdom from the point of view of a plant, but meets with critical disdain – a great deal of jokes about vegetating, like watching grass grow, etc etc – and remains the last genuinely ambitious album from Stevie Wonder. A fitting close to the decade from him.

Madness play dates in New York and California with reasonable success – an incongruous Two Tone cult based around mohair suits, scooters and ska music will survive in Los Angeles for several years. **Bob Dylan**'s evangelical-flavoured material

Top, the Boomtown Rats; bottom, U2.

1979 - HEADLINE NEWS   NOV 28: The UK mortgage rate hits a record 15% • DEC 4: The Ayatollah Khomeini is declared absolute ruler of Iran – the Shah has been in exile since January

'I want my...I want my MTV'

The Eighties

1980s

Sylvie Simmons

By the Eighties, pop music was part of the fabric of life. It was everywhere. On countless new radio stations. On numerous movie soundtracks. On airline in-flight services. In restaurants, in supermarkets and even in lifts. And, perhaps by way of escape, or at least in an attempt to choose what to listen to, suddenly everyone seemed to be plugged into a Walkman as they went about their daily lives.

This explosion of music found its way into the tabloid press as the papers started covering the antics of pop stars as major news stories and into an overwhelming number of new music and style magazines. And, most importantly of all, it found its way on to television. When MTV, the music video channel, was launched in the US in the summer of 1981 it changed our view of music overnight. Suddenly it was important what music looked like, as well as how it sounded. Even though the introduction of the compact disc had improved the quality of recordings enormously, it was how artists presented and packaged themselves that really mattered. In the Seventies, the last thing that any self-respecting rock musician would have thought about was what they looked like – it was the music that mattered. But all the Eighties megastars – **Madonna** and **Michael Jackson**, **Prince** and **George Michael**, **Def Leppard** and **Motley Crue** – not only had the videos, they had The Look (and a host of advisers, stylists and trainers to help them achieve it). The only megastar who didn't was **Bruce Springsteen**, though his whole sweat-under-the armpits, grime-under-the-nails, checked-shirt, live-show approach could be seen as an anti-style statement, and therefore a style in itself.

Yes, style was one of the buzzwords of the Eighties, with 'Style-Bibles' like The Face and i-D, UK magazines for the hip adult market and Smash Hits for the kids, underlining even further the visual emphasis. As for the music, the Eighties witnessed an astounding variety of different styles and genres, from new psychedelia to acid house, disco to death metal, goth rock to hip hop, folk to technopop, reactions and revivals following on from each other and often colliding at an alarming rate. The most important of them, though, was rap. What started out as a black punk movement was to establish itself as the musical revolution of the decade.

◄ Dire Straits: 'Money For Nothing'

The Eighties arrived with punk and new wave spitting and sneering in tow – new ska, new romantics, even a new wave of British heavy metal, jostled each other for space in the UK charts. But, for the most part, the old guard didn't seem to take too much notice of what was going on. A handful of established rock stars were provoked into releasing albums detailing the pain and suffering of being rich and famous – **Billy Joel**'s 'Glass Houses', **Jackson Browne**'s 'Hold Out', **Paul Simon**'s 'One Trick Pony', **Bob Seger**'s 'Against The Wind', the **Rolling Stones**' 'Emotional Rescue' and the biggie, **Pink Floyd**'s 'The Wall'. Some, including **Emerson, Lake & Palmer** and the **Eagles**, went as far as to break up. However, the big established names continued to dominate, especially in the States. 1980's *Grammy Awards* were almost perversely conservative considering the abundance of excellent new acts: Best Male Pop Vocalist **Kenny Loggins**; Best Pop Female **Bette Midler**; Best Pop Group, believe it or not, **Barbra Streisand** duetting with the **Bee Gees Barry Gibb**; Best Rock Vocalist **Billy Joel**; Best Rock Group **Bob Seger & The Silver Bullet Band**. The Grammy for Best Newcomer (along with three more

Grammies including Record Of The Year) went to soft-rocker **Christopher Cross**, whose debut album gave him the huge AOR hits 'Ride Like The Wind' and 'Sailing.' The only winner under pensionable age was **Pat Benatar**, a 27-year-old opera-trained New Yorker who had a million-selling US single with the pop-rock song 'Hit Me With Your Best Shot'.

In January 1980, with their single 'Brass In Pocket' topping the charts and fronted by uncompromising, leather-clad Chrissie Hynde from Akron, Ohio, the **Pretenders** embark on a 30-date British tour to coincide with the release of their self-titled debut album. It enters the UK charts at Number 1. Fifteen years after 'As Tears Go By', **Marianne Faithfull** makes a comeback with her album 'Broken English'. The critics quite rightly drool over the album's collection of songs, which covers everything from sex to the Baader-Meinhoff terrorist group and includes a version of **John Lennon**'s 'Working Class Hero' – sung more than adequately for an upper-class, ex-convent school girl. The singer tells the press that she's over the heroin addiction that led to her departure from the music world and adds that the royalties from 'Sister Morphine', the song she wrote for the Stones' album 'Sticky Fingers', have been what sustained her through the past ten years. "Don't tell me", she says, "that drugs don't pay."

▲ Pretenders - the Talk of the Town in 1980.

On January 16, **Paul McCartney** – touring Japan for the first time since the **Beatles** played there in 1966 – is arrested when he lands there with nearly half a pound of marijuana in his suitcase. Prisoner Number Twenty-Two, as he is suddenly known, faces up to seven years behind bars. When his father-in-law and lawyer, Lee Eastman flies out, the Japanese authorities elect to send Macca away rather than send him down. McCartney is deported and the tour is cancelled.

Pink Floyd's concept album, 'The Wall', Britain's Number 1 album since it was released last month, starts the first of a 15-week run at the top of the US charts as the band begins its world tour. Not exactly the most gruelling of schedules, they play just four locations – New York, Los Angeles, Dusseldorf and London. During their spectacular show, a thirty-foot wall is built across the stage to symbolize the isolation of fame...this barrier is dismantled brick by brick as the band plays on. The review in *Rolling Stone*

I Heard the News Today, Oh Boy...

"(Paul McCartney) turned up at the door. I said 'Look, do you mind ringing first? I've just had a hard day with the baby, I'm worn out, and you're walking in with a damn guitar'." (John Lennon)

In November 1980, after five years of domestic bliss as a house-husband, **John Lennon**, the man whose music galvanized the previous decade, came back with an album that told the world he was really quite happy not making music, thank you very much, and preferred staying holed up with Yoko Ono in the Dakota Building, their exclusive Manhattan apartment looking after their son Sean. Judging by the response to 'Double Fantasy' (named after a tropical flower that the Ono-Lennons spotted in the Bahamas) and by subsequent tragic events, Lennon really ought to have stayed where he was. Music critics, who had anticipated the ex-Beatle's new release as if it were the second coming, were not enthusiastic about 'Double Fantasy'. Sales of the record – the first release on music industry mogul David Geffen's new label Geffen Records – rapidly started to fall away.

On December 8, a strange young man stood waiting outside the Dakota Building alongside the regular fans. Mark David Chapman was clutching a copy of the album as well as JD Salinger's novel, *Catcher In The Rye*. When Lennon came out on to the street, Chapman asked for his autograph. Six hours later, when the star returned, the young man shot him five times – Lennon died of blood loss shortly

John Lennon shot dead - imagine the unimaginable.

afterwards. A bizarre photograph of the ex-Beatle unwittingly signing his name for the fan who would later kill him flashed across front pages and TV screens over the world. John Lennon was 40 years old.

While mourners held candle-lit vigils outside the Dakota Building for nights on end, 'Double Fantasy' shot to Number 1 in both Britain and the States. On December 14, 100,000 people gathered in New York's Central Park to pay homage. As the public address system boomed out 'Give Peace A Chance', Yoko Ono requested that mourners across the world hold a vigil of ten minutes silence for peace.

For baby boomers who had grown up on his music, Lennon became a martyr for the peace movement; his murder was an 'assassination' – as in the case of President John F Kennedy. Conspiracy theorists published books blaming the American government and it became a cliché to talk about what you were doing at the time you heard Lennon had been shot. Personal bodyguards experienced an unprecedented business boom as Lennon's fellow rock stars discovered the significance of 'stalkers' – disturbed, obsessive fans – almost overnight. A spate of biographies – including the notorious *The Lives Of John Lennon* by the late Albert Goldman, which paints Lennon as a drug-addled, homosexual, mother-fixated bully and Yoko as an evil and scheming figure – hit the stores. The single '(Just Like) Starting Over' was a big posthumous hit. The following June, Chapman ignored his lawyer's advice and pleaded guilty to murder. He was given 20 years to life.

Marianne Faithfull, upper class heroine, makes a comeback with 'Working Class Hero', featured on her critically-acclaimed album 'Broken English'. Faithfull, daughter of an Austrian baroness, had her first hit in 1964 with a cover of the Jagger/Richard song 'As Tears Go By', and her first fame as Mick Jagger's girlfriend

magazine describes the show as "an enormously impressive testament to a band that doesn't mind playing second fiddle to a lot of white blocks."

In the *American Music Awards*, **Michael Jackson** wins in the Favourite R&B Album, Favourite Single and Favourite Male R&B Artist categories. Meanwhile in the UK, pop's Mr Clean **Cliff Richard** is included in January's New Year's Honours List. The Queen presents

him with an OBE (The Order of the British Empire).

On February 19, while the band are in Britain recording, **AC/DC** vocalist **Bon Scott** chokes to death on his own vomit in the back of a friend's car in London after a night of heavy drinking.

Patti Smith, New York punk poetess and high priestess of anarchy, marries **Fred 'Sonic' Smith** of the **MC5**, the legendary Detroit band of 'Kick Out The Jams' fame on

March 1. Conveniently for her, she doesn't have to change her name: inconveniently for fans, she opts to retreat from the music business. In March too, **Pink Floyd**'s 'Another Brick In The Wall' tops the US and UK singles charts. The song with its chorus of kids chanting 'We don't need no education' is banned in South Africa, after being adopted as an anthem by militant black school-children.

In April, David Geffen, founder of

APR 24 : Eight US servicemen die in a failed attempt to rescue the 52 American hostages seized with the Ayatollah Khomeini's approval five months ago in Iran

Asylum Records, launches his new record label, Geffen. He tells *Rolling Stone*, "People are just doing it badly and I think I can do it better." His first three signings are **Donna Summer**, **Elton John** and **John Lennon**. **Genesis**' album 'Duke', featuring drummer **Phil Collins** on lead vocals, tops the UK charts – the band's first-ever British Number 1. Two months after the death of their vocalist, **AC/DC** announce his replacement – Brian Johnson, ex-**Geordie**. In April they start work on a new album, 'Back In Black', whose title suggests they're still in mourning. While touring the US in the same month, **Pretenders** vocalist **Chrissie Hynde** meets an old idol of hers in a New York nightclub: **Ray Davies** of the **Kinks**. Romance ensues.

On May 18, on the eve of the band's first US tour and shortly after the release of their second album, 'Closer', **Joy Division** frontman **Ian Curtis** commits suicide. Formed a year ago, the Manchester band's brilliant first single 'Love Will Tear Us Apart', with Curtis' detached, fragile vocals, was a huge indie hit, and their excellent debut album, 'Unknown Pleasures', won them a large cult and critical following. The pressure of following it up, coupled with epilepsy and depression, are cited as the reasons Curtis hangs himself in his bedroom. The body is found with **Iggy Pop**'s 'The Idiot' winding round Curtis' turntable and Werner Herzog's melancholic film *Stroszek* winding through his video machine.

June 9 is the day a thousand punks march in London, to mark the anniversary of **Sex Pistols** bassist **Sid Vicious**' death. Sid's mum can't make the big parade; she's in hospital dealing with her own drug problems. Meanwhile, across the pond, cowboys are all the rage, thanks to the summer's smash hit film *Urban Cowboy*. Starring **John Travolta** and Debra Winger, its soundtrack is one of America's 20 top-selling albums of the year. A new (and painful) Western craze, bucking mechanical bulls, makes an appearance – trendies try to ride them at parties. Everywhere there are overdressed people looking – and walking – like Liberace impersonating John Wayne. Country and western music is suddenly in vogue. The Sissy Spacek film *Coal Miner's Daughter*, the rags-to-riches story of country singer **Loretta Lynn**, wins an Oscar.

Iron Maiden, leaders of the New Wave of British Heavy Metal movement. The band - named after the medieval torture device - formed in London in the late Seventies as a way of keeping the metal banner flying when punk still reigned supreme. They built up a strong grass-roots following on the ▼ pub circuit.

Heavy Metal's New Wave

At least as far as the British rock press was concerned, heavy metal died in 1980. Punk and new wave had been specially invented to kick the bloated corpses of dinosaurs like **Journey**, **Foreigner**, **Styx** and **Yes** into touch.

Fine in principle if not quite in practice: Styx's new concept album, 'Paradise Theater', went to Number 1 in the States, and Yes' album 'Drama' – with **Geoff Downes** and **Trevor Horn** of **Buggles** ('Video Killed The Radio Star') in place of vocalist **Jon Anderson** and keyboardist **Rick Wakeman** – was a big US and UK hit. Ageing arena bands and faceless 'corporate rockers' were still the norm. That is, until a number of young, hungry rock bands with the stamina, attitude and tight pants their predecessors lost long ago started to appear in Britain. They'd gathered under the banner NWOBHM – the

New Wave Of British Heavy Metal.

At the start of 1980, EMI Records in Britain released 'Metal For Muthas' – a compilation album of new bands like **Iron Maiden**, **Samson**, **Angelwitch** and **Sledgehammer**. MCA returned fire with its own collection, 'Brute Force' . 'Metal Mothers II', 'Metal Explosion', 'Heavy Duty' and 'The New Electric Warriors' compilations followed, all within the space of a year. Iron Maiden's self-titled debut album was hailed as the hottest metal album of the year and went Top 5 in Britain, aided by extensive touring with OldWOBHM-ers **Judas Priest** and **Kiss**. And **Def Leppard** – who, like Iron Maiden, released an acclaimed independent EP the year before – made it to Number 15 in the UK charts with their debut album, 'On Through The Night'.

The Blues Brothers - the off-the-wall comedy film starring Saturday Night Live comics John Belushi and Dan Aykroyd and a stellar musical cast including James Brown, Aretha Franklin and Ray Charles - is a worldwide smash and a staple on tour bus video machines.

June also sees the release of one of the year's biggest movies – and hit records – *Fame*. The story of a bunch of aspiring New York performing arts students, it's essentially an excuse for lots of limbs and leotards and catchy music like the title track sung by **Irene Cara**. The same month, *The Blues Brothers* movie is released to lousy reviews. Never mind, it grosses $13 million in its first week. A spin-off from the American TV series *Saturday Night Live*, the film stars comedians John Belushi and Dan Aykroyd as musicians who reunite their band to save an orphanage and features cameo appearances from **James Brown**, **Aretha Franklin**, **John Lee Hooker**, **Cab Calloway**, **Ray Charles**, Pee Wee Herman and Twiggy. **Peter Gabriel**'s third self-titled solo album tops the UK charts and is an unexpected Top 20 hit in the States – particularly unexpected for Atlantic Records, who dropped the singer after hearing the demo tapes which they declared to be uncommercial. The LP includes a song that will become an anti-apartheid anthem: 'Biko'. Based around a chorus of South African tribal singing, it heralds the former **Genesis** singer's growing interest in world music.

July marks the release of 'Searching For The Young Soul Rebels', the debut album by **Dexy's Midnight Runners** – post-punk angry young soulmen. Especially angry is frontman Kevin Rowland, who snatches the album's master tapes from producer Pete Wingfield and refuses to return them until a better deal has been negotiated. Rowland later takes out ads in the British music papers to vent his spleen on the album's critics.

By way of contrast, the country's fashion cognoscenti have taken to dressing up in pantomime costume as 'Ant Fever' starts to sweep the UK. **Adam & The Ants**' sound pulsates to an African tribal beat, with lots of Burundi drums; their look is a romantic mix of Red Indian chic, highwayman accessories and Hollywood pirate. Adam Ant, one of the most marketable pop idols in years, is a protégé of **Sex Pistols** svengali **Malcolm McLaren**. Following the huge success of their indie album 'Dirk Wears White Sox', the Ants sign a major label record deal in July and start working on a new album.

Joy Division's second album, 'Closer', is a posthumous Top 10 summer hit for **Ian Curtis**. **Simon Le Bon** joins **Duran Duran** as vocalist, replacing **Stephen 'Tin Tin' Duffy**. He's no show business virgin. As a child, Le Bon, now a 21-year-old drama student, starred in a TV commercial for the soap powder, Persil. **AC/DC**'s new album 'Back In Black' is released in August. It tops the UK charts for two weeks.

David Bowie gets rave reviews for his appearance on Broadway in September, as John Merrick, the Victorian sideshow freak who was known as *The Elephant Man*. At the same time, his album 'Scary Monsters And Super Creeps' tops the UK charts. The unsettling single 'Ashes To Ashes' is his first Number 1 UK single since 'Space Oddity', to which it is a kind of belated sequel. On September 25, the eve of their US tour, **John Bonham**, **Led Zeppelin**'s drummer, is found dead in bed in guitarist **Jimmy Page**'s house in Windsor after a 12-hour drinking session. The autopsy reports the cause of death as pulmonary edema – inhalation of vomit to you and me.

Norwegian pop trio **A-ha** release their debut album in October. With the not-too-catchy name of 'Fakkeltog', it's perhaps a good thing it is only released in Norway. To widen their appeal, the band recruits singer **Morten Harket** and relocates to London. Also releasing their debut album this month are Australians **INXS**. It features their Aussie hit 'Just Keep Walking'. Ian Craig Marsh and Martyn Ware are about to take this advice and leave the **Human League** to form **Heaven 17** – the name comes from Anthony Burgess' book, *A Clockwork Orange*. As part of their preparations for the 'Women And Children First' US tour, testosterone-charged rockers **Van Halen** take out insurance against paternity suits.

October 11, and the **Police**'s third album, 'Zenyatta Mondatta',

JUL 19 : The Olympic Games are held in Moscow. The US, West Germany and Japan boycott in protest at the USSR's invasion of Afghanistan.

John Bonham, Led Zeppelin's hard-living drummer.

spends its first of four weeks at Number 1 in the UK charts. The band have their first US Top 10 hit with the easily-digestible white reggae song 'Don't Stand So Close To Me', former teacher **Sting**'s teasing tale of an illicit teacher-pupil attraction.

In November, with 'The Tide Is High' – more radio-friendly white reggae – topping the UK singles charts, **Blondie** release their album 'Autoamerican'. It soars into the Top 10 on both sides of the Atlantic.

Blondie, the New York new wave band fronted by a bleached-blonde, mini-skirted former *Playboy* bunny, **Deborah Harry**, playing with and against the bimbo stereotype in an ironic art-pop way, have been stars in Britain since the Seventies. This year they make their US breakthrough. The music is stunningly slick and emotionless and quite wonderful. Celebrated rock-critic Lester Bangs doesn't agree and writes in his book *Blondie*, "If the main reason we listen to music in the first place is to hear passion expressed – as I've believed all my life – then what good is this music going to prove to be?... What are we confirming in ourselves by doting on art that is emotionally neutral?" Whatever we may be confirming in ourselves, the band starts a long run of hit singles, Deborah Harry signs a lucrative endorsement deal with Muirjani designer jeans and 'Call Me' is even covered by the **Chipmunks**,

which must mark as one of the drawbacks of fame.

In December, the **Clash** release 'Sandinista' – a triple album that would have made a brilliant single album and which the band insists is released at the price of a double LP – to mixed reviews. It reaches Number 19 in the UK and starts to climb the US charts. In the same month, following an endless succession of rumours in the music papers, **Led Zeppelin** issue a statement announcing their decision to break up. Before this announcement, some people had speculated that the band intended to continue with either **Carl Palmer** of **ELP**, **Paul Thompson** of **Roxy Music** or **Cozy Powell** of just about everyone, taking drummer **John Bonham**'s place. Others spoke of vocalist **Robert Plant**'s plans to quit the band, reportedly blaming guitarist **Jimmy Page**'s interest in the occult for John Bonham's death – one of a long list of tragedies to befall the band.

Waking Up with a Monster

In August 1980, in the middle of a Leicestershire race course, Britain's annual Metal mudbath, *The Castle Donington Monsters Of Rock* festival, was born. It was fathered by ex-**Deep Purple** guitarist **Ritchie Blackmore**, who wanted an appropriate outdoor event for his band **Rainbow** to play that summer.

Evidently he'd lived abroad so long he'd forgotten what English summers were like. A week of torrential rains turned the site into a giant swamp. Bands – Rainbow were joined on the bill by **Judas Priest**, **Scorpions**, **Saxon**, **April Wine** and **Touch** – were spotted surreptitiously taking off their wellington

boots and donning more suitable rock star footwear as they climbed onstage. In an unusual summer mishap, Touch's vocalist swallowed a bee while he was singing. Worse still, following their Donington appearance, the band itself disappeared without a trace.

Reviews of the festival were dreadful, but it still went ahead the next year and every other throughout the Eighties with audiences ranging from 60-100,000 – except for 1989, when it was cancelled after the deaths by crushing of two fans during **Guns N'Roses**' set the year before. Donington took over from the Reading Festival as Britain's top annual heavy metal pilgrimage.

MARCH: Debut album from synth-poppers Orchestral Manoeuvres In The Dark.

MAY 16: Elvis Presley's doctor George 'Dr Nick' Nickopoulos is indicted in Memphis for over-prescribing huge amounts of drugs to Elvis, Jerry Lee Lewis and nine other patients. Elvis is said to have been given 12,000 pills in the last 20 months of his life.

SEPTEMBER: UB40 follow up three hit singles with a successful debut album. Their name comes from the number on the form needed to claim unemployment benefit in the UK.

OCTOBER: Debut album from Australian rock band INXS.

NOVEMBER: U2 follow up three flop singles with their debut album, 'Boy'. It's a critics' favourite and sells steadily as the Irish band start touring heavily.

DECEMBER 29: Singer-songwriter Tim Hardin dies of unknown causes.

NOV 4 : Ronald Reagan is elected as US President after a landslide victory

The most important new musical breakthroughs in 1981 were technological. Sony introduced the Walkman pocket stereo cassette recorder during this year; second-hand music and 'Walkman overspill' became a way of life on public transport and America launched the 24-hour channel devoted to music videos, MTV.

1981 was also a year in which the most notable new entries in the US charts were all by women. Ex-punk band the **GoGos**, after a glamorous make-over into pop stars, had one of the biggest-selling albums of the year with 'Beauty And The Beat'. **Joan Jett**, ex-guitarist with heavy metal girl group the **Runaways**, similarly slimmed-down and prettified, had a huge hit with 'I Love Rock'n'Roll' with her new band, the **Blackhearts**. On the singles front, **Sheena Easton**'s '9 To 5' (re-named 'Morning Train' for US release to avoid confusion with the Dolly Parton song of the same name) went platinum in the States, as did **Kim Carnes**' 'Bette Davis Eyes', and **Olivia**

Before re-emerging in 1981 with one of the year's biggest hit records, 'I Love Rock'n'Roll', Joan Jett languished in cult obscurity alongside fellow guitarist Lita Ford in the Runaways, American svengali Kim Fowley's all-girl heavy metal jailbait band.

Kim Wilde – Britain's new head girl in 1981.

Newton-John's 'Physical'. **Fleetwood Mac** vocalist **Stevie Nicks**' 'Bella Donna' album was one of the best-sellers of 1981 in the States. In Britain, that honour went to 'The BBC Album Of The Royal Wedding', as the long-running royal soap opera of Chuck and Di began.

'Lace, ruffles, ribbons and bows are all the rage right now', proclaims the headline on the *Sunday Times* fashion page as 1981 dawns. Former art student Stuart Leslie Goddard, better known as **Adam Ant**, tops the UK album charts with his major label debut, 'Kings Of The Wild Frontier'. The percussion-heavy dance music storms the UK airwaves, while the face – the perfect pin-up, complete with cheese-slicing cheekbones and primal make-up – hijacks every magazine cover in sight. Overnight, Adam makes the move from peripheral punk to pop idol of the masses. Antmusic is everywhere.

Everywhere in Britain, that is. In America, the charts are dominated by a 13-year-old, middle-of-the-road rock band from Illinois who named themselves after an antique fire engine. In February, **REO Speedwagon**'s 'Hi Infidelity' album – a collection of songs about vocalist Kevin Cronin's wife's marital betrayals – knocks **John Lennon**'s 'Double Fantasy' off the top of the US charts and settles in for an amazing 15-week stay at Number 1. Meanwhile disharmony reigns in Sweden too, as Benny Andersson and Frida Lyngstad of **Abba** start divorce proceedings.

In March, **Roxy Music**'s tribute to John Lennon, a cover of 'Jealous Guy', hits the Number 1 spot in the UK only weeks after Lennon's new 'Double Fantasy' single, 'Woman' and the four-year-old 'Imagine', vacated the position. Also in the Top 10 is 'Kids In America', the first single by new artist **Kim Wilde**, daughter of

FEB 13 : Australian press magnate Rupert Murdoch buys the London Times for £11 million

Video Killed the Radio Star

In the summer of 1981, a new TV channel appeared for the first time on the screens of millions of cable subscribers across the States and changed the face of music almost overnight.

MTV – music videos, 24 hours a day, seven days a week – was launched on August 1 with **Buggles**' all-too-appropriate 'Video Killed The Radio Star'. A nation's youth instantly became addicted to three-minute stabs of music and visuals; MTV's five original VJs (video jockeys) – an actress, a bartender, two ex-radio DJs and a college graduate – became overnight stars; and fans, musicians and the entire record industry had to rethink their approach to music. Thanks to MTV, the video became as important as the song itself, if not more so. In the post-MTV age, it was next to impossible for your single to become a hit without a promotional video.

'Promo' videos weren't an entirely Eighties phenomenon; they were already being made back in the Sixties by the big bands – the **Beatles**, the **Stones** – too busy to make all the worldwide TV appearances that audiences demanded. And their importance in terms of sales was shown back in 1975, when **Queen**'s celebrated 'Bohemian Rhapsody' video aired on the BBC's Top Of The Pops while the band was off touring and sent them instantly to the top of the charts. But there had been music video shows before MTV – ex-**Monkee** and music video pioneer **Michael Nesmith**'s half-hour Popclips was a popular American cable TV show. Promo videos are basically commercials and people have always said they prefer the commercials to the shows. MTV was simply the first broadcaster to come up with the lucrative idea of launching a TV channel running nothing but commercials.

MTV cost $20million to set up. It was a brilliant idea because the programming – ie. videos – came free. One major record label, Polygram, initially baulked at the idea of providing material for nothing, but was soon forced to change its mind when MTV's influence on the record-buying public became evident.

MTV was making stars of a whole host of new bands – young, good-looking bands who wouldn't scare the TV viewers away. Britain's new romantic bands, for example: **Duran Duran** were one of the first groups to be played on heavy rotation. And America's own breed of videogenic stars: the new heavy metal bands. Before MTV, there were legions of faceless, ageing, stadium acts – their unattractiveness was no barrier to success in the days when it was just a set of speakers between you and them, nor was it a problem when they played in venues so big you couldn't see what they looked like. But when MTV burst into the young music fan's bedroom, the look of the band became all important. After MTV, a host of image-conscious bands such as **Motley Crue**, **Ratt**, **Quiet Riot** and **Def Leppard** chased each other up the charts.

The result of MTV's success is that rock and pop are now established as a visual medium. Some people even ask, 'Did you see the new video by...?' rather than 'Have you heard the new record by...?' And, when all is said and done, pop videos at least ensure that a great many large-chested young women in bikinis and mini-skirts are seldom out of work.

Sixties pop idol **Marty Wilde** (his hit 'Hello Little Girl' was actually written to celebrate her birth!). The Wildes like to keep things in the family – dad Marty produces Kim's debut song, which brother Ricky wrote.

In April, reggae superstar **Bob Marley** is awarded Jamaica's Order Of Merit. His son Ziggy accepts it on his behalf, since Marley Senior is seriously ill with brain and lung can-

cer (diagnosed last year when his health forced him to cancel two shows at Madison Square Garden). May 11, Bob Marley dies in Miami, Florida, at the age of 36. His body is flown home to Kingston Jamaica – the place he left at the age of 14 – where it lies in state in Kingston's National Arena on May 20 and 21. He is buried with full state honours.

At a record company conference

in Los Angeles in the same month, **Ozzy Osbourne** bites the head off a live dove. "I was jetlagged," offers Ozzy by way of explanation. The bird-biting episode causes a furore, and there's a brief sadistic fashion for throwing biteable things – some living, some not quite – on stage as his band starts its US tour. Someone tosses him a live bat. Thinking it's a toy, Ozzy bites off its head. A couple

---

ROCK'N'ROLL record

JANUARY: Sarah Dallin, Keren Woodward and Siobhan Fahey give up their day jobs to perform as an a capella act called Bananarama.

FEBRUARY: Mick Jagger walks off the set of German director Werner Herzog's film Fitzcaraldo after five crew members are killed during filming.

FEBRUARY 9: Bill Haley of 'Rock Around The Clock' fame dies of a heart attack, aged 56.

APRIL 27: Ex-Beatle Ringo Starr marries actress Barbara Bach.

JULY16: Songsmith Harry Chapin dies in a car crash aged 38.

SEPTEMBER 19: Simon and Garfunkel reunite for a concert in New York's Central Park .

NOVEMBER: Jean Michel Jarre becomes the first western pop musician to play China.

NOVEMBER 21: Olivia Newton-John's 'Physical' goes to the top of the US charts for the first of ten weeks.

The whole world watches Prince Charles' fairytale marriage to Lady Diana Spencer take place at Westminster Abbey on July 29. 'The BBC Album Of The Royal Wedding' is one of the best selling albums of the year in Britain.

of dates have to be cancelled as the singer is sent for painful rabies shots.

Adam & The Ants' single 'Stand And Deliver' enters the UK charts at Number 1 in May and holds onto the position for five weeks.

But chart competition soon arrives in unlikely-looking form. **Motorhead**'s live album 'No Sleep Till Hammersmith' enters the UK charts straight at Number 1 – the first heavy metal album ever to do so. Recorded onstage during their 1980 tour, the LP features live versions of classic Motorhead tracks such as 'Ace Of Spades', 'Bomber' and 'Overkill.'

The **Specials** – leading lights of

the ska movement and a band who make dance music with meaning – top the charts for three weeks in July with their single 'Ghost Town'. The bleak lyrics about urban life coincide with an outbreak of rioting in several British inner-city areas in the summer. Meanwhile across the Atlantic, *The Decline Of Western Civilization* – Penelope Spheeris' documentary film about the LA Punk scene, featuring bands like **Black Flag**, **Germs**, **X** and **Fear** – is premiered to much critical acclaim. **REM**, a new band from Athens, Georgia, release their debut single. *Village Voice* magazine hails 'Radio Free Europe' as the independent single of the year. The **Jacksons** – reunited with eccentric

brother Michael – launch their 36-city Triumph tour in Memphis, Tennessee. And the **Tom Tom Club** – a sideline for Tina Weymouth and Chris Frantz of **Talking Heads** – have a Top 10 UK hit in July with the single 'Wordy Rappinghood'.

The fourth annual *International Reggae Sunsplash* Festival in Jamaica on August 6 is billed as a tribute to **Bob Marley**. Four of his children appear onstage under the name of the **Melody Makers.**

Jean Michel Jarre and synthesizer in China.

Elsewhere, **Deborah Harry** releases her debut solo album 'Koo Koo', its sleeve – featuring the Blondie vocalist's beautiful head pierced by four large pins – is designed by controversial artist HR Giger of *Alien* fame. **Olivia Newton-John** has a star unveiled on the Hollywood *Walk Of Fame*. **Lionel Richie**, who has just released his final album, 'In The Pocket', with the **Commodores**, enjoys a massive US hit when he duets with **Diana Ross** on 'Endless Love' – the song stays an endless nine weeks at Number 1. On August 25, Mark David Chapman is sen-

A shot rings out in St. Peter's Square, Rome, on May 13, and his holiness Pope John Paul II is wounded. A Turkish terrorist is later charged with the assassination attempt.

tenced to 20 years to life in prison for the murder of **John Lennon**.

Over in England, **Neil Tennant**, assistant editor of pop magazine *Smash Hits* meets keyboard player **Chris Lowe** in a music shop and they discuss forming a band which will be called the **Pet Shop Boys**. The **Rolling Stones**' new album 'Tattoo You' is released at the start of September and shoots to Number 2 in the UK charts and Number 1 in the States, where it will lodge for nine weeks. The band plays a warm-up date under the monicker **Blue Monday & The Cockroaches** at a tiny club in Massachusetts. Trouble breaks out when 4,000 fans try to get into the 350-capacity venue and eleven people are arrested. The 50-date US tour is launched a week later in Philadelphia's JFK Stadium before a 90,000-strong crowd. Opening act **Journey** release their new album 'Escape'. It goes to the top of the US charts, spending the first of 53 weeks in the Top 20.

But the biggest British single of the year comes from a recently formed band from the north of England. Electropop group **Soft Cell** – whose debut single released six months back failed to chart – re-work the **Gloria Jones** soul song 'Tainted Love' to good effect and take it to Number 1 in Britain and a dozen other countries around the world.

After a short but hugely successful career, leading ska band the **Specials** break up in October. Neville Staples, Lynval Golding and Terry Hall form a new band, **Fun Boy**

Three. Not long after, leading new wave of British heavy metal band **Iron Maiden** part company with vocalist Paul Di'anno and replace him with Bruce Dickinson of **Samson**.

Queen have their first Number 1 single since 'Bohemian Rhapsody' in November with 'Under Pressure', their 'spontaneous' duet with **David Bowie** who co-wrote the song. Queen

also become the first-ever group to top the British singles, album and video charts at the same time, when their 'Greatest Hits' album starts its six-year residency in the listings.

In 1981, two soul fans from Lancashire - Marc Almond and David Ball, collectively known as Soft Cell - had the biggest-selling single of the year. Their electro-soul cover of 'Tainted Love' was a Number 1 in scores of countries around the world.

Genesis Chapter Two

It didn't look too hopeful on paper. An ageing drummer – who'd spent the previous 11 years in a progressive rock band, and whose past experience included a role in a stage production of Humpty Dumpty, a tour of duty promoting Smith's Crisps round Britain which involved demonstrating a dance called Do The Crunch

Phil Collins crying all the way to the top.

and a job as extra in the **Beatles**' film A Hard Day's Night – releases a solo album inspired by the acrimonious break-up of his marriage.

But when **Phil Collins** of **Genesis**' debut solo effort, 'Face Value', was released on February 21, it went straight to Number 1 in the UK charts (the first day of a 274-week stay). The haunting, drum-heavy single 'In The Air Tonight' was only kept off the top spot by **John Lennon**'s 'Woman'. By the summer, Collins had accumulated three UK hit singles. In July his album went gold in the States and stood at Number 7 in the charts.

A former child actor, Collins joined Genesis as drummer in 1970. When **Peter Gabriel** left five years later, the band spent 18 months looking for a new vocalist, auditioning more than 400 singers before giving Collins the job. Collins continued working on his solo album while writing and performing with Genesis.

The result was the new Genesis album 'Abacab' which was released in September and spent two weeks at Number 1 in the UK charts, giving the band three hit singles as well as their first-ever US Top 10 hit. All this was not bad for a Londoner who lost his job as the Artful Dodger in the Sixties stage production of Oliver because his voice broke…

Roland Orzabal and Curt Smith – confronting their Fears.

Billy Idol – who left **Generation X** earlier in the year following the failure of their single 'Dancing With Myself' and moved to New York – releases his debut solo album, 'Don't Stop'. It includes a cover of **Tommy James & The Shondells**' 'Mony Mony' and a solo version of 'Dancing With Myself', appropriately enough.

Back in Britain, **Tears For Fears** – put together by former ska bandmates Curt Smith and Roland Orzabal and named after a chapter in an Arthur Janov *Primal Scream Therapy* book – release their debut single, 'Suffer Little Children'. **ABC**'s debut single 'Tears Are Not Enough' makes the UK Top 20, while **Haircut 100**'s debut single 'Favourite Shirts (Boy Meets Girl)' makes the Top 5. LA glam-metal band **Motley Crue** take a leaf out of the punk bands' book and release their debut album, 'Too Fast For Love', on their own independent Leathur label in December. It took three days and $7000 to make.

New Order, the band formed from the ashes of **Joy Division**, release their debut album 'Movement' at the end of the year. It tops the UK indie charts and makes the regular Top 30.

OCT 6 : Egyptian leader Anwar Sadat is assassinated during a military parade in Cairo

1980s Trash

The bride was young, slim, beautiful and blonde. The groom was older, rich, renowned. It was the wedding that the Eighties, in need of some escapism, was waiting for. Forget Charles and Di, this was Bill and Mandy!

Mandy Smith first hit the headlines in August 1986, when the *News Of The World*, the UK's salacious tabloid, printed an interview with the then-16-year-old in which she claimed that she and **Rolling Stones** bassist, Bill Wyman, 49, began an affair when she was just 13. Three years later, on June 2, 1989, with Wyman's 28-year-old son from his first marriage as best man, the two were joined in holy matrimony in a secret ceremony in Suffolk. The same evening they made a not-so-secret appearance on TV chat show *Wogan*. Among the wedding presents

was a Zimmer frame from comedian Spike Milligan.

The Andy and Fergie of pop weddings was **Madonna**'s short-lived stab at matrimony with actor Sean

Penn. The star met "the coolest guy in the universe" in February of 1985, and married him six months later in a cliff-top ceremony as helicopters full of news crew hovered overhead. In March 1986, the newlyweds flew to London to start filming *Shanghai Surprise*. The tabloids dubbed them "The Poison Penns" after Penn nearly strangled a member of the paparazzi and ran over the *Sun*'s photographer's foot. By December the following year, the material girl had filed for divorce. She changed her mind, filed again in January 1988, before changing her mind yet again. Third time lucky, in January 1989 – while dropping the assault charges she had taken out against him – she finally served Penn with the papers. If all this wasn't enough to upset the Pope, the same year the Vatican was in an uproar over Madonna's sex-and-religion video for 'Like A Prayer'.

Jerry Lee Lewis showed himself to be a big supporter of marriage in the Eighties. In June 1983 he married his fifth wife, 25-year-old Shawn Stevens. Two months later, Shawn was found dead in their home. A grand jury investigation said there was no reason to suspect foul play, although an article in *Rolling Stone* in October the following year alleged that there were suspicious circumstances surrounding her death, including blood-stained clothes, broken glass and bruises. By now, Lewis had already moved on to wife number six. The 'wild man' of rock'n'roll married 22-year-old Kerrie McCarver in April 1984.

In September 1984, **Janet Jackson** and El DeBarge from the

Jacksons-esque group **DeBarge**, eloped. The marriage was annulled seven months later.

But it was Janet's brother **Michael Jackson** who took up most of the tabloid space in the Eighties, as one outlandish story after another dominated front pages around the world – some of them true. Such as the incident in January 1984 when the singer's hair caught fire while shooting a commercial for Pepsi (a soft drink his Jehovah's Witness faith forbade him to actually drink). Marlon Brando's son Miko – working as Jackson's bodyguard – put the flames out, but Jackson was rushed to hospital with second degree burns to the skull. President Ronald Reagan sent him a telegram saying he was pleased the star was "not seriously hurt".

In September 1986, the *National Enquirer* printed a front-page picture of Jackson in what it claimed was an oxygen chamber, with the headline: "Jackson's bizarre plan to live to 150." The singer said he was just trying out the machine he'd bought for a local hospital burns unit with the money Pepsi paid him as compensation for his accident. Then, in 1987, reports appeared that

▼ The other Royal Couple: Madonna and Sean Penn. The singer and the actor embarked on a short-lived career as man and wife.

▲ Judas Priest, the Birmingham heavy metal band, found themselves on trial in California.

Jackson had offered $50,000 to buy the remains of the Elephant Man – the deformed Victorian John Merrick, immortalized in David Lynch's 1980 film of the same name – from The London Hospital. The headquarters of the Jehovah's Witnesses issued a statement in May the same year saying they no longer considered the singer to be of their faith.

The following year, the British tabloids were filled with shock stories about Jackson's plastic surgery. As he came to London in July 1988 to unveil his dummy at Madame Tussaud's waxworks, Jackson denied everything, and went to Hamleys toy store to buy an official Michael Jackson doll (it came complete with one white glove).

As the decade came to a close, speculation over the biggest success story of the Eighties kept on rolling. When Jackson split from his manager at the start of 1989, there were reports the man had asked for a $60 million settlement not to reveal the secrets of the singer's private life. And in July the same year, **LaToya Jackson**'s manager Jack

Gordon claimed that Michael had offered his sister $5 million not to publish her controversial autobiography, *La Toya: Growing Up In The Jackson Family*.

Yet another home-grown scandal generated by *The Sun* turned out to be a lie. In March 1987, the tabloid printed front-page stories claiming that **Elton John** had indulged in sex and drugs orgies with male homosexuals. The singer sued them for libel. The following October, *The Sun* admitted the stories were false, printed an apology and paid Elton £1 million.

A Texas teenager charged in December 1982 with murdering his aunt gave his defence as mental illness caused by listening to too much **Pink Floyd**. Then, in December 1986, **Judas Priest** and CBS Records were unsuccessfully sued by the family of two teenagers who shot themselves, claiming their sons had been driven to it after spending six months listening to the album 'Stained Class'. And a California supreme court judge threw out the lawsuit brought against **Ozzy Osbourne** over his song 'Suicide Solution', said to be responsible for the death of an American youth.

In May 1988, a month after being released on bail on charges of assault with intent to murder his wife, **James Brown** was released on bail after a car chase in South Carolina. It was his fifth arrest in 10 months. He was charged with assault, resisting arrest, possession of weapons and the drug PCP. Brown was a member of the President's Council Against Drugs. At the end of the year, the singer was sentenced to two concurrent six-year jail sentences following another car chase, this one across two states.

A good deal of Eighties scandals were drugs related. **Boy George** appeared at an anti-apartheid concert in London in July 1986 – inexplicably covered in flour. He introduced himself as "your favourite junkie". His brother

leaked the story of George's heroin addiction to the tabloids, and George was arrested with singer Marilyn and let off with a fine.

Meanwhile, a New York musician friend, Michael Rudetski, was found dead of a drug overdose in the singer's London home.

Comedian **Richard Prior** accidentally set fire to himself in February 1980 while 'freebasing' cocaine. And the same month, a thousand punks marched in London on the anniversary of **Sex Pistols**' bassist Sid Vicious's drug-induced death. Sid's mum couldn't make it. She was in hospital with drug problems herself.

In an interview with the *Washington Times* in June 1989, **Public Enemy**'s Professor Griff told the reporter that the Jews are responsible for the "majority of the wickedness that goes on across the globe". Demands that frontman Chuck D denounce their 'Minister of Information' were refused.

The same month, **Chrissie Hynde** of the **Pretenders** claimed it was meat eaters causing the world's evils. Asked at a Greenpeace press conference what she'd done for the environment, the vegetarian vocalist said, "I firebombed McDonalds". Shortly afterwards a McDonalds in Milton Keynes, England was firebombed. The burger chain threatened to sue the singer until she issued a statement saying she had spoken "joking and fictitiously".

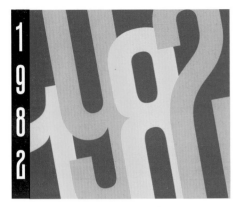

The Stranglers' gentle ode to heroin shoots up the charts.

Paul McCartney's appearance on *Desert Island Discs* set a nostalgic tone for 1982. On the BBC radio show where Very Important People are invited in hushed and reverential whispers to choose music to take with them to a desert island, the records he selected to take with him were all blasts from the past: rock-'n'roll classics such as **Chuck Berry**'s 'Sweet Little Sixteen', **Elvis Presley**'s 'Heartbreak Hotel' and **Little Richard**'s 'Tutti Frutti'. His only concession to recent recordings was **John Lennon**'s rather insipid 'Beautiful Boy'.

McCartney wasn't the only one looking back this year. Although Britain's theatrical new romantic movement was gathering momentum in the clubs, two Seventies dinosaurs were making a comeback: the Supergroup and Heavy Metal. The American heavy metal scene, once dominated by ageing stadium rockers, moved increasingly underground with the appearance of two new shock rock bands: **Twisted Sister** from New York and over in Los Angeles **WASP**, the 'psychodrama' band formed by Blackie Lawless, who had once enjoyed five minutes of fame as a touring drummer for the **New York Dolls**.

And in Britain the NWOBHM (new wave of British heavy metal) made its big breakthrough with **Iron Maiden**'s 'The Number Of The Beast'. The band's first album with new vocalist Bruce Dickinson knocked **Barbra Streisand** off the top of the UK charts and provided them with their first hit single, 'Run To The Hills'. German metal band the **Scorpions** also had their biggest chart success to date with their album 'Blackout', which reached Number 11 in the UK charts and the Top 10 in the States.

Elsewhere, new bands ride high at the start of the year in the British charts – **Madness**' remake of **Labi Siffre**'s 'It Must Be Love', is Top 5 in January; whilst the **Stranglers**' gentle waltz-time paean to heroin, 'Golden Brown', reaches Number 2 in February, giving them their biggest UK hit.

May, however, heralds the return of the supergroup. **Asia** – a Seventies-style pomp band featuring Steve Howe and Geoff Downes, ex-**Yes** man, Carl Palmer, ex-**ELP** and John Wetton, ex-**King Crimson** – hit Number 1 in the US charts with their eponymous debut album, and stay there for over two months.

Back in Britain, the **Cure**'s fourth album 'Pornography' is their first to make the UK Top 10 in May. Their success doesn't look like lasting long. On tour in France, pallid front-man Robert Smith quarrels with bassist Simon Gallup and the band breaks up. Same month, same country, Joe Strummer, the **Clash**'s singer, goes AWOL and the band's UK tour has to be postponed. When the music press later speculates that his disappearance was a publicity stunt, Strummer reveals that he flew to Paris where his girlfriend's mum is in jail. Meanwhile, 'Combat Rock' nestles at Number 2 in the UK album charts.

Paul McCartney reunites with Beatles producer, George Martin, for the album 'Tug Of War', which enters the UK charts at Number 1. It features a tribute to John Lennon, a

This is Planet Earth

"It's about overthrowing greyness and putting some colour back into life." Simon Le Bon, **Duran Duran**.

Their look was theatrical – futuristic pirate garb, extravagant hairdos, exotic make-up and trousers that would get you arrested in a dozen countries. Their sound was sub-**Bowie** with a twist of **Kraftwerk** thrown in – synthesizer-dominated electropop with catchy tunes and fronted by that Look. The new romantics were a reaction against punk which was itself a reaction against the we-can-change-the-world optimism of the Sixties and the big-money pop of the Seventies. Where punk was raw, harsh and ugly, the new romantics were smooth, clean, beautiful. Where punk was no-future, no-celebrity, the new romantics were optimistic, materialistic, wannabes.

The first of the self-conscious, design-conscious British bands to flaunt the new romantic label were **Spandau Ballet**. Regulars on the London nightclub circuit, the upwardly-mobile, extravagantly-wardrobed young Londoners released their debut single in 1982. Before Spandau Ballet came along, to be called a 'poser' was an insult for a musician. Suddenly, it was the whole point.

Rubbing shoulderpads with Spandau were a number of bands, each of whom approached the style/pop problem with varying

Duran Duran, leaders of the New Romantic pack.

degrees of wit and self-consciousness: **Depeche Mode** (their name is French for 'fast fashion') whose first two albums both made the Top 10; **ABC**, whose Trevor Horn-produced debut album went to Number 1, the **Human League**, **Soft Cell** and **Haircut 100**, the group who, against all odds, made 'Val Doonican' Arran sweaters hip and whose debut album 'Pelican West' sold over 300,000 copies in its first week of release.

But prettiest of them all were Duran Duran. Named after a character in the film *Barbarella*, these five cute boys from Birmingham's elitist nightclub scene first clambered on the national stage in 1982 with the release of their single 'Planet Earth'. They were the perfect pop package: aspiring to be jet-setters whilst still betraying all the signs of not being long out of high school. With their cheekbones only just emerging through the puppy fat, they played a clean, charismatic pop through which futuristic 'Space Invaders' noises could just about be heard. Unsurprisingly, they were snapped up by EMI, the record label that once had the **Beatles** and the **Sex Pistols**.

If jet-setting, narcissism, luxury, affluence, no hint of irony or self-deprecation and flaunting your celebrity were the hallmarks of the new romantics, Duran Duran were the movement's archetype. Their references were James Bond and the Monaco monarchy. Their videos, where they lived out soft porn teen-boy fantasies, like 'Rio' with its yachts, champagne and beautiful girls, played an intrinsic part in their huge success. Said keyboardist Nick Rhodes, "We're about entertainment and we're about free enterprise and doing something for yourself instead of being pulled down by everybody else." 'Rio', their second album, released in May with the band on its second world tour, hit Number 2 and stayed in the UK charts for the rest of the year.

Princess Diana loved them; the critics hated them; but their records kept on selling. By the end of the year, with their slick videos a permanent feature on MTV, they'd begun their ascent in the US.

Dressed for success - Depeche Mode.

APR 2 : Argentina invades the Falkland Islands. Britain declares war

1982 · HEADLINE NEWS   JUN 14: British forces regain command of the Falkland Islands

reunion with **Ringo Starr**, an appearance by **Carl Perkins** and a duet with **Stevie Wonder** on 'Ebony And Ivory', which tops the UK and US singles charts. 'Complete Madness', a compilation of **Madness**' hits plus an accompanying video, goes to Number 1 in the UK in May, and gives the band their US breakthrough.

June is an awful month for the **Pretenders**. On the 14, they fire bassist Pete Farndon because of his drugs problems. Two days later, guitarist James Honeyman-Scott, 25, dies of a drugs overdose. Chrissie Hynde flees to the States, where boyfriend Ray Davies is touring with the **Kinks**. Later this month, the Hacienda – a nightclub owned by indie label Factory Records and partly financed by **New Order** – opens in Manchester, England.

The Wall, the movie version of the **Pink Floyd** album, directed by Alan Parker and starring **Bob Geldof** as Pink, premieres in London in July. Its flavour is captured by one critic as "the longest-ever rock video, and

certainly the most depressing". Unusually, World music takes centre stage in the UK this summer as the first *World Of Music Arts And Dance* festival – WOMAD – takes place at Shepton Mallet in Somerset, July 16-18. The festival's backer is **Peter Gabriel**, who uses money he made from **Genesis** to introduce (or rather reintroduce: George Harrison went that route 10 years ago) global culture to British audiences.

The man in the beret, **Captain Sensible** of the **Damned**, has a Number 1 single with his daft version of 'Happy Talk' from the musical *South Pacific*. Sheffield dance-pop band **ABC**'s debut album, 'Lexicon Of Love', produced by maestro Trevor Horn, hits the Number 1 spot in Britain in July. And **Soft Cell**'s 'Tainted Love' boomerangs back into the charts for the third time. In the US, its 43 consecutive weeks on the chart sets a new record.

In August **Dexy's Midnight Runners** top the UK charts for four weeks with 'Come On Eileen', taken from their second album 'Too Rye-

Ay', a mixture of soul and Irish blarney with a three-piece fiddle section added to the line-up. **Motley Crue** become the first of the new wave of American heavy metal bands to land a major deal. Elektra Records reissue the Los Angeles band's debut album 'Too Fast For Love' in August after the indie label Leathur Records sells out all of the 20,000 copies it printed. Liverpool pays tribute to the **Beatles** by naming four streets on a new housing estate after them. None of the remaining three group members attends the August inauguration of John Lennon Drive, Ringo Starr Drive, George Harrison Close and Paul McCartney Way.

Frank Zappa and his unusually named daughter, Moon Unit, have a surprise hit in September with 'Valley Girl'. The song satirizes the attitudes of the rich teenage girls who haunt the shopping malls of Los Angeles suburb, the San Fernando Valley. It introduces new and useful phrases into the English language such as 'gag me with a spoon' and 'grody to the max'. But the biggest thing in America right now is **John Cougar**. No longer the Seventies glam-rocker, more a sleeves-rolled-up, blue-collar Mid-western Springsteen, Cougar becomes the first artist to have a US Number 1 album ('American Fool') and two Top 10 singles ('Hurts So Good' and 'Jack And Diane') at the same time. Meanwhile **Bruce**

Dexy's Midnight Runners – post-punk angry young soul men. Especially angry is frontman Kevin Rowland who took out ads in the British music press to vent his spleen against rock critics, and those who banned alcohol from the venues they played.

Over four thousand Moonies say "I do" in Madison Square Garden, New York.

JANUARY 30: Bluesman Lightnin' Hopkins dies at the age of 69.

FEBRUARY: The Police donate proceeds from their San Francisco show to Sir Freddie Laker to help save his airline.

FEBRUARY 4: Sensational Scottish rocker Alex Harvey dies.

MARCH: Filming begins on The Hunger, Tony Scott's vampire film starring David Bowie.

MARCH: R&B singer Teddy Pendergrass crashes his Rolls Royce. He is paralyzed from the waist down.

APRIL: Strawberry Fields, the memorial to John Lennon in New York's Central Park, is opened by Yoko Ono.

APRIL: Graceland, Elvis Presley's mansion in Memphis, Tennessee, opens its doors to the public for the first time.

SEPTEMBER: The Who release their final studio album 'It's Hard'. They embark on a US tour with the Clash.

▲ Elvis Presley's mansion, Graceland, opens its doors to the public on June 7.

Springsteen's 'Nebraska', released this month – his solo acoustic album recorded earlier in the year on a four-track in his New Jersey home – lags just behind, going Top 5 on both sides of the Atlantic.

Sting releases his first solo single, 'Spread A Little Happiness' – taken from playwright Dennis Potter's *Brimstone And Treacle*, the film in which he stars as a strange young man who worms his way into the life of a respectable couple whose daughter lies in a coma. Blue-eyed soul specialist **Paul Young** leaves the hard-gigging **Q Tips** for a solo career. And **Yazoo**, the band formed this year by ex-**Depeche Mode** keyboardist Vince Clarke and R&B singer **Alison Moyet**, zoom to Number 2 with their debut album 'Upstairs At Eric's'.

Foolishly encouraged by this year's supergroup revivals, Chris Squire and Alan White of **Yes** recruit South African vocalist-guitarist Trevor Rabin and original keyboard player Tony Kaye (who left in 1971) in September for their new band, **Cinema**. When Yes vocalist Jon Anderson, who has been working with Greek synthesizer star **Vangelis**, decides to join them, they all decide to make it an official Yes reunion. Bye bye, Cinema.

Two of the biggest new wave bands break up in October. The demise of **Blondie** has been predicted following vocalist **Deborah Harry**'s solo album and movie career. (Her major movie debut comes this month in David Cronenberg's ultra-weird *Videodrome*. Says Harry, "When I was a little kid I always wanted to be a movie star, because rock groups didn't exist.") More of a shock is **Paul Weller**'s announcement that the **Jam** are splitting up at the height of their success. He's lost sympathy with the band's musical direction, he says, so he's formed the soul band **Style Council**

with keyboardist Mick Talbot. The Jam decide to go ahead with the UK shows they've already set up – which includes six sold-out nights at Wembley Arena – and call it a farewell tour.

Peter Gabriel takes part in a **Genesis** reunion concert in Milton Keynes in October, to make up some of the money that this summer's *WOMAD* festival lost. The following month, the first Jamaican World Music Festival is held in Montego Bay in November. Its varied bill includes the **Clash**, the **Beach Boys**, the **Beat**, **Gladys Knight & The Pips** and the **Grateful Dead**. It also features **Squeeze**'s last appearance before they split up.

In November too, Andy Partridge of **XTC** – who has twice collapsed on stage this year, once from a stomach ulcer and once from exhaustion – announces that the band will never play live again. And sure enough, when Terry Chambers quits no replacement is mooted. **Janet Jackson**, youngest of the Jackson clan, launches a television sitcom career in the States and releases her self-titled debut album. She promotes both by touring American high

Jul 1 : At the largest wedding ceremony in history, 2,075 couples are married by the Reverend Sun Myung Moon at a Moonie wedding in Madison Square Garden, New York

1982 – HEADLINE NEWS

schools and telling pupils they ought to stay in school.

The same month, Australian band **Men At Work** – touring the US as openers for **Fleetwood Mac** – release the single 'Who Can It Be Now?' which climbs to the summit of the US chart followed by the album 'Business As Usual'. Already Number 1 down under, it starts a 15-week run at the top of the US charts, first time ever for a debut album. Following an unsuccesful suicide attempt, **Marvin Gaye** bounces back with 'Sexual Healing', a Top 10 hit in Britain and Number 1 on the US R&B charts. The record is released on a new label after long negotiations, which include discussions with the

American tax office, to whom Gaye owes a great deal of money.

Madonna signs a deal with Sire Records and releases her first single, 'Everybody' in November. Beginning her irresistible rise to stardom, she promotes it by dancing and lip-synching at New York nightclub, the Danceteria.

On the other side of the Atlantic, the **Smiths** are formed when **Morrissey** – ex-president of the UK **New York Dolls** fan club and author of the book *James Dean Isn't Dead* – teams up with guitarist Johnny Marr, veteran of several Manchester bands. They play their first show at a local club, the Ritz. **Frankie Goes To Hollywood** make their first national

appearances in the UK – a live session on Radio 1 and a spot on the TV show *The Tube*, playing an early version of a song called 'Relax'. They attract the attention of record producer (and *Tube* theme song composer) Trevor Horn.

In December, the **Cure**'s Robert Smith rejoins **Siouxsie & The Banshees** and leaves with them on a tour of the Far East. 'Coda', an album of unreleased **Led Zeppelin** material repackaged by Jimmy Page, is a Top 10 UK and US hit in December. And an unassuming little album by a former member of the **Jackson 5** released this month doesn't do too badly either – **Michael Jackson**'s 'Thriller'...

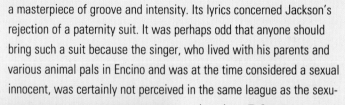

Michael Jackson's 'Thriller' - the biggest-selling album of all time, the video, 'The Making Of Michael Jackson's Thriller', the biggest-selling pop video of all time.

Glove Story

In August 1982, **Michael Jackson** and **Quincy Jones** plus the cream of LA session men went into the studio to start work on a new album. The result, 'Thriller', was released on December 1st. It shot into the charts, making Number 1 in the US, the UK and every major western country. The album went on to top the US charts for 37 weeks, an unprecedented run for a contemporary pop album, spawned a record-breaking seven Top 10 US singles, won eight Grammy Awards and sold over 40 million copies worldwide.

The first extract from the album – 'The Girl Is Mine', a mawkish duet with **Paul McCartney** recorded in Los Angeles a year earlier – contained no indication of the brilliance of the rest of

'Thriller'. The title track turned into a mini musical horror film, complete with voiceover by horrormeister Vincent Price. 'Billie Jean' was

a masterpiece of groove and intensity. Its lyrics concerned Jackson's rejection of a paternity suit. It was perhaps odd that anyone should bring such a suit because the singer, who lived with his parents and various animal pals in Encino and was at the time considered a sexual innocent, was certainly not perceived in the same league as the sexual predator **Prince**.

However with 'Beat It', which astutely featured **Edward Van Halen** on guitar, Jackson achieved the perfect cross-over. The ingenious videos for 'Billie Jean' and 'Beat It', with choreographed gang-violence featuring actual LA gang members, were the first by a black artist to get major airplay on MTV, a fact which guaranteed the album phenomenal sales. The workaholic vegetarian man-child with Diana Ross's face and one sequinned glove had made the most successful pop album of all time.

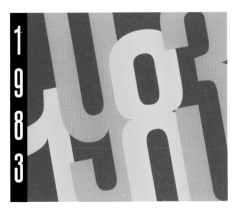

"1983," *Rolling Stone* magazine wrote in its end-of-year issue, "showed more clearly than ever that MTV sells looks at least as much as sound. Perhaps, its greatest achievement was to create a rock'n'roll format as attractive to young women – virtually disenfranchised in AOR's heyday – as to young men." As if to underline the point, New Wave Of British Heavy Metal band **Def Leppard** – MTV favourites and, it seemed, as popular with the girls as the boys – spent most of the year on the US charts with their third album 'Pyromania'.

Meanwhile, out on the streets, **Michael Jackson**'s 'Thriller' went nuclear as the single 'Billie Jean' hit the Number 1 spot on both sides of the Atlantic, and the innovative video – featuring mesmerizing dance steps by Jackson – finally got shown on

MTV. The MTV playlist was accused of racism – with some justification since most videos of the time showed pretty white boys like **Duran Duran**. Threatened with the withdrawal of promo material by Jackson's record company CBS, MTV relented and screened the clip. The reaction was amazing. Through sheer weight of popular demand, the video was soon hardly ever off the air. And MTV proved its importance in the marketplace as the album's sales went through the roof. All this opened the way for other black artists to reach MTV and its huge crossover market.

This time last year he was playing his old rock'n'roll records for the BBC radio show *Desert Island Discs*. January 1983 finds **Paul McCartney** buried away with **Michael Jackson** in a London studio, as the Macca-Jacko's duet 'The Girl Is Mine' is riding high in the US charts. They're already writing material for McCartney's next album.

In February, **Eddy Grant**, former **Equals** frontman, racks up a huge US hit with the single 'Electric Avenue' from his UK hit album, 'Killer On The Rampage'. One of America's biggest black crossover acts, **Lionel Richie**, wins the best Pop/Rock and

Eddy Grant topped the UK and US charts in 1982.

best Soul/R&B categories at the *American Music Awards*. Across the Atlantic at the *BRIT Awards*, **Yazoo** are voted Best British Newcomer and **Pete Townshend** gets a Lifetime Achievement award. Despite his immense wealth, the **Who** guitarist takes a part-time job as technical adviser to the literary publishing house of Faber & Faber.

Echo & The Bunnymen's third album, 'Porcupine', gives them their first real UK and US chart success. And **Eurythmics** – the duo formed from the ashes of the critically-acclaimed **Tourists** – have a big hit both sides of the Atlantic with their second album 'Sweet Dreams (Are Made Of This)'. The video for 'Who's That Girl', scripted by Dave Stewart and Annie Lennox, features a guest appearance by pop trio **Bananarama**, among other mysterious femme fatales.

When Essex girl Alison 'Alf' Moyet put an ad in the music papers she was looking for a "rootsy blues band". What she got was synthesizer wizard Vince Clarke, who'd just left hit band Depeche Mode. Together as Yazoo they became ▼ an instant success

MAY 6 : West German news magazine Stern obtains and publishes what it claims are Hitler's diaries

Chrissie Hynde gives birth to her daughter by **Ray Davies** and troops straight back to work: her immediate projects are a new line-up for the **Pretenders**, and a new hit single, 'Back On The Chain Gang'. On April 14, Pete Farndon, the bass player fired from the Pretenders a year ago, dies in his bathtub after an overdose of drugs. He was in the process of forming a new band with Topper Headon of the **Clash**. In April, too, the movie *Flashdance* is released. It's panned by the critics but voted a huge success by everyone else: the soundtrack will become one of the biggest-selling albums of the year. Helped by the hit single, 'Flashdance: What A Feeling', sung by **Irene Cara** – the single's video is a compilation of clips from the film – the album tops the US charts. **Sade** Adu leaves the funk group **Pride** to form her own band. **Metallica** fire guitarist Dave Mustaine, replacing him with Kirk Hammett, ex-**Exodus**. By way of response, Mustaine forms his own band, **Megadeth**.

In May, **Metallica**'s debut album, 'Kill 'Em All' (changed from its original title of 'Metal Up Your Ass') is released. The band is heralded as the spearhead of the new American metal genre, thrash. The same month, a new thrash band comes into existence in New York: namely **Anthrax**. **New Edition** are enlisted in Boston by producer Maurice Starr. Conceived as a new **Jackson 5**, the band features five kids between the ages of 13 and 15 who know how to dance as well as sing. Their debut single 'Candy Girl' tops the UK charts. There's even a British version of the Jacksons called **Five Star** and, like the Jacksons, they are put together and managed by their father, a former session guitarist. **REM**'s first full-length album is released. Entitled 'Murmur', it becomes a mainstay of US college radio, and nudges into the Top 40. No such hedging for **David Bowie** whose album, 'Let's Dance', heads straight for the top of the UK and US charts. The cool and stylized dance single of the same name, produced by **Chic**'s Nile Rodgers, becomes his only single to top the charts in Britain and America. Bowie also

launches his Serious Moonlight tour.

Also in May, **Pink Floyd** release 'The Final Cut' – the title proves all too prophetic, when the band suddenly falls apart at the seams and Roger Waters makes his famous acrimonious departure. Nonetheless the track 'Not Now John' hits Number 30 in the UK charts, only the band's fifth hit single in 16 years of making records.

In June, the self-titled debut album by New York black vocal trio **Run DMC** is the first-ever rap album to go gold. Rap, whose roots are in doo-wop and 'toasting', grew up on the street in America's black inner-cities in the late Seventies, primarily as a reaction against the increasingly bland commercial black music played on the radio. The percussive lyrics are half-sung, half-spoken over a beat-heavy backing track. Four months after getting their BRIT award

George Michael and Andrew Ridgeley of Wham! looking like ads for toothpaste and washing powder. The pop-dance duo met on the first day of term at Bushey Meads Comprehensive School in north London and formed their first band at the height of the punk movement

Jam Master Jay, MC Darryl 'D' McDaniels and Joseph 'Run' Simmons know a lot about gold. Run-DMC's debut album - turned down by all the major labels and released on New York's Profile Records - spent over a year on the US charts, the first rap album certified gold.

as Best British Newcomers and just after the release of their second album, electro-pop duo **Yazoo** split up. Chanteuse **Alison Moyet** signs a solo deal. **Japan** – pretty-boy art rockers from the **Roxy Music** school and leading lights of the new wave of British synthesizer bands – break up. They release a double live album recorded on their last tour, 'Oil On Canvas.'

The biggest band of the summer in Britain is **Wham!** Their album

'Fantastic' storms into the UK charts at Number 1 in July, as the band starts its first major tour – sponsored by a sportswear company. Over in the States, the new US metal bands rule. **Quiet Riot**'s cover of **Slade**'s 'Cum On Feel The Noize' helps their debut album 'Metal Health' become one of the biggest-selling albums of the year. **Los Lobos**, a Mexican-American band from East Los Angeles, release the indie album, 'A Time To Dance'. Produced by T-Bone

Burnett and Steve Berlin of the **Blasters**, it sells 50,000 copies. The band use the profits to buy a second-hand van and embark on a US tour.

In August, **Big Country** release their debut album 'The Crossing'. It soars into the Top 5. The Scottish band, with its big guitars and heroic, anthemic rock, are the polar opposite of the predominant synthesizer groups. They play the Reading Festival with another blaze-of-glory

ZZ Top - middle-aged, hairy, unsubtle and overweight - the ▽ fans went crazy.

Every Girl's Crazy 'Bout a Sharp-Dressed Man

"We're just a little ol' blues band from Texas..."

Blues boogie trio **ZZ Top** – Billy Gibbons, Dusty Hill and Frank (beardless) Beard – have been playing together since they formed in Texas in 1970.

Thanks to constant touring, their albums have sold very nicely and their shows – like the *Worldwide Texas Tour*, featuring cactus, buffalo and longhorn steer onstage – are among the biggest grossers in rock. But it wasn't until 1983 that their big commercial break-through came with the release of their eighth album: 'Eliminator'. The "little old blues band from Texas" was transformed overnight into the coolest band on the planet and the unlikeliest-looking pop stars ever.

Recorded in Memphis, Tennessee, and released in April, the album shot into the American Top 10, staying on the charts for 183

weeks. In the UK, it hit Number 3 and spent a total of 135 weeks in the charts there. The songs – with synthesizers added to their usual blues-metal boogie for the first time – were witty, sleazy, infectious and fun. The single 'Gimme All Your Lovin'', released in May, presented MTV with the first of a brilliant trilogy of videos directed by Tim Newman, which cemented the band's now-familiar image as cool, bearded Muppets, and strange purveyors of the American Dream in the form of cars, guitars and gorgeous girls.

'Sharp Dressed Man' and 'Legs', parts two and three of the trilogy, followed in close succession; the latter was, appropriately enough, picked up for a Leggs pantyhose commercial. Beards, boiler-suits and synchronized movements, not forgetting The Car (a '33 Ford), became video images of the year. And the band won *Billboard*'s Best Video award, as well as selling seven million copies of the album to boot.

1983 - HEADLINE NEWS   OCT 5 : Lech Walesa, the moving force behind the outlawed Polish Solidarity union, is awarded the Nobel Peace Prize

pomp rock band, the **Alarm** from Wales. Rock critics christen this new rock movement 'positive punk.'

In September, veteran heavy metal band **Kiss** take off the make-up that was their trademark and appear bare-faced for the first time on MTV. It's seen as a way of wresting back some of the attention that's being heaped on metal's new wave, who have been walking all over the old wave. **Paul Young**'s debut solo album 'No Parlez' hits Number 1 in the UK. It includes soulful covers of **Joy Division**'s 'Love Will Tear Us Apart', **Nicky Thomas**' 'Love Of The Common People' and **Marvin Gaye**'s 'Wherever I Lay My Hat', Young's first chart-topping single.

Also in September, **UB40**'s cover version of the **Neil Diamond** song 'Red Red Wine' is their first British Number 1. **Madonna**'s self-titled debut album hits the US charts, while the single 'Holiday' provides her with her first hit. A benefit concert for ARMS (Action for Research into Multiple Sclerosis) is held in London. Playing alongside ex-**Faces** MS sufferer **Ronnie Lane** are **Charlie Watts** and **Bill Wyman** of the Stones, **Jeff Beck**, **Kenney Jones**, **Joe Cocker**, **Ray Cooper**, **Steve Winwood**, **Andy Fairweather-Low** and **Eric Clapton**.

Unable to say no, **Yes** make a comeback bid in October with the US chart-topping single, 'Owner Of A Lonely Heart'. **Spandau Ballet**'s album 'True', having already topped the UK charts, is a Top 5 US hit. And **New Order**'s 'Blue Monday', a fixture in the charts since its release in April, becomes Britain's biggest-sell-

ing 12-inch single ever – 600,000 copies in the UK alone. The band's album 'Power Corruption And Lies' goes Top 5. Indiana-born rocker **John Cougar** changes his name. As his album 'Uh-huh' goes Top 10 in the States, the singer reverts to his family name of **Mellencamp**.

As the band embarks on its first US tour, **Big Country**'s 'The Crossing' goes Top 20 in the States in November. Back in Britain, the **Teardrop Explodes** disintegrate. Eccentric frontman and connoisseur of psychedelic drugs, **Julian Cope** goes solo. **Prince** starts shooting his film *Purple Rain* in his hometown of Minneapolis.

In December, having filed for bankruptcy following the failure of her critically-lauded band **Blue Angel**, **Cyndi Lauper** signs a solo deal and releases her debut album, 'She's So Unusual'. With the album on its way to becoming the best-selling record in history – 16 million copies and five Top 10 singles by the year's end – **Michael Jackson**'s *Thriller* video premieres to a background of huge hype on MTV. The 14-minute epic, directed by Jon Landis with a million-dollar budget and 54 make-up artists, features Michael transforming into a werewolf and a zombie and uttering

the famous line, "I'm not like other boys." When the leading man incurs the wrath of the leaders of the Encino Kingdom Hall of Jehovah's Witnesses, Jackson adds the disclaimer: "Due to my strong personal convictions I wish to stress that this film in no way endorses a belief in the occult".

The end of the year marks the release of a video of the video, *The Making Of Michael Jackson's Thriller*, which after being on sale for just two weeks, is certified platinum – the first music video to achieve this status. On New Year's Eve, 36 years after George Orwell's novel was published, **Van Halen** release their new album, '1984'.

Marillion, forerunners of New Progressive Rock started life, in perfect Prog Rock fashion, as an instrumental group named after a JRR Tolkein novel, Silmarillion. With a shortened name and the addition of statuesque singer Fish, the band hit the Top 10.

U2

With the single 'New Year's Day' at Number 10 in the UK charts and a sold-out British tour under their belts, **U2** released their third album 'War' in March 1983. Produced by Steve Lillywhite, the album had everything: passion, glory, gravity, bombast and angst. Fuelled by these ingredients, it entered the UK charts at Number 1.

The band was formed in Dublin in 1976 by schoolboys Paul Hewson (**Bono**), Dave Evans (**The Edge**), **Adam Clayton** and **Larry Mullen**, whose 'Musicians Wanted' note left on the Mount Temple High School noticeboard sparked the whole thing off. Soon they won a talent contest sponsored by Guinness which led to a record deal. Success didn't happen overnight: their first three singles were flops and, although their debut album 'Boy' (produced by Lillywhite and released in November 1980) wasn't a huge hit either, their constant gigging was starting to pay off. Their second album, 'October', released a year after its predecessor, got to Number 11 in the UK charts.

In April '83, with a second single, 'Two Hearts Beat As One', in the Top 20, the band started out on a two-month arena tour of the States. 'New Year's Day' became their first single to make the US charts (though barely nudging the Top 50). But the shows played to large crowds and earned rave reviews from the American rock press. The band reaped more praise for its appearance at the US Festival in California and its headlining appearance in August at the open-air festival *A Day At The Races* in Dublin's Phoenix Park.

So when a live album, which actually managed to capture the band's intense and charismatic stage presence, was released in November, it was no surprise that it was a hit – especially, as it was accompanied by an equally powerful performance video. 'Under A Blood Red Sky', produced by Jimmy Iovine and recorded at shows in Germany, Boston and the *Red Rocks* Festival, Colorado, hit Number 2 in the UK charts, their second hit album of the year, and climbed into the US Top 30. It was to become one of the best-selling live sets ever, but failed to stem the flow of U2 bootleg recordings.

▲ U2 on stage, where they made their reputation. Fronted by charismatic vocalist Paul Hewson. He took the rather more rock'n'roll name of Bono Vox from a billboard advertising a hearing aid retailer. The band's early gigs comprised mostly covers at local pubs in Dublin.

1983 - HEADLINE NEWS   OCT 25 : 1,200 marines and 700 Army Rangers invade the small Caribbean island and former British colony of Grenada in a bid to stop the island becoming a Soviet satellite

1980s Underground

In the Eighties an underground scene all but ceased to exist. Modern media showed it had an insatiable hunger for novelty and any good new idea was snapped up, consumed and rapidly spat out. The turnover in trends was relentless.

The keyword for music in the Eighties was 'variety': a mind-boggling mish-mash of styles, fashions and movements looking backwards and forwards all at the same time, as rock music chewed up its own history and regurgitated it in a thousand new forms. There was punk, post-punk, ska, new soul, technopop, anti-techno guitar-based rock, reggae, white reggae, glam rock, goth rock, rap, hip hop, house, acid house, new psychedelia, folk, protest rock, the new wave of British heavy metal, thrash metal, death metal, rap metal, all manner of mix and match music.

All these genres, sub-genres and crossover genres started out as

▲ MTV brought about a revolution in music as visuals became as important as the sound.

underground movements. They didn't stay that way for long, for two main reasons. Firstly, media became incredibly diverse and all-pervasive in the Eighties. Media thrives on the new, so any fledgling movement that appeared on the scene was immediately picked up and promoted. The Eighties brought in MTV (Music Television, which needed a quick and constant turnover of new music to keep its viewers glued to their sets). There was more and more radio coverage. And, with computers and desktop publishing making it so much cheaper and easier to produce magazines, the number of music and youth culture-oriented publications multiplied, all of them scrambling for exciting trends and fashions to lure in new readers. Teen mags, at the start of the decade, helped make stars of bands like **Culture Club**, whose dandified decadence emerged from the underground night-club scene. Hip magazines, with articles on US gangland fashion and New York subway graffiti artists, helped break the underground movements rap and hip hop into the mainstream.

And the record labels stepped in willingly to supply new product. More and more bands were being signed and recorded by more labels in the Eighties than ever before. Look at the difference between the record stores of the Sixties – small for the most part, the records categorized into maybe rock, pop, classical and jazz.

Compare them to the record superstores of the Eighties, with their mind-boggling number of separate sections (not to mention variable formats: vinyl, cassette or compact disc).

▲ The young British heavy metal band Def Leppard were an international success.

As the Eighties began, punk was a good example of an underground cult that had been brought to the surface (some would say dragged against its will, as the mainstream can appropriate anything it lays its hands on). Although the Los Angeles scene – **Germs**, **Fear**, **Black Flag**, **X** – was still somewhat subterraneous, the **Clash** were now a mainstream US hit in the States, and Beverly Hills shops sold designer-ripped dresses held together by safety-pins.

The major underground musical movement at the start of the decade – ironic when you consider that punk was probably born as a direct reaction to Seventies excesses – was heavy metal. The new wave of British heavy metal bands had grass roots followings, played pubs and clubs, and made no-budget records for their own independent labels. It wasn't long, though, before the groups who spearheaded the movement, like **Def Leppard** and **Iron Maiden**, went on to major success.

The Los Angeles glam metal scene started as an underground movement too:

Motley Crue and **Ratt**, like their British metal counterparts, released albums as indie bands, but did not stay that way for long (except in Britain where bands like **Tigertailz** and **Marionette** kept their cult status – and consequent low profile). Thrash metal started in Britain in 1981 with **Venom**'s album 'Welcome To Hell'. Although no British thrash band has had more than an underground following, American bands like **Metallica**, **Slayer** and **Anthrax** picked up on the sound and made it a huge commercial success.

New progressive rock reared its head as an underground movement in 1983-4 with bands like **IQ**, **Pallas**, **Solstice**, **Pendragon** and **Marillion**.

underground clubs in 1983-4, had their mainstream stars: **Southern Death Cult** became the **Cult**, successful on both sides of the Atlantic. The **Sisters of Mercy** gave birth to the **Mission**, European stars. And the **Damned** had hit albums and singles in the middle of the Eighties.

Rap and hip hop started out as black New York underground movements at the start of the Eighties, but by the end of the decade had infiltrated pop (**Blondie**, for example), crossbred with heavy metal (**Run-DMC** and **Aerosmith**'s collaboration on 'Walk This Way' heralded the successful rap metal movement promoted by America's Def Jam label), installed itself in the charts (six platinum rap albums in the US in 1988), dominated dance (the ultra-gymnastic break-dancing, body-popping and moon walking) and completely taken over the fashion world with the b-boys look of track suits, trainers and backwards baseball caps. The music was developed in dance clubs as DJs came up with ways to blend records together so as not to stop the flow of the dancing, and made new sounds by manipulating and 'scratching' the records on the turntables. The DJs teamed up with MCs who added words – a combination of bragging and descriptions of ghetto life, going back to the blues.

Blues kept its underground status for the first half of the decade, but entered the mainstream with the success of yuppie favourite **Robert Cray** by the mid-Eighties. Folk music, similarly low-key, was dragged out into the bright lights by **Suzanne Vega** in 1986-7, and by the success of protest singers/folkies/former buskers **Billy Bragg** and **Tracy Chapman** in 1988.

In 1987-88, the UK "baggy" movement was still out of the mainstream, though not for long. **Happy Mondays**' indie/dance crossover album 'Bummed' – the music's wild, trancey rhythms spiked with sequels and hid-

den curlicues of sound best appreciated on the mild hallucinatory drug Ecstacy – heralded the soon-to-be huge Acid House movement, with its hands-in-the-air warehouse parties, all-night raves and Sixties-revival psychedelic clubs and posters.

Oh yes, the Eighties also saw an infinite number of Fifties, Sixties and Seventies revivals: re-made, re-modelled, re-mixed re-matched and re-issued. As soon as the mainstream discovered them, the underground movements of the Eighties would subdivide yet again, like amoeba, into something new. Just about staying ahead of the pack. But only just.

▲ Thrash, the heaviest of heavy metal, began in Europe with the band Venom.

▼ Robert Cray, son of a US serviceman, started singing the blues after watching Albert Collins perform at his high school in Georgia.

▲ The Sisters Of Mercy featured Oxford-educated Andrew Eldritch and L.A. punk Patricia Morrison.

The latter took it into the British charts. Meanwhile, in the US the Paisley Underground – **Green On Red**, **Gun Club** and **Rain Parade** among others – bubbled away below the surface until the **Bangles** made it platinum.

Even the goths, with their black clothes and dramatic white make-up and a number of their own vampirical

By 1984, video had taken over the pop business in the States, in a bloodless but all-encompassing coup. A number of blockbuster albums appeared in 1984 – **Prince** sold 10 million copies, **Van Halen** 6 million, **Huey Lewis** 5 million, **Bruce Springsteen** 4 million, **Tina Turner**, **Cyndi Lauper**, **John Cougar Mellencamp** and the **Cars** sold over 2 million each – and music videos were given much of the credit for raising sales. The huge discrepancy between sales at the top and the bottom end of the market was put down to the smaller bands not having the huge budgets needed to make a video. It was all a lifetime away from the days when **Queen** made their 'Bohemian Rhapsody' video for £5000. Big Brother may not have been watching you in 1984, but you were sure as hell watching Big Brother.

As the year opens, **Yes**' 'Owner Of A Lonely Heart' sits astride the US singles chart. The **Pretenders** album 'Learning To Crawl', their comeback following the deaths of James Honeyman-Scott and Pete Farndon, moves into the American Top 10. On the other side of the pond, **Billy Bragg** – alias The Bard Of Barking, former busker at London Tube stations and erstwhile member of punk

outfit **Riff Raff** – is strumming his way up the charts with his debut solo album, 'Life's A Riot With Spy Vs Spy'. It's already topped the indie charts for the past two months.

At the annual *American Music Awards* in January, **Michael Jackson** receives a record seven awards as favourite in just about every category. Ten days later, the singer is hospitalized with second degree burns to his skull after pyrotechnics set his hair on fire during the shooting of a Pepsi commercial. President Reagan sends a telegram to the hospital saying how pleased he is that the star is "not seriously hurt."

In February, **Culture Club**'s 'Karma Chameleon' floats at the top of the US charts for the first of three weeks as their album 'Colour By Numbers' hovers

just behind Michael Jackson's 'Thriller' on the album listings. Fronted by androgynous new romantic **Boy George**, Culture Club win the Best British Single and Best British Group awards at the *BRIT Awards*. **Annie Lennox**, who wins the BRIT for Best Female Artist, shares the cover of American magazine *Newsweek* with Boy George as 'gender-bending' starts to attract major media attention across the Atlantic. **Van Halen** have their first US Number 1 with 'Jump', an infectious song that features synthesizers for the first time. And **Whitesnake**'s

▼ Boy George of Culture Club. The man who dressed like a geisha girl, sang like a soul man, inspired the tabloids to coin the term 'gender bender' and said he preferred a cup of tea to sex.

Jimmy Somerville formed electro-dance band Bronski Beat with fellow Glaswegian Steve Bronski and Londoner Larry Steinbachek. Their debut single 'Smalltown Boy', dealing with homosexual alienation, was followed by the hit album 'Age Of Consent'.

'Slide It In', a UK Top 10 album, starts to climb the US charts.

In March, **Lionel Richie** signs an $8.5 million sponsorship deal with Pepsi. **Deep Purple**'s classic Mark II line-up – featuring Ian Gillan on vocals, Ritchie Blackmore on guitar, Jon Lord on keyboards, Roger Glover on bass and Ian Paice on drums – reforms for an album and a world tour. And guitarist Joe Perry reunites with **Aerosmith**, whom he left in 1979. The **Smiths**' self-titled debut album, striking a chord with a generation of alienated and disaffected youth, goes to Number 2 in the UK charts.

On April Fool's Day, the day before his 45th birthday, **Marvin Gaye** is tragically shot to death in his parents' home in Los Angeles. His father is arrested and charged with murder. The singer's funeral on April 5 at Forest Lawn is attended by **Stevie Wonder**, **Smokey Robinson**, **Quincy Jones**, **Ray Parker Jr** and Gaye's former father-in-law, Motown chief Berry Gordy.

Gaye is cremated the next day and his ashes scattered over the Pacific Ocean by his ex-wife Anna and their three children.

Jerry Dammers and John Bradbury, the remnants of the **Specials** when three of the band left to form **Fun Boy Three**, release the single 'Nelson Mandela' in April, under the monicker **Special AKA**. The political anthem, which demands freedom for the imprisoned South African ANC leader, goes Top 10 in the UK. Also in April, **Bon Jovi** and the **Red Hot Chili Peppers** release their self-titled debut albums, and **Nick Cave** unleashes his first album with the **Bad Seeds**, 'From Here To Eternity'. It includes his cover of **Elvis Presley**'s 'In The Ghetto.' And the **Scorpions** release their most successful album yet. 'Love At First Sting' is a UK Top 20 item and another US Top 10 hit.

The **GoGos** break up in May after just three albums. Lead singer **Belinda Carlisle** announces she will pursue a solo career. Barefoot

Sixties star **Sandie Shaw**, persuaded out of retirement by her biggest fan **Morrissey** and backed by the Smiths, reaches Number 27 in the UK with her version of 'Hand In Glove.' The **New Kids On The Block** are discovered in Boston by **New Edition** producer Maurice Starr, where they have been singing under the name of **Nyunk**. He renames them as fast as he can after one of their song titles. On the third anniversary of his death in May, the **Bob Marley** compilation album 'Legends' is released. It enters the UK charts at Number 1 – the reggae superstar's biggest-ever success.

In June, the Smiths have their first UK Top 10 hit with the single 'Heaven Knows I'm Miserable Now', its lyrics the very essence of Morrissey miserabilism. **Bronski Beat**'s debut album, 'Age Of Consent', is a Top 5 hit. The title reflects Scottish falsetto frontman Jimmy Somerville's concern with gay issues. Capitol Records refuse to release **WASP**'s single 'Animal (Fuck Like A Beast)'. The band releases it on an independent label. Although banned – in fact probably because it is banned – it sells well.

In July, **Sade** releases her first album, 'Diamond Life', a collection of sophisticated jazz-pop. It is one of the most successful debuts ever by a female artist and makes her one of the richest women on the UK pop scene. The **Jacksons** reunite with brother Michael for what they announce will be "our final farewell tour as a family" to promote the largely uninteresting album, 'Victory'. The 40-city tour starts on July 6 in

JUN 2 : Virgin Atlantic, the airline owned by Virgin Records boss Richard Branson, makes its first flight – London to New Jersey – for a bargain £99

Kansas City. **Bruce Springsteen**'s seventh album, 'Born In The USA', a collection of all-American, honest-Joe anthems, propels him to megastardom. It starts its seven week reign at Number 1 in the US charts just as the tour begins, with **Nils Lofgren** brought in to replace **Miami Steve Van Zandt**, who has left to form his own band.

In August, with her album 'Private Dancer' at Number 2 in the UK, Number 3 in the US and the single 'What's Love Got To Do With It' climbing towards the Top 10, **Tina Turner** performs at a McDonalds convention in Canada. This unglamorous gig is all down to a contract

she signed before she made the comeback of the decade. Her new album features a mix of producers and special guests/Tina Turner fans from **David Bowie** to **Heaven 17**, **Mark Knopfler** to **Jeff Beck**. The music, commercial, adult-oriented pop, is far tamer than her early sexy R&B stuff – Turner herself reportedly objects to the wimpiness of some of the songs – but her voice and personality are as resilient as ever and it's a huge success. A true case of persistence finally paying off, it's 24 years since Turner had her first entry in the pop charts.

The **Bangles** release their first full-length album, 'All Over The

Place'. Distinguished by harmonies and jangly guitars, it includes a cover of **Katrina & The Waves**' 'Going Down To Liverpool'. On the wider stage, a small matter of two and a half billion TV viewers around the world watch **Lionel Richie** perform his hit 'All Night Long' accompanied by 200 dancers at the closing ceremonies of the LA Olympic Games.

The first annual *MTV Video Awards* show is held in New York in September. Hosted by **Bette Midler** and Dan Aykroyd, it features live performances by **Madonna**, **Tina Turner**, **Rod Stewart** and **ZZ Top**. Among the biggest winners is jazz-funk keyboardist **Herbie Hancock,** who earns five awards for his 'Rockit' video. **U2**'s album 'The Unforgettable Fire' – recorded in the ballroom at Slane Castle in Ireland, produced by **Brian Eno** and **Daniel Lanois** and even more grandiose than its predecessor – enters the UK charts at Number 1. **Tina Turner** has her first-ever US Number 1 in September with the million-selling single 'What's Love Got To Do With It'. She agrees to appear in Australian director George Miller's third Mad Max movie, *Mad Max: Beyond Thunderdome*, with Mel Gibson.

In November, **Madonna** flirts with her reputation and her public by calling her second album, 'Like A Virgin'. **Wham!** have their first US hit with 'Wake Me Up Before You Go Go' – their UK summer Number 1. The **Jesus & Mary Chain** – much loved by the British music press, not least for their unpredictable gigs that often last less than half an hour and end in riots – release their debut single

The man they call 'The Boss' hard at work on stage. Bruce Springsteen's brilliant and epic-length live shows with the E Street Band helped propel his album 'Born In The USA' to the top of the charts

Frankie say wear a T-shirt. And buy a record. Frankie Goes To Hollywood - who took their name from a headline about Frank Sinatra's film career - take over the charts, the shops and the press in 1984.

ROCK'N'ROLL
record

What Frankie Says Goes

More than a mere pop group, **Frankie Goes To Hollywood** were an all-conquering phenomenon. First there was the Frankie Music – three Number 1 singles and a debut album that shipped platinum on advance orders alone. Then there was the Frankie Lifestyle – acted out in interviews and videos banned by the BBC. Next, there was the Frankie Philosophy - emblazoned across the chests of millions of Britons who bought the 'Frankie Say' T-shirts. And finally there was the Frankie Hype – from the rantings of ZTT ideas man Paul Morley, former *NME* journalist, to the endless 12-inch remixes, three or four of each song.

In their short career, Frankie had one record banned, two videos outlawed, and became the only act besides the **Beatles** and **John Lennon** to hold the Number 1 and 2 positions on the British charts. For one brief, glorious moment, they were the biggest group in Britain: the biggest thing to come out of Liverpool since the Fab Four. But a section of the UK press still dubbed them 'The Foul Five'.

Frankie were brilliantly produced by Trevor Horn, who had a Number 1 hit as one of **Buggles** in 1979 with 'Video Killed The Radio Star' and later went on to join **Yes**, and were allegedly masterminded by former *NME* writer Paul Morley. Their first single, 'Relax' , was released in October of 1983. By December, as it slowly inched its way up the charts, it was banned by Radio 1 because of problems over its lyrics – although the words were mostly lost in the lush swamp of sound. Said a BBC spokesman, "The lyrics of the song are sexually explicit and not suitable for a show with a family audience." The video, with its tongue-in-cheek debauchery and simulated sex, was described by the BBC as "nasty to say the least" and got the same censorious treatment. Tabloid newpapers put 'The Frankie Phenomenon' on their front pages with headlines like 'Gay Sex Tops Pops' and 'Gender Benders', all making wonderful copy. As ex-*NME* journalist Julie Burchill wrote at the time, no one should be too surprised. "The last sexless record to get into the Top 40 was by the **Singing Nun**."

In January, 'Relax' topped the charts and stayed there for five weeks. Its sales in the UK passed a million. In June, the follow-up, 'Two Tribes', entered the charts at Number 1, rekindling the fortunes of 'Relax' and sending it whizzing up the chart again to the runner-up position behind 'Two Tribes'. Frankie became the first group ever to have its first two singles go platinum. The video – featuring a wrestling match between US and USSR Presidents Reagan and Chernenko, and starring lookalikes – aroused more controversy. The Soviet embassy claimed it was "gravely offended". Meanwhile, the police snapped up early photos of the band onstage to see if the simulated fellatio contravened the Obscenity Act.

Frankie's long-awaited debut album, 'Welcome To The Pleasuredome', was released in November and went straight in at Number 1, as did their Christmas ballad 'The Power Of Love' in December, making Frankie only the second group ever after fellow-Liverpudlians **Gerry & The Pacemakers** to have their first three singles hit the top spot.

"We want to be controversial," the band insisted over and over again. "Pop music has been boring for too long", declared singer Holly Johnson, "and we came along and gave it a quick kick in the backside."

Movie Tie-ins

Movies and music were beginning to enjoy an increasingly incestuous relationship. Eight film soundtrack albums went platinum in 1984 – more than in 1981, 1982 and 1983 put together. The relationship was two-way: clips from movies were used to promote the records from the soundtrack and pop videos made ideal commercials for the film.

Take *Footloose*. The film was released in February. Its director admitted to having watched MTV religiously before making the movie, and it showed. Three singles were released before the film opened – including the title track, sung by **Kenny Loggins**, which reached the Number 1 spot in the US. All the publicity pulled people into the cinema, which in turn helped push three more singles (including Ann Wilson of **Heart** and Mike Reno of **Loverboy**'s ballad duet, 'Almost Paradise') into the charts. The five-million-selling album took over from **Michael Jackson**'s 'Thriller' at Number 1.

Among the year's biggest-selling singles were **Stevie Wonder**'s 'I Just Called To Say I Love You', from the film *The Woman In Red*, **Glenn Frey**'s 'The Heat Is On' and the **Pointer Sisters**' 'Neutron Dance' from *Beverly Hills Cop* and the title track to *Ghostbusters*, sung by **Ray Parker Jr**. A perfect example of the cross-fertilization between music and film, *Ghostbusters* was a top movie that spawned a top single which was then made into a video essentially to advertise the movie, and so on and so forth.

Other hit movie-music combos this year included *Breakdance: The Movie*, **Talking Heads**' *Stop Making Sense*, **Paul McCartney**'s *Give My Regards To Broad Street* and *This Is Spinal Tap*, a spoof-documentary about an ageing British heavy metal band on tour in America – the line between rock parody and rock reality gets more blurred when the actors start playing as a live band for real – and the Big One: **Prince**'s *Purple Rain*.

Before long television started to get in on the act. *Miami Vice*, one of the biggest and coolest programmes on TV, had a high-volume rock music soundtrack, often featuring guest appearances by rock musicians in acting roles including **Phil Collins**, **Sheena Easton**, Gene Simmons of **Kiss**, **Power Station**, **David Johansen** and Glenn Frey (who starred as a drug-running pilot in an episode inspired by his own song 'Smuggler's Blues'). The series – which revolved around a black cop and a white cop, who dressed like young yuppies and chased glamorous-looking crooks through glamorous-looking locations in glamorous cars – leant heavily on music video editing techniques and pop promo camera angles.

'Upside Down', which cost £174 pounds to make, sells over 35,000 copies and whizzes up the indie charts. The **Who** break up – or rather fizzle out – with the release of the live album, 'Who's Last'. **Paul McCartney**'s "musical fantasy drama" movie *Give My Regards To Broad Street* is premiered. It is panned by the critics and becomes a box office disaster. The accompanying album includes re-recordings of old **Beatles** and McCartney hits. A measure of how bad the movie is, is that even with songs of this pedigree, the LP doesn't make the Top 20. Louis Farrakhan, controversial founder of 'The Nation Of Islam', tells *People* magazine that **Michael Jackson**'s "Jheri-kurl, female-acting, sissified-acting expression is not wholesome for our young boys, nor our young girls". And another spiritual leader, **Marvin Gaye**'s father (a former Pentecostal minister), is sentenced to five years in prison for voluntary manslaughter.

In December, Rick Allen, **Def Leppard**'s drummer, crashes his Corvette Stingray just outside Manchester in the north of England. His left arm is torn off by the impact. Surgeons sew the limb back on but have to amputate it three days later when infection sets in. Vince Neil, **Motley Crue**'s vocalist, crashes his Ford Pantera in California, killing his passenger Nicholas 'Razzle' Dingley of the group **Hanoi Rocks** and seriously injuring the occupants of the car he ran into. Found to be under the influence of alcohol, Neil is arrested and charged with vehicular manslaughter.

William Reid chucked in his job at a cheese-packing plant in Glasgow and his brother Jim gave up working for Rolls Royce to form the Jesus And Mary Chain in 1983. A year later they release their debut album - a huge indie hit.

Sheila E followed in the wake of earlier Prince protégées like Vanity and Apollinia, is the latest beautiful female performer to enter the royal court. The Minneapolis maestro worked on her debut album, 'The Glamorous Life'.

▼

Cyndi Lauper's 'All Through The Night', which hits Number 5 in December, is her fourth US Top 5 single in a row this year – the others are 'Girls Just Want To Have Fun', which made Number 2 in March, the ballad 'Time After Time', Number 1 in June, and her ode to female masturbation, 'She Bop', which hit Number 3 in September. 'We All Stand Together', credited to **Paul McCartney & The Frog Chorus**,

croaks into the UK Christmas charts.

After watching a BBC TV report on the famine in Ethiopia, **Bob Geldof** of the **Boomtown Rats** writes a song with **Midge Ure** of **Ultravox** called 'Do They Know It's Christmas?', and rounds up everyone in the UK music industry to record it. An all-star line-up under the name of **Band Aid** includes **Phil Collins**, **George Michael**, **Sting**, **Paul Young**, **Paul Weller**, **Jody Watley**,

Marilyn and members of **U2**, **Culture Club**, **Duran Duran**, **Bananarama**, the **Boomtown Rats**, **Status Quo**, **Spandau Ballet**, **Kool & The Gang** and **Heaven 17**. The song enters the charts at Number 1 where it stays for five weeks, right through to the end of the year, selling three-and-half million copies, including over one million in one week alone, and becoming Britain's biggest-selling single ever.

Prince

In July 1984, the movie *Purple Rain* opened in the US and Britain. Its soundtrack album sold a million copies on the first week of release and it topped the US charts for 24 weeks. Spawning three hit singles, two of them chart-toppers, including one of the biggest-selling singles of 1984, the album then went on to win an Oscar. And **Prince** – the small, sexy, androgynous dandy with a taste for purple, ruffles, Edwardian tailcoats and minimalist underwear – its author, songwriter, producer, arranger and leading man, became a megastar.

One of the most fascinating artists of the Eighties, the pocket-sized legend was born Prince Rogers Nelson in Minneapolis in June 1958, just two months before **Michael Jackson** with whom he's often been compared – the comparison owes as much to each star's eccentricity and perfectionist streak, as it does to their age, size, skin colour and prodigious talent. Like Jackson, Prince writes, sings, dances and exercizes total control over both the business and artistic side of his career. His record deal with Warner Brothers in 1978 amazingly allowed him complete artistic autonomy, and he made the most of it, playing all the instruments, writing all the songs, and building his own myth with as much care as he devoted to each track he recorded. Early in his career he stopped doing regular interviews, adding further mystery to his enigmatic personality. The interviews he

did do encouraged a romantic view of his life history, about his parents and growing up in Minneapolis, details which were stretched further out of shape to provide the plot for *Purple Rain*.

'When Doves Cry', the brilliant first single, stayed at the top of the US charts for six weeks in July, selling two million copies. It was Prince's biggest success in Britain too, reaching Number 4 in the charts. The second single, 'Let's Go Crazy', released in September with a video of film excerpts, became another US Number 1. A month later, the million-selling 'Purple Rain', its video made up of some of the film's powerful concert footage, hit Number 2 in the US and Number 8 in the UK. The album went ten times platinum, its massive gravitational force pulling the two-year-old '1999' back to the chart.

Critics, who loved Prince and wanted to praise him but found the film narcissistic and plotless, latched on to the stunning concert footage as the reason to recommend it. Not that people needed much persuading; the film took $60 million at the box office in its first two months of release in America and made more money in 1984 than the hugely popular *Ghostbusters*. Prince continued doing what he does best, making music, leaving at the end of the year on a 100-date US tour, accompanied by the latest of his female discoveries, **Sheila E**, daughter of **Santana** percussionist Pete Escovedo.

1980s Crazes

At the end of the Seventies, the **Sex Pistols** produced 'Anarchy In The UK', three minutes of sheer vitriol and nihilism that reflected the prevailing British climate of despondency and unemployment. The voters, however, responded to these uncertain times by ushering in a Conservative government in 1979. Margaret Thatcher became UK Prime Minister for the rest of the next decade, while Ronald Reagan was voted in as US President, spending the maximum eight-year term in office.

A return to 'Victorian Values' called for by the new ruling party in the UK was matched by a new conservatism in America, embracing censorship and the growing Born Again Christian movement. AIDS was introduced to the public as a sexually transmitted disease of potentially plague proportions that would put paid to the trendy permissiveness of the Sixties and Seventies. And, if that was not enough, the Cold War seemed to be getting worse. In 1980, the US refused to attend the Moscow Olympic Games.

Hardly surprising then that as the decade opened, escapism was big business. The biggest thing on television in the UK and US was *Dallas*, an American TV series about a wealthy Texan family called the Ewings. In November 1980, eighty million people in the US alone watched the episode where it was revealed exactly who shot smug baddie JR.

The biggest movie of 1980 was *Fame*, Alan Parker's film about the struggles and aspirations of teenagers at a New York performing arts school. Striking a real Eighties chord with its do-it-yourself, winner-takes-all philosophy, the film showed relentlessly cheerful kids, gyrating to relentlessly cheerful music in relentlessly cheerful leg-warmers (a huge fashion hit on both sides of the Atlantic).

Meanwhile, at home and in the playground, people were struggling to master *Rubik's Cube* – the biggest craze of the first two years of the Eighties, a block of moveable coloured squares named after its Hungarian inventor, Erno Rubik – and the ultra-escapist *Dungeons & Dragons*, a complicated fantasy medieval board game.

'Personal' became a key word in the Eighties. Whereas the previous decade still held on to the concepts of community and togetherness that the Sixties claimed as their own, the Eighties was the decade of Self: self-improvement, self-motivation, self-help manuals. There's no such thing as society, the individual is all, said Margaret Thatcher. Appropriately enough, in 1981 Sony introduced the personal pocket stereo cassette player, the Walkman. 'Walkman overspill', the tinny noise exuding from headphone wearers oblivious to the world around them, entered the general vocabulary.

In July 1981, a fairytale wedding took place at St Paul's Cathedral in London – ironically against a backdrop of some of the worst inner-city riots mainland Britain had seen. Prince Charles married Lady Diana Spencer. The monarchy – previously seen as something distant and detached and only good for opening fêtes – was suddenly of great interest to the general population. Royalty descended to the level of pop stars as the tabloid press printed every detail of the young couple's lives. Di, a huge fan of pop music, was said to spend her day dancing with her Walkman on.

In 1982, the hottest new things were video games. In the US alone this year, $5 billion and the equivalent of 75,000 years were spent playing the machines at the video arcades that had taken over from the old pinball and slot-machine amusement parlours. The two most popular games were *Pac Man* – a coloured pie with a mouth that chomped its way through a maze, eating dots in its path – and *Space Invaders* – the shooting down of enemy spaceships, *Star Wars*-style. With their bright colours, high speed and electronic sound effects, the machines were exciting, absorbing and ultra-addictive.

Home videos started to catch on this year as video cassette tapes became more readily available for rent. Yet another reason to stay at home, it led to a decline in cinema attendance: movie-going went down 26

▲ Be there or be square. Another one succumbs to the addiction of solving the puzzle of Rubik's Cube.

▼ Hear today – the Sony Walkman personal cassette player takes over the world.

percent on the previous year. Only the blockbusters – like this year's huge hit, ET, Stephen Spielberg's film about a space alien who befriends a boy in the LA suburbs – seemed to get people off their couches.

There were incredible advances in technology this decade. Sophisticated equipment for leisure and pleasure become increasingly affordable. The Eighties was the decade of gadgets: from digital watches to computers to cappuccino machines. In 1983, the first compact disc machines went on sale in the US. Their Japanese inventors claimed that the discs – recorded digitally and read by a laser beam – had no sound distortion and were indestructible.

Breakfast TV made its debut in Britain with *Breakfast Time* on the BBC and ITV's *Good Morning Britain*. Audiences were small at first, but it was very quick to catch on. But not as quick as aerobics. The fitness craze became a household word. Jane Fonda's work-out video cassettes were huge sellers on both sides of the Atlantic. And the biggest fashion was two-piece jogging suits – cotton or towelling for daytime wear, silk ones, worn perhaps with some jewellery (medallions for men), for evening.

In 1984, Yuppies appeared on the scene. An American word standing for

Young Urban Professional, it became synonymous with greed, selfishness and upward mobility. Yuppies wore designer clothes, drove hi-tech cars (BMWs or Porsches, always equipped with car phones), had high-speed jobs (stock market, entrepreneurs) and went nowhere without the year's hottest item, the Filofax – a portable information system (we used to call them diaries and address books) held together in a leather-covered ring binder.

The Yuppies' drug was, of course, Cocaine – *the* drug of the Eighties. Sniffing the white powder, derived from the South American coca plant, was *de rigueur* at parties.

All this selfishness and decadence was bound to lead to a backlash. Sure enough, **Bob Geldof**'s Live Aid concert in the summer of 1985 headlined a growing sense of global community and political consciousness. A number of awareness and money-raising concerts appeared in the second half of the decade, winning support for Amnesty International, Nelson Mandela and Greenpeace. Ecology became a household word. Being Green was all the rage.

Probably the biggest *failed* fad of the decade was British entrepreneur Clive Sinclair's electric tricycle, the C5. Made entirely of plastic and run on an ozone-friendly battery, it was introduced in 1985 as a means of revolutionizing city transport. Trouble was, drivers found it cold, wet and slow. Production of the C5 was halted within 12 months.

When the Chicago Bears played the Dallas Cowboys at Wembley Stadium in August 1986, a crowd of 80,000 fans turned up and American football became the new UK craze. There were 100 teams in Britain by

the end of the year, and an enormous audience for televised US games.

1987 introduced three new words to the English language: *glasnost* (openness), *perestroika* (reconstruction) and Gorbiemania. The Western world loved Gorbachev, the first cuddly, user-friendly Soviet leader, who talked of reforming the communist system and of the East and West becoming good neighbours. Meanwhile, it was the Australian soap *Neighbours* which really caught on in the UK, with regular audiences of 20 million Brits.

The biggest book of 1988 was *Bonfire Of The Vanities*, Tom Wolfe's satirical look at New York life. The most talked-about film was *Fatal Attraction*, which was seen as heralding a backlash against feminism and predatory unmarried, professional women. But the biggest box-office hit starred Bob Hoskins and a floppy-eared cartoon mammal: *Who Framed Roger Rabbit*.

The decade ended with "Europe's biggest-ever street party" at the Berlin Wall in November – where East Berliners were given the right to cross into the West for the first time. There was much talk of how satellite television, a wonderful new technology, had been able to show this happy, united community to the rest of the world. In 1989, Rupert Murdoch launched the first independent satellite TV station in Britain, Sky TV. Hailed as the brave new world of television, old films and even older sit-coms made up its staple diet. There was not exactly a rush to buy satellite dishes.

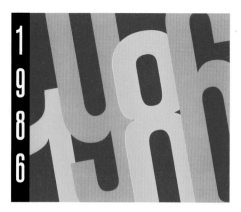

1986 was by and large a time when rock music trod water, as the successful acts of 1985 settled in for another year. Heavy metal, rap and movie soundtrack albums continued to rule the charts, while benefit concerts dominated the arenas. And the TV cop series *Miami Vice* went from strength to strength, with guest appearances by a bizarre variety of musicians – from **Little Richard** playing an evangelist to **Leonard Cohen** as the head of Interpol. Censorship hadn't gone away either. TV evangelist Jimmy Swaggart denounced a total of about three dozen rock and pop magazines from the pulpit including *Rolling Stone*, causing the giant Wal-mart chain to refuse to stock any of them.

In January, the First Annual *Rock & Roll Hall Of Fame* ceremony is held in New York. Awards are presented to rock'n'roll founders **Little Richard**, **Chuck Berry**, **James Brown**, the **Everly Brothers**, **Jerry Lee Lewis** and **Fats Domino**. **Buddy Holly**, **Sam Cooke** and **Elvis Presley** are inducted posthumously. Among performers present in the flesh are **Neil Young**, **Julian Lennon** and **Billy Joel**. **Stevie Wonder** organizes three major concerts on January 15 in Washington DC, Atlanta and New York, to celebrate the newly inaugurated US public holiday observing the birthday of Martin Luther King.

Meanwhile in the UK, *Red Wedge*, a coalition of Socialist-minded musicians including **Paul Weller**, **Billy Bragg** and the **Communards**, embarks on a tour to raise money and election support for the British Labour Party. The **Clash** break up. Their final album, 'Cut The Crap', makes the UK Top 20 but doesn't get past Number 88 in the States, partly as a result of being panned by critics. The **Pet Shop Boys**' 'West End Girls' tops the UK singles charts for two weeks. Back in the US, **Janet Jackson**, filing for divorce from El DeBarge, releases her new album 'Control'. Produced and co-written with Jimmy Jam and Terry Lewis of **Time**, it reveals a new tougher, more street-wise Janet.

Sigue Sigue Sputnik, named after a Russian street gang and put together by Tony James, ex-**Generation X**, as a kind of latter-day **Monkees** with cheekbones and futuristic outfits, are showered with publicity and record deals before they've even played a note. In February, they release their debut single, 'Love Missile F1-11', produced by Giorgio Moroder. It sails on a sea of hype to Number 2 in the UK charts.

A month after the release of the EP 'Live?!*@ Like A Suicide' on their indie Uzi Suicide label, **Guns N'Roses** sign to Geffen Records in March after a mad scramble from most major record companies for their signatures. Newlyweds **Madonna** and **Sean Penn** start shooting their new film, *Shanghai Surprise*. As the tabloids trail them in London, Penn nearly strangles one member of the paparazzi and runs over the *Sun* photographer's foot. The press promptly dubs them "the Poison Penns". **George Harrison** – whose Handmade Films is producing the movie and who makes a cameo appearance in it as a nightclub

 Pet Shop Boys - vocalist Neil Tennant and keyboardist Chris Lowe - started the year with a hit, 'West End Girls' knocked Shakin' Stevens' 'Merry Christmas Everyone' off the top of the UK charts. It went on to hit the Number 1 spot in eight other countries, including the United States.

'Hey Hey We're The Punkees'. Generation X escapee Tony James and his futuristic glam band Sigue Sigue Sputnik. Their debut single, 'Love Missile F1-11', was propelled by promotion and publicity to Number 2 in the British charts.

Nine years after his debut solo album, former Genesis frontman Peter Gabriel finally grabbed his first chart-topping LP when 'So' entered at Number 1, on the back of the stunning single 'Sledgehammer' - a song best-known for its mind-boggling, stop-motion, clay-animation video.

The end of an era. Seventy-two thousand fans poured into London's Wembley Stadium in June to say goodbye to one of the best-loved bands of the decade: Wham! George Michael left to pursue a solo career, he'd already scored two solo chart-toppers with 'Careless Whisper' and 'A Different Corner'.

singer – holds a press conference to try to calm things down.

Also in March, the **Bangles** arrive at Number 2 in the US and UK charts with 'Manic Monday', a song written for them by **Prince**. **James Brown** has his biggest-ever hit in the States with 'Living In America', the theme song from *Rocky IV* which he sang at Sylvester Stallone's personal request. **Duane Eddy**'s re-recording of his 1959 hit 'Peter Gunn' with arrivistes the **Art Of Noise** goes Top 10 in the UK. And **Cliff Richard** clings to the UK Number 1 spot for three weeks with a spoof re-make of his 1959 hit single 'Living Doll', re-recorded with **Hank B Marvin** of the **Shadows** as well as comedy team the **Young Ones**. Money raised from half a million sales goes to *Comic Relief*'s efforts on behalf of Ethiopian famine victims.

Heavy metal weighs in for

Ethiopia in April. Singer **Ronnie James Dio** records the single 'Stars' with a collection of heavy rock performers including **Motley Crue** and **Ted Nugent**. A Number 1 US album for **Heart** this month – their self-titled, first album for their new record label is the band's first chart-topper in an 11-year recording career. Their single, 'These Dreams', is also the

first to make the UK charts. And the same goes for **Van Halen**'s '5150'. Named after the New York police code for the criminally insane, it's their first album to feature David Lee Roth's replacement, **Sammy Hagar** and includes the radio-friendly singles 'Love Walks In' and 'Why Can't This Be Love'.

Michael Hutchence of **INXS** makes his movie debut in April in the spaced-out *Dogs In Space*. A song from the film, 'Rooms For The Memory', becomes a solo hit in Australia. Marie Fredriksson and Per Gessle from Sweden form **Roxette**, named after a **Dr Feelgood** song. Their debut album, 'Pearls Of Passion', is only released in Sweden but sells over 100,000 copies. The **Pixies** form in Boston after Black Francis and Joey Santiago place an ad for musicians "into **Husker Du** and **Peter, Paul** and **Mary**".

In May, Prince decides to return to live performing after all and sets off on the Parade tour. **Elvis Costello** releases his rootsy album, 'The King Of America', recorded live in the studio with the cream of US session men including Elvis Presley's old guitar player, **James Burton**. **Peter Gabriel**'s single 'Sledgehammer', accompanied by a stunningly innovative and wildly expensive clay-mation video, climbs into the Top 5, while his fifth LP, 'So', enters the UK charts at Number 1 – his first chart-topping album. A concert is held in Dublin to benefit the Irish unemployed. **U2** are among the performers.

In June, **Wham!** play their farewell concert in front of 72,000

World', subtly amended to 'Everybody Wants To Run The World', as the theme song for *Sports Aid*, a worldwide running event held to raise money for Ethiopian famine relief. And the man who started the whole charity thing off, **Bob Geldof**, is dubbed Sir Bob, Knight of the British Empire, in the Queen's birthday honours list in June.

Leaders of the pack in July are **Janet Jackson**'s 'Control' – Number 1 in the US – and **Madonna**'s album 'True Blue', which spends five weeks at the top of the US and the UK charts. Meanwhile the top position on the US singles charts is held by **Simply Red**'s 'Holding Back The Years'; it just misses the mark in Britain and stalls at Number 2.

On the film front, July sees the premiere of **Prince**'s new movie *Under The Cherry Moon* – a silly, black and white exercise in narcissism with Prince starring as an American gigolo in France – and also of *Sid And Nancy*, Alex (*Repo Man*) Cox's true life drama based on the lives and deaths of **Sex Pistols** bassist **Sid Vicious** and his girlfriend Nancy Spungen. Released in the same month is *True Stories*, an innovative musical tour of Texas, which **David Byrne** of **Talking Heads** wrote, directed and stars in. **David Bowie** takes on a new image as King Of The Goblins in *Labyrinth* directed by Muppets man Jim Henson. *Top Gun*, however, starring Tom Cruise and the cream of the US airforce's jet fighters, proves to be the biggest draw of the summer. The film gives **Berlin** a Number 1 hit with 'Take My Breath Away' and leads to record sales of Ray Ban sunglasses. The **Psychedelic Furs** have a US hit

1986 - HEADLINE NEWS

FEB 25 : President Marcos flees Manila for the United States after Corazon Aquino is elected President of the Philippines

fans at Wembley Stadium. Their final record 'The Edge Of Heaven/ Where Did Your Heart Go' – tops the charts. **ELP** reform in June, with drummer **Cozy Powell** taking over from **Carl Palmer** as the missing 'P'. The album 'Emerson, Lake & Powell' makes the Top 50 both sides of the Atlantic. The **Police** reform to play on the Amnesty International Conspiracy Of Hope tour. Among the other performers are benefit concert regulars **Peter Gabriel**, **U2**, **Jackson Browne**, **Bryan Adams** and **Lou Reed**. Gabriel and Sting also perform at the Artists Against Apartheid concert in June before a 250,000-strong crowd on Clapham Common in London. Organized by **Jerry Dammers** of **Special AKA**, it features, among others, **Elvis Costello**, **Boy George**, **Billy Bragg**, **Hugh Masekela** and **Sade**.

Tears For Fears release a new version of their big hit of last year, 'Everybody Wants To Rule The

Top Gun was the biggest film of 1986. Based in an elite naval aviation academy, its attractions were aerial dog-fights as exciting as any video game - and actor Tom Cruise. The movie made Cruise a major star and gave Berlin a Number 1 hit with the theme song.

The return of the girl group. Bananarama - Sarah Dallin, Keren Woodward and Siobhan Fahey - topped the US charts with their first collaboration with the hit-making production team of Stock, Aitken and Waterman, 'Venus'.

If Muzak be the Food of Love

MTV wouldn't touch it, radio ignored it and the rock press had written it off as yuppy dinner party muzak, upmarket musical wallpaper with intellectual pretensions. In spite of such neglect, new age – floaty, pastoral, vaguely cosmic, meditative, grown-ups' music – was one of the biggest-selling genres of 1985.

New age was always designed to appeal to an older, richer, more leisured audience, who were raised on but had now outgrown traditional pop and rock music, the odd **Dire Straits** album excepted. California was at the forefront of the movement, though Britain could be said to have start-

ed the whole thing off with **Mike Oldfield**'s world conquering 'Tubular Bells' in 1973. Britain's main new age label was Coda, which defined its brief as 'from Elgar to Eno' and released albums by **Claire Hammill** and **Rick Wakeman** of **Yes**, among others. But the main source of new age was California label Wyndham Hill, founded by guitarist Will Ackerman. Customers for top sellers **Michael Hedges**, **Liz Storey** and Japanese musician **Kitaro** were not confined to the States. They could also be found served up with Marks & Spencer quiche and capuccinos in the UK any night of the week.

with 'Pretty In Pink' – a song from their 1981 album 'Talk Talk Talk' – after it was used in John Hughes' hit movie of the same name. Former Van Halen frontman **David Lee Roth** has a Top 5 US hit with his solo mini-album 'Eat 'Em And Smile', while **Bananarama**'s first collaboration with hitmaking machine Stock, Aitken & Waterman, a cover of **Shocking Blue**'s 'Venus', yields a Top 10 hit in Britain, a Number 1 smash in America.

In August, as the great rock survivor **Tina Turner**'s star is unveiled on the *Hollywood Walk of Fame*, the singer publishes her autobiography. *I Tina* is a

fascinating and sordid account of her 16-year-marriage to Ike and her rise to stardom as a solo artist. **Metallica**'s album 'Master Of Puppets' breaks into the US and UK Top 50. **Chris De Burgh**'s 'Lady In Red', a song about Mrs De Burgh, tops the UK charts; the tabloids report that Prince Andrew and Fergie took the single with them on their honeymoon. Former **GoGo Belinda Carlisle** releases her debut solo album 'Belinda', in which she metamorphoses from bubbly, baby-fat, wild child punk to sophisticated, high-heeled, worked-out yuppy.

U2 guitarist **The Edge** records a soundtrack album with **Sinead O'Connor**, 'The Captive'. Meanwhile, he and the band start work on a new album, 'The Joshua Tree', with **Brian Eno** and **Daniel Lanois** once again producing. **Niggaz With Attitude**, a rap band formed this year in the Compton area of Los Angeles,

APR 14 : The US launches an air raid on Libya in an attempt to punish leader Colonel Gaddafi for sponsoring terrorism. 39 people are killed including Gaddafi's baby daughter

1986 · HEADLINE NEWS

187

release their debut single, 'Boyz N' The Hood', an uncompromising look at life in the LA ghetto. **Eric B & Rakim** have a hit with their first single, 'Eric B For President'. Their debut album, 'Paid In Full', leads to a court case when former **James Brown** sideman, Bobby Byrd, objects to the use of part of 'I Know You Got Soul' without permission and demands royalty payments.

Black rap trio **Run-DMC** sign a six-figure sponsorship deal with Adidas sports shoes. In September they become the first rap act to go platinum when their album 'Raising Hell' enters the US Top 10. The band's cross-over breakthrough comes with the rap-metal single 'Walk This Way', a cover of a nine-year-old **Aerosmith** song. The witty

Amazing Graceland

Inspired by the township music he heard on bootleg tapes, **Paul Simon** ignored the United Nations' cultural boycott of South Africa to go to Johannesburg and record with some of the country's best black vocal and instrumental groups. The resulting album 'Graceland', a mix of traditional South African music and American pop (it also featured contributions from **Los Lobos**, **Linda Ronstadt** and the **Everly Brothers**), was released in October. It hit Number 3 in the US and topped the UK charts for the first of five weeks.

Up to this point, Simon's solo career hadn't been going too brilliantly. Most of the time, he was never allowed to forget **Art Garfunkel**, with whom he periodically – and seemingly reluctantly – united for successful one-off reunion shows and albums that quickly outsold his own eclectic blend of reggae, salsa, world music, pop and jazz. 'Graceland', critically acclaimed, earned him a platinum disc, a Grammy for Album Of The Year and the BRIT Award for Best International Solo Artist. His breaking of the UN cultural boycott also caused a furore and Simon held a press conference to explain his position – basically, his belief in the healing power of music – and to state that the ANC and the UN had both taken him off their blacklists, but Anti-Apartheid supporters still picketed his UK tour.

Meanwhile the vocal group **Ladysmith Black Mambazo** were offered their own recording contract as a result of their brilliant contribution to 'Graceland'. Simon co-produced their album, 'Shaka Zulu', which earned the group a UK Top 40 placing.

APR 26 : 15,000 people are evacuated from the Ukraine after the nuclear power plant in Chernobyl blows up

1986 · HEADLINE NEWS

JANUARY 4: Phil Lynott of Thin Lizzy dies of heart failure; he is 34 years old.

FEBRUARY 23: The Rolling Stones play at the tiny 100 Club in London in memory of their keyboard player Ian Stewart.

APRIL: The late Sam Cooke has his biggest hit with 'Wonderful World', after it is used in a Levi's TV commercial.

MAY: The Monkees reform, without Michael Nesmith, and embark on a 145-date 20th anniversary tour.

MAY: Gloria Estefan & Miami Sound Machine release their first English album, 'Primitive Love'.

MAY 16: Elvis Costello marries Cait O'Riordan of the Pogues.

AUGUST: Bob Geldof marries Paula Yates.

NOVEMBER: Roger Waters takes his former bandmates to court, claiming they have no right to use the Pink Floyd name.

▲ Girl group the Bangles started and ended the year with hits - 'Manic Monday', written for them by Prince, and 'Walk Like An Egyptian' by Liam Sternberg. Originally called the Bangs, the L.A. band featured Susanna Hoffs, Michael Steele and sisters Vicki and Debbi Peterson.

One man and his guitar, Paul Simon made some of his most popular and critically-acclaimed music on his seventh solo album 'Graceland', recorded in South Africa with local musicians. He found himself in trouble with anti-apartheid groups for breaking the UN ◀ cultural boycott.

video, with Steven Tyler and Joe Perry of Aerosmith making guest appearances, gets plenty of airplay on MTV and the single reaches the US Top 5.

Michael Jackson is the star of the 15-minute 3-D film *Captain Eo* – directed by Francis Ford Coppola and produced by George *Star Wars* Lucas – which premieres at Disneyland in California and Disneyworld in Florida in September. The same month, the cover of the *National Enquirer* carries a photo of Jackson in an oxygen chamber, with the headline: 'Michael Jackson's bizarre plan to live to 150'. At the annual *MTV Awards*, **A-ha** walk off with trophies for Best Concept Video, Best New Artist Video, Best Special Effects, Best Direction, Most Experimental Video and the Viewers' Choice Award for 'Take On Me'. Their video for 'The Sun Always Shines On TV' takes the prizes for Best Editing and Best

Cinematography. **Madness** announce that they're splitting up. September 27, **Metallica**'s bassist, 24-year-old Cliff Burton, is killed when the band's tour bus crashes in Scandinavia.

In October, **Bon Jovi**'s third album 'Slippery When Wet' starts an eight-week stay at Number 1 in the US charts and becomes one of the biggest-selling rock albums of the decade. Recorded with Bruce Fairbairn in Vancouver, it's packed with infectious singalong pop-rock anthems, like 'You Give Love A Bad Name' – their first UK hit last month – and the even bigger 'Livin' On A Prayer', songs which cross them over from the male-dominated metal audience to the pop girl crowd, miraculously without alienating either side. **Elvis Costello** makes up his differences with the **Attractions** and releases his second album this year, 'Blood And Chocolate'. An entirely different animal from May's release

'The King Of America', the LP is produced by **Nick Lowe** and includes a song co-written by Costello with his new wife, **Cait O'Riordan** of the **Pogues**. Also this month, **Ultravox** release their final album. 'U-Vox' is a UK Top Ten hit but doesn't make a dent in the US charts.

Madonna's latest film, *Shanghai Surprise*, opens in November to unanimously dreadful reviews. The adventure film about stolen opium is "awesome in its awfulness", according to one critic. **Boston** come back with their first album in eight years. 'Third Stage' sells three million copies in its first month of release and spends four weeks at Number 1 in the US. As a result, the band's previous two albums – first released in 1977 and 1978 – re-enter the charts. **Bruce Springsteen** delivers a knockout punch to the bootleggers with his five-album set 'Live 1975-85'. Compiled from 21 concerts over a 10-year period, it includes for the first time his own versions of 'Because The Night', covered by **Patti Smith**, and 'Fire', a hit for the **Pointer Sisters**. **Metallica** replace the late Cliff Burton with Jason Newsted, ex-**Flotsam & Jetsam**. Four years after 'Don't You Want Me', November sees the **Human League** back on top of the US chart with a Jimmy Jam/Terry Lewis composition, 'Human'

In December, **Bobby Brown** forsakes **New Edition** for a solo career. Their last record together is the covers album 'Under The Blue Moon'. The **Bangles** have their second big hit this year with 'Walk An Egyptian', which reaches Number

A good year for the oldies with the **Grateful Dead** having the most successful album in their 22-year history; **Robbie Robertson** of the **Band** made a successful comeback, **George Harrison**'s 'Cloud Nine' went Top 10 in Britain and the **Beatles**' back catalogue was released on CD. Life was not so good for the **Rolling Stones**, though. Mick Jagger and Keith Richard conducted trench warfare against each other through the pages of the tabloids – Mick told Britain's *Daily Mirror* about Keith, "I don't think we can work together any more" and Keith told *Mirror* rival the *Sun* that the frontman should "stop trying to be like Peter Pan and grow up."

And, more than ever before, commercial sponsorship was underwriting the big name tours in 1987. **Whitney Houston** and **Duran Duran** went out on the road under the Coca Cola banner, while **Michael Jackson**, **Lionel Richie**, **Tina Turner** and **David Bowie** all toured for Pepsi. Other deals meant that **Run-DMC** were now sponsored by Adidas sportswear and **Genesis** by Michelob beer.

The year opens with the **Bangles** still at the top of the US charts with 'Walk Like An Egyptian'. Four weeks

at Number 1, it's their biggest American hit to date.

In March, the **Beastie Boys** debut album 'Licensed To Ill' (toned down from its original title 'Don't Be A Faggot') is the first rap album to top the US charts. It stays at Number 1 for seven weeks. **U2**'s album 'The Joshua Tree' is released and immediately enters the UK charts at Number 1, going platinum within 48 hours. Harsher and more echoey than before, it features evocative tracks like 'Where The Streets Have No Name', 'I Still Haven't Found What I'm Looking For' and 'With Or Without You', their first chart-topping US single. In April, the album goes to Number 1 in the States – U2 are the first Irish band to achieve this feat – and stays there for nine weeks.

In April, **Frankie Goes To Hollywood** announce that they will part for nine months to work on solo projects: a temporary separation that ends up being a divorce. **Holly Johnson** performs without the band

for the first time at an AIDS benefit in London, and signs a solo recording deal. **Bob Geldof** stars in an AIDS awareness commercial that does the rounds of a dozen independent cinemas in England. Holding up a condom, uncompromising Sir Bob declares, "Some people say these will kill your sex life. When your sex life is killing you, what choice do you have?... Don't play sexual chicken, stick one of these things on your dick." Geldof – with **Herbie Hancock** and **Andy Summers** of the **Police** in his backing band – performs at an AIDS benefit show at Wembley Arena (after a *Live Aid*-style benefit concert for April 3, International AIDS Day, that has been talked about since December has fails to materialize). Also on the bill: **Elton John**, **Aswad**, **Tom Robinson**, **Sandie Shaw**, **Meat Loaf**, **Womack & Womack**, **Herbie Hancock**, **Kim Wilde**, Holly Johnson, **Boy George** and **George Michael**, who brings **Andrew Ridgeley** onstage for a **Wham!** reunion. Says Michael, "My generation

▶ Suzanne Vega was the first of a new generation of little women with big guitars who made folk music hip again. Her self-titled debut album in 1985 was a UK hit, but it was the follow-up, 1987's 'Solitude Standing', that made her a worldwide star.

Public Enemy - Chuck D., Flavor Flav, Terminator X and Professor Griff - were the most uncompromising rappers on the circuit. Their aggressive form of urban rap earned them the description, "The Black ▼ Panthers of rap".

mustn't be a generation whose kids ask us in years to come why we didn't do anything to stop the spread of the disease in the mid-Eighties."

In May, Ad-Rock of the **Beastie Boys** is arrested in Liverpool during the band's UK tour. He's accused of hitting a female fan in the face with a can of beer. The British tabloids pile on a few more sins, accusing the band of insulting crippled and mentally handicapped children, not to mention causing an outbreak of theft of VW car ornaments which copycat fans wear as medallions. Nonetheless, the hit single '(You Gotta) Fight For Your Right (To Party)' propels the Beasties' album into the UK Top 10. The toughest, most uncompromising rap album to date appears on the scene this month: **Public Enemy**'s 'Yo! Bum Rush The Show'. Manager/producer Bill Stephney describes his boys as "the Black Panthers of rap". They join the Beastie Boys on the US leg of their tour. Meanwhile, a morbidly obsessed **Michael Jackson** is

reported to have offered to buy the remains of John Merrick, the Elephant Man, from the London Hospital for $100,000.

'Solitude Standing', folk-waif **Suzanne Vega**'s bittersweet second album, makes Number 2 in the UK and Number 11 in the US as she embarks on an 11-month world tour in May. And **Happy Mondays** – the Manchester band whose name was inspired by a **New Order** song but who came last in a *Battle Of The Bands* contest at New Order's Hacienda club – release their debut, 'Squirrel & G-Man Twenty Four Hour Party People Plastic Face Carnt Smile (White Out)'. Produced by **John Cale**, the album is popular with rock journalists who are paid by the word but otherwise it is ignored.

Oldies **Bob Dylan** and the **Grateful Dead** team up in June for one of the year's most successful tours of the States. The Dead play with Dylan as his backing band as well as playing a (much longer) set of their own. It's all too easy for **Simple Minds** who release their third UK platinum album in a row. Entitled 'Live In The City Of Light', it's recorded in Paris and Sydney and enters the UK charts at Number 1. **Whitney Houston**'s second album 'Whitney' also sails effortlessly into the US charts at Number 1 for a ten-week stay.

David Bowie, **Genesis** and **Eurythmics** play at a festival held in June on the

western side of the Berlin wall. East German police arrest 50 people who've gathered on the other side to watch the show and start chanting "The wall must go." Alex Cox, director of *Sid And Nancy*, releases his new film *Straight To Hell*. A dreadful spoof spaghetti Western, which should have been called *Straight To Video,* it stars Dennis Hopper with **Elvis Costello**, **Joe Strummer**, the **Pogues**, **Grace Jones** and **Courtney Love**.

July sees the release of another rather dire Madonna movie, *Who's That Girl,* in which the blond ambitious one fails to convince as a recently-sprung jail inmate. **Joan Jett** and Michael J Fox play a brother and sister rock act in the film *Light Of Day.* As far as critics are concerned, Jett steals the show. *La Bamba*, a movie about the life of Mexican-American pop idol **Ricthie Valens** (who died in the same plane crash as **Buddy Holly**) has its US

La Bamba, the biopic about Ritchie Valens (played by Lou Diamond Phillips), the impoverished Mexican-American who at the age of 17 becomes a teenage pop idol, also featured L.A.-based Mexican-American band Los Lobos ('The Wolves') as 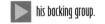 his backing group.

premiere. The soundtrack album, featuring **Los Lobos**, goes to Number 1 in the States, while their cover of **Valens**' 'La Bamba' is a Number 1 single in Britain.

In the summer of 1987, five of *Billboard*'s top six albums are by heavy metal bands. Number 1 band **U2** are followed in the chart by **Whitesnake** ('Whitesnake '87'), **Motley Crue** ('Girls Girls Girls') **Poison** ('Look What The Cat Dragged In') and **Ozzy Osbourne** ('Tribute'). Also high in the charts are **Cinderella, Deep Purple, Ratt, Tesla, Van Halen, Europe, Iron Maiden** and **Stryper**. Big hair bands still rule – although the new breed of thrash metal bands like **Metallica** and **Megadeth** are also starting to do well. **Heart**'s biggest-ever single, 'Alone' – the ballad that **Lemmy** of **Motorhead** confesses makes him cry – tops the US charts in July.

Also in July, **Terence Trent D'Arby** – the man who tells the *NME* "I think I'm a genius" – releases his debut album, 'Introducing The Hardline According To Terence Trent D'Arby'. It goes into the UK charts at Number 1. D'Arby was born in New York and joined the army in 1980 (he was stationed in Germany with **Elvis Presley**'s old regiment), when he put his first band together. He moved to London in 1986 to sign a solo record deal and work with Martyn Ware of **Heaven 17**, who produced his debut.

In August, MTV makes its debut in 14 countries in Europe. The first video played is **Dire** Straits' 'Money For Nothing'. Husky-voiced **Dusty Springfield** returns to the UK Top 10 after years away with 'What Have I Done To Deserve This', a duet with the **Pet Shop Boys**. And **Kylie Minogue**, 19-year-old award-winning Australian soap opera actress, performs **Little Eva**'s 'Locomotion' at the opening of a major football game in Sydney. Released as a single, it races to Number 1 down under for the first of seven weeks. With *Neighbours* one of the most popular programmes on British television, **Bananarama** producers Stock, Aitken & Waterman invite Kylie to their London recording studio and international stardom is assured.

Salt 'N' Pepa, two former New York shop assistants, release their debut album, 'Hot Cool & Vicious', an infectious mix of hip hop and humour. Also in August, **LL Cool J**'s 'Bigger And Deffer' album goes platinum in the States; it features the first ever rap ballad and the man's

David Coverdale had been destined for the big time since he sang with Deep Purple in the Seventies. But his band Whitesnake had to wait until 'Whitesnake 1987' went platinum to join the stadium rock elite.

Everybody in Britain followed everybody in Australia and sat glued to their TV sets whenever Kylie and Jason hit the screen. With Neighbours topping the television ratings, hit producers Stock, Aitken and Waterman made a beeline for sometime singer Kylie Minogue.

Buy George!

In November 1987, **George Michael** released 'Faith', his first solo album. It was an impressive debut. Michael, who produced and played most of the instruments himself, had gone firmly for credibility since leaving **Wham!**. The man who won the *Daily Mirror* reader's award for 'Best Bottom of 84' and who was then parodied with former partner Andrew Ridgeley as a pair of singing shorts-clad buttocks by TV programme *Spitting Image*, proved himself to be a sophisticated singer and songwriter.

Georgios Panayiotou and **Andrew Ridgeley** were schoolfriends in the London suburb of Bushey, when they formed the bubblegum club-funk group that was to become one of the biggest pop sensations of the Eighties. Wham! broke up in 1986, after Michael had already had two solo Number 1 singles (three if you count 'Careless Whisper', credited to George Michael on the UK release and 'Wham! featuring George Michael' in the States) and appeared individually with **Smokey Robinson**, **Stevie Wonder**, **Elton John** and **Aretha Franklin** (his duet with the latter, 'I Knew You Were Waiting (For Me)', topped the UK chart in February).

George Michael's first post-Wham! solo single was released in June – to a good deal of controversy. The BBC's Radio 1 would only play the former teen idol's 'I Want Your Sex' after 9pm, and MTV in the States first banned, then re-edited the video, which featured George romping naked with girlfriend Kathy Jeung. Accused of irresponsibility during the AIDS era, the singer insisted that the video promoted monogamous relationships. The single (featured in the movie *Beverly Hills Cop II*) hit Number 3 in the UK charts and Number 2 in the US, kept from the top by a partial airplay ban.

'Faith' entered the UK charts at Number 1 in November and spent four weeks at the top of the US charts. Fourteen times platinum, it was the most successful album ever in the US by a British solo act.

Salt (Cheryl James) and Pepa (Sandra Denton) - the first female rap stars. The New York duo were working together as telephone sales girls when a friend invited them to rap on 'The Show Stopper', a reply to Doug E. Fresh's hit 'The Show'. Their performance won them a record deal.

first big hit single, 'I Need Love', recorded with **LA Posse**. **Def Leppard**'s 'Hysteria' album, four years in the making and beset by no end of tragedies and problems, enters the UK chart at Number 1, spending the first of 95 weeks in the listings. After a career singing advertising jingles and doing backing vocals for the likes of **Lionel Richie**, **Richard Marx** releases his debut single, 'Don't Mean Nothing'; it goes Top 5 in the States.

Having told *NME*, "Whoever says that the **Smiths** have split shall be severely spanked by me with a wet plimsoll" after reports of battles with **Johnny Marr**, **Morrissey** announces that the Smiths have indeed split. The singer signs a solo deal with EMI; Marr hooks up with the **Pretenders**. The Smiths' final studio album, 'Strangeways Here We Come', goes to Number 2 in the UK.

It's tough following up a 47 million-selling album. To judge by **Michael Jackson**'s example it takes four years hard work. In September his new album 'Bad' is finally ready; it instantly materializes at Number 1 on both sides of the Atlantic. The title track is the first single, and its 17-minute black-leather, crotch-grabbing video shows a tougher, tighter Jackson. The singer starts his 12-month world tour, sponsored by Pepsi, in Tokyo. While all this is going on, **REM**'s fifth album, 'Document', turns into their first US Top 10 record.

A TV tribute to **Roy Orbison** is screened. Shot at a hotel bar in Los Angeles, it has Orbison playing with an all-star backing band including

MAR 30 : A Japanese insurance company buys Van Gogh's 'Sunflowers' for $39.9 million, the highest price ever paid for a painting

▲ Michelle Pfeiffer, Cher and Susan Sarandon - the man-hungry Witches of Eastwick - conjure up the Devil: Jack Nicholson.

Bruce Springsteen, **Elvis Costello**, **Tom Waits**, **Jackson Browne**, **Bonnie Raitt**, **kd lang** and **Jennifer Warnes**. 'The Big O' re-records his Sixties classics for the album 'In Dreams: The Greatest Hits', produced by T-Bone Burnett.

In October, **Frankie Goes To Hollywood**'s 'The Power Of Love' is used as the backing track to British TV's first condom commercial. As **Chuck Berry** has a star unveiled on the *Hollywood Walk of Fame* in LA, the film biography *Chuck Berry: Hail! Hail! Rock'n'Roll* opens in the US. It features appearances by **Eric Clapton**, **Robert Cray**, **Etta James**, **Julian Lennon**, **Linda Ronstadt**, **Little Richard**, **Roy Orbison**, the **Everly Brothers**, **Willie Dixon**, Bruce Springsteen and its musical director **Keith Richard**.

In the same month, **Cher** – back in the UK charts for the first time in 14 years with 'I Found Someone' – starts filming *The Witches Of Eastwick* with Jack Nicholson and Michelle Pfeiffer. The **Christians**' self-titled debut album goes into the

UK charts at Number 2, helped by two smooth soul-rock hit singles, 'Forgotten Town' and 'Hooverville.' The **Pixies** release their debut mini-album 'Come On Pilgrim', which tops the UK indie charts. **Sting**'s album 'Nothing Like The Sun', with guests including Eric Clapton, **Ruben Blades** and **Mark Knopfler**, makes Number 1 in the UK. It's dedicated to Sting's mother, who died during the recording. **Prince**'s duet with **Sheena Easton**, 'U Got The Look' hits Number 2 in the US. The sexy video fuels rumours that the two are an item.

Belinda Carlisle's 'Heaven Is A Place On Earth', from her second solo album, goes to Number 1 in December. It comes with a weird video directed by actress Diane Keaton. This year's Christmas hit is 'A Very Special Christmas', a collection of seasonal songs by Sting, Bruce Springsteen, **John Cougar Mellencamp**, **Eurythmics**, **Bon Jovi**, **Bryan Adams**, **Stevie Nicks**, **Whitney Houston**, **Bob Seger**, the **Pointer Sisters**, the **Pretenders**, **Madonna**, **Alison Moyet**, **U2** and **Run-DMC**. Proceeds go to the Special Olympics.

▲ Freddie Mercury sings with a new Queen - opera diva Monserrat Caballe.

Bad Boys Run Riot

"A rock band even nastier than the Beastie Boys is heading for Britain" – The *Daily Star*.

They called it 'street rock', this new rock beast dressed in **Aerosmith**, **Stones**, **Sex Pistols** and **New York Dolls** cast-offs that strutted out of Los Angeles and into the charts world-wide. Kind of a funny name considering that Los Angeles doesn't even have streets, just free-ways and airport runway-sized boulevards. Street rock was really nothing more than good old rock'n'roll played by younger bands. Only it was selling in amounts that most good old rock'n'roll bands could never have dreamed of.

Guns N'Roses, described as "The Stones meets The Sex Pistols", were the kings of street rock. They messed around with drugs, drink and sex at a time when heavy rock's godfathers (**Alice Cooper**, **Ozzy Osbourne**, Aerosmith et al) had all climbed on the wagon. "People think we're dangerous," declared vocalist Axl Rose, who put the band together in Los Angeles after hitch-hiking to Hollywood from Indiana, with old schoolfriend Izzy Stradlin'. Slash, Duff McKagan and Steven Adler from LA band **Road Crew** completed the line-up.

The mini-album they first released on their own Uzi Suicide label, 'Live?!*@ Like A Suicide', was re-released at the start of 1987 by Geffen, the label that won the battle to sign them. Guns N'Roses then got the opening slot on **Iron Maiden**'s US tour, but had to leave half-way through when vocalist Axl Rose lost his voice and guitarist Slash was packed off to Hawaii to sort out his drug problem.

In May, pugnacious Axl got into a fight with members of the Los Angeles Police Department. He didn't win and was taken to hospital,

recovering just in time for the band's headline appearance at the London Marquee in June. On the plane ride over, Slash almost set fire to himself when he fell asleep and dropped his cigarette on the seat. When the band received a bad write-up in a magazine, macho Axl demanded directions to their office so he could piss on the journalist's desk. "A rock band even nastier than the Beastie Boys", spouted the *Daily Star*, "Los Angeles band Guns N'Roses are led by the outrageous Axl Rose, who has an endearing habit of butchering dogs..."

In August, their debut album, 'Appetite For Destruction' was released. The rock press raved. Feminist groups protested about the 'robot rape' sleeve, the picture of a battered young woman with her underwear around her ankles. Several stores refused to stock the album. It promptly climbed the UK and US charts.

With their single 'Welcome To The Jungle' picking up airplay fast, the band toured the US this time with **Motley Crue**. The tour had to be cancelled when Crue bassist Nikki Sixx collapsed from a massive heroin overdose, and GN'R flew back to Britain, this time for their own headlining tour – with Fred Coury of **Cinderella** sitting in for drummer Steven Adler, who had broken his hand in a bar-room brawl. Their Hammersmith Odeon show was a sell-out.

At a time when the new wave of heavy metal was starting to become every bit as stale and clichéd as the old wave, Guns N' Roses injected a new vigour and intensity. They brought us back to the days when technicolour overdoses, stains on the carpet, policemen in the lobby and doctors at the hotel door in the early hours of the morning were all part of the show – the kind of things that separated Rock from Pop. And in the process they become the biggest rock'n'roll band of the decade.

Axl Rose, Guns N'Roses volatile lead singer, inflames the audience.

OCT 19 : Fifty billion pounds are wiped off share values as the Stock Market crashes on Black Monday. Wall Street also has its worst day ever with the Dow Jones index plummeting over 20 percent

Some of the strangest and most lasting images of the Eighties were of a young black man from Gary, Indiana. The single white sequinned glove. The oxygen chamber. The waxwork dummy. The white gauze face mask and dark glasses peering around hotel curtains. The gaunt, haunted face surgically altered to somewhere between **Diana Ross** and **LaToya**. The too-thin arm photographed around the space alien ET and around other best friends including Elizabeth Taylor, Bubbles the Chimp, Muscles the snake and a host of little boys.

Michael Jackson was born in August 1958, the seventh child of the large Jackson family. Barely out of kindergarten, he was pushed to the front of the **Jackson Five** and led them to the top of the charts during the golden years of Motown. By the age of 14 he was a millionaire. By the Eighties he had sold more records than any performer alive. One album alone, 'Thriller' (1982) sold over 40 million copies, topping the US charts for a mind-boggling 37 weeks and reaching the Number 1 spot in every major record-buying country in the world.

'Thriller' gave Jackson an unprecedented seven US Top 10 singles – an achievement that owed as much to the Eighties emphasis on visuals as to the songs. The first extract from the album – 'The Girl Is Mine', a somewhat mawkish duet with **Paul McCartney** – was well received, but it wasn't until the follow-up, 'Billie Jean', that it was obvious that we were dealing with something special.

As we were regularly informed by a sneering media, Jackson was at least two sandwiches and a sausage roll short of a picnic. But for all his eccentricities he was a shrewd businessman – a man who could buy the **Beatles'** publishing out from under Paul McCartney and secure a $5-million sponsorship deal from Pepsi when, as a Jehovah's Witness, he couldn't drink the stuff. He was also the person who received a telegram from the then US president, Ronald Reagan, declaring: "Your faith in God and adherence to traditional values are an inspiration to all of us". Maybe a little odd, but hardworking, moral, an all-American success story for the Eighties – Jackson was also its most talented singer, songwriter, dancer and all-round performer. The Nineties, alas, were to prove a roller-coaster ride.

▲ The press dubbed him 'Wacko Jacko' for his eccentric looks and lifestyle

Michael Jackson

Madonna

No-one quite embodies the Eighties like the 'Material Girl' from Detroit, **Madonna** Louise Ciccone. In the old days, if she was lucky, a girl like Madonna – young, attractive, could sing a bit, act a bit – might have been picked up by some male showbiz svengali and schooled for stardom. Madonna schooled herself. She didn't wait for luck. "She pulled herself up", as **Bette Midler** remarked in her introduction to Madonna's performance at Live Aid in 1985, "by her bra straps."

Smart, disciplined, ruthless and hard-working, Madonna's methods mimicked the yuppies whose rise and fortunes coincided with her own. She pushed, bullied and manipulated her way to the top. She mixed and matched philosophies with a defiantly Eighties abandon – the forceful woman who could pose for girlie mags, the whore who was Like A Virgin. Feminists didn't know whether to support her or condemn her for using her body to promote her career. Madonna didn't give a damn. "From when I was very young", she once said, "I just knew that being a girl and being charming in a feminine sort of way would get me a lot of things, and I have milked it for everything I could." Young girls rushed to buy into her look and her outlook – they understood.

Although her first album, 'Madonna' (1983) was a relative success, it was the next two – 'Like A Virgin' and 'True Blue' – that set the tone she was to follow through-

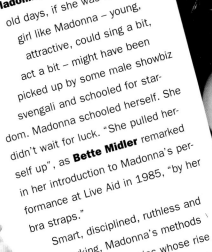

◄ Never before had one woman so dominated the charts. She paved the way for the likes of Janet Jackson, Whitney Houston and even Kylie.

out the Eighties. She marketed herself like any other youth-orientated commodity, using sex with impunity, updating herself regularly, altering her look in an attempt to keep at the forefront of fashion. She made movies that were slammed by the critics and videos that were slammed by the Vatican. She didn't care. She made statements that were slammed by everybody and she still didn't care. No other pop star, except maybe **Prince**, was as self-possessed as Madonna. Above all, the Eighties was the decade of the Self.

The music – you sometimes forget she made music – was for the most part a clever and disposable confection. But the symbols Madonna gave us were some of the strongest of the decade: the crucifixes, the coy lace undies, the muscles and, of course, the perfect belly button.

◄ Madonna, the Material Girl from Motor City, USA, pulled herself up by her bra-straps right to the top of the charts.

PriNCE

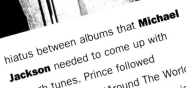

Minneapolis-born **Prince** Rogers Nelson – later Prince, and then plain Nelson – later Prince, and then plain As a teenager Prince led a migratory existence, running away from his stepfather to live with his father, then his aunt and on to various friends. His career has been similarly nomadic. Constantly exploring new musical avenues, surprising, annoying and entertaining people with whatever he comes up with.

He signed to Warner Brothers as an 18-year-old in 1978. His debut, 'For You' ran ridiculously over-budget and was not a commercial success, but it did hint at the young man's budding talent. He finally hit his commercial stride when his third album 'Dirty Mind' appeared in 1980. This was the same year that Ronald Reagan won a landslide victory in the US presidential elections; a time when America was engulfed in a wave of 'hard work', 'responsibility' and 'God-fearing family values' sponsored by the Moral Majority. Into this climate came Prince – a man who sang about sex with his sister and sex with just about everybody else, telling us all he wanted to do was to take off his clothes and party!

Prince followed up this success with the aptly titled 'Controversy'; another album that guaranteed that the eyes of the world were firmly fixed on his crotch area. A year later he released '1999' which gave him two major hit singles – 'Little Red Corvette' and the infectious title track – and a huge cross-over audience on which he was to unleash his masterpiece 'Purple Rain'.

The movie of that name, written by and starring Prince, was assumed to be his true life story. It opened in the summer of 1984 in the US and in the UK. Its soundtrack album sold a million copies in the first week of release and topped the US charts for the first of 24 weeks. It spawned three hit singles, two of them chart-toppers, one of them, 'When Doves Cry', was the biggest selling single of the year. In exemplary Eighties audio-visual fashion, the movie sold the music, the music sold the movie and the video sold both. Prince was a megastar.

A particularly prolific one at that. Not for him the four-year

hiatus between albums that **Michael Jackson** needed to come up with enough tunes. Prince followed 'Purple Rain' with 'Around The World In A Day' in 1985, 'Parade – Music From Under The Cherry Moon' in 1986, 'Sign O' The Times' in 1987, 'Lovesexy' in 1988 ('The Black Album' was also recorded that year but was recalled after being pressed up) and the soundtrack to the movie *Batman* in 1989.

He also found time to write songs for his female entourage: **Sheila E**, **Apollonia**, **Wendy and Lisa** and **Sheena Easton**. Other Prince-penned hits included the **Bangles**' 'Manic Monday', **Chaka Khan**'s 'I Feel For You' and **Sinead O'Connor**'s version of 'Nothing Compares 2 U', the latter two both peaked at Number 1 in Britain, higher than any of his own material.

What with outputting an LP every year, regularly touring, starring in films and writing/producing hits for his various protégés, it was inevitable that Prince's work was often inconsistent. But, the man himself was always fascinating: on a musical and mythical level he continued to invent and re-invent himself – he was the ultimate Eighties self-made hero.

▼ Prince in typical sexy pose. The man from Minneapolis was synonymous with sex and sensuality.

◀ When Prince was ten years old, his parents took him to see James Brown play, an influence that lives on in Prince's excellent live shows.

George Michael spent the first part of the decade making bubblegum funk-pop and frothy fun videos. He spent the second half making his name as a serious singer and songwriter, and both halves at the top of the charts. His was one of the most successful careers of the Eighties and, in many ways, one of the most representative.

Georgious Panayiotou first started singing with schoolfriend Andrew Ridgeley when they went to the same suburban London state school at the age of 16. It was 1979. Britain was suffering a recession; punk was at its zenith. George and Andrew just wanted to have fun: the antithesis to punk, they were well-dressed, well-coiffured, their nails and teeth were sparkling clean. The pair formed a band with the prophetically yuppie name the **Executive** before settling on **Wham!** In a burst of Thatcheresque enterprise, they got on their bike, hired a portable studio and made demos in Andrew's parents' living room – among them a song entitled 'Wham! Rap (Enjoy What You Do)' which espoused a blithe optimism that had all but vanished from Britain at this time.

Wham! were nice, smart, normal boys-next-door – attractive, unthreatening, photogenic fun. Teen magazines, tabloids, TV loved them. The little girls adored them. Their debut pop-dance album, cheerily titled 'Fantastic', entered the UK charts in the summer of 1983 at Number 1.

In a designer decade, Wham! were the perfect designer band (George the perfect designer stubble!) Like most successful pop bands, a perfect commodity. But unlike earlier pop bands, they weren't designed by outsiders, they manufactured themselves, and George was increasingly the one at the drawing board. While he was still in Wham! he released his first solo single – 'Careless Whisper' – deemed too serious for the duo. The song topped both the US and UK charts for three weeks and won him the prestigious Ivor Novello Award for Songwriter Of The Year.

The cut-off point for Wham! probably came with Live Aid in 1985. George, who had already duetted with **Smokey Robinson** and **Stevie Wonder**, performed without Andrew but with **Elton John**. They continued the collaboration on Elton's album later in the year. By the year's end, Wham! had decided to split.

George's solo debut, the resolutely grown-up album 'Faith', spent 12 weeks at the top of the US charts, selling more than eight million copies and won him a second Ivor Novello Award and a Grammy for Album Of The Year. Before long, the Sunday Times had named him as one of the richest men in Britain. At the end of the decade, the immigrants' son from north London was worth, they said, £65 million.

◀ George Michael – once known as the blond half of Wham! – forged a successful solo career as a respected singer-songwriter.

George Michael

Trouble at the Milli

It couldn't fail really. German writer/producer Frank Farian, the man who masterminded the massively successful Seventies pop band **Boney M**, discovered two gorgeous black hunks, Rob Pilatus and Fabrice Morvan, and **Milli Vanilli** came into being. Soon they sounded as good as they looked. Their debut album, 'All Or Nothing', made the UK Top 10. Retitled 'Girl You Know It's True' for American release, it sold six million copies in the US alone and gave them three Number 1 singles: 'Baby Don't Forget My Number', 'Girl I'm

Milli Vanilli – the number one lip-synchers of the Eighties.

Gonna Miss You' and 'Blame It On The Rain'. The duo were presented with the Grammy award for Best New Artist. That was before being told they had to give their trophy back.

Farian had just revealed that the album was one of the biggest scams of the Eighties rock scene. Neither of the two photogenic lip-synchers, he announced, actually sang on the album. The entire record had been made with faceless German session musicians. Milli Vanilli, one of the biggest pop sensations of 1989, made an ignominious exit.

1989 was a turbulent year for Guns N'Roses (pictured: lead guitarist Slash). Arrests, fights, accusations of racism and homophobia, and a celebrated gig opening for the Stones where Axl threatened to fire the whole band.

---

wicked, fiddling Uncle Ernie. But who is cast truest to type?

With their new album 'Disintegration' at Number 3 in the UK and climbing into the US Top 10, the **Cure** launch their biggest American tour in August amid rumours that it will be their last. (Robert Smith has fired Lol Tolhurst and is insisting the band sails to the States on the QE2 since he's afraid of flying). The reviewer from *Rolling Stone* catches the basic contradiction of a Cure concert better than anyone else, "Never before had so many people enjoyed having so little fun at a rock show." Also in August, **Liza Minnelli** has her first British Top 10 hit for her collaboration with the **Pet Shop Boys** on 'Losing My Mind'. **Tears For Fears** make the Top 5 in the UK and the US with their psychedelic **Beatles**-ish 'Sowing The

Seeds Of Love'. Heart-throb **Chris Isaak** releases his third album, 'Heart Shaped World'; it features the song 'Wicked Game', used in both the TV movie, *The Preppie Murder*, and the ultra-weird David Lynch film *Wild At Heart*. Following **McCartney**'s lead, **Bon Jovi** release their album 'New Jersey' in the USSR on the government's Melodiya label; they're paid the maximum Soviet licensing fee of $9600.

Guns N'Roses guitarist Izzy Stradlin' is arrested and charged with urinating in the aisle of an aeroplane, an offence which is compounded by his smoking in the No Smoking section. In September, Izzy is involved in a fist-fight with **Motley Crue** vocalist Vince Neil backstage at the *MTV Awards*. The Crue – whose album 'Dr Feelgood' spends two weeks at the top of the US charts and is also

JANUARY 1: A TV movie, The Karen Carpenter Story, revives interest in the Carpenters; a Greatest Hits album is released and tops the UK charts.

FEBRUARY: Former folk-pop star Cat Stevens, now known by his Moslem name Yusuf Islam, is back in the news after supporting the Iranian fatwa, or death sentence, on author Salman Rushdie.

JUNE 2: Bill Wyman of the Rolling Stones, 52, marries Mandy Smith, 18, after dating her for five years.

JULY: Blues great John Lee Hooker makes his comeback with an album, 'The Healer'.

JULY: LaToya Jackson's husband and manager Jack Gordon claims that Michael Jackson offered his sister $5 million not to publish her autobiography, Growing Up In The Jackson Family.

SEPTEMBER 22: Songwriter Irving Berlin dies of natural causes. He is 101 years old.

▲ Tanks poured into Tiananmen Square in Beijing in June as troops opened fire on demonstrators.

Number 4 in the UK this month – are there to present the heavy metal award. The Best Video Of The Year Award goes to **Neil Young**'s 'This Note's For You' – in spite of MTV having banned it when it first came out in 1988.

Also in September, the **Bangles** split up. And geriatric rockers **Jefferson Airplane** reform – instantly winning *Rolling Stone*'s Most Unwelcome Comeback award. The album 'Jefferson Airplane' features the classic but now wizened Sixties line-up of Grace Slick, Paul Kantner, Marty Balin, Jorma Kaukonen and Jack Casady but all is not as chummy as it seems; many of the members recorded their tracks individually and mailed them in to the producer. Another sad old rocker who refuses to mellow with age is **Ozzy Osbourne**, who is arrested and charged with attempting to kill his wife Sharon. He is released on condition he enrols on a detoxification programme. His wife subsequently drops all charges.

Opening for the **Rolling Stones** at the LA Coliseum in October, Axl Rose of **Guns N'Roses** fires the rest of the band on stage for, he alleges, "dancing with Mr Brownstone" –

meaning they've been messing around with serious drugs. He announces, "This may be my last gig with Guns N'Roses." Meanwhile, wholesome **Kate Bush**'s album 'The Sensual World' is Number 2 in the UK in October. It features the suddenly fashionable **Trio Bulgarka**, the much-lauded traditional Bulgarian singers with their Macbethian cackles and surreal harmonies, as well as classical music's new *enfant terrible*, violinist **Nigel Kennedy**. Meanwhile in the US, **Janet Jackson**'s 'Rhythm Nation 1814' spends the first of four weeks at Number 1. After years of decline, the **B52s** have a Top 5 US hit in November with the Don Was-produced 'Love Shack', and a Top 10 UK and US album, 'Cosmic Thing'. The same month, **Chris Rea**'s 'Road To Hell' album – its title song supposedly inspired by the London orbital M25 motorway – is the British Number 1. **Lenny Kravitz** releases his debut album, 'Let Love Rule' – a mix of punk, soul, heavy rock, funk

and psychedelia. It includes a song he wrote with his new wife Lisa Bonet, an actress on *The Cosby Show*.

Rockers Against Drug And Alcohol Abuse is a club with a growing membership – **Bon Jovi**, **Skid Row**, the **Scorpions** plus the bands from the Moscow Music Peace Festival – release an album of cover songs in December, 'Stairway To Heaven/Highway To Hell'. Proceeds go to the Make A Difference Foundation. Also in December, fellow Christians **Van Morrison** and **Cliff Richard** have a hit with their spiritual duet, 'Whenever God Shines His Light'. And Cliff appears on a second version of 'Do They Know It's Christmas?' produced by Stock, Aitken & Waterman. **Band Aid II** also features **Kylie Minogue**, **Jason Donovan**, Chris Rea, **Sonia**, **Lisa Stansfield**, **Marti Pellow** of **Wet Wet Wet** and **Matt Goss** of **Bros**. It enters the UK charts at Number 1.

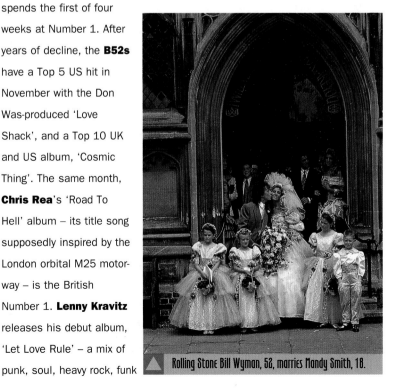

▲ Rolling Stone Bill Wyman, 52, marries Mandy Smith, 18.

'I'm ready for what's next'

The Nineties

In the Nineties, the remix culture of the late Eighties spread like wildfire. It was time for artists and labels to capitalize even further on the CD boom by issuing re-mastered versions of back catalogue albums. No recording was sacred. Established superstars such as **Eric Clapton** and **Rod Stewart** received their biggest career boosts in years with the release of acoustic re-workings of old material recorded for MTV's Unplugged series. And, for a new generation of artists, the back pages of musical history became a treasure trove of sounds and textures to be sampled.

This trend was most obvious in European house music and American hip hop, which both relied heavily on sampled funk grooves and beats. But many artists, working outside the dance and rap fields, also derived their sound from blends of earlier music even if they didn't use actual samples. For instance, groups such as **Crowded House**, **World Party** and **Oasis** owed an enormous debt to the **Beatles**, though each personalized their sound by skilfully weaving the Beatles influence in among other stylistic shadings, from psychedelia to punk.

As the decade progressed, litigation became an increasingly significant aspect of the music industry, with artists suing labels, fans suing artists and music being increasingly drowned out by the sound of lawyers cackling with glee. All areas of operation in the industry allowed themselves to be fitted up with legal straitjackets — while those responsible for its artistic development busied themselves wringing the last drop of profit from recycled product.

With the dominance worldwide of MTV, virtually the only acts to achieve widesprea success were to be those for whom music came, with a few exceptions, a poor second to dance. As **Buggles** had predicted a decade earlier, video had effectively killed off the radio star, though there were greater ironies than that. In the Sixties, audiences would go to see tours such as the Stax-Atlantic revues, in which a succession of great singers would take the front of the stage while go-go dancers frugged away on raised platforms behind. By the Nineties the dancers had moved to the front of the stage, while many singers were not on the stage at all. Indeed some, as in the case of Milli Vanilli, were permanently in some recording studio back in Germany. Some called this progress.

1990s

Andy Gill

◄ U2: 'Zoo Station'

1990

In 1990, music was less self-contained than it had been for many years and became increasingly dependent on outside influences such as movie tie-ins and adverts.

Indeed a substantial proportion of the year's Number 1 hit singles profited from connections with commercials (**Steve Miller Band**'s 'The Joker', Number 1 a mere 17 years after its first release), movies (the **Righteous Brothers**' 'Unchained Melody', 25 years after its first release, and **Partners In Kryme**'s 'Turtle Power'), and even from the year's soccer World Cup, for which **New Order** teamed up with the England football squad to score their first-ever UK Number 1 hit with 'World In Motion'.

There was still room for a few quality hits throughout the year, however, most notably **Sinead O'Connor**'s spellbinding interpretation of a **Prince** song, 'Nothing Compares 2 U', and **Elton John**'s first Number 1, 'Sacrifice', in a career stretching back two decades. The most successful dance-oriented Number 1s came from **Snap!**, whose 'The Power' became a staple of sports TV run-downs, and **Adamski**'s 'Killer', which first introduced the vocal talent of the statuesque **Seal** to the world. The year also saw the rebirth of new age music, this time in the unlikely guise of 'ambient techno' acts like the **Orb** and the **Grid**. And, sensitive as ever to the subtle changes in the dance market, the **KLF** pulled off the double coup of having a UK hit single with 'What Time Is Love?' whilst releasing a successful album of ambient new age music, 'Chill Out', with a cover which spoofed **Pink Floyd**'s 'Atom Heart Mother'.

In an unpredictable commercial atmosphere, holding operations were the order of the day for established artists such as **David Bowie** and **Bob Dylan**, who embarked upon tours showcasing the wealth of their back catalogues; while others, such as **Lou Reed**, **Robert Plant** and **Jimmy Page** effected high-profile reunions of their old bands, namely the **Velvet Underground** and **Led Zeppelin**, albeit on a strictly temporary basis. As the year progressed, sales patterns suggested the American market, in particular, was splitting along racial lines like society itself. Hip hop and upscale soul's dominance of the black market was mirrored by the rise to prominence in the US pop album charts of 'New Country' acts such as **Garth Brooks**, **Clint Black**, **K T Oslin** and **Mary-Chapin Carpenter**. The baffling cross-market success of baggy-trousered rapper **MC Hammer** however, indicated that, with a catchy funk sample – in his case, lifted from **Rick James** – and a daft enough dance, anything was possible. The decade starts as it means to go on, with legal action uppermost in

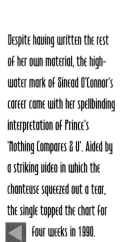

Outselling even Michael Jackson, Garth Brooks spearheaded the 'New Country' boom with a winning blend of soft rockabilly and old-style traditionalist country attitude which found widespread populist appeal in an American market increasingly split along racial lines.

Despite having written the rest of her own material, the high-water mark of Sinead O'Connor's career came with her spellbinding interpretation of Prince's 'Nothing Compares 2 U'. Aided by a striking video in which the chanteuse squeezed out a tear, the single topped the chart for four weeks in 1990.

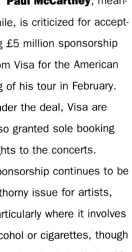

Doyens of the Manchester 'baggy' indie-dance scene, the Stone Roses kept up rock'n'roll's laissez-faire attitude to law and order, making the decade's first pop appearance in court on charges of criminal damage.

While their own star waned steadily through the decade, New Kids On The Block served as the prototype for successive waves of conveyor-belt pop idols, the assiduous promotion of which obscured the rapidly rising popularity of more fringe musical styles, like rap.

industry minds. On January 31, the **Stone Roses** get their claim in early to be the first pop group of the new decade to appear in court, when they appear on charges of doing criminal damage to their former record label head's car and offices. Enraged by the man's opportunist reissue of a their 1987 track, 'Sally Cinnamon', in order to cash in on their new fame, the band are accused of splattering paint on his property. They are granted conditional bail.

Paul McCartney, meanwhile, is criticized for accepting £5 million sponsorship from Visa for the American leg of his tour in February. Under the deal, Visa are also granted sole booking rights to the concerts. Sponsorship continues to be a thorny issue for artists, particularly where it involves alcohol or cigarettes, though many bands claim that, with-

out the ability to underwrite tours in this manner, it would be difficult to stage concerts and no one would get to see them.

Things ain't what they used to be in the industry generally. An infatuation with new formats obscures the fact that globally the record industry is not investing as much money in new blood as it should. Satisfied with the tried and tested conveyor-belt approach which produces endless

batches of teen idols in the mould of **New Kids On The Block**, the business fails to acknowledge the rise in popularity of alternative musics, most notably rap, which will dominate charts as the decade progresses.

Future business problems are signalled by the failure of in-store music compilation facilities such as Personics – which allows the public to make up its own compilation cassettes from a range of music – to make significant headway in either the US or UK markets. A good idea in theory, in practice the facility depends too heavily on being able to offer as wide a selection of music as possible. The system is doomed after several record companies decline to let their artists' material be available for compilation – a precedent set to bedevil future format launches.

Belatedly, in February, BBC Radio 1 announces its intention to alter its notorious playlist, so that it more accurately reflects the increasing chart dominance of dance-oriented singles. One man who will not be doing too much dancing in the fore-

seeable future, however, is rebel-rocker **Billy Idol**, whose right leg has been so badly crushed in a motorbike accident this month that amputation has to be considered. Seven hours of surgery save the leg, but he loses a prominent part in Oliver Stone's bio-pic about the **Doors**. A month later, **Gloria Estefan** suffers serious spinal injuries when her tour bus crashes in Pennsylvania. She will recover but the injury puts her out of action for the rest of the year.

Other stars are more fortunate: **Bruce Springsteen** and Patti Scialfa announce the impending arrival of a little Springsteen, while **Bob Dylan** plays what prove to be his best British live shows in years in a short February season at the Hammersmith Odeon. **Prince** starts work on yet another movie, *Graffiti Bridge* and, in March, **David Bowie** starts his Sound And Vision world tour in Quebec, just one of several career retrospectives planned for 1990. At an AIDS benefit in America,

American Rap Group Battles Obscenity Charges

The unhappy relationship between rap music and the law reached a new low in August 1990 when Luther Campbell, leader of rap group **2 Live Crew**, was arrested on obscenity charges after a performance in Hollywood, Florida.

This was just the latest in a series of incidents which had been dogging the group's provocative live shows: 2 Live's act featured graphically simulated sex-play between the group, their dancers and their female fans. In Boston, earlier in the year, two shows were initially cancelled, then reprieved at the last minute. When they received permission to play in the city, a local councillor unsuccessfully demanded that they should only be allowed to

Them so horny: 2 Live Crew, Banned In The USA.

play in the city's red light district. On another occasion, three band members were arrested after performing at an 'adults only' show.

Trouble had been building for 29-year-old Campbell – who was once sued for $300 million by *Star Wars* director George Lucas for using the stage name Luke Skyywalker – ever since the release of the group's album 'As Nasty As They Wanna Be', which boasted several sexually-explicit raps like the single, 'Me So Horny', a million seller despite a blanket airplay ban. Judges in Florida and Greenville, South Carolina, declared the LP obscene, resulting in the prosecution of seven record shop owners for selling the offending article. It wasn't the first time that 2 Live Crew's records had fallen foul of the law. In 1987, an 18-year-old shop assistant, Laura Ragsdale, was arrested for selling the group's record 'It's What You Want' to a minor; charges were eventually thrown out of court, but the publicity helped start the

group's bandwagon rolling.

Though this latest action resulted in the 47-store HMV chain in Canada and the 117-store Western Merchandisers chain removing the album from their racks, both the single and album profited from the furore, with the latter selling an estimated two million copies. Small wonder that Campbell, whose assets for 1989 were estimated at a cool $11 million, is now one of Florida's more successful self-made black businessmen, with three record labels, a studio, a construction company, three discos and various real estate investments in his portfolio.

Born-again Christian Jack Thompson, a Miami attorney, has been a prime mover in agitations against Campbell's group, whose music he believes "comes straight from hell and smells like smoke", claiming it fosters "the brutalization of women and children". One Miami DJ was harassed so badly by attorney Thompson that he eventually won a court order preventing him from even mentioning his name. The conservative pressure group the American Family Association has also lobbied strongly against the album, which was defended on First Amendment free-speech grounds by Civil Liberties campaigners and rock stars such as **David Bowie** and **Bruce Springsteen**. The latter even allowed the 2 Live Crew to sample his most famous song for their protest single 'Banned In The USA', which went straight into the American Top 20.

In November, Campbell and the Crew were acquitted of obscenity charges after prosecuting attorney John Jolly declined to produce expert witnesses to testify as to the album's obscenity, deeming it self-evident. According to him, the facts spoke for themselves.

Curtis Mayfield, tragically paralyzed by collapsing equipment at an outdoor show in New York.

Curtis Mayfield Paralyzed in Stage Accident

Legendary soul singer and songwriter **Curtis Mayfield** was paralyzed from the neck down after a lighting rig collapsed on him at an outdoor concert in Brooklyn, New York, on August 13, 1990.

The former **Impressions** lead singer, best known for his single 'Move On Up' and the soundtrack to the film *Superfly*, was all set to perform at a Martin Luther King memorial concert at Wingate High School football field in Flatbush, Brooklyn, when a strong gust of wind dislodged unstable scaffolding, knocking overhead lights down on top of Mayfield and seven others. Mart Markowitz, the New York State Senator who organized the concert, blamed the weather rather than negligence: "As Mayfield was about to come onstage, an overwhelming wind hit us and blew the speakers off the stage, and the lighting crashed down".

The 48-year-old singer was rushed to the local King's County Hospital, where it was discovered that the accident had left him with a broken neck, three shattered vertebrae and serious head injuries. He was subsequently transferred to the Shepherd Spinal Center near his home in Atlanta, Georgia. Ironically, the accident occurred the day before Mayfield's 'Return Of Superfly' soundtrack — featuring a version of the famous title track recorded with rap star **Ice-T** – was due to be released by Capitol Records. As if to prove it never rains but it pours, the singer's home was burnt down shortly after the tragic accident. On the good news front, stars from all branches of the music industry pledged to contribute to two tribute albums of Mayfield's songs, the proceeds of which, it's hoped, will help offset huge medical bills.

Nelson Mandela with wife Winnie: The International Tribute To A Free South Africa Concert on April 16 was one of the year's most invigorating and wide-ranging concert parties at ▼ Wembley Stadium.

meanwhile, **Patti Smith** appears on stage for the first time in 12 years; she sings 'Power To The People' and 'A Hard Rain's Gonna Fall'. In one of the more bizarre turn-ups in a career noted for unorthodoxy, **Frank Zappa** is briefly appointed Cultural Liaison Officer for Czechoslovakia. The new Czech president, playwright Vaclav Havel, is, like many of his countrymen, a **Mothers Of Invention** fan of long standing and offers Zappa the post when the composer visits the newly-capitalist country to set up distribution for his record labels. Allegedly following pressure by the US government, Havel is subsequently forced to rescind the appointment.

Spring 1990 brings in a new mood of altruism with the staging of two tribute concerts in Britain. On April 16, Nelson Mandela's Birthday Tribute Concert takes place at Wembley in front of the man himself: two house bands organized by George Duke and Daniel Lanois are used to back a variety of artists including **Simple Minds**, **Bonnie Raitt**, **Peter Gabriel**, **Neil Young**, **Tracy Chapman**, **Anita Baker** and the **Neville Brothers**. On May 5, the John Lennon Tribute Concert gets underway, featuring **Yoko Ono**, **Lou Reed**, **Joe Cocker**, the **Christians**, **Wet Wet Wet**, **Terence Trent D'Arby**, **Kylie Minogue**, **Hall & Oates** and **Lenny Kravitz**, and is televized live from Liverpool. In less generous mood, **Genesis** are criticized in April for having caravan and tent-dwellers evicted from their Scottish estate, Pennyghael, on Mull.

The British government, meanwhile, continues its attack upon acid-house raves, with the third and final reading, in May, of the Public Entertainments (Increased Penalties) Bill. Under this measure, the holding of an unlicensed function becomes a criminal rather than civil offence, with increased penalties to match: offenders will be liable to fines of up to £20,000, six months' imprisonment and confiscation of equipment. May 27 sees the staging on Spike Island in Cheshire of an outdoor concert by the **Stone Roses**, their final appearance before an extended period out of the limelight which will allow copyists like the **Charlatans** to steal

their 'Madchester' (used to describe the crazy scene in Manchester at this time) thunder. This the Charlatans do very successfully, when they enter the UK album chart at Number 1 with their debut 'Some Friendly'. At the annual Glastonbury Festival in June, however, music is upstaged by a pitched battle between security guards and the 'peace convoy' travellers, who claim the right to free attendance.

Perhaps the most surprising of the many band reunions that take place during the decade is that of the **Velvet Underground**, whose members re-group to attend an Andy Warhol retrospective on June 15 in Paris, at which they perform a 15-minute version of the old Velvets classic 'Heroin'. The summer of big outdoor concerts continues with

Roger Waters' staging of *The Wall* at Potzdamer Platz, adjacent to the former Berlin Wall and near the site of Hitler's bunker. Heavy with the irony of building another wall – only to knock it all down again as the show proceeds – the concert proceeds with contributions from the **Band**, **Van Morrison**, **Sinead O'Connor** and **Bryan Adams**. **Jimmy Page** and **Robert Plant**, meanwhile, reunite at Knebworth, the site of **Led Zeppelin**'s final performance 11 years earlier, in an all-British show which also stars **Eric Clapton**, **Elton John**, **Cliff Richard**, **Status Quo**, **Genesis**, **Dire Straits**, **Paul McCartney** and **Pink Floyd**.

Radio 1 continues to remodel itself: in July, the BPI (British Phonographic Institute) loses control of the station's chart, which has

The February demonstration in Trafalgar Square against the 'Bright Bill' was but the first of a succession of protests against increasingly illiberal establishment measures aimed at restricting the right to party.

Thousands Protest at New Bill

These days in the UK, you really do have to fight for the right to party. More than 5,000 ravers attended a demonstration in Trafalgar Square in February 1990 to protest against MP Graham Bright's proposed new bill aimed at criminalizing unlicensed acid-house parties.

The demo was masterminded by Worldwide Productions CEO Tony Colston-Hayter – known to the tabloids as 'Acid's Mr Big' – who persuaded the organizers of events such as Sunrise, Biology, Energy, World Dance and Back To The Future to join forces in the Freedom To Party Campaign. In order to legitimize their functions if the bill became law, Colston-Hayter has also set up ADPPro (the Association of Dance Party Promoters) as an umbrella organization for rave organizers.

Acid-house dances originally became known as parties because

the British Public Entertainment Act of 1982 made it illegal to hold public entertainment without a licence. As private parties, these events went beyond the long arm of the law and were therefore legal. Recently, however, local councils have been encouraged to make use of the Private Places of Entertainments Act of 1967 (a locally-enforcable act originally used by London councils to shut down cinemas showing pornography), which makes it illegal to hold a private entertainment for financial gain without obtaining a licence. Mr Bright's private member's bill, the Public Entertainments (Increased Penalties) Bill, proposed changing the holding of unlicensed functions from a civil to a criminal offence, which could result in massive fines, confiscation of equipment and up to six months' imprisonment.

ROCK'N'ROLL
record

JANUARY 19: Mel Appleby of sibling singing duo Mel & Kim dies of pneumonia.

APRIL: Lou Reed and John Cale team up for the first time since the Velvet Underground to pay tribute to Andy Warhol with 'Songs For Drella'.

MAY: Madonna releases 'I'm Breathless'. One of three spin-off soundtrack albums connected to the Dick Tracy movie, it features tracks written by Stephen Sondheim.

JUNE 9: 'Hold On' by Wilson Phillips hits the US Number 1 slot exactly 25 years after The Beach Boys were at the top with 'Help Me Rhonda'.

AUGUST 27: Stevie Ray Vaughan dies in a helicopter crash, aged 35.

OCTOBER: The Red Hot And Blue AIDS Awareness Project releases its first album, a compilation of Cole Porter covers.

Roger Waters Stages The Wall in Berlin

One of the largest concerts in memory was held on July 21 1990 at Potzdamer Platz in Berlin, the original site of Hitler's Bunker, when former **Pink Floyd** songwriter **Roger Waters** staged an extravagant version of the group's meisterwork *The Wall* in front of about 200,000 people.

Like Woodstock, the event was declared a free concert after thousands of tickets had already been sold, many to East Germans who could ill afford the expense. An all-star cast, including **Van Morrison**, **Bryan Adams**, **Sinead O'Connor** and the **Band**, performed selections from the album, as an enormous fake wall 600 feet long and 100 feet high, made up of 2,600 blocks of styrofoam, was built in front of the stage and then knocked down for the finale.

Gerald Scarfe constructed enormous animated

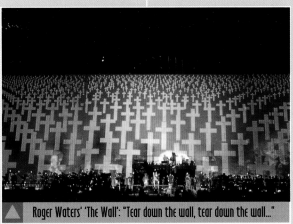

▲ Roger Waters' 'The Wall': "Tear down the wall, tear down the wall..."

grotesques, including a towering teacher-hammer figure and a six-storey pig specially for the event, which was dogged by power failures. For reasons best known to himself, singer **Thomas Dolby** performed a bungee-jump during a dramatized version of Franz Kafka's *The Trial* featuring appearances from such renowned thespians as Albert Finney and Tim Curry. War hero, Group Captain Leonard Cheshire, VC, served as MC, introducing the event as a flock of mini-parachutes were launched into the air, and other celebrities played cameo roles – including Jerry Hall, who made her appearance during the song 'Oh My God, What A Fabulous Room'. Ironically, one of the last remaining sections of the Berlin Wall functioned as a backstage barrier, separating the stars from the prying attentions of the audience.

been compiled for it by Gallup; in future, the chart will be compiled by a *Music Week* magazine offshoot called the Chart Information Network. Also in July, **Tom Waits** wins his case against Frito-Lay for using a Waits soundalike in radio ads. He receives a cool $2,475,000 compensation. **Curtis Mayfield** is less fortunate: in August, at an outdoor concert in Brooklyn commemorating Martin Luther King, a lighting rig falls on the singer, paralyzing him from the neck down.

In October, heavy metal group **Judas Priest** are cleared of bizarre charges – relatives claim that a snatch of backward-played vocals on

one of their tracks had caused the attempted suicide of two of their American fans. One fan died by self-inflicted shotgun blast, while the other needed wholesale reconstructive surgery after he blew his face off. Sadly, the surviving fan was to successfully commit suicide three years later.

Also in October, the **Stone Roses**' case from the beginning of the year concludes with them being fined £12,000. And after an unbroken stretch of four and a half consecutive years in the Top 100, producers Stock, Aitken & Waterman find themselves drifting in a month when they are completely unrepresented by any

single in the chart.

In November, on the other hand, **MC Hammer** completes an unbroken stretch of 21 weeks atop the US LP charts with 'Please Hammer Don't Hurt 'Em', which has sold somewhere in the region of six million copies during its tenure at the top. Conversely, **Milli Vanilli**, are ordered to hand back the Grammy Awards they won last year, after the discovery that they didn't sing on their own records. **2 Live Crew**, meanwhile, are acquitted of obscenity charges, paradoxically, a mere three weeks after a record retailer was convicted for selling 'obscene material' in the form of their album.

1990 – HEADLINE NEWS   DEC 17 : Aristide becomes Haiti's first democratically elected President

1990s Trash

In the Nineties, the usual rock-biz staples of sex, drugs and Rolls Royces in the swimming pool were overshadowed by sleazy business deals that echoed the payola scandals that had engulfed rock'n'roll pioneer DJ Alan Freed decades earlier.

The old sex and drugs story continued to run although increasingly celebrities were let off the hook by the American psychological industry and confessional talk-shows such as *Oprah* and *Donahue*, which allowed them to blame all their faults on supposed depredations experienced in childhood. Secluded in substance-abuse-treatment centres like the Betty Ford Clinic, these fallen stars were just about living proof that there was one law for the famous and another for the little people.

A case in point: Motown funk star **Rick James**, the man responsible for, among other things, the riff behind **MC Hammer**'s 'U Can't Touch This', was convicted in November 1993, along with his girlfriend Tanya Anne Hijazi, of drug and sex offences committed upon a female 'sex slave' against her will. While the unknown Hijazi ended up serving time, Rick's expensive attorney secured his client the relatively easy option of attending a rehabilitation programme.

The offence itself was by no means an isolated incident, with rappers especially prone to charges of sexual assault. Movie-star rapper **Tupac Shakur** (aka **2-Pac**) was accused with friends of gang-rape, while **Jodeci** singers Kay Cee and DeVante Swing faced charges of aggravated criminal sexual contact and unlawful possession of weapons after threatening two teenage girls who had refused to accommodate their sexual desires.

Elsewhere, celebrities such as **Axl Rose** and **Michael Jackson** sought forgiveness for eccentric or unruly behaviour by accusing their parents of abusing them as children – though such claims became suspect in the mid-Nineties when the phenomenon of False Memory Syndrome became as notorious as anything the stars might have done. Whatever its basis, Jackson's multi-million-dollar pay-off to Jordy Chandler, the teenage boy who accused him of sexual assault, did nothing to diminish doubts about the case. Suspicions were further exacerbated when former bodyguards, housekeepers and even Jackson's sister **LaToya** came forward – all eager to provide their own confirmation of the rumours, for the right price! Certainly, when Jackson sensationally married **Elvis Presley**'s daughter Lisa Marie in 1994, a by-now sceptical world simply smirked at what

▲ LaToya Jackson seemed eager to spill her brother's beans, for the right price.

▲ Tupac Shakur's self-proclaimed 'Thug Life' resulted in charges of sexual assault.

▶ Jimmy Somerville fought back against a feeble but influential wave of homophobia.

appeared to be a cynical ruse to stress the star's supposed heterosexual manliness and deflect attention away from earlier problems. The younger Presley's membership of the Scientology cult added an extra layer of tabloid interest to this bizarre union which quickly appeared to be on the rocks.

Most male stars, with the honourable exceptions of **Jimmy Somerville**, **Elton John**, **Erasure**'s Andy Bell and the **Pet Shop Boys**' Neil Tennant, were reluctant to admit to any other than the most red-blooded hetero instincts, and with good reason: the lingering view of AIDS as a 'gay

advocated the killing of homosexuals, while **Shabba Ranks** suffered several career traumas when TV shows on both sides of the Atlantic boycotted him after he voiced medieval views on sexuality.

Female sexuality, on the other hand, experienced something of a golden age of libertarianism in the Nineties. Lesbianism didn't seem to excite the same level of distaste as male homosexuality, while female rockers brought a new explicitness to expressions of their sexuality. **Madonna**'s Sex book of 1992 was the most high-profile incident in this new sex war, though equally important inroads were made by **Liz Phair**, who brought a bracing frankness to her discussion of inter-gender relationships, and **L7**'s Donita Sparkes, who bared her butt on British TV's The Word. Trash hit rock bottom with the release of **Nine Inch Nails**' Trent Reznor's promotional video featuring gruesome sado-masochistic acts including genital mutilation. Immediately banned in the UK, it was not that much of a surprise from the man who chose to record his album 'The Downward Spiral' in the house where the Manson Family disembowelled Sharon Tate.

Drug stories became commonplace again in the Nineties although compared to the jet-set, high-living Seventies when cocaine was still a rich people's thing, the potent cocaine derivative, crack, caused enormous social problems amongst the underprivileged black community in America. For white kids, the drug of choice at this time was heroin. As the Seattle-based grunge sound grew in influence, so the city's widespread smack habit became pathetically fashionable despite a string of overdose deaths among musicians. Even such clean-cut types as the **Lemonheads**'

Evan Dando admitted to usage.

In Britain, the dance underground found a new favourite drug, the amphetamine derivative MDMA, or Ecstasy, which enabled ravers to

▲ L7's Donita Sparkes bared her butt for feminism on TV's The Word.

dance all night in a non-stop feverish whirl. Dance tracks of the era often contained sly allusions to the drug, most notably in the **Shamen**'s claim, in 'Ebeneezer Goode', that "Es are good"; though more recent medical findings suggest that the supposedly benign 'love drug' may turn out to have more harmful long-term effects than originally thought.

The record industry had its own problems. While the activities of American pluggers and promoters have always been covered by a thin film of sleaze, in Britain industry bodies have usually tried to ensure that their dealings have been above board. Nevertheless, the Nineties saw both London Records and Rhythm King Records being fined substantial sums for chart-hyping, while even the beleaguered BRIT Awards, the industry's equivalent of the American Grammies, was subject in 1993 to accusations of attempted vote-rigging, the very year in which its new 'electoral college' was supposed to make such activities impossible.

▲ The Lemonheads' Evan Dando: the cleanest cut heroin user in rock?

plague' encouraged a feeble but nevertheless influential wave of homophobia from acts as disparately dim as **Marky Mark** and the **Happy Mondays**. The most deep-rooted and extreme attitudes belonged to the Jamaican ragga community: **Buju Banton** was excoriated for his single 'Boom By-By', which

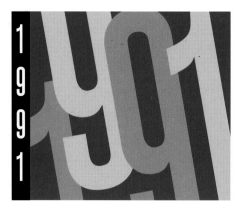

1991 was the Year Of Death, in which more rock legends than ever before expired. This increasing number of rings on the tree trunk of rock-'n'roll was highlighted by the growing ill health afflicting once youthful artists who had imperceptibly moved into middle-age.

On a musical level, rock's midlife crisis was symbolized by a succession of sub-standard album releases from middle-aged AOR acts like **Genesis**, **Dire Straits**, **Sting**, **Eric Clapton** and **Michael Jackson**, and weak offerings from other mainstream favourites such as **Guns N'Roses** and **Simple Minds**. The unprecedented success of **Bryan Adams**, whose '(Everything I Do) I Do It For You' spent an unseemly 16 weeks at the top of the singles chart, was widely perceived as epitomizing the general stagnation of the music scene.

With the possible exception of **U2** (who moved on from the discovery of spurious American 'roots' with 'Rattle & Hum' to the more experimental, European-influenced 'Achtung Baby'), nobody in the mainstream, it seemed, had any idea of where music was going. Most people settled for lukewarm retreads of their previous work. Further indication of the general lack of direction in pop

FEB 26 : Kuwait-sponsored forces defeat Iraq in the six-month Gulf War • MAY 7 : Civil War breaks out in Yugoslavia

▲ The Manic Street Preachers built a substantial following on thinly-rehashed punk outrage.

and rock could be gleaned from numerous desperate attempts to kick-start a punk revival. Several compilations of old punk favourites appeared, retro tours featuring duff old punk outfits like **Sham 69** and **999** did a round of the regions and 'new punks' such as the **Manic Street Preachers** courted outrage in hackneyed punk fashion. In the event, only the **Clash** profited much from the trend, getting their first Number 1 single with the reissued 'Should I Stay Or Should I Go', which followed the tried and tested jeans-advert route to the top.

Genuine 'new punk' was arriving down other avenues however, as hardcore techno music, evolved from the late Eighties acid-house scene, made its deepest inroads yet into chart territory. This happened via acts like **Altern-8**, **LFO**, **Orbital** and the **Prodigy**, all of whom built up significant grass-roots followings before

becoming pop successes. Most notably, the **KLF** released a string of huge hits throughout the year, starting in January with their Number 1, '3AM Eternal', and concluding in December with the extraordinary Christmas hit, 'Justified And Ancient', which featured country legend **Tammy Wynette** on vocals.

The other significant UK 'underground scene' of 1991 began in rock's silly season – namely the spring – when few records of merit are ever released, enabling a clutch of Home Counties, student-style guitar bands (**Ride**, **Chapterhouse**, **Slowdive** etc) to seize centre stage with their insipid offerings. Colloquially known as 'shoegazers' because of their general desultory air and the close attention they had to pay to basic fretting, the shoegazers married imperfect technique to a love of flange and chorus effects. They were shown up for the dilettantes

MARCH: R.E.M. release 'Out Of Time', their breakthrough album.

MARCH 14: R&B songwriter Doc Pomus dies in New York, aged 65.

APRIL 20: Steve Marriott, singer with the Small Faces and Humble Pie, burns to death at his home in Essex, aged 44.

MAY: Ice-T's 'O.G. Original Gangster' album is released, along with the soundtrack to his film debut New Jack City.

JUNE 1: David Ruffin, lead singer with the Temptations, takes a crack-cocaine overdose in Philadelphia, aged 50.

JUNE 29: Bryan Adams' '(Everything I Do) I Do It For You' reaches Number 1.

JULY: Nirvana's multi-million selling album 'Nevermind' is released.

NOVEMBER 24: Freddie Mercury, singer with Queen, dies of AIDS in London, aged 45.

REM vaulted to prominence with their 'Out Of Time' album, despite doing little or no promotional work besides a secret London show under the pseudonym Bingo Hand Job.

Ozzy Osbourne, cleared of "culpably exciting" a fan to commit suicide

they were, when textural extremists **My Bloody Valentine** released their second album 'Loveless', a dense, difficult work which cost a rumoured £250,000 to record, a staggering sum for an indie release.

1991 was the year in which Hollywood realized the crossover rebel appeal of rap stars, and started featuring rappers in their movies. **Ice Cube** was moody and magnificent in John Singleton's urban drama *Boyz N The Hood*, while **Ice-T** played against type (and his better judgement) as a wild cop in the guns'n'-drugs actioner **New Jack City**. **MC Hammer**, by contrast, got his own children's cartoon series, **Hammerman**, just as his 15 minutes of fame were coming to an end. The new year begins well for **Bob Dylan**. After selling out eight nights at London's Hammersmith Odeon between February 8 and 16, he returns to America where, on February 20, he, along with a posthumous **John Lennon**, is given a Lifetime Achievement Award at the annual Grammy awards. Things are also looking up for **James Brown**, who is paroled from jail in March: the parole board describe him as a "model prisoner" after all his good work inside – this included organizing the prison band!

To promote their new album 'Out Of Time', **REM** play two low-key gigs on March 14 and 15 at London's Borderline Club under the nom-de-gig Bingo Hand Job. Taking a slightly different promotional tack, **Paul McCartney** plays MTV's **Unplugged** series on April 3, later releasing the results as an 'official bootleg' live album in a limited edition of 500,000.

The spring of 1991, however, proves to be a dark time, with a wave of deaths hitting some of the most crucial figures in rock music history. In March, R&B songwriter Doc Pomus, long confined to a wheelchair, dies aged 65 in New York. In April, Leo Fender, father of the Telecaster and Stratocaster, dies aged 83; **Steve Marriott**, singer with the **Small Faces** and **Humble Pie**, burns to death in a fire at his home in Essex; Martin Hannett, seminal producer responsible for many of the recordings of **Joy Division**, **New Order**, **Happy Mondays**, **Buzzcocks**, the **Stone Roses**, **Magazine** and **U2**, dies aged 42 in Manchester, from a heart attack sustained following a chest infection, and **Johnny Thunders**, one-time **New York Doll** and **Heartbreaker**, dies aged 38 in a New Orleans hotel. The following month, Will Sinott of the **Shamen** drowns on May 11 while swimming in the sea off Tenerife, and former **Byrds** singer **Gene Clark** succumbs in Los Angeles, aged 49. June sees the deaths of **Stan Getz**, aged 64, and former **Temptations** singer **David Ruffin**, who is killed by a drug overdose in Philadelphia, aged 50 – mysteriously, he is dumped at the local hospital by a limousine driver who swiftly departs without giving his name. The **Stone Roses** enjoy a happier visit to court, being freed on May 20 from their contract with Silvertone Records, and awarded costs of £700,000 – whereupon they immediately sign to Geffen Records for an advance alleged to be in the region of £2 million. In a macabre echo of the previous year's case involving **Judas Priest**, **Ozzy Osbourne** is finally cleared in an Atlanta court of 'culpably exciting' a young fan to shoot himself through his 1986 song 'Suicide Solution'.

JUL 4 : IBM develops the Static Random Access Memory microchip, enabling new speeds of computer operation • JUL 5 : BCCI bank collapses amidst accusations of fraud

Less welcome for British exports like Ozzy, however, is the US Justice Department's June announcement of plans to cut by two-thirds the number of visas available to foreign artists, which should take effect in October.

A British Phonographic Institute investigation reports in June that it has to fine two companies, London Records and Rhythm King Records, for chart hyping. London are fined £50,000 for hyping the **High**'s 'More', and Rhythm King £5,000 for hyping **S Express**' 'Find 'Em, Fool 'Em, Forget 'Em'. The investigators found that copies of the two records had been "deliberately purchased in order to enhance their chart positions", and both record companies are threatened with expulsion from the BPI if they don't comply with the verdicts.

On June 28 and 29, **Paul McCartney** and Carl Davis' oratorio is performed by a 90-piece orchestra and 230-strong choir at Liverpool Cathedral, to commemorate the 150th anniversary of the Liverpool Philharmonic. In July, the latest British sensation, **EMF**, top the US singles charts with their debut release 'Unbelievable', which receives heavy airplay despite the semi-audible use of a well-known

EMF: ****ing 'Unbelievable'.

four-letter word in the chorus. In Britain, Canadian rocker **Bryan Adams** sustains a record-breaking spell of 16 weeks at Number 1 with his single '(Everything I Do) I Do It For You', which goes on to sell in the

Ice Cube Raises Racial Heat

With the release of his controversial new album 'Death Certificate' in America on October 31, rapper **Ice Cube** brought the subject of racism into uncomfortably close focus. No longer prepared simply to complain at the disadvantaged position of the black population, the rapper went recklessly on the offensive: the track 'Black Korea' was an apparent call for the torching of Korean-owned shops in black neighbourhoods and 'No Vaseline', aimed at his former colleagues in **NWA**, seemed little more than an incitement to the band to kill their Jewish manager, Jerry Heller.

In response to the latter, the rapper was accused by the Simon Wiesenthal Centre, a Los Angeles-based, human rights organization, of using lyrics which "threaten and promote violence". The SWC called on the four major US record retail chains to stop selling the LP, which had advance orders of over a million and in fact entered the album charts at Number 2, one place higher than **MC Hammer**'s new album — an indication of the changing face of rap tastes in America. Despite earlier complaints about records by **Madonna**, **Public Enemy** and **Professor Griff**, this was the first time the SWC had actually advocated the banning of a record. Brian Turner, president of Priority Records, which distributed

Ice Cube: "a macho put-down kind of thing".

the album in America, told the *Los Angeles Times*: "'Death Certificate' is not anti-semitic. The allegations made by the Simon Wiesenthal Centre are absolutely invalid. Ice Cube's lyrics represent nothing more than a macho put-down kind of thing that stems from a long-standing feud between Cube and his former group NWA and their manager, Jerry Heller."

Ice Cube himself was disingenuous. "I'm not against Jews," he argued, "I'm just doing what they do in the media. When they describe someone, they often say he's black or Korean or Muslim. That's all I'm doing. I don't like [Heller], but it's not because he's Jewish."

The 'Black Korea' track — which despite British distributor Island's success in defending NWA's recent album against obscenity charges, was removed from the album's British release — aroused outrage amongst America's Korean community, which swiftly organized itself to lobby against the rapper. In December, by threatening a nationwide boycott of the brewery's products, it succeeded in losing Ice Cube his position as figurehead for St Ides malt liquor. Their '40 ounce' bottles were marketed specifically at black youth and Ice Cube had been chosen to spearhead their TV advertising campaign.

Rap Albums Impounded by British Police

In a June 4 raid on Polygram's Chadwell Heath depot, 13,000 copies of 'Efil4zaggin', the second album by Los Angeles rap group **NWA** (Niggaz With Attitude), were impounded by the Metropolitan Police's Obscene Publications Squad under Section 3 of the Obscene Publications Act, days before its planned UK release.

The album, which had previously entered the American charts at Number 1, kept up the aggressive stance of the group's debut 'Straight Outta Compton', with titles like 'To Kill A Hooker' and 'Findum Fuckum And Flee'. Hopes that the recording industry would rally round Island Records to oppose the police action in the courts were dashed when, in a pathetic echo of the Recording Industry Association of America (RIAA)'s craven response to demands that certain albums be 'stickered' to indicate questionable content, the August meeting of the British Phonographic Institute (BPI) voted not to support Island and their distributors, Polygram, when the case came to magistrates court in September.

Nonetheless, the obscenity case was eventually settled in Island's favour in November, when Geoffrey Robertson QC, famed for his eloquence in the *Oz* magazine trial two decades earlier, defended the album as simply "the black equivalent of our rugby songs". "This style of rap is street journalism," he claimed. "The stories are told in street language which is ironic, bitter, sarcastic, rude and crude, not in vacuous moon-and-June rhymes like Perry Como and Elvis Presley." He brandished copies of porn magazines bought in a local Redbridge newsagent to establish the difference between the LP and pornography, claiming that, though the lyrics were "vivid, disturbing and shocking", they were "a million miles away from pornography". "The album arouses fear and concern, distaste but not lust," he said. "No-one in their right minds, or indeed in their wrong minds, could be sexually aroused by this record."

Magistrates ordered that the impounded records should not be forfeited, and awarded costs of £1000 to Island and £350 to Polygram, against the police. A civil liberties spokesperson described the result as being of massive significance, adding "It's time to review the whole working of the Obscene Publications Act, which gives the police carte blanche. NWA were lucky that Polygram were big enough to take on the Crown Prosecution Service – independent record producers couldn't possibly afford it." For their part, the unhelpful BPI were castigated as "balding pedants and ingrates" by triumphant Island MD Marc Marot.

▲ Bryan Adams: record-breaking run.

region of 10 million copies around the world. In November, however, the singer takes out a 'cease and desist' order against David Duke, the former Ku Klux Klansman and would-be Governor of Louisiana, preventing Duke from using the single in his election campaign.

Concert troubles bedevil bands in the summer. On July 2, **Guns N'Roses** singer **Axl Rose** attacks a camera-wielding punter at a concert in St Louis, provoking a riot. After the show is aborted, Rose is charged with assault and property damage. 51,000 punters, meanwhile, are left out in the cold, owed a total of £1.275 million, when a **Prince** concert planned for August 31 at Blenheim Palace is cancelled. Prince has apparently been paid an advance of £325,000 for the no-show. More satisfied customers, presumably, are the estimated 750,000 who attend the final date of **Paul Simon**'s Born At The Right Time tour in Central Park on August 15.

The never-ending battle between musicians and the taxman claims its latest casualty when country star **Willie Nelson** is landed with a back-tax demand for $16 million in August. The singer, who rose to widespread fame when he wrote 'Crazy' for **Patsy Cline**, plans to pay off the debt by selling a solo album, 'Who'll Buy My Memories?', down the telephone line: Each copy ordered pays off $6 of the debt. Business proves rather better for the **Rolling Stones**, who in November sign a three-album deal with Virgin worth £25 million.

Premier Independent Distributor Goes Broke

After months of legal and financial to-ing and fro-ing, Rough Trade Records and Rough Trade Distribution were finally wound up on May 31 1991. These companies, formed in the late Seventies by alternative entrepreneur Geoff Travis, were instrumental in spreading the new punk-rock music of the era. The function Rough Trade served was to provide outlets for independently-made music both on their own label – which initially featured avant garde new wave acts such as **Cabaret Voltaire**, **Kleenex** and **Metal Urbain** – and more importantly to act as a clearing-house for the rash of small labels which blossomed in punk's wake. The collapse of the organization effectively signalled the end of a fertile and optimistic period in grass-roots music production in the UK.

In the Eighties, the label experienced unprecedented success with the **Smiths**, while the distribution arm was perfectly placed to capitalize upon the growth of independently-made dance records later in the decade, which spawned Number 1 hits for artists such as **Yazz**. But the company's success ultimately proved its downfall. Changes were made to its egalitarian personnel structure – since its earliest days the company had been run as a co-operative, with managing director Travis receiving the same salary as the organization's shop assistants and cleaners – and in attempting to expand to cope with the unprecedented Eighties success, like many other businesses of the era, Rough Trade found itself over-extended and unable to pay its creditors. The company eventually wound up owing some £3.6 million to over 60 indie labels, including a whopping £800,000 to Mute Records, whose phenomenally succesful acts **Depeche Mode** and **Erasure** had effectively been carrying Rough Trade for several years.

Despite calls for Rough Trade to be declared bankrupt, the largest of the indie labels – 4AD, Big Life, Situation Two and Mute among others – came up with a last-minute package to bail the company out. The old Rough Trade Distribution would be replaced by a new company, Rough Trade Marketing (RTM), which with the help of a £1 million-plus deal with the other largest independent distributors Pinnacle and APT, would continue to handle sales and marketing of those labels, while the back catalogue of the company's publishing arm Rough Trade Music was sold to Cherry Red Records for a little over £50,000.

Later in the year, in November, the American arm of Rough Trade was also put up for sale. An 80-page inventory listing the company's assets includes unfulfilled contracts and back catalogue material by **Pere Ubu** and the **Butthole Surfers**. The New Jersey firm Scorpio Music were believed to be leading bidders for the company.

The arrangement also gives Virgin the rights to much of the Stones' back catalogue.

One of the sleazier rock trials of the decade looms when Motown star **Rick James** is arrested in August on charges of imprisoning and torturing a 24-year-old woman during a three-day orgy in July at his Hollywood home. He and girlfriend Tanya Anne Hijazi face charges of false imprisonment, suspicion of assault with a deadly weapon, terrorist threats, supplying narcotics and forced oral copulation, for which bail is set at $1 million. Having met the woman at a party and invited her home, James and Hijazi allegedly tied her up, threatened her with a gun and burnt her with a crack pipe. She was then allegedly forced to smoke crack and have oral sex with Hijazi while the singer watched.

In America, **NWA**'s summer ascendancy passes on to indie grunge band **Nirvana**, who surprise many by taking their second LP 'Nevermind' to a Top 5 chart position before the year's heavyweight releases take over. In September, **Guns N'Roses** end the long wait for their follow-up to the hugely successful 'Appetite For Destruction' by releasing not one but two double-albums, 'Use Your Illusion I & II'. In general, the response is that, just as most double albums could be usefully trimmed to single-album length, so these two doubles might better make one, or at a stretch two, single albums. **Simply Red**'s 'Stars' follows in October, before **U2**, with 'Achtung Baby', and **Michael Jackson**, with 'Dangerous', lock horns for the public's attention in November. The mounting disaffection with Jackson's attitude, however, becomes more personal in December

 Rough Trade founder and indie guru Geoff Travis found the organization he had started was ill-equipped to deal with the sudden commercial expansion of the independent dance scene. The pioneering alternative company was bailed out for years by its more successful indie colleagues such as Mute and 4AD Records.

► The Queen is dead: a year studded with rock deaths climaxes in November with the passing of Queen's Freddie Mercury, from AIDS. The group mourn the loss of "the greatest and most beloved member of our family".

A decade of legal wrangling over ownership of the late Bob Marley's estate finally concludes with the remaining family, including son Ziggy (right), prevailing; Ziggy names his newborn son Justice in ► celebration.

when his brother Jermaine releases the single 'Word To The Badd', a thinly-disguised attack on his brother, accusing him of only thinking "about number one" and asking, "was your colour wrong?".

Following months of speculation about his health, in November **Frank Zappa** is diagnosed as suffering from inoperable prostate cancer. A statement is read out by his daughter Moon Unit at the Ritz in New York, after Zappa fails to show up for his own 50th birthday celebrations featuring a concert called Zappa's Universe. "He's been fighting successfully," she announces. "There are occasional periods when he's not feeling well, and it's unfortunate this one happened to coincide with the event."

Less sympathetically supported by his family is that other Sixties genius, ex-**Beach Boy**

Brian Wilson, who in December is forced to sever all links with controversial therapist/business adviser Eugene Landy after his brother Carl, mother Audree and daughters Carnie and Wendy (of **Wilson Phillips**) threaten to take him to court, claiming he is mentally incompetent to run his own business affairs. The settlement is reached on the day he is due to stand trial in Los Angeles. The Wilsons claim Landy brainwashed Brian into making him chief beneficiary in his will; an independent conservator will now be appointed to handle Wilson's financial affairs and Landy is forbidden to contact him for two years, which means the dissolution of their Brains & Genius company.

Another long-running family dispute which finally grinds to a halt in December is that involving the estate of the late **Bob Marley**. After a decade of wrangling over ownership, Jamaican Supreme Court Justice Clarence Walker rejects a bid of $15.2 million from MCA Music Publishing in favour of a joint bid of nearly $4 million less from Marley's widow Rita, children Ziggy, Cedella and Stevie, together with Chris Blackwell's Island Logic company.

Trouble initially arose because Marley left no will when he died in 1981, and a document allegedly assigning musical assets to Rita was found to be a forgery. That's why the Attorney General of Jamaica appointed an administrator to sell off the assets, but it isn't until July that the

Marley/Blackwell bid is mounted. Explaining his decision, Justice Walker says that Marley's legacy is "a treasure-house of priceless music which must be of sentimental value to his descendants". Blackwell expresses satisfaction that Marley's children have received their due inheritance. And, in celebration of the result, **Ziggy Marley** names his newborn son Justice.

Eric Clapton and his band act as backing group for **George Harrison** at the latter's December concerts in Japan, the ex-**Beatle**'s first tour since 1974. But a year replete with tragedy ends on a sad note with the death of **Queen** singer **Freddie Mercury** from AIDS on November 24. "We have lost the greatest and most beloved member of our family," announce the group in a statement. "We feel overwhelming grief that he has gone, sadness that he should be cut down at the height of his creativity, but above all great pride in the courageous way he lived and died." His finest moment, 'Bohemian Rhapsody' is re-released and becomes the only hit to top the UK chart on two separate occasions.

NOV 5 : Robert Maxwell, publisher and pension-plunderer, drowns • NOV 12 : Indonesian troops massacre mourners at a funeral in East Timor

257

1990s Underground

In the Nineties, virtually all branches of what would once have been considered 'underground' in previous decades came roaring overground to dominate youth culture on both sides of the Atlantic.

In America, the inroads made in the early Eighties by punk outfits like the **Germs** and **Black Flag** finally paid off big-time with the huge success of the grunge scene which originated in Seattle and spread rapidly across the entire country. Groups like **Nirvana**, **Pearl Jam** and

Soundgarden suddenly made the poodle-haired, spandex-trousered heavy metal bands of the Eighties seem dated and absurd, bringing to the genre an earthier rebelliousness which went some way beyond the hackneyed, bad-boy posturings of **Motley Crue** and **Poison**. More importantly, these new bands attempted to articulate the frustrations of a generation which had seen its hopes and aspirations rudely curtailed. Unlike previous generations, these American teenagers were constantly told that they should not expect to have a better standard of living than their parents – although, compared to those of equivalent age in other countries, American youth was still a lot better off than most.

This 'Generation X', as some called it, related to grunge's abject nihilism – it gave 'slackers' justification for their slouching and sulking. There was no real comparison between this and the nihilism of the Seventies punk generation, which was altogether more energetic and focused. It could hardly be coincidental that while the punk drug of choice was amphet-

amine (speed) – a chemical motivator – the grunge drug of choice was the more pernicious heroin, the 'no future' drug par excellence.

In Britain, the crusty/raver underground movement begun in the late Eighties grew increasingly influential in the Nineties, even as the authorities took ever more drastic measures aimed against it. Government rushed through parliament a succession of ill-thought-out bills restricting traditional rights of movement and congregation.

As with punk and grunge, the soundtrack to the rave movement was in part dependent on its drugs of choice. In one direction, under the influence of the amphetamine derivative

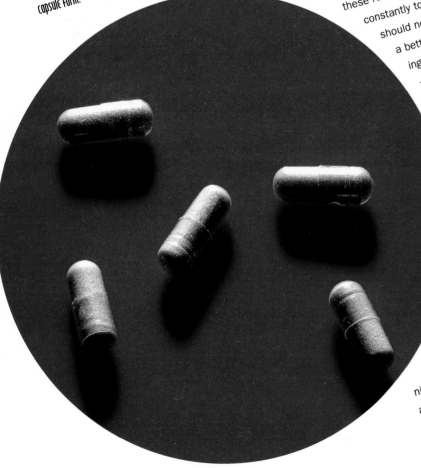

▼ Ecstasy was available in both tablet and capsule form.

◄ The low-key approach of grunge bands like Soundgarden made earlier spandex-clad metal bands seem absurd.

Kurt'n'Courtney became rock's most turbulent couple in 1992, with reports of heroin abuse during the latter's pregnancy outraging readers of Vanity Fair magazine, while Cobain's drug and psychological problems increasingly worried his colleagues and acquaintances.

ing month, Prince outdoes himself in the oddity stakes by naming his new album with a squiggly device which incorporates both the male and female symbols: Warners are forced to issue US newspapers with floppy disks containing printable versions of the title. For her part, **Madonna** delivers the first fruits of her Warners deal, a book and an album. Bound in aluminium and featuring a series of explicit erotic photographs of the star herself, the book, *Sex*, not surprisingly excites rather more media interest than the album, 'Erotica', and is used to test the obscenity laws in Cincinnati, where two years earlier Robert Mapplethorpe's explicit photo exhibition prompted similar action.

Not everybody is impressed with Madonna, however. Former **Pink Floyd** songwriter **Roger Waters**, for one, roundly lambasts her in *Details* magazine: "She's made all these rotten records, and she's this awful, ugly, dull person who, by virtue of the fact that she's completely fearless and shameless and blatant and cheap and bad, has become successful," he rants. "She develops this grandiose theory of herself as being important, and makes *Truth Or Dare*, which I had to stop watching because it was so unpleasant and embarrassing and awful. It's like she had a multi-barrelled gun, and hasn't just shot herself in the foot, but shot

herself everywhere and blown her own head off, and no-one seems to have noticed."

Much as they love themselves, both Madonna and **Prince**, however, fail to ignite widespread public interest within the American public, which suddenly seems besotted with the country-music performers colloquially known as 'hat acts' due to their fondness for huge cowboy hats. Handsome newcomer **Billy Ray Cyrus**' LP 'Some Gave All', which features the dance-craze hit 'Achy Breaky Heart', is finally toppled off the top of the US album charts after 17 weeks by **Garth Brooks**' LP 'The Chase'. The hankering after an older, simpler way is also reflected in the latest releases by **Bob Dylan** ('Good As I Been To You') and **Neil Young** ('Harvest Moon'), whose albums reiterate specific aspects of their earlier work. In Young's case, this is a belated continuation of the cosy country-rock of his most successful LP, 'Harvest', whereas Dylan's represents a return to the solo acoustic traditional folk and blues covers of his debut album. **Eric Clapton**, too, succumbs to the roots-music virus, enjoying his greatest success in years with the album of acoustic blues covers recorded for MTV's *Unplugged* series. This is the second release this year to be spawned by the series, **Mariah Carey** having experienced some success with an acoustic EP in July.

To celebrate his 30 years with the company, CBS throw an all-star tribute concert for Bob Dylan at Madison Square Garden on October 16, featuring alongside the Bard him-

self superstars like **Stevie Wonder**, **Lou Reed**, Neil Young, **Tom Petty**, **George Harrison**, **Chrissie Hynde** and Eric Clapton. The event, however, is hijacked by **Sinead O'Connor**, who is barracked by the audience for tearing up a picture of the Pope on the *Saturday Night Live* TV show. She responds with silence, followed by an angry, shouted version of **Bob Marley**'s 'War'. This, and the subsequent poor reception accorded her album of torch-song covers, 'Am I Not Your Girl?', prompts O'Connor to announce her retirement from the music business. "There is no longer any point in trying to use music as a means of communicating with people," she avers. "I will not do that until the fight to create the circumstances under which we can have the freedom to express ourselves is finished. Until this happens, I'm not writing any more fucking songs, and I'm not singing any more fucking songs." The retirement, however, ends prematurely when she appears onstage the following month with rap group the **Disposable Heroes Of Hiphoprisy**.

In October, **Kurt Cobain** finally admits to using heroin, telling the *Los Angeles Times*, "I chose to do drugs, but I have nothing good to say about them. They are a total waste of time. People who use drugs are fucked." He claims a stomach disorder left him "sitting in a corner by myself looking sick and gloomy...I was trying to fight against the stomach pain, trying to hold food down. People looked at me and assumed I was some kind of addict." A doctor prescribed Cobain methadone tablets

SEP 16 : Having wasted around £12 billion propping up the pound, the UK drops out of the European Monetary System, effectively devaluing sterling

1992 - HEADLINE NEWS

Police Protest at 'Cop Killer' Song

The release in April of the eponymous album by rapper **Ice-T**'s thrash-metal band **Body Count**, which included the track 'Cop Killer', started a furore which grew and grew through subsequent months. The Los Angeles riots, which followed the acquittal in April of the LAPD police officers accused of assaulting Rodney King, produced a climate in which the song's anti-police sentiment found both vociferous supporters and vociferous detractors. In June, an LA city councilwoman called for the album to be withdrawn, while a Texas police group called for a wholesale boycott of all Time-Warner product, including the corporation's big summer movie, *Batman*. Glen White, of the Dallas Police Association, called for police to demonstrate at Time-Warner's annual shareholders meeting on July 16.

In a keynote speech to the New Music Seminar in New York, Ice-T characterized the complaints as illiberal, claiming his critics were trying to deprive him of his freedom of speech: "What they're really trying to do is shut down my platform – they do not want me to be able to speak to the masses". He said the song 'Cop Killer' was a condemnation of racism and police brutality, elaborating "We give the police the power of God. I don't understand how we allow them to have this power – they're nothing but public servants, like a fireman or a mailman". The LA police union contradicted his claim, saying the LP "does nothing but arouse the passions of the criminal element who make the streets of Los Angeles unsafe". Their view was echoed by actor Mickey Rourke, who said of the May riots that "the blood of Los Angeles falls on those who instigated this revolt – the malicious prophets of black cinema and rap music".

In July, an electioneering George Bush denounced 'Cop Killer' as sick and went on to proclaim war "against those who use film or records or TV or video games to glorify killing law enforcement officers". If taken too literally, Bush's stand could have led to the outlawing of virtually the entire output of the American film industry over the past two decades. Disgraced former Reagan aide Colonel Oliver North, meanwhile, called for all 50 state Governors to bring criminal proceedings against Time-Warner. In response to the mounting pressure, Warner MD Jerry Levin memo'd his staff: "We won't retreat in the face of threats of boycotts or political grandstanding. We stand for creative freedom...we believe that the worth of what an artist or journalist has to say does not depend on pre-approval from a government official". At the company's general meeting, however, proceedings were theatrically suspended when Charlton Heston, a company shareholder, insisted on reading out aloud the lyrics to another song from the album, 'KKK Bitch'.

The pressure ultimately had its desired effect. On August 4, following a week in which three bomb threats had been made to the record company offices, Ice-T reluctantly withdrew the 'Cop Killer' track from the album. "At the moment the cops are in a criminal mode," he announced. "They've raised a lot of death threats against Warner Brothers Records. It's like somebody else is fighting my battle." Unsold copies were to be returned, and the sleeve re-designed, though the rapper stated he would give away free copies of the offending track at his live shows. As a result, 60 police officers joined anti-Ice protestors outside his North Hollywood show. "I'm like the Mayor of America right now," claimed the rapper. "I could probably run for President. I got a country split right down the middle, and who's to say I don't have the majority?"

In support of Ice-T's sentiment, US indie groups including **Sonic Youth**, **Ministry**, **Anthrax** and the **Beastie Boys** placed a full-page ad in industry paper *Daily Variety* headed "How Does Dan Quayle Spell Censorship? I-C-E-T". The final word, however, went to the *Wall Street Journal*, which reported that Warners was considering a new policy against distributing music deemed "inappropriate". They later announced their intention to issue a public-service television special on the Body Count issue, called *Popular Culture: Rage, Rights and Responsibility*. Moderated by a Harvard law professor, it would feature a discussion panel which would include Ice-T.

For the rapper, who later moved his record company over to a new distributor, the repercussions of the brouhaha continued throughout the rest of the year, most notably affecting Body Count's support slot on the huge **Guns N'Roses/Metallica** tour, one of the year's biggest-grossing projects. Fearing their presence might harm ticket sales, concert promoter Brian Murphy, vetoed their appearances at the two Los Angeles shows, claiming the group to be "an inappropriate act, given the circumstances of where the shows are taking place". **Axl Rose** of Guns N'Roses attacked Murphy's decision as "shallow-minded", and in response, at the San Diego concert, Ice-T performed 'Cop Killer' after reading out, then screwing up, a letter from the San Diego Police Officers Association requesting that he refrain from performing the offending song.

A harrowing sado-masochistic video for 'Happiness In Slavery', by Trent Reznor's industrial techno-thrash outfit Nine Inch Nails, was banned by the BBC for its explicit depiction of genital mutilation. Mmmm, nice!

Ice-T: "At the moment, the cops are in criminal mode".

when his stomach became upset following a detox programme to which the singer was obliged to return during a break in **Nirvana**'s tour schedule. **Cobain** claims his recent fatherhood has changed his priorities and perspective totally. "I knew that when I had a child I'd be overwhelmed, and it's true, holding my baby is the best drug in the world," he says. "I don't want my daughter to grow up with people telling her that her parents were junkies."

Also suffering from poor health at this time is **Frank Zappa**. Prostate cancer forces the cancellation of shows in Berlin and Vienna so that the composer can return to America for treatment. "I was in bad shape, but I'm better now," he announces later. "I'm not in a hospital, I'm in my kitchen. I'm not dead, and I have no intention of checking out any time this week or within the foreseeable future."

October in Chicago and presidential candidate Bill Clinton taps into the youth market, visiting **U2** backstage before their show. Interviewed for MTV by **Megadeth**'s Dave Mustaine, Clinton receives the endorsement of **Madonna**'s Fan Club, to which he responds: "I think this endorsement sends a loud and clear message to the Bush/Quayle campaign: Poppy don't preach". Clinton is ultimately the main beneficiary of a widespread Rock The Vote campaign, which has run TV adverts featuring Madonna, **REM**, the **Red Hot Chili Peppers**, **Deee-Lite**, U2,

Queen Latifah, Robin Williams and Spike Lee – all likely Clinton supporters – and events such as the free concert put on for 29,000 fans in Seattle by **Pearl Jam**, at which they were joined by Nirvana's Dave Grohl and Chris Novoselic. In November, aided by his campaign theme, **Fleetwood Mac**'s 'Don't Stop', Clinton wins the US Presidency.

In Britain, political activity continues on a more grass-roots level with the **Orb** and **Primal Scream** co-headlining a miners' benefit show at Sheffield Arena, and Donita Sparks of female hard rock band **L7** shocking the nation by dropping her trousers – she isn't wearing panties – on youth TV show *The Word* during a performance of 'Pretend We're Dead'. "I did it as an act of protest because I wasn't allowed to be in the bum contest," she says, referring to one of the programme's saltier items. "So I not only gave them a bum, I gave them a beav as well."

Not all sexual peccadilloes are as welcome on British screens, however, with the British Board Of Film Classification banning a **Nine Inch Nails** video. The video, for 'Happiness In Slavery', features self-confessed masochist performance artist Bob Flanagan undergoing extreme torture from a robotic machine. Using special effects, the video appears to show Flanagan's hands and chest being penetrated by sharp objects, a mechanical claw tearing at his skin and – gulp! – cutting wheels severing his genitals. The drama climaxes with his body falling into a coffin and being turned into mincemeat. NIN frontman **Trent**

Reznor, defending the video, endorses its portrayal of "a world in which people willingly submit to ritualized S/M relationships with devouring machines".

Also on the receiving end of a ban is ragga star **Buju Banton**, who is refused permission to appear at the WOMAD Festival because of the sentiments expressed in his song 'Boom By By', which appears to call for the shooting of homosexuals. Scheduled to appear at the festival in Brighton in December, Banton is invited to offer a retraction after gay pressure groups complained to the festival organizers. He replies, "I do not advocate violence against anyone, and it was never my intention to incite violent acts with 'Boom By By'. However, I must state unequivocally that I do not condone homosexuality, as this lifestyle runs contrary to my religious beliefs."

After a year of diligent touring, U2 are acclaimed in December as the biggest live draw of 1992, accruing a whopping $64 million from 70 US shows. They are followed by **Metallica** ($32 million from 53 shows), **Guns N'Roses** ($29 million from 36 shows), hardy perennials the **Grateful Dead** ($27 million from 45 shows) and, somewhat surprisingly, **Neil Diamond** ($26 million from 63 shows). In the UK, a more modest record is set when, with their single 'No Christmas', the **Wedding Present** become the first artists to have 12 new singles enter the chart in a year. None of them however spend more than two weeks in the listings and only one, 'Come Play With Me', makes the Top 10.

1990s Crazes

Some indication of the desperation of rock in the Nineties came with the most noticeable youth culture craze of the era – the widespread interest in body piercing and scarification (the cutting of one's flesh in a supposedly decorative way).

In Western culture the practice had been largely confined to the ears of women, sailors and gypsies until the early Seventies, when male rockers keen on appropriating some of that gypsy rebel spirit began sporting simple earrings. Towards the end of that decade, the practice started spreading to other areas of the body, with punks wearing safety-pins as an anti-style

statement with a high outrage factor. Others, like the **Human League**'s Phil Oakey, adopted pierced nipples for their alleged erotic potential.

The practice grew particularly rife amongst artists on the fringes of the burgeoning electronic and avant garde music scene, with

Psychic TV's Genesis P. Orridge, in particular, revealing he even had metal pins through his genitals. It was this, the more extreme end, of piercing which grew in popularity through the late Eighties and into the Nineties, with the "crusty" sub-culture of dreadlocked travellers and ravers developing the practice to new limits, often as an accompaniment to tattoos. Ears became girdled with dozens of tiny rings; studs were punched through tongues and noses; eyebrows, lips and belly-buttons – most famously **Madonna**'s – blossomed with little lumps of metal. X-Ray charts the pop world over were thrown into confusion by the level of human-metal interaction.

Though rarer, scarification carried just as much impact as piercing. Such was the rationale behind the action of the **Manic Street Preachers**' Richey James, who in the course of an interview with the NME after a Norwich gig on May 15 carved the phrase "4

▶ *"Roomy enough for you, sir?" Baggy trousers beyond Madness' wildest dreams became the height of fashion for the scallies of the Madchester scene and hip rappers from Los Angeles to London.*

▲ *Piercing and scarification of the most sensitive parts of the body became de rigueur in the Nineties.*

Real" into his arm with a razor blade. Intended as an assurance of the group's sincerity, the action inevitably evoked memories of **Sid Vicious** scarring himself on stage in America with pieces of broken glass. When, a few years later in 1994, James was hospitalized, allegedly with the classic self-disgust disorder anorexia, the comparison became decidedly more uncomfortable.

Fashion-wise, floppy was the way of the Nineties, with baggy jeans and loose tops de rigueur amongst the 'scallies' of the Manchester-based indie-dance scene whose figureheads were the **Stone Roses** and **Happy Mondays**. Across the Atlantic, the Seattle-based grunge scene revived the long-abominated plaid check shirt as a fashion garment. As a punkish anti-fashion statement, this was a witty adaptation of the lumberjack shirt traditionally favoured by the area's logging industry, and it also served to suggest a link with 'grunge

godfather' **Neil Young** who, it seemed, had never thought about wearing anything other than plaid throughout his long and varied career.

At the opposite extreme, tight Lycra outfits were the order of the day for the more athletically-inclined, especially the bicycle shorts which were affected by many who had never even sat on a bike. Ludicrous garments which only suited the young and fit, they were soon adopted for use by footballers, who wore them coyly peeking beneath their baggy football shorts.

As regards headgear, there was really only one essential item through

out the Nineties: the baseball cap, worn either backwards, rapper-style, or straightforwardly forwards, though a few sad souls showed their irrepressible wackiness by wearing the peak sideways. The legend on the cap was all-important: with the possible exception of **Ice-T**, no artist could flaunt their own name or album title and retain any vestige of cool, and non-musical references were in general the order of the day. Particularly favoured were logos suggestive of working-class occupations: that cap with "Al's A1 Brake and Lube" could add much-needed street-cred to the reputation of a nice middle-class boy from the suburbs.

▶ Stretchy lycra cycling shorts were affected by men whose behind had never touched a saddle.

▶ Hole's lead singer Courtney Love was romantically linked with Julian Cope from the Teardrop Explodes before getting hitched to Grunge godfather Kurt Cobain.

In 1993, the bad reputation rap music had worked so hard to foster finally came home to roost. Bands were beset by a host of legal problems, weighed down with recriminations and attacked from every side. Even though the constant publicity enabled rappers like **Ice-T** and **Ice Cube** to take further steps towards mainstream movie stardom, their musical careers suffered in various ways. At Ice Cube's January show in Seattle's Paramount Theatre, fights between rival gangs escalated into a gun battle outside the venue, leaving 12 injured. In February, Ice-T finally parted company with Warner Brothers. Later in the year, trouble spread to Britain, with riots breaking out at a concert by bad-boy slaphead rappers **Onyx**.

Nothing, however, could halt the impressive ascendancy of rap in the American charts, with **Dr Dre**, **Cypress Hill** and **Snoop Doggy Dogg** reaping the rewards of popularity of a new strain of dope-smokin', gun-totin' gangsta rap. The American charts were in any case more volatile in 1993 than they had been for some time, with successive releases by artists as disparate as **Depeche Mode**, **Janet Jackson**, **Pearl Jam** and the aforementioned gangsta-rappers breaking sales records.

Depeche Mode, with 'Songs Of Faith And Devotion', became the only act on an independent label ever to go straight to Number 1, Janet Jackson sold 350,000 copies of 'Janet' in one week as she followed the Essex boys to the top. Meanwhile, Pearl Jam broke **Guns N'Roses**' two-year-old record for a single week's sales when they shifted 950,000 copies of 'Vs' in one week, and Snoop Doggy Dogg becomes the first artist ever to have a debut album enter the chart at Number 1.

With business this good, it was no surprise that music-business lawyers continued to profit from a welter of litigation. **U2** introduced a new wrinkle to the already grizzled visage of rock-biz disputes when they announced in April that they intended to take legal action against the UK's Performing Rights Society, claiming they were owed millions of pounds from live shows across Europe. The group wanted to collect its own songwriting royalties on live performances in future, concluding after lengthy attempts to audit the PRS that the organization was "inauditable".

Artists came and went. The **Pixies** split up into the **Breeders** and **Frank Black**, **Suede**'s debut album was garlanded with praise and **Prince** retired when Warners declined to release a special mini-album on his birthday, June 7. Though the **KLF** were no more, Bill Drummond and Jimmy Cauty continued to conduct publicity stunts, most notably when their K Foundation gave £40,000 to prize-winning sculptor Rachel Whiteread for the year's worst work of art, twice the amount she

had already received from the Turner Prize for being their artist of the year.

In Britain, rave culture continued to dominate grass-roots musical activity, with the Club Dog in Finsbury Park offering a blueprint for contemporary multi-cultural music events, featuring trance, techno, industrial and rock musics in seamless co-existence. The Planet Dog label grew out of the club, as did the Midi Circus Tour featuring **System 7**, **Orbital**, the **Drum Club** and **Aphex Twin**, the Cornish techno genius whose lengthy ambient albums and predilection for buying old military tanks built him into a cult figure. Away from legal venues, however, the UK government continued to crack down on rave culture, with plans for a raft of con-

▲ *Pearl Jam became the fastest-selling band in America when they shifted 950,000 units of their second album 'Vs' in a single week, besting Guns N'Roses' two-year-old record.*

tentious new legislation intended to outlaw outdoor parties.

The grunge scene swept all before it in America, with **Pearl Jam** and **Nirvana** comfortably outselling all rock acts apart from **Aerosmith**. Nirvana's **Kurt Cobain** and his wife **Courtney Love** cut a dazed swathe through the gossip columns. And the year created a tremendous amount of showbiz scandal, with people like **Adam Clayton**, **Axl Rose**, **Eddie Vedder** and **David Lee Roth** all involved in dubious doings of one form or another. However it was the child-abuse allegations against **Michael Jackson** that made the really big story of the year; crippling the star's world tour, ruining his sponsorship deal with Pepsi and sending him into hiding.

Starting the new year off where he left the old, **George Michael** – in tandem with old **Wham!** partner **Andrew Ridgeley** – issues another writ against Sony, alleging royalty

underpayments of £386,000 relating to Wham! and £958,000 back royalties on his 'Faith' album. A small portion of that would have been useful to another of George's singing partners, **Aretha Franklin**, who is hit with a $225,618 tax bill on her 1991 accounts. The IRS relent in the case of **Willie Nelson**, however, who gets a partial reprieve in February on his $16m tax bill: he has to pay $2.5 million immediately, and $1.5 million over the next three months. A far cry from the situation of warm-hearted **Sinead O'Connor**, who auctions off her Los Angeles mansion, donating the money to Somalian famine relief.

At the Grammy Awards, the major winners are **Arrested Development**, **U2**, the **Red Hot Chili Peppers**, **Peter Gabriel** and **Eric Clapton**. In Britain, though, anger greets the equivalent BRIT Awards when nominations for Best Newcomer overlook the likes of **Suede**, **PJ Harvey**, **Nirvana**, the **Manic Street Preachers** and **Carter USM** in favour of **KWS** and **Undercover**. There are widespread accusations of a 'fix' when Warners acts receive five of the possible six nominations for Best International Solo Artist, and 1992's runaway success story, the **Shamen**, are not nominated in any category. This discrepancy causes the Award show's spoof-DJ presenters Smashie & Nicey to describe the proceedings as "vote-rig-mungous". Their suspicions are later confirmed when two major acts on an unnamed label are stripped of their awards by the Electoral Reform Society, who find evidence of block-voting. BRITs (and Warners) chairman Rob Dickins

comments, "There's nothing specifically illegal about block-voting, but it's something we've tried to discourage with the BRITs." Next year, the voting panel will be substantially widened to include critics, journalists, TV programmers and niche groups in the music business.

For most of the year, U2 are busy taking their Zooropa tour around the world, annoying world leaders with incessant nightly phone calls and generally making a nuisance of themselves. In August, they are joined onstage at Earls Court by outlawed author Salman Rushdie and, in Germany, they flout local laws forbidding the display of Nazi imagery by including clips of Leni Riefenstahl's Hitler-era documentaries *Olympia* and *Triumph Of The Will* as backdrops to their June shows. It is a different matter for Perry Farrell, whose new band **Porno For Pyros** run into trouble with their first album's sleeve design which contains a yantra, a pagan symbol involving a device similar but opposed to, a swastika, inside a Star Of David. Acceding to Warner Brothers' request to change the sleeve, Farrell says, "I do not in any way, shape or form have any relationship with the swastika. The thing I liked about the yantra was that it had both the Jewish and Nazi symbols together, and you've got to have both positive and negative in your life".

In complete agreement with Farrell, presumably, are that increasingly notorious rock couple Kurt'n'Courtney, who command more than their fair share of press attention throughout the year, as **Nirvana**

Arrested Development were one of the major winners at the Grammies, where their rootsy, agrarian rap stylings were rewarded as one of the few truly positive developments in a genre increasingly dominated by dystopian gangsta-rap. ▼

Government Clamps Down on Crusties and Ravers

Following widespread trouble the previous year, the British Government led by Prime Minister John Major announced their intention of giving the police much wider powers to combat unlicensed outdoor parties and travellers' convoys. These new measures will enable police to: turn back people anywhere within a five-mile radius of a site; confiscate sound equipment used on the site; break up convoys of six or more vehicles and arrest people who refuse to leave a site.

The government initiative came after a £25-a-head January rave at Peter De Savary's Littlecote House, near Hungerford, turned into a near-disaster when freezing fog descended on the valley, causing many of the 20,000 ravers to suffer hypothermia — though ironically, as a legitimate, paid event, such a rave would not fall under the purview of the new government measures.

The rave collective **Spiral Tribe** pulled out of their proposed January 23 concert at Brixton Academy because the limitations of playing a legal venue were too great. "We have only ever organized free illegal underground parties, and that is what we are all about," said a spokesperson for Spiral Tribe. "We have given the legal system a chance and it does not work. In this country the laws are creatively stifling. We will continue our free illegal policy until they lock us up or change the law."

In March, however, 13 members of the Spiral Tribe collective were committed to court to answer public nuisance charges arising from May 1992's week-long Castlemorton rave in Worcestershire, which attracted between 20,000 and 50,000 people. The defendants faced a maximum penalty of life imprisonment under common law, in a trial which may cost taxpayers up to £4 million. As a result of constant police harassment, however, the Tribe have taken their sound-system into exile in Europe. A spokesperson said, "The way we have been received over there is incredible — we've been welcomed with open arms. We put on a party in Amsterdam and I had a very pleasant breakfast with the chief of police — we spent the whole time taking the piss out of the British authorities. They couldn't believe how uptight this country is. In France, the mayor of the town we were in came to the party with his daughter!"

Sadly, later in the year, proposed Summer Solstice celebrations at Stonehenge on June 18-20 were marred by violent clashes between police and travellers, when the authorities enforced a four-mile exclusion zone around the site. The organizers of this year's Glastonbury Festival, meanwhile, have banned rave crews from attending because of licence restrictions which limit the time loud music can be played.

The various Megadog events took the multi-media aspects of the rave movement to new levels in 1993...

...while despite the introduction of more stringent police powers for controlling unlicensed parties, and violence at the Summer Solstice celebrations at Stonehenge, the Glastonbury Festival proceeded relatively smoothly. The Festival was, however, forced to prohibit rave crews' sound systems in order to comply with licence restrictions.

struggled to finish their follow-up to the mega-platinum 'Nevermind'. In February, they attempt to stop production of an unofficial Nirvana biography called *Flower Kissin', Kitty Pettin', Baby Kissin', Corporate Rock Whores*, leaving threatening messages on the answerphone of authors Britt Collins and Victoria Clarke. The same month, **Kurt Cobain** tells US gay magazine *The Advocate* he feels he is "definitely gay in spirit", and would be pursuing a bisexual lifestyle were it not for **Courtney Love**.

In April, Cobain's group reach an out-of-court settlement with the original Sixties group **Nirvana**, whose hits include 'Rainbow Chaser'. There are problems, however, with the new Nirvana album, with strong rumours of record company displeasure at Steve Albini's production. Geffen, who want to draft in Andy Wallace to add "a more commercial sheen" to the tapes, face trouble from Albini, whose contract stipulates that nobody may tamper with his work. Nirvana themselves deny any such pressure, claiming they simply want the vocals a bit louder on some tracks. "Steve has made a career out of being anti-rock-establishment," they insist, "but being commercial or anti-commercial is not what makes a good rock record. It's the songs, and until we have the songs recorded the way we want them, Nirvana will not release this record."

In February, **Ice-T** departs from Warner Brothers when they prove reluctant to release his 'Home Invasion' album. "What they were indirectly asking me to do was jeop-

ardize my integrity," mutters the rapper, "so I asked them to release me from the contract." Warner president Mo Ostin comments, "The decision was a difficult one for all concerned, but in the final analysis we believe that this was the best way to resolve our creative differences." Oliver North, of the right-wing Freedom Alliance, celebrates, "An action like this demonstrates the power that the average American shareholder can bring to bear against mega conglomerates like Time Warner." Later in the year, the repercussions of the affair will strike further home, when rap group the **Geto Boys** and pantomime horror-metal group **GWAR** are both dropped by Warners because of fears of a 'Cop Killer'-style outcry over obscene lyrics. GWAR's label boss Brian Slagel reveals Warners now require an advance inspection of lyrics before releasing an album. "There's definitely been a change at Warner Bros. since the Ice-T incident," he complains. "They're just not going to distribute records they think they're going to have problems with." Warner executive Bob Merlis admits, "We've been very sensitized by circumstances. We must be aware of what we release and how we release it."

Ice-T's situation is better, however, than that of Nigerian bandleader **Fela Kuti**, who is arrested and charged with 'conspiracy and murder' by the Nigerian police, after the body of one of Fela's employees, allegedly killed by one of his entourage in a dispute over money, is discovered. In Germany, meanwhile, 500 police seize 30,000 CDs, records and

tapes as well as quantities of guns and ammo in raids on record company offices, studios and musicians' homes, part of a crackdown on 'Nazi music' centred on 28 neo-Nazi bands such as **Stoerkraft** and **Radikahl**.

In May, **Prince** announces his retirement from recording at the age of 34, claiming he wishes to concentrate on films, theatre, nightclubs and interactive media. A spokesperson says, "I don't think people should fret over this news. Prince announced he was retiring from touring in 1984, and he came back. I don't think this is a permanent retirement. He is just having a break, and that might be a good thing after being so prolific over the years." The diminutive genius's action is rumoured to be because Warners refused to put out a mini-LP on his birthday, June 7 – on which date he presents himself with a peculiar new name, identical to the squiggle with which he titled his last album.

Also in May, **Madonna** is invited to play in the People's Republic of China, provided her concert includes no nudity or "indecent exposure". She accedes, because she wants to visit the country anyway. Meanwhile, after she duets with **Red Hot Chili Peppers**' singer Anthony Kiedis at an AIDS benefit concert in Los Angeles, it's strongly rumoured Kiedis may seek a solo deal with her Maverick label.

Kurt'n'Courtney hit the headlines again in July, when Cobain is arrested after police are called to the couple's Seattle house following complaints of loud noise by neighbours. The police find the pair arguing over

Rise of Ragga Brings Problems

The enormous success of ragga in 1993 revolutionized reggae music, with artists such as **Shabba Ranks**, **Chaka Demus & Pliers** and Asian ragga-rapper **Apache Indian** all enjoying success. It did not come without problems. Ragga, a form of reggae made with digital instruments, is a kind of Jamaican cousin to rap music, and certain of rap's characteristics also apply to it, notably the non-PC attitude towards women, who are invariably viewed with leering lasciviousness in the 'slack' lyrics, as well as a fondness for firing guns.

In March, enthusiasm for ragga reached unprecedented levels, with hits by **Shaggy**, **Snow** and Shabba Ranks at Numbers 1, 2 and 3 in the charts. The latter, however, was banned from appearing on the BBC's *Top Of The Pops* following homophobic remarks he made on youth-TV show *The Word*, where he maintained that gays "deserved crucifixion" and that "if God had meant men to be gay, he'd have created Adam and Steve, not Adam and Eve". Shabba was also in trouble in America, where the Gay and Lesbian Alliance Against Defamation got him banned from appearing on the *Tonight Show* for the same reasons.

On accusations of sexism, South London ragga star **General Levy** claimed that "If you talk to the people who buy the music, the girls who go to dance halls and dance to it, they don't find it offensive. It tends to be the people looking at the music from the outside who find it offensive."

It wasn't the sexism that worried most outside observers, however, but the gunplay which had become a feature of ragga culture. On April 12, at the height of ragga's UK success, two men were gunned down at ragga shows in London and Bristol over the Easter weekend. A spokesperson for Heavyweight Promotions, who specialize in reggae and rap, claimed that 'gun salutes' were a commonplace part of the Jamaican ragga scene, and were intended to show approval of the music: "Guns have been a part of this scene for years, there's no point moralizing about it. It's not the music industry's responsibility to solve the problem."

In general, the ragga industry was determined to downplay the problem. A spokesperson for Hardzone, who represent Shabba and Snow, claimed, "If you put a rock band on at a venue for 2,000 people and 8,000 turned up, you would have trouble there too," while Greensleeves Records' Christopher Sedgewick pointed out that there were "many thousands of ragga dances held each year at which there is no trouble."

Other sections of the reggae community, however, were worried at the importation of gun culture into the UK. "This is Britain and we don't tolerate guns in a public place," said Tony Williams, organizer of the Reggae Industry Awards. "Nobody wants that." At the Hammersmith Palais Easter Monday show, most guns were kept out of the venue by metal detectors and 30 security guards. The gunman was believed to have been amongst 50 gatecrashers let in to ease congestion, when a large number of 'walk-up' punters attended on the night without buying tickets in advance.

Ragga superstar Shabba Ranks' open flaunting of his homophobia took the shine off his enormous success, but was the least of the problems afflicting the genre in a year which saw shootings become an almost commonplace part of the ragga scene.

Actor Johnny Depp's Hollywood club The Viper Room, scene of River Phoenix's drug-overdose death, decked out for a memorial service in his honour.

JANUARY: Cream reform for a one-off Rock'n'Roll Hall Of Fame show.

FEBRUARY: Heavy metal band Megadeth receive the Doris Day Award, as campaigners for animal rights.

MARCH: The Velvet Underground announce their reformation.

APRIL: Saw Doctors keyboard-player Tony Lambert wins £850,000 on the Irish State Lottery.

APRIL: Holly Johnson, former Frankie Goes To Hollywood singer, reveals he is HIV+.

APRIL 30: Mick Ronson, one-time Spider From Mars, dies of liver cancer, aged 47.

NOVEMBER: Snoop Doggy Dogg's 'Doggystyle' becomes the first debut album ever to enter the US chart at Number 1.

DECEMBER 4: Frank Zappa dies of prostate cancer, aged 53.

▲ 1993 was the year in which Bjork graduated from cult indie singer to mainstream style icon.

the presence of guns in their home – **Cobain** had apparently thrown **Love** to the floor after she threw a glass of orange juice in his face. Police confiscate three guns and several ammunition clips, and Cobain is detained temporarily and later released on $950 bail, before the couple are referred to the city's Family Violence Project. There's no such inconvenience for **Lisa Stansfield**, however, after she breaks ex-**Pogue Shane McGowan**'s nose during a backstage altercation in Dublin.

The world is stunned in August when **Michael Jackson**, the superstar regarded as 'childlike' by many, is accused by 13-year-old Jordy Chandler of child molestation. When

it is admitted by parents of the star's other child acquaintances that Jackson did indeed sometimes fall asleep with their children, "the way tired children do", many wonder whether this is the correct way for a

35-year-old man to behave. As media interest mounts, Jackson cancels the Far East dates of his world tour in September, alleging "headaches and exhaustion", and goes into hiding. In November, he admits himself to a London clinic for treatment of an alleged addiction to painkillers. His situation worsens, however, when five former bodyguards sue him for wrongful dismissal because, they allege, they "knew too much". An *Entertainment Weekly* survey, meanwhile, reports that although only 25% of those asked believe the child abuse allegations, only 21% would be less likely to buy Jackson product and a mere 10% would stop their children listening to his records or watching his videos.

In October, **Rick James** is found guilty of assault, torture and imprisonment in the sex-prisoner case, but sentencing is postponed until new charges from two other women can be investigated. James eventually manages to avoid a prison sentence by agreeing to enter a drug rehabilitation programme – a judgement which must really delight his girlfriend

Tanya Anne Hijazi, co-defendant in the case, who receives a four-year jail sentence. Sixties soul star **Wilson Pickett**, meanwhile, receives a one-year sentence and 200 hours of community service after knocking down an 86-year-old pedestrian whilst drunk-driving in New Jersey. Maybe he crosses paths in jail with rapper **Slick Rick**, who is serving ten years for murder. In October, Slick Rick is allowed out on a work-release programme to cut tracks for his new LP. And, in December, the man with all the talk becomes eligible for parole after serving only two years of his sentence.

Other sections of the showbiz world keep their minds on higher things, however. **Michael Stipe**, Shirley MacLaine, Richard Gere, Sharon Stone, Meg Ryan and Cindy Crawford all attend an October public address by the Dalai Lama in Los Angeles. Hopefully it will have taken their minds off matters material and mundane. In recently published figures, **Phil Collins** is reportedly the highest-earning British rock star, receiving a director's salary of £12,680,000 in 1992 from his parent company Philip Collins. **Elton John** and **Eric Clapton** are the only other Brit-rockers to make the Top 10, with year's earnings of £8,008,211 and £3,867,474 respectively. **George Michael** isn't mentioned, but the smart money says his fortune will diminish substantially in the court action against Sony which he launched earlier this month. Meanwhile, in *Business Now* magazine, **Bono**'s worth is given as somewhere in the region of £70 million,

with **The Edge** on £60 million and **Adam Clayton** on a mere £55 million. Poor old **Larry Mullen**, sadly, isn't quoted. Blown it all on beer and smokes, probably, unlike Adam Clayton, who the Sunday tabloids reveal has indulged in sex-and-drug orgies with £300-a-night hookers after busting-up with girlfriend Naomi Campbell.

In November, **Guns N'Roses** cause a stir by including a track written by murderous Sixties hippie guru Charles Manson, 'Look At Your Game, Girl', on their LP of cover versions, 'The Spaghetti Incident?' Patti Tate, sister of murdered actress Sharon, threatens an injunction to prevent Manson receiving any royalties, then Phil Kaufman, who produced some recordings for Manson in the Sixties, claims he owns the rights to the song in question, which Manson allegedly signed over to him in 1971. Kaufman, who earned notoriety by stealing and cremating the body of **Gram Parsons**, ex-**Flying Burrito Brothers**, who died of drug abuse in 1973, has no qualms about taking the money and running: "[Manson's] 'family' made three attempts on my life," he claims. "That should be worth something."

Meanwhile, inquiries into another ancient death, that of **Jimi Hendrix** in September 1970, are re-opened following the promptings of a former Hendrix girlfriend, Cathy Etchingham.

Hendrix's father Al, now in his 70s, is unimpressed by the new investigation, while Alan Douglas, manager of the Hendrix estate, criticizes it as unnecessary: "Whether someone did or did not telephone an ambulance at whatever time is meaningless now. I don't know why she can't let it rest."

The year concludes on a sad note, with the death of **Frank Zappa** following a protracted struggle against cancer of the prostate. The guitarist and composer was one of the most articulate and outspoken critics of music censorship in America, and his passing surely leaves the forces of darkness sleeping a little more comfortably, knowing he won't be around to cross verbal swords with them.

Who's a naughty boy, then? Following a bust-up with supermodel girlfriend Naomi Campbell, U2's Adam Clayton was revealed by the tabloids to have indulged in sex-and-drug orgies with expensive hookers.

Snoop Surrenders at MTV Awards

Rapper **Snoop Doggy Dogg**, wanted in connection with the death of gang member Philip Woldemariam, gave himself up to the police after serving as one of the presenters at the *MTV Music Awards*. Dogg managed to hand out the award for Best R&B Video to **En Vogue** before handing himself over to the authorities. The following day the rapper was released on bail, to be arraigned on October 1.

Snoop, aka Calvin Broadus, was believed to be the driver of a car containing his bodyguard McKinley Lee, when the latter shot Woldemariam following an argument. The defendants pleaded self-defence, claiming that Woldemariam, who had allegedly threatened the rapper earlier, was going for his gun, though the immediate circumstances of the killing remained shrouded in mystery.

The shooting was but the latest in a long line of violent crimes and disturbances involving rappers and rap concerts. In February, Snoop Doggy Dogg's producer **Dr Dre** (aka Andre Young) was hit with several law suits following a New Orleans hotel-room brawl — for which he faced 18 months in prison for battery on a police officer. In 1991, Dre faced further charges for an assault on TV rap show presenter Dee Barnes, who served a civil suit for $20 million before Dre settled in September on a six-figure out-of-court settlement, an hour before jury selection for his trial was due to start. In August, Young had pleaded "no contest" to a criminal suit on the same charge, for which he was fined $2,500 and ordered to do 240 hours community service, as well as being put on probation for two years. He was also jailed for 90 days for a 1992 assault in which he broke a man's jaw.

▲ Gun totin' Snoop Doggy Dogg.

Trouble at rap concerts became almost commonplace in 1993. Besides the gun battle in January outside **Ice Cube**'s Seattle show, there was a riot at a **House Of Pain** concert in April in Baltimore, when the group refused to play after one of their roadies was hospitalized by the venue's bouncers. A **Run-DMC/Naughty By Nature** show in Richmond, Virginia the same month was marred by the shooting of a 17-year-old student outside the venue, who had just come to collect a friend.

Also at the start of 1993, **Marky Mark** paid an undisclosed sum to a man whose jaw was allegedly broken after he was kicked in the face by the rapper. Shortly after, **NWA**'s MC Ren (aka Lorenzo Patterson) was landed with a $16 million paternity suit judgement in favour of a 16-year-old woman who bore a child after Patterson and others allegedly raped her after a 1989 show in Birmingham, Alabama. In August, trouble spread to Britain, with a riot at a Hammersmith Palais concert by bad-boy gangsta rappers **Onyx**, when 300 fans tried to gatecrash the show. Later, in October, Onyx rapper Sticky Fingaz (aka Kirk Jones) allegedly assaulted a passenger on a New York-bound flight as the plane was preparing for take-off from Chicago — he had taken umbrage at a request to remove his personal stereo headphones in line with flight rules. He now faces a misdemeanour battery charge as a result.

The rap industry's annual Jack The Rapper convention, at the Marriott Marquis Hotel in Atlanta, was riven with mayhem. Much of the trouble was said to be caused by **Luther Campbell**'s **2 Live Crew**, who apparently instigated fights and vandalized hotel furniture. In November, **Public Enemy**'s clock-toting Flavor Flav (aka William Drayton) was charged with attempted murder following a shooting incident near his New York home. He was arrested and held for two days after shooting at neighbour Thelouizs English, whom he suspected of sleeping with his girlfriend. He was later admitted to the Betty Ford Clinic for help with a 'chemical dependency' associated with cocaine.

The same month, actor/rapper **2-Pac** (aka Tupac Shakur) was arrested for the alleged shooting of two policemen in Atlanta and charged with two counts of aggravated assault before being released on bail of $55,000. Then in December Shakur, under investigation for the alleged forcible sodomy of a 20-year-old woman in New York, faced further investigations following a police search of his hotel room which uncovered a video of the rapper having sex with a (possibly underage) girl who, according to reports, appeared to be under the influence of drink or drugs.

Finally, the year drew to a close with fights breaking out on a boat hired for the launch party for **Snoop Doggy Dogg**'s album The captain called the police when "approximately 150 people were fighting on the dock". The rapper's LP went on to sell 803,000 in its first week of release, proving that there is no such thing as bad publicity.

Nirvana

Formed in Seattle in 1987, **Kurt Cobain** and Kris Novoselic's group underwent a string of name-changes – Skid Row and Fecal Matter among them – before settling on **Nirvana**, the name under which they record-ed their debut album 'Bleach' for the local Sub Pop label in 1989. Having tried several local drummers, in August 1990 they stabilized their line-up by drafting in Dave Grohl, securing their future by following their friends **Sonic Youth** in signing to David Geffen's DGC label for an advance of $287,000. Initially attracted to **R.E.M.** pro-ducers Scott Litt and Don Dixon, they stuck with Butch Vig (who had produced the six-track demo which secured the DGC deal) when making their sophomore album 'Nevermind'. A potent blend of punk-infused metal riffs and hummable teen melodies, 'Nevermind' proved an instant success when released in October 1991, being certified platinum in little over a month while the group toured feverishly, visiting Europe three or four times in a matter of months, either as support to Sonic Youth or, later, as headliners in their own right. It was the phenomenal success of the single 'Smells Like Teen Spirit', however, which sent sales into overdrive. A distinctive roar of alienation with a catchy chorus, the song was quickly adopted as the anthem for the grunge generation which grew up in their wake. There was a harbinger of future problems, though, towards the end of the year, when the band cancelled several European dates after Cobain was struck down with a viral infection. 1992 began well for the band, with an appearance on Saturday Night Live and tours of Australia, New Zealand and Japan building on the chart-topping success of 'Nevermind', which went on to sell over four million copies in America. In February, singer Kurt Cobain wed **Hole** singer **Courtney Love** in Waikiki, Hawaii, and the couple announced they were expecting a child. A few months later, however, the troubles began to mount up for the band: in May, an English duo of the same name, best known for their late-Sixties hit 'Rainbow Chaser', sued Nirvana for using their name (the case was eventually settled out of court); in June, Cobain was rushed to hospital after a con-cert in Belfast, allegedly suffer ing from ulcer pains; and though the couple's daughter Frances Bean was born without complications at Cedars Sinai Hospital in Los Angeles on August 18, their celebrations were cut short when a Vanity Fair cover story reported that Love had admitted using heroin during her pregnancy.

The year continued in up-and-down fashion: the group were well-received at the Reading Festival, where they headlined the final day, and at the MTV Music Video Awards, where they picked up a couple of trophies and Cobain got into an argument with Guns N'Roses singer **Axl Rose**. In December, **Killing Joke** filed a suit claiming that Nirvana's 'Come As You Are' lifts a riff from their song 'Eighties', but buoyed by a string of hit singles and an impending album of out-takes and archive material to be called 'Incesticide', 'Nevermind' finally reached the British Top 20 in January of 1993. In February, the group won Best International Newcomer Award at the annual BRIT Awards, and another chart hit was chalked up in March with a limited-edition single, 'Oh, The Guilt'.

In May, Croatian native Kris Novoselic became a temporary foreign correspondent for *Spin* magazine, filing a report from war-torn Zagreb. At home, however, all was not well with Kurt and **Courtney**: Cobain was arrested on June 4 when police were called to their Seattle home to settle a domestic dispute which had blown up over Cobain's gun collection; he was detained temporarily and later released on $950 bail. Meanwhile work continued on

their real follow-up to 'Nevermind'. DGC were reportedly unhappy with the tracks recorded by former **Big Black** frontman Steve Albini for the album, and there was talk of re-recording them with another producer or re-mixing them to obtain a commercially viable release. Their worries eventually proved groundless, as the resulting album 'In Utero', despite being banned from some chain-stores for its explicit cover art, debuted at Number 1 in both the US and UK album charts when it was finally released towards the end of September. The year ended on an upbeat note with the recording, on November 18, of an acoustic concert for transmission in MTV's Unplugged series. Helped by second guitarist Pat Smear, cellist Lori Goldston and the **Meat Puppets**' Kirkwood brothers, the show featured sensitively rearranged versions of Nirvana songs like 'Come As You Are' and 'All Apologies' along with covers of **David Bowie**, the Meat Puppets and **Leadbelly** songs.

In 1994, the pressures which had been building up in the Cobain/Love relationship finally exploded, with tragic results. Struggling with a persistent heroin addiction (which he blamed on his stomach pains), Cobain's natural depression increased when he felt slighted by his wife. On March 4 in Rome, the singer was rushed to hospital yet again after taking an overdose; his wife and friends initially claimed it was accidental, but on March 18, police were once again summoned to the couple's

Seattle home to remove a selection of drugs and four guns after Cobain threatened to kill himself. A misguided friend supplied him with replacement guns, and less than a month later, on the morning of Friday, April 8, Cobain's body was found, dead from self-inflicted gun-shot wounds, by an electrician carrying out security work on the house. Released in November 1994, the 'Unplugged In New York' album followed 'In Utero' in topping both British and American charts. A plan to include further out-take material on the album was abandoned by Novoselic and Grohl.

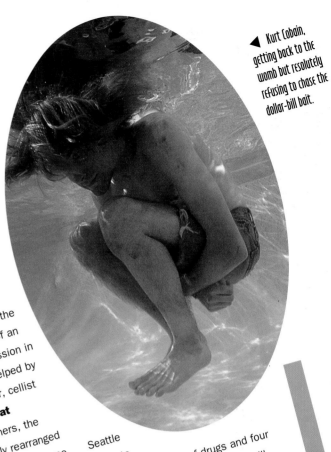
▶ Kurt Cobain, getting back to the womb but resolutely refusing to chase the dollar-bill bait.

▶ Fraught with problems, the stage became one of the few places Kurt Cobain could feel completely free.

Nirvana

Against a year-long backdrop of intermittent protest against the proposed Criminal Justice Bill, portions of which were drafted specifically to prevent outdoor raves, British pop regained some of its self-respect with the rise of **Oasis** and **Blur**, whose new albums tapped into the kind of classic songwriting skills that spawned the British beat boom of the Sixties.

Casting a huge shadow over the year's events, however, was the April suicide of **Nirvana**'s **Kurt Cobain**, to which fellow musicians responded in different ways: Cobain's wife, **Courtney Love**, took to posting rambling, semi-literate messages on the Internet, **Pearl Jam** singer Eddie Vedder married his longtime girlfriend Beth Liebling in Rome, in what some saw as an attempt to add some stability to his life, and **Oasis** singer, Liam Gallagher, opined that Cobain was "just a sad cunt who couldn't handle the fame".

Michael Jackson's marriage to Lisa Marie Presley which was rumoured to be on the rocks by the end of the year, was outdone in weirdness terms only by the antics of the Norwegian 'Satanic black metal' scene, which was responsible for a spate of arson attacks on churches and at least two related murders.

Meanwhile, in two separate books published around its 25th anniversary, **Rolling Stone Brian Jones**' death was finally revealed to have been a case of murder, the alleged culprit being Jones' former builder.

The courts were kept as busy as ever by disgruntled rock stars in 1994, despite **George Michael**'s costly failure to extricate himself from his Sony contract: **Prince**, **Metallica**, **U2**, **Pearl Jam** and others were involved in disputes with record companies or other industry agencies; a sizeable posse of rockers sued to prevent their songs being used in adverts (though **Bob Dylan**, amazingly, allowed the accountants Coopers & Lybrand to use a version of his 'The Times They Are A-Changin'' in an ad), and gangsta-rappers continued their financial support scheme for lawyers, with **Tupac Shakur**'s numerous court cases demonstrating a particularly assiduous dedication to this worthy cause.

Apart from Kurt Cobain, the year was relatively low on rock-related deaths, with few other significant artists shuffling off this mortal coil. This decrease was more than compensated for by the number of accidents and hospitalizations – particularly relating to broken legs – which were an unusual feature of an otherwise fairly uneventful year.

The year begins with **Prince**, or The Artist Formerly Known As Prince, placing adverts in papers around the world searching for The Most Beautiful Girl In The World to "spend the holidays" with him; hopefully, his relations with any respondent run more smoothly than his relationship

with Warner Brothers, which breaks down when the company drops his Paisley Park label. In April, he releases the single, 'The Most Beautiful Girl In The World' on his own NPG label, distributed in Europe by a small German company; it becomes his first British Number 1, assisted by heavy publicity that includes the opening of a Prince merchandise shop in London's Camden Town, in the basement of which the diminutive purple one has entombed a time-capsule of Princely ephemera.

As his dispute continues with the company – he became a director of Warners when he signed his last contract – Prince spends much of the year in workaholic mode, trying to conclude his remaining four-album commitment to them in record-quick time. He is buoyed a little in September when 'Purple Rain', with 11 million sales, officially becomes the biggest-selling single-artist soundtrack of all time. For public appearances though, he has the word 'SLAVE' printed across his face, an echo of **George Michael**'s assertion regarding his own relationship with Sony, the unsuccessful conclusion of which leaves the singer some £3 million pounds lighter in legal fees. Still,

 The Charlatans all but disappeared from public view in 1994, quite literally in the case of keyboard player Rob Collins, who was sentenced to eight months' imprisonment for armed robbery.

at least George doesn't have to go to jail, unlike the **Charlatans**' keyboard player Rob Collins, who is sentenced to eight months in January for armed robbery. Industry wags were moved to comment that though they knew the group career had taken a bit of a downturn, they hadn't realised its members were quite that strapped for cash.

In January, **Michael Jackson** concludes the Jordy Chandler affair with an out-of-court settlement worth $20 million over 40 years, including a million each for the boy's parents, $3 million for Jordy's attorney Larry Feldman and $15 million for Jordy himself. Hopes that this would settle matters once and for all are dashed later in the year when another child starts proceedings against Jackson on similar child-abuse grounds, and Jordy's stepfather, David Schwarz, files another suit alleging the singer destroyed his family. There is widespread revulsion when a promotional exercise backfires badly – Jackson and Lisa Marie visit a chil-

Along with Bjork, the Stereo MCs were the main winners at the BRIT Awards, an indication of the dominance of the dance-scene-derived pop in the British music scene of the 90s. ▼

dren's hospital in Hungary during a break from filming a video which portrays Jackson as a freedom fighter rescuing the Eastern bloc from communism. Not that the singer allows public derogation to spoil his fun: in July, he and his wife buy a 75-room pink palace in Atlanta, bigger than Graceland and Neverland put together, for a cool $11 million.

In the awards season, **Bjork** and the **Stereo MCs** are the main winners at the BRIT Awards with two trophies each, while **Van Morrison** is awarded an Outstanding Contribution Award. In America, **Bob Marley** is inducted into the Rock'n'Roll Hall of Fame. The benefit season, meanwhile, gets well underway in March and April: an Imperial Cancer Fund benefit at London's Clapham Grand on March 2, to commemorate the death of publicist Philip Hall, features **Suede** guitarist Bernard Butler guesting with the **Manic Street Preachers**, and a one-off reunion of **Shane MacGowan** and the **Pogues**. Also to raise money for cancer care, the **Alexis Korner** memorial show at Buxton Opera House on April 17 features **Robert Plant**, **Charlie Watts**, **Bill**

Wyman, **Paul Jones**, **Jack Bruce** and **Chris Barber**, while the same day, the **Wonder Stuff**'s Malcolm Treece runs the London Marathon to raise funds for cancer research. And going against the habit of a lifetime for the second time in two months, **Bob Dylan** follows the March relaxation of his policy of refusing to allow his songs to be used in commercials by donating a cheque for $20,000 to build a school playground for handicapped children in Rockford, Illinois, the first charitable donation he's been known to make.

In April, rock's less charitable instincts were on show when Bard Eithum, aka Faust, of the Norwegian death-metal outfit **Emperor**, is sentenced to 14 years in prison for stabbing a gay man to death in Lillehammer two years previously. On April 18, the trial begins of another death-metal rocker, Varg Vikernes, aka Count Grishnackh, of the band **Burzum**, who is accused of stabbing to death his one-time colleague Oystein Aarseth. Vikernes, who visited Aarseth's apartment armed with an axe, a bayonet and seven knives and stabbed him 23 times, was apprehended after boasting about the crime to British heavy metal magazine **Kerrang!**, some of whose journalists are subsequently threatened themselves. At his trial, Vikernes, 21, blames the affair on "the Jews who killed my father Odin", and is sentenced to the maximum available 21 years. The Satanic Terrorist movement, founded by Vikernes and Aarseth in chummier times, is said to be involved in a number of arson attacks on churches, a pastime copied by English band **Necropolis**, members of whom are jailed for between two and three years for the desecration of Kent churches. British thrash-rockers **Napalm Death**, however, do their bit to redress the political balance at a July festival in Tallin, Estonia, by beating up Russian Nationalist band **Corrosive Metal** for their racist and fascist comments.

April, by tradition "the cruellest month", sees the start of the spate of injuries which will build up throughout the year, with **Rage Against The Machine** bassist Timmy C breaking his arm in a mountain bike accident and **Cranberries'** vocalist Dolores O'Riordan breaking a leg skiing. The following month, ex-**Dead Kennedy** singer **Jello Biafra** has a leg broken by former punks who accuse him of selling out and **Public Enemy** DJ **Terminator X** breaks a leg in a motorbike accident; it is also announced that singer **Ella Fitzgerald** had both legs amputated last year because of a diabetes-related illness. Later in the year, new **Iron Maiden** frontman Blaze Bayley breaks a knee in the traditional motorbiking manner, while **Auteurs'** songwriter Luke Haines busts both ankles leaping off a wall in Spain.

Other rockers requiring medical treatment include **John Mellencamp**, who needs heart surgery in October and **David Crosby**, who is given a new liver in a seven-hour transplant operation at the UCLA Medical Center on November 22. And, days before he is found guilty on sex abuse charges,

actor/rapper **Tupac Shakur** is shot five times – in the head, groin and hands – when mugged of jewellery worth $40,000 in New York. Against his doctor's advice, Shakur checks out of hospital immediately, allegedly for his own safety, but has to return for more treatment the next day. It is the culmination of a bad time for Shakur, who appeared in court on December 8 wearing a bulletproof vest, to learn he faces between two and seven years in jail on the sex abuse charges; he is already due to spend ten days in jail over Christmas on the Atlanta police-shooting charge, and also has to appear in court in Los Angeles on December 20 to answer weapons-possession charges.

Also in need of medical care is **Glenn Frey** of the **Eagles** – their comeback tour is halted in October when he requires stomach surgery. This is a huge blow to the group, which re-formed for an album and tour after members had appeared as **Travis Tritt**'s backing band in the video for a track on an Eagles tribute album. However, the tour's itinerary of 70 shows (at up to a whopping $105 a seat) is not the most suc-

cessful comeback of the year; with five million sales of their new album 'The Division Bell', and a total gross of £125 million from the album and accompanying 100-date tour, **Pink Floyd** put themselves back at the head of the rockers' earnings league. This is in spite of a disaster at the opening date of their three-night stint at London's Earl's Court, when the collapse of a bank of seating sends 1000 fans plummeting to earth: 60 people are hurt, eight with serious back injuries. Survivors later quip, "The Floyd were fine, but the support was crap!"

While the Eagles and, in Britain, **Traffic** are re-forming, the usual rash of departures afflicts various bands. **Pearl Jam** sack drummer Dave Abbruzzese, ultimately replacing him with Josh Freese despite rumours linking both **Nirvana**'s Dave Grohl and one-time **Red Hot Chili Pepper** Jack Irons; Paul Hester leaves **Crowded House** for personal reasons, said to be connected with the group's continuous tour schedule; guitarist Bernard Butler leaves **Suede**, citing personal differences with co-songwriter Brett Anderson; the **Wonder Stuff** finally call it a day, with frontman Miles Hunt rumoured to be starting a new career

 Pink Floyd's album 'The Division Bell' was their most successful release in years, but their concert tour got off to a bad start at Earl's Court when a bank of seating collapsed, sending 1,000 fans plummeting to earth. Sixty people required medical attention.

Blur's 'Parklife', along with Oasis' 'Definitely Maybe', restored some self-respect to British pop by tapping into the kind of classic songwriting skills that spawned the British beat boom of the Sixties.

JANUARY: Harry Nilsson, singer of 'Without You', dies in Los Angeles following a huge heart attack.

MARCH 22: Disco godfather, Dan Hartman dies of an AIDS-related disease, aged 42.

APRIL 8: 27-year-old Kurt Cobain is found dead at home in Seattle.

MAY: BBM, a reincarnation of Cream with Gary Moore replacing Eric Clapton start their first tour.

MAY: George Michael loses his court case against Sony.

AUGUST: 25 years after the event, Jimi Hendrix's Woodstock performance is released in full.

OCTOBER 17: Page and Plant's MTV Unledded show is screened.

DECEMBER: The Beatles release their first album in over 25 years, 'Live At The BBC'.

as an MTV presenter; and **Saw Doctors**' keyboardist Tony Lambert also finally sees sense, leaving the band a year after winning £850,000 on the Irish Lottery. Staying with his band, however, despite being hospitalized in July for "nervous exhaustion" is **Manic Street Preachers**' lyricist Richey James, who subsequently admits problems with alcohol and self-mutilation.

Following the death by overdose of bassist Kristen Pfaff, former **Fall** guitarist Brix Smith is hotly tipped as her replacement in **Courtney Love**'s group **Hole**. The rumour is scotched when she rejoins the **Fall** at an Edinburgh concert. Melissa Auf Der Mauer joins Hole instead. Following **Kurt Cobain**'s suicide, Courtney Love continues to behave in her usual erratic, outrageous manner: she is romantically linked with both Evan Dando of the **Lemonheads** (who later denies he is being considered to play Cobain in one of several planned film biographies of the singer) and Billy Corgan of **Smashing Pumpkins**. She also accompanies **R.E.M.**'s Michael Stipe to the MTV Film Awards – though Stipe later reveals he refused her request to look after her daughter if she should die, believing compliance might encourage the clearly depressed singer to take her own life. Though Hole's album 'Live Through This' was well received, Love seems to spend much of the year conducting futile arguments on the Internet and, as if she hadn't suffered enough, in June she is harassed by a stalker convinced he is destined to marry her and become the new singer in

Nirvana. She is granted an injunction against the man, as is **Madonna** against a similar stalker who suffers from the delusion that he is the superstar's husband. Apparently, Todd Lawrence, 26, would turn up at Madonna's house shouting, "Hi honey! I'm home!"

1994 isn't a particularly good year for festivals. In June, the Pyramid Stage at Glastonbury is burnt to the ground, to be replaced for the festival by a hired stage – the same one used at London's rain-drenched Pavarotti In The Park show. In August, meanwhile, descriptions of the huge Woodstock 2 festival range from disaster to fiasco: on the first night, the security team abandon the event, allowing over 100,000 to get in free; a scheme whereby only specially-minted "Woodstock Money" can be used for purchases inside the arena goes woefully wrong (the scheme's distributor ends up hospitalized for nervous exhaustion); and there is no forethought or provision for the inevitable downpour which turns the event into a mudbath. The best acts at the festival are said to be **Bob Dylan**, the **Red Hot Chili Peppers** – who appeared wearing giant lightbulbs on their heads – and **Nine Inch Nails**, who reflect the spirit of the event by appearing covered in mud.

MTV's 'Unplugged' series continues to attract top stars: **Bjork** sings 'My Funny Valentine' and versions of songs from her 'Debut' album, Nirvana's session spawns a chart-

topping album, **Jimmy Page** & **Robert Plant**'s Unledded session features revised versions of old **Led Zeppelin** tracks given an Arabic flavour by the involvement of Egyptian musicians and even Bob Dylan bows to the inevitable, recording a couple of sessions for transmission on Christmas Eve.

Dylan is one of several stars heavily involved in litigation in 1994, mostly concerning the appropriation of songs for use in commercials. Perry Farrell, who owns the trademark to Lollapalooza, wins a dona-

▲ Woodstock 94: disaster or fiasco?

tion to a rain-forest charity from the J Walter Thompson advertizing agency, who use the name in an advert for a Ford car; the **Jesus & Mary Chain** sue Reebok for using part of their song 'Reverence' in an advert for footwear; and **Tom Waits**, a veteran of this kind of litigation, wins further cases brought against his former publisher Third Story Music for allowing two of his songs, 'Ruby's Arms' and 'Heart Attack And Vine', to be

JUL 17 : Brazil beats Italy in the soccer World Cup final held in the United States. It's the first time the competition is settled by a penalty shoot-out

1994 - HEADLINE NEWS

used in adverts for shaving cream and jeans, respectively.

Always contrary, **Dylan** allows accountants Coopers & Lybrand to use a song of his, but is less happy when computer company Apple call a new software programme of theirs DYLAN, claiming some sort of ownership of the word; being long dead, poet Dylan Thomas, whose name

Dylan appropriated in the first place, is unavailable for comment but is likely to be turning in his grave at Mr Zimmerman's cheek. A similar software-related suit is brought by the **Jefferson Airplane** against Berkeley Systems for using the 'flying toaster' image (similar to those used on the cover of the Airplane's 1973 live album '30 Seconds Over Winterland')

in its screen-saver programme After Dark. The group allowed Berkeley to use the image for five years, but are spurred into action when Berkeley sue another software company for copying what they consider their copyrighted image. In a more open-and-shut case of copyright, **Michael Bolton** loses a case brought by the **Isley Brothers**, who claim his song

Presley/Jackson: weird is as weird does. ▼

Jackson/Presley Marriage Stuns World

Despite earlier denials from representatives of both parties, it seems that **Michael Jackson** and Lisa Marie Presley, daughter of **Elvis**, were indeed married on May 26 in the Dominican Republic.

Annoyed at denials which effectively cast him as a liar, the official who presided over the nuptials, Judge Hugo Alvarez Perez, confirmed that the extraordinary wedding did actually take place at his home, after the couple's initial desire to be married aboard an aeroplane was stymied through his lack of jurisdiction in such areas. Originally planned for May 18, following stringent security checks of the premises and the evacuation of Judge Perez's family and staff, the occasion was re-scheduled for 10am on May 26. Thus ensured of privacy, the bride and groom were brought from their separate villas to the Judge's home at the island's resort of La Romana.

The ceremony, which normally takes over half an hour, was concluded in 11 minutes and the judge later expressed himself disconcerted at the casual attitude of both participants. "It was like a big game to them," he said. "Before I could even begin the ceremony, Lisa Marie suddenly walked out of the room. When she eventually returned, her witness Eva Darling (wife of Lisa Marie's ex-husband's brother Thomas Keough) announced 'The couple will not kiss'. I thought this was absurd. They also didn't even hold hands or touch, and never looked into each other's eyes at all. I kept pushing them to kiss at the end, and finally there was one small peck on the cheek." Jackson later admitted that when the judge had asked him, "Do you take Lisa Marie to be your wife?" he had responded not with the traditional "I do" but a more ambivalent "Why not?" The couple and their entourage were apparently in such a hurry to leave that they forgot their marriage

certificate, which had to be collected later by a lawyer.

For the occasion, Lisa Marie wore a pale beige strapless dress, while Michael sported black jeans and black shirt, with his hair pulled back into a ponytail. A Band-Aid across the bridge of his nose was disguised with heavy make-up foundation, and the judge described him as looking like "an alien ... he is the first groom who ever came before me wearing more make-up than the bride; his skin was unlike any other human I have seen – almost like parchment."

Jackson, a 35-year-old presumed virgin, first met Lisa Marie when he went to an Elvis Presley performance in Lake Tahoe in 1973, when he was 15 and she a small child. Their relationship blossomed after Jackson contacted her in late December 1993 with a view to covering a Presley song for his forthcoming 'Jackson Family History' LP; regular dates ensued, including a holiday weekend at Donald Trump's Mar-A-Lago estate in Palm Beach, Florida.

Since the wedding, speculation has been rife about the couple's relationship. Lisa Marie, who was divorced from her previous husband Danny Keough only 20 days before the Jackson/Presley marriage, is a member of the Church of Scientology, which is known to prize celebrity converts such as Tom Cruise and John Travolta – Michael is rumoured to have already undergone part of the Church's 'cleansing' process. For his part, Jackson is understandably keen to promote a more obviously normal, heterosexual image following the damaging child-abuse allegations he suffered last year, though the awkward 45-second kiss he and Lisa Marie shared publicly at the MTV Awards ceremony merely aroused suspicions that the couple were not quite as relaxed in each other's company as they wished to suggest.

 Wet Wet Wet's Marti Pellow: their version of the Troggs' 'Love Is All Around' stalled one week short of Bryan Adams' record of 16 weeks at the top of the UK singles chart.

'Love Is A Wonderful Thing' was plagiarized from their 1966 song of the same name; Bolton churlishly suggests afterwards that the decision went against him because four of the jurors were black. And **Michael Jackson** is sued for $5 million by sportswear company LA Gear for the non-appearance of adverts for which the singer had already been advanced $2 million. Presumably, he has more pressing matters on his mind. Poor old Lol Tolhurst, meanwhile, is left with legal bills in the region of £1 million when he loses his case against his former bandmates in the **Cure**. This is the same amount rumoured to have been burnt by the **KLF** on the Scottish Isle Of Jura in an attempt to make a serious point about the value of money or to gain maximum publicity, depending on your point of view.

U2 receive a boost in their battle with the Performing Rights Society when the Irish Competition Society declared the PRS monopoly unfair, turning down the PRS's application to continue collecting royalties in Ireland. In America, **Pearl Jam** spend much of the year in dispute with the Ticketmaster ticket agency, over the agency's refusal to accept a $1.80 maximum booking fee on their shows. In June, Stone Gossard and Jeff Ament testify before the House Government Operations information sub-committee, claiming Ticketmaster's monopoly on American stadia – already being con-

sidered for an anti-trust suit by the US Justice Department – prevents them giving their fans a low-cost show. They are supported in their assertions by **Aerosmith**'s management, which alleges the company offered to split the proceeds of an artificially-inflated "service charge" with them. Pearl Jam further claim that the **Rolling Stones** did in fact take a cut of the huge $5 service charge on tickets for their tour.

Amidst all this unpleasantness, there are a few happier moments: **M People** edge out **Pulp** to win the Mercury Prize, unreleased **Jim Morrison** songs and poems are found in a Paris apartment, where he left them over two decades ago, **R.E.M.** sell out their British stadium tour in a mere five hours whilst shifting a colossal 200,000 copies in a week of their album 'Monster', and **Wet Wet Wet**'s chart-topping run with 'Love Is All Around' concludes one week short of **Bryan Adams**' record 16 weeks: the song's composer, ex-**Trogg** Reg Presley, a dedicated cerealogist, says he intends to spend his windfall studying corn-circles.

The undoubted success story of 1994, however, is **Oasis**, who spend much of the year accruing the kind of headlines publicists can only dream of. As the August 30 release of their debut LP 'Definitely Maybe' approaches, they go on a classic rock-star rampage, smashing up hotels in London and Sweden, and getting involved in fights at the first show of

their national tour in Newcastle, where a punter jumps onstage and punches guitarist and songwriter Noel Gallagher in the face – whereupon the band piles into the audience after the attacker; a crowd of 300 later attack the group's van as they depart. The group has the last laugh, however, when their LP sells 150,000 copies in the first three days of release, going straight to the top of the charts.

Their Manchester colleagues, the **Stone Roses**, are less successful when 'Second Coming', the long-awaited follow-up to their debut album, is released after nearly five years of silence. The album, which reflects guitarist John Squire's new-found fascination with **Jimmy Page** and **Jimi Hendrix**, has a mixed reception, compounded by their decision to promote it with only one interview, in the homeless persons' paper *The Big Issue*, and the concurrent release of a double album of material recorded for BBC radio shows by the **Beatles**.

Oasis' Noel Gallagher was chinned onstage at Newcastle, but got the last laugh when the group's album 'Definitely Maybe' shifted 150,000 units in three days, one of the fastest-selling debuts of all time.

NOV 6 : George Foreman regains the World Heavyweight Boxing Crown at the age of 44 • DEC 12 : Over 500 die in two cinema fires in the space of two weeks

Top 5 UK Albums

The first weekly UK LP charts started in November 1958. All points scored by an album during its Top 10 chart run are included in the year that it first charted (except for 1959 which includes albums already charting when the year started).

1959
1. South Pacific SOUNDTRACK
2. Buddy Holly Story BUDDY HOLLY
3. Gigi SOUNDTRACK
4. My Fair Lady ORIGINAL BROADWAY CAST
5. Cliff Sings CLIFF RICHARD

1965
1. The Sound Of Music SOUNDTRACK
2. Mary Poppins SOUNDTRACK
3. Rubber Soul BEATLES
4. Help BEATLES
5. Rolling Stones No.2 ROLLING STONES

1971
1. Electric Warrior T. REX
2. Motown Chartbusters Vol. 5 VARIOUS
3. Sticky Fingers ROLLING STONES
4. Fog On The Tyne LINDISFARNE
5. Imagine JOHN LENNON

1960
1. The Black And White Minstrel Show GEORGE MITCHELL MINSTRELS
2. G.I. Blues ELVIS PRESLEY
3. Me And My Shadows CLIFF RICHARD
4. Oliver ORIGINAL CAST
5. Elvis Is Back ELVIS PRESLEY

1966
1. Best Of The Beach Boys BEACH BOYS
2. Aftermath ROLLING STONES
3. Revolver BEATLES
4. Going Places HERB ALPERT & THE TIJUANA BRASS
5. Pet Sounds BEACH BOYS

1972
1. Greatest Hits SIMON & GARFUNKEL
2. All Time Hits Of The Fifties VARIOUS
3. Never A Dull Moment ROD STEWART
4. Dynamic Hits VARIOUS
5. Fantastic Hits VARIOUS

1961
1. Blue Hawaii ELVIS PRESLEY
2. The Shadows SHADOWS
3. The Young Ones (Soundtrack) CLIFF RICHARD
4. Another Black And White Minstrel Show GEORGE MITCHELL MINSTRELS
5. Best Of Barber And Bilk Vol. 1 CHRIS BARBER AND ACKER BILK

1967
1. Sergeant Pepper's Lonely Hearts Club Band BEATLES
2. The Monkees MONKEES
3. More Of The Monkees MONKEES
4. British Motown Chartbusters VARIOUS
5. Are You Experienced JIMI HENDRIX EXPERIENCE

1973
1. Tubular Bells MIKE OLDFIELD
2. Band On The Run WINGS
3. And I Love You So PERRY COMO
4. Aladdin Sane DAVID BOWIE
5. Goodbye Yellow Brick Road ELTON JOHN

1962
1. West Side Story SOUNDTRACK
2. Out Of The Shadows SHADOWS
3. Pot Luck ELVIS PRESLEY
4. The Best Of Ball, Barber And Bilk KENNY BALL , CHRIS BARBER AND ACKER BILK
5. Bobby Vee Meets The Crickets BOBBY VEE & THE CRICKETS

1968
1. The Best Of The Seekers SEEKERS
2. John Wesley Harding BOB DYLAN
3. Greatest Hits HOLLIES
4. Greatest Hits DIANA ROSS & THE SUPREMES
5. Bookends SIMON & GARFUNKEL

1974
1. The Singles 1969-1973 CARPENTERS
2. Rollin' BAY CITY ROLLERS
3. Elton John's Greatest Hits ELTON JOHN
4. Engelbert Humperdinck - His Greatest Hits ENGELBERT HUMPERDINCK
5. David Essex DAVID ESSEX

1963
1. Please Please Me BEATLES
2. With The Beatles BEATLES
3. Summer Holiday (Soundtrack) CLIFF RICHARD
4. Meet The Searchers SEARCHERS
5. Greatest Hits SHADOWS

1969
1. Led Zeppelin 2 LED ZEPPELIN
2. Abbey Road BEATLES
3. British Motown Chartbusters Vol. 3 VARIOUS
4. Johnny Cash At San Quentin JOHNNY CASH
5. Easy Rider SOUNDTRACK

1975
1. The Best Of The Stylistics STYLISTICS
2. Once Upon A Star BAY CITY ROLLERS
3. Atlantic Crossing ROD STEWART
4. Horizon CARPENTERS
5. Golden Greats JIM REEVES

1964
1. Rolling Stones ROLLING STONES
2. Beatles For Sale BEATLES
3. A Hard Day's Night BEATLES
4. The Bachelors And 16 Great Songs BACHELORS
5. Lucky 13 Shades Of Val Doonican VAL DOONICAN

1970
1. Bridge Over Troubled Water SIMON & GARFUNKEL
2. Greatest Hits ANDY WILLIAMS
3. Motown Chartbusters Vol. 4 VARIOUS
4. Led Zeppelin 3 LED ZEPPELIN
5. Let It Be BEATLES

1976
1. Greatest Hits ABBA
2. Arrival ABBA
3. Golden Greats BEACH BOYS
4. Hotel California EAGLES
5. A Night On The Town ROD STEWART

1977
1. Rumours FLEETWOOD MAC
2. A Star Is Born BARBRA STREISAND /SOUNDTRACK
3. The Sound Of Bread BREAD
4. Golden Greats SHADOWS
5. Disco Fever VARIOUS

1978
1. Saturday Night Fever SOUNDTRACK
2. Grease SOUNDTRACK
3. Parallel Lines BLONDIE
4. The Album ABBA
5. Night Flight To Venus BONEY M

1979
1. Reggatta De Blanc POLICE
2. Discovery ELECTRIC LIGHT ORCHESTRA
3. Manilow Magic BARRY MANILOW
4. Breakfast In America SUPERTRAMP
5. Voulez-Vous ABBA

1980
1. Kings Of The Wild Frontier ADAM & THE ANTS
2. Flesh And Blood ROXY MUSIC
3. Guilty BARBRA STREISAND
4. Double Fantasy JOHN LENNON
5. Greatest Hits ROSE ROYCE

1981
1. Dare HUMAN LEAGUE
2. Greatest Hits QUEEN
3. Stars On 45 STARSOUND
4. Love Songs CLIFF RICHARD
5. Pearls ELKIE BROOKS

1982
1. Thriller MICHAEL JACKSON
2. Kids From Fame KIDS FROM FAME
3. Love Songs BARBRA STREISAND
4. Rio DURAN DURAN
5. Complete Madness MADNESS

1983
1. Can't Slow Down LIONEL RICHIE
2. No Parlez PAUL YOUNG
3. An Innocent Man BILLY JOEL
4. Let's Dance DAVID BOWIE
5. Fantastic WHAM!

1984
1. Born In The USA BRUCE SPRINGSTEEN
2. Diamond Life SADE
3. Legend BOB MARLEY & THE WAILERS
4. Alf ALISON MOYET
5. Like A Virgin MADONNA

1985
1. Brothers In Arms DIRE STRAITS
2. No Jacket Required PHIL COLLINS
3. Songs From The Big Chair TEARS FOR FEARS
4. Whitney Houston WHITNEY HOUSTON
5. Be Yourself Tonight EURYTHMICS

1986
1. Graceland PAUL SIMON
2. True Blue MADONNA
3. Silk And Steel FIVE STAR
4. The Whole Story KATE BUSH
5. A Kind Of Magic QUEEN

1987
1. Tango In The Night FLEETWOOD MAC
2. Bad MICHAEL JACKSON
3. The Joshua Tree U2
4. Popped In Souled Out WET WET WET
5. Introducing The Hardline According To TERENCE TRENT D'ARBY

1988
1. Kylie KYLIE MINOGUE
2. Anything For You GLORIA ESTEFAN & MIAMI SOUND MACHINE
3. Tracy Chapman TRACY CHAPMAN
4. Push BROS
5. Money For Nothing DIRE STRAITS

1989
1. ...But Seriously PHIL COLLINS
2. A New Flame SIMPLY RED
3. Sleeping With The Past ELTON JOHN
4. Enjoy Yourself KYLIE MINOGUE
5. The Road To Hell CHRIS REA

1990
1. The Immaculate Collection MADONNA
2. In Concert LUCIANO PAVAROTTI /PLACIDO DOMINGO/ JOSE CARRERAS
3. The Very Best Of Elton John ELTON JOHN
4. Only Yesterday CARPENTERS
5. Listen Without Prejudice Vol. 1 GEORGE MICHAEL

1991
1. Stars SIMPLY RED
2. Out Of Time R.E.M.
3. Greatest Hits EURYTHMICS
4. Queen's Greatest Hits 2 QUEEN
5. Dangerous MICHAEL JACKSON

1992
1. Automatic For The People REM
2. Back To Front LIONEL RICHIE
3. Diva ANNIE LENNOX
4. Cher's Greatest Hits: 1965-1992 CHER
5. Up RIGHT SAID FRED

1993
1. Music Box MARIAH CAREY
2. Bat Out Of Hell II MEAT LOAF
3. So Close DINA CARROLL
4. End Of Part One (Their Greatest Hits) WET WET WET
5. One Woman - The Ultimate Collection DIANA ROSS

1994
1. Our Town- Greatest Hits DEACON BLUE
2. Cross Road - The Best Of BON JOVI
3. The Division Bell PINK FLOYD
4. Twelve Deadly Cyns...And Then Some CYNDI LAUPER
5. Carry On Up The Charts - The Best Of BEAUTIFUL SOUTH

Top 5 US Albums

The first **weekly** US LP charts started in March 1956. All points scored by an album during its Top 10 chart run are included in the year that it first charted (except for 1956 which includes albums already charting when the year started).

1956
1. Calypso HARRY BELAFONTE
2. My Fair Lady ORIGINAL CAST
3. Elvis Presley ELVIS PRESLEY
4. Belafonte HARRY BELAFONTE
5. Elvis ELVIS PRESLEY

1957
1. Around The World In 80 Days SOUNDTRACK
2. Loving You ELVIS PRESLEY
3. Love Is The Thing NAT 'KING' COLE
4. Elvis' Christmas Album ELVIS PRESLEY
5. Ricky RICKY NELSON

1958
1. South Pacific SOUNDTRACK
2. The Music Man ORIGINAL CAST
3. Gigi SOUNDTRACK
4. Sing Along With Mitch MITCH MILLER
5. Tchaikovsky: Piano Concerto No. 1 VAN CLIBURN

1959
1. The Sound Of Music ORIGINAL CAST
2. The Kingston Trio At Large KINGSTON TRIO
3. The Music From Peter Gunn HENRY MANCINI
4. Here We Go Again! KINGSTON TRIO
5. Heavenly JOHNNY MATHIS

1960
1. The Button Down Mind Of Bob Newhart BOB NEWHART
2. G.I. Blues ELVIS PRESLEY
3. Sold Out KINGSTON TRIO
4. String Along KINGSTON TRIO
5. Nice 'n' Easy FRANK SINATRA

1961
1. West Side Story SOUNDTRACK
2. Camelot ORIGINAL CAST
3. Blue Hawaii ELVIS PRESLEY
4. Breakfast At Tiffany's (Soundtrack) HENRY MANCINI
5. Exodus SOUNDTRACK

1962
1. Peter, Paul & Mary PETER, PAUL & MARY
2. Modern Sounds In Country And Western Music RAY CHARLES
3. The First Family VAUGHN MEADER
4. My Son, The Folk Singer ALLAN SHERMAN
5. Jazz Samba STAN GETZ/CHARLIE BYRD

1963
1. (Moving) PETER, PAUL & MARY
2. In The Wind PETER, PAUL & MARY
3. Days Of Wine And Roses ANDY WILLIAMS
4. The Singing Nun SINGING NUN
5. Trini Lopez At PJ's TRINI LOPEZ

1964
1. Mary Poppins SOUNDTRACK
2. A Hard Day's Night BEATLES
3. Hello, Dolly! ORIGINAL CAST
4. Meet The Beatles BEATLES
5. Goldfinger SOUNDTRACK

1965
1. The Sound Of Music SOUNDTRACK
2. Whipped Cream & Other Delights HERB ALPERT & THE TIJUANA BRASS
3. Going Places HERB ALPERT & THE TIJUANA BRASS
4. Beatles '65 BEATLES
5. Help BEATLES

1966
1. Doctor Zhivago SOUNDTRACK
2. The Monkees MONKEES
3. What Now My Love HERB ALPERT & THE TIJUANA BRASS
4. S.R.O. HERB ALPERT & THE TIJUANA BRASS
5. Rubber Soul BEATLES

1967
1. Sgt. Pepper's Lonely Hearts Club Band BEATLES
2. More Of The Monkees MONKEES
3. Diana Ross & The Supremes Greatest Hits DIANA ROSS & THE SUPREMES
4. Headquarters MONKEES
5. The Doors DOORS

1968
1. Hair ORIGINAL CAST
2. The Graduate (Soundtrack) SIMON & GARFUNKEL
3. In-A-Gadda-Da-Vida IRON BUTTERFLY
4. Wichita Lineman GLEN CAMPBELL
5. Time Peace/The Rascals' Greatest Hits RASCALS

1969
1. Blood Sweat & Tears BLOOD, SWEAT & TEARS
2. Abbey Road BEATLES
3. Led Zeppelin II LED ZEPPELIN
4. Johnny Cash At San Quentin JOHNNY CASH
5. Green River CREEDENCE CLEARWATER REVIVAL

1970
1. Jesus Christ Superstar VARIOUS
2. Abraxas SANTANA
3. Woodstock VARIOUS
4. Cosmo's Factory CREEDENCE CLEARWATER REVIVAL
5. Chicago II CHICAGO

1971
1. Tapestry CAROLE KING
2. Ram PAUL McCARTNEY
3. Pearl JANIS JOPLIN
4. Every Picture Tells A Story ROD STEWART
5. Mud Slide Slim And The Blue Horizon JAMES TAYLOR

1972
1. Harvest NEIL YOUNG
2. Honky Chateau ELTON JOHN
3. You Don't Mess Around With Jim JIM CROCE
4. Chicago V CHICAGO
5. Rhymes & Reasons CAROLE KING

1973
1. Goodbye Yellow Brick Road ELTON JOHN
2. John Denver's Greatest Hits JOHN DENVER
3. Band On The Run WINGS
4. Dark Side Of The Moon PINK FLOYD
5. Brothers And Sisters ALLMAN BROTHERS BAND

1974
1. Back Home Again JOHN DENVER
2. The Sting (Soundtrack) MARVIN HAMLISCH
3. Elton John - Greatest Hits ELTON JOHN
4. Caribou ELTON JOHN
5. Not Fragile BACHMAN-TURNER OVERDRIVE

1975
1. Fleetwood Mac FLEETWOOD MAC
2. Red Octopus JEFFERSON STARSHIP
3. Captain Fantastic And The Brown Dirt Cowboy ELTON JOHN
4. One Of These Nights EAGLES
5. That's The Way Of The World (Soundtrack) EARTH, WIND & FIRE

1976
1. Frampton Comes Alive! PETER FRAMPTON
2. Songs In The Key Of Life STEVIE WONDER
3. Hotel California EAGLES
4. Wings At The Speed Of Sound WINGS
5. Boston BOSTON

1977
1. Rumours FLEETWOOD MAC
2. Saturday Night Fever SOUNDTRACK
3. Simple Dreams LINDA RONSTADT
4. Slowhand ERIC CLAPTON
5. The Stranger BILLY JOEL

1978
1. Grease SOUNDTRACK
2. Double Vision FOREIGNER
3. 52nd Street BILLY JOEL
4. Some Girls ROLLING STONES
5. Minute By Minute DOOBIE BROTHERS

1979
1. The Wall PINK FLOYD
2. Breakfast In America SUPERTRAMP
3. The Long Run EAGLES
4. In Through The Out Door LED ZEPPELIN
5. Spirits Having Flown BEE GEES

1980
1. Hi Infidelity REO SPEEDWAGON
2. Glass Houses BILLY JOEL
3. Crimes Of Passion PAT BENATAR
4. Double Fantasy JOHN LENNON
5. Against The Wind BOB SEGER & THE SILVER BULLET BAND

1981
1. 4 FOREIGNER
2. Escape JOURNEY
3. Paradise Theater STYX
4. Tattoo You ROLLING STONES
5. Bella Donna STEVIE NICKS

1982
1. Thriller MICHAEL JACKSON
2. Business As Usual MEN AT WORK
3. Asia ASIA
4. H2O DARYL HALL & JOHN OATES
5. American Fool JOHN COUGAR MELLENCAMP

1983
1. Can't Slow Down LIONEL RICHIE
2. Synchronicity POLICE
3. Sports HUEY LEWIS & THE NEWS
4. Pyromania DEF LEPPARD
5. Flashdance SOUNDTRACK

1984
1. Born In The U.S.A. BRUCE SPRINGSTEEN
2. Purple Rain PRINCE
3. Private Dancer TINA TURNER
4. Like A Virgin MADONNA
5. Heartbeat City CARS

1985
1. Whitney Houston WHITNEY HOUSTON
2. No Jacket Required PHIL COLLINS
3. Brothers In Arms DIRE STRAITS
4. Heart HEART
5. Songs From The Big Chair TEARS FOR FEARS

1986
1. Slippery When Wet BON JOVI
2. Control JANET JACKSON
3. Licensed To Ill BEASTIE BOYS
4. Top Gun SOUNDTRACK
5. Third Stage BOSTON

1987
1. Hysteria DEF LEPPARD
2. Dirty Dancing SOUNDTRACK
3. Faith GEORGE MICHAEL
4. Appetite For Destruction GUNS N' ROSES
5. Bad MICHAEL JACKSON

1988
1. Forever Your Girl PAULA ABDUL
2. Don't Be Cruel BOBBY BROWN
3. Hangin' Tough NEW KIDS ON THE BLOCK
4. New Jersey BON JOVI
5. Cocktail SOUNDTRACK

1989
1. Girl You Know It's True MILLI VANILLI
2. Janet Jackson's Rhythm Nation 1814 JANET JACKSON
3. The Raw & The Cooked FINE YOUNG CANNIBALS
4. Full Moon Fever TOM PETTY
5. ...But Seriously PHIL COLLINS

1990
1. Please Hammer Don't Hurt 'em M.C. HAMMER
2. Mariah Carey MARIAH CAREY
3. Wilson Phillips WILSON PHILLIPS
4. To The Extreme VANILLA ICE
5. No Fences GARTH BROOKS

1991
1. Ropin' The Wind GARTH BROOKS
2. Gonna Make You Sweat C&C MUSIC FACTORY
3. Nevermind NIRVANA
4. Time, Love And Tenderness MICHAEL BOLTON
5. Unforgettable NATALIE COLE

1992
1. Some Gave All BILLY RAY CYRUS
2. The Bodyguard SOUNDTRACK
3. Unplugged ERIC CLAPTON
4. Breathless KENNY G
5. Totally Krossed Out KRIS KROSS

1993
1. Music Box MARIAH CAREY
2. The Sign ACE OF BASE
3. Janet JANET JACKSON
4. The Chronic DR. DRE
5. Bat Out Of Hell II : Back Into Hell MEAT LOAF

1994
1. The Lion King SOUNDTRACK
2. August & Everything After COUNTING CROWS
3. II BOYZ II MEN
4. Purple STONE TEMPLE PILOTS
5. Not A Moment Too Soon TIM MCGRAW

The publishers would like to thank the following sources for their kind permission to reproduce the pictures in this book:

Colorsport; J Taylor Doggett; Chris Dreja; Ronald Grant Archive; Hulton Deutch Collection; London Features International/Matt Anker, Kristin Callahan, Fin Costello, Kevin Cummins, Nick Elgar, G. E. Friedman, David Fisher, Simon Fowler, Frank Griffin, Curt Gunther, Gie Knaeps, Lawrence Lawry, Colin Mason, Kevin Mazur, Ilpo Musto, Phil Nicholls, Michael Ochs Archive, Annelise Possin, Steve Rapport, Ken Regan, Derek Ridgers, Tom Sheehan, Geoff Swaine, Arnold Williams; Mirror Syndication International; NASA; Pictorial Press/Waring Abbott, George Chin, Todd Kaplan, Jeffrey Mayer; Barry Plummer; Range/Bettmann/UPI; Redferns/Richie Aaron, Fin Costello, Erica Echenberg, Mick Hutson, Stephen Morley, David Redfern, Ebet Roberts; Retna/Ray Stevenson; Rex/Eugene Adebari, Christopher Brown, Steve Fenton, Bruce Fleming, Dave Hogan, Nils Jorgensen, James Kelly, Andrew Murray, Brian Rasic, Crispin Rodwell, Neil Stevenson, Jeff Werner; Rough Trade Records; Science Photo Library/Alexander Tsiaras.

Every effort has been made to acknowledge correctly and contact the source and/or copyright holder of each picture, and Carlton Books Limited apologises for any unintentional errors or omissions which will be corrected in future editions of this book.